T0367862

CHINA vs. U.S.

A Political Analysis of U.S.–China Competition, a Police State vs. a Democracy

BRAD PEERY

ARCHWAY
PUBLISHING

Archway Publishing books may be ordered through booksellers or by contacting:

Archway Publishing
1663 Liberty Drive
Bloomington, IN 47403
www.archwaypublishing.com
1 (888) 242-5904

ISBN: 978-1-4808-6637-9 (sc)
ISBN: 978-1-4808-6638-6 (e)

Library of Congress Control Number: 2018909025

Print information available on the last page.

Archway Publishing rev. date: 8/24/2018

CONTENTS

PROLOGUE

Media Bias, Trump Russian Collusion, Brad Peery Background and Blogs

Trump Russian Collusion

A House FISA Memo Shows That High Level Employees In The DOJ Used Illegal Methods To Defeat Trump And Start The Mueller Russian Investigation

The Mueller Russian investigation has through February 2018 so far not shown any Trump collusion with Russia, but even a baseless investigation weakens the U.S. internationally and helps China and others that are seeking to reduce worldwide U.S. influence.

*Trump, during his presidential campaign, claimed that he was being spied on by the Obama administration. He was widely criticized by most of the media. It appears he was correct. During the campaign, the Democratic National Committee (DNC) was in need of funds, and Hillary Clinton basically funded and controlled the DNC. During the campaign, Bernie Sanders was discriminated against by the DNC. Should socialism as espoused by Bernie Sanders prevail within the Democratic Party, this will likely lessen the effectiveness of the U.S. in confronting Chinese ambitions.

The Hillary Clinton campaign and the DNC paid for a Fusion "dossier" on Donald Trump that was based largely on unsubstantiated Russian declarations. It was presented to the FBI, despite the fact it was unverified, paid for by the Democratic National Committee, and Hillary Clinton, and the financing sources were not disclosed to the FISA Court.

The memo states that in December 2017, then FBI deputy director Andrew McCabe testified that "no surveillance warrant would have been sought" from the FISA court "without the Steele dossier information."

*House memo states disputed dossier was key to FBI's FISA warrant to surveil members of Team Trump, Fox News, By Alex Pappas, Catherine Herridge, and Brooke Singman, February 2, 2018

****Fusion GPS co-founder Glenn Simpson told the Senate Judiciary Committee that the author of the opposition research dossier on then-candidate Donald Trump and Russia was acting on his own volition when he went to the FBI, because he was concerned that a presidential candidate was being blackmailed, according to the 312-page transcript of his testimony. Sources familiar with House and Senate investigations say this is the FBI's dossier talking point 24 months after agents were first briefed in July 2016, as Donald Trump battled Hillary Clinton for the White House.

Simpson told a Congressional committee in closed-door testimony in August, 2016, which was released publicly in January, 2018, that he did not know how the FBI would react when ex-British intelligence agent Christopher Steele, the author of the dossier, went to the bureau in July 2016.

This was a political indictment of Trump that was used by the highest echelons of the FBI to get a FISA warrant, from the most secret court in the U.S. The purpose of the FISA warrant was to spy on a Trump campaign official, Carter Page. It was not disclosed to the FISA court that the dossier was paid for by Clinton and the DNC, and was unverified. Because it was paid for by Clinton and the DNC, it was probably illegal to use it because of the funding sources.

**Fusion co-founder: Dossier author feared Trump was being black-mailed, CNN Politics, By Jeremy Herb, Manu Raju and Marshall Cohen, CNN, Updated January 10, 2018
***The most recent witness was FBI Deputy Director Andrew McCabe, who spent nearly eight hours in December, 2017 in a closed session before the House Permanent Select Committee on Intelligence. Republicans believe they have unearthed a scandal inside the bureau's top echelons over its determination to target Trump associates based on flimsy evidence and improper Justice Department contacts.

Republican committee members pressed Mr. McCabe about a dossier that was financed by the Democratic National Committee and the Clinton campaign based on gossip-tinged information from paid, unidentified Kremlin operatives. Mr. McCabe declined to criticize the dossier's 35 pages of salacious and criminal charges against Donald Trump and his aides, but he said it remains largely unverified, according to a source familiar with ongoing Congressional inquiries.

Sources speculated to The Washington Times that it would be embarrassing for Mr. McCabe to condemn a political opposition research paper on which his agents based decisions to open a counterintelligence investigation and interview witnesses. Some press reports said the FBI cited the dossier's information in requests for court-approved wiretaps. Mr. McCabe retired in March 2018, without reaching his retirement age.

Justice Department Inspector General Michael E. Horowitz is investigating whether Mr. McCabe should have recused himself from the Clinton email investigation in 2015 and 2016. Mr. McCabe's wife, an unsuccessful 2015 Democratic candidate for Virginia state Senate, received more than $700,000 in campaign donations from two PACs, one of which was controlled by Gov. Terry McAuliffe, a close Clinton ally. Mr. McCabe was fired by Attorney General Jeff Sessions, which was recommended by the Office of Professional Responsibility. He was two days away from his retirement and will lose his accrued pension benefits.

***Embattled FBI admits it can't verify dossier claims of Russia, Trump campaign collusion,** The Washington Times, By Rowan Scarborough, December 25, 2017

**** Other Hillary Clinton issues exist. Bill Clinton met with Attorney General Roberta Lynch at the time that Clinton's private emails were being investigated. They supposedly met accidentally, and Lynch claimed to have discussed "grandchildren, golf and travel" and Lynch stated that they did not discuss Hillary's email server issues or the Benghazi attacks, a report about which had been released the previous day.

****Bill Clinton, AG Loretta Lynch meet on tarmac in Phoenix**, CBS News, By Emily Schultheis, June 29, 2016

There are also allegations that Hillary Clinton used pay-to-play tactics to gain access to her as Secretary of State in return for contributions to the Clinton Foundation.

*****According to the New York Daily News, Federal investigators spent a substantial amount of time considering reopening an investigation into allegations that the Clinton Foundation promised political favors for donations. FBI agents were looking at whether donors were improperly given access to Hillary Clinton while she was serving as secretary of state, . "The Feds shut down an initial dive into the nonprofit and Clinton, who ran the State Department from 2009 through 2013, two years ago. The renewed investigation is being run out of the FBI's field office in Little Rock, Ark., where the foundation has offices".

*****FBI investigating Clinton Foundation for pay-to-play: reports, New York Daily News, By Christopher Brennan and Denis Slattery, Updated, January 5, 2018

******Peter Strzok and Lisa Page, both FBI employees discussed a strategy, that probably involved Andrew McCabe, and probably occurred in his office, that would be an insurance policy in the event that Trump, whom they disliked intensely, won the election. According the WND, Senate Judiciary Committee chairman Chuck Grassley, R-Iowa, is soliciting answers from the Justice Department about a text from one of the FBI's top Russian counterintelligence experts discussing an "insurance policy" in the event that presidential candidate Trump won the presidential election.

According to WND, after months of attacking then-candidate Trump and stating that Democratic nominee Hillary Clinton "just has to win", Peter Strzok and FBI lawyer Lisa Page exchanged a text about a so-called "insurance policy" against a possible Trump win.

******FBI On Hot Seat Over 'Insurance Policy' Against Trump Election, WND, By Chelsea Schilling, 12/14/2017

The Special Counselor Mueller investigation into Trump collusion with the Russians also has other possible conflicts, which were discussed previously. Also no charges have been filed against Trump.

ArmchairTechInvestor Opinion

This book has covered the activities of some of the highest officials in the Department of Justice and their activities in opposition to the election of Donald Trump, including those of James Comey, the FBI director fired by Trump. The firing of Comey resulted in the appointment of the Special Counsel Robert Mueller to investigate possible collusion of the Trump campaign, despite no evidence has been disclosed that substantiate such claims. One of the actions of Comey was the leaking of a memo through a professor friend to the New York Times that included his interpretation of private meetings with Trump, which may have been contained classified information, and been an illegal activity.

Other subjects covered by this book are the questionable actions by Bill and Hillary Clinton and the dossier financed partly by Clinton, which was used by the Clinton campaign through the offices of the Department of Justice and the FBI to fight the election of Donald Trump.

Media Bias

Media Bias & Trump Overstatements Both Occur: How Does That Distort The Reporting Of World Events?

There is clearly a media bias against President Trump. It can be characterized by Harvard's Shorenstein Center study that showed that 93% of the stories about Trump have been negative. In a neutral media environment, one would only expect 50% of the stories would be negative. However, the media needs to cover stories in a controversial way to generate interest and controversy, so there is a certain rationale for their behavior. Since Trump won the presidential election on a conservative agenda, one can presume that there is a liberal media bias, or Trump has done miserably in his performance. If the media is misrepresenting the actual situation, it is likely to catch up with them. The American public is often informed in other ways, such as over the Internet. Trump has clearly had his successes, particularly internationally and in the U.S. judicial system, but the media has not covered them.

Going against Trump is the intransigence of the Democrats in Congress, who have so far been unwilling to develop anything other than a very liberal agenda that was developed during the presidential election, with Senator Bernie Sanders driving their agenda towards socialism. The first deviation from this policy occurred in February, 2018, when a 2-year budget was approved that substantially increased funding for the military, and also increased social spending.

Socialism has not worked anywhere, and recent results in Europe show the downside of socialism. Even China and Russia could have been socialist countries, but the have evolved to support competitive markets that they try to control. President Trump has not had any success so far in getting approval of healthcare, tax reduction, or other programs that would impact the economy. However, some regulation relief and the prospect tax reductions have clearly been a factor in the strong stock market performance, which are all beneficial to the near and long-term prospects for businesses.

ArmchairTechInvestor Opinion

There is a dichotomy between what happens in the political arena and between what happens in world events. What Trump calls "fake news", such as the possible collusion between Russia and President Trump that resulted in a special prosecutor, Robert Mueller. President Trump attempts to take credit for events for which his administration has had little impact, such as a job growth, and the performance of the economy. However, the prospects of the tax cuts could have been influential in producing a strong stock market and economy.

The media has been focused on happenings that distract from reporting on the real issues that the U.S. faces, such as confronting the adversarial activities of China, Russia, ISIS, Iran and North Korea. The Democrats in the U.S. Senate have refused to help in developing U.S. policy, and the Republicans in the Senate are split, so no major legislation as of February, 2018, has been passed, other than the tax cuts.

Media Bias: Both CBS And CNN Distort Comey Testimony.

The liberal media and the Democrats are trying to take Trump down, and distortions by the liberal media are an important element of that joint effort. The Democrats have been totally obstructionist. The liberal media takes content out of context, and in many cases distorts the situation to the detriment of President Trump and his administration. An illustration of this was given earlier in this book by analyzing ABC's reporting of Trump's State of the Union Address.

James Comey submitted a copy of the testimony he gave in a public setting, early in the Trump Presidency. President Trump's claimed that Comey said on three occasions that Trump was not being investigated by the FBI with regard to the investigation into Russian involvement in the elections in 2016.

Comey's testimony described encounters when Trump said he hoped the FBI would "see its way clear" to clear General Flynn, who was let go by Trump because he lied to VP Pence about some Russian contacts. Trump and Comey said that honest loyalty was what was agreed to by both parties. CBS and CNN both took this encounter out of context and said that Trump was demanding that was the FBI drop the Investigation. The language and Trump's statements contradict this interpretation.

Obstruction of justice by Trump is also a manufactured situation designed to smear Trump by just raising the question. There has so far been no credible evidence of criminal wrong doing by Trump.

The investigation of involvement of the Trump campaign in collusion with the Russians appears to be another manufactured situation that so far has no basis in fact. However, it has resulted in Jeff Sessions, the Attorney General, recusing himself from the investigation, and a special prosecutor being appointed. All of this has happened despite there being no data to reflect this is even a possibility. The special prosecutor is a former colleague of James Comey, another indication of the politicized situation in Washington. The Republicans have been very weak in confronting this baseless assault by the Democrats and the liberal media on the Trump administration.

The Liberal Media Bias Has Been Documented: The Most Covered President Ever Has Extremely Negative Media Coverage

A study by Harvard's Shorenstein Center, a widely respected organization that chronicles media coverage, has provided details of Trump media coverage. The Center examined the tone and content of media coverage of President Trump for his first 100 days in office.

CNN, NBC, Fox and CBS were the four media companies covered in the study. Among the liberal media, CNN and NBC were the worst with 93% of their coverage being negative. Marginally better was CBS, which also provides liberal media biased coverage, was one percentage point better, with 92% negative coverage. Fox News is viewed as conservative media company. It was the only major media company that came close to being unbiased, with 52 percentage of its Trump coverage being negative.

The liberal news programs it appears have gone from being reporters of world events, to distorting their coverage to build controversy and promote the Democrats and their liberal political agenda.

The newspapers studied were The New York Times, The Washington Post, and The Wall Street Journal. The New York Times, and The Washington Post, are liberal newspapers, but slightly less biased than CNN, NBC and CBS, with 87% and 83% negative coverage respectively. The Wall Street Journal provides investment news coverage to its subscribers, and for that reason, appears to be relatively objective in its coverage of news events. Despite this objectivity, The Wall Street Journal still provided 70% negative coverage of President Trump.

The Liberal Press Vs. President Trump

In general, the media is strongly biased against Mr. Trump and his policies. The media is so biased continually that it is difficult to chronicle their inaccuracies, because there are so many. This book is more focused on the results that are being achieved, but we will occasionally comment on the inaccuracies. CNN, the New York Times, the Washington Post, NBC, CBS and ABC are the most inaccurate of the reporting media that we have been following. We consider the Wall Street Journal to be the most reliable print media, and Fox to be the least unbiased of the national networks.

ArmchairTechInvestor Opinion

ArmchairTechInvestor's original objective was to examine the liberal media coverage of Trump. Instead, this book looks at the Trump objectives and results. Many of the positive results are in the Middle East, but Asia, Europe, Africa and Latin America are covered also. We are also looking at the realities of the positive performance of the U.S. economy and the U.S. Government. So far, the military and deregulation, plus the approval of a Supreme Court Justice, and many appellate court justices (13 by February, 2018) are Trump administration achievements.

Brad Peery Background and Blogs

The blog ArmchairTechInvestor was created by Brad Peery, a former U.S. Senate candidate, who challenged Lowell Weicker in the 1982 Connecticut Senate Primary. The other candidates were Robin Moore, the author of the Green Berets, and Prescott Bush. When Prescott Bush came into the race, financing became unavailable to candidates not connected to traditional financing sources that lobby U.S. Congressional representatives to promote their causes. Money drives politics.

Mr. Peery has a love for politics, and provides an analyst perspective of the issues being faced by the Trump Presidency.

The author has over 40 years of experience in the investment industry. He was the first Wall Street telecom analyst in 1972. He followed the telecom industry for over 30 years. His broker-dealer was an underwriter in over 200 telecom syndicates in the 1990s, His investment banking firm managed partnerships that invested through both U.S. and offshore entities. His investment banking firm also invested in over 20 private early-stage broadband communications companies.

The telecom industry, being global, allowed Mr. Peery to be a worldwide telecom economist. This required understanding the economic issues that faced companies trying to do business in countries such as

China and India. He was an advisor to companies that included American Express, Wellington, T Rowe Price, and many other large money managers. Underwriting partners included Merrill Lynch, Morgan Stanley, Alex Brown, and many other large underwriters.

He was recently an advisor to companies in the medical technology area, and to a company, ChromaWay, which is developing colored coins, a blockchain technology application that allows many kinds of assets to be transferred securely, and inexpensively worldwide over the bitcoin blockchain network. Blockchain technology will be the underlying technology that will move banks and other financial institutions into the blockchain currency opportunity and improve the FinTech technology being pioneered by bitcoin technology.

Etherium is another blockchain application that has made improvements over bitcoins, and has its own currency, ethers. Litecoin and Ripple are two other currencies and blockchain technologies that are being developed.

Brad is currently developing two Blogs, ArmchairPolitician.US and ArmchairTechInvestor.com. The ArmchairPolitician.US blog postings are about President Trump's Policies and their success in being implemented, the role the liberal media and the Democrats are having in blocking that success, and details of foreign policy objectives, domestic economic and defense policy, and regulation in area such as the environment, energy, business, and the economy. This blog is structured in a way that this could be the first of several books that will look objectively at U.S. political issues, and worldwide technology developments.

The second blog, ArmchairTechInvestor.com, is a summary of the companies and countries, such as China, that are developing or supporting emerging technologies that will likely be game changing. These include quantum computing, artificial intelligence, small nuclear power plants, robots, drones, cognitive computing, holograms, and internet of things (IoT), plus others.

We have been writing about U.S.-Chinese relations and U.S. relations with China has become a book, **China vs. U.S. 2018, A Police State vs. A Democracy**. The China book will outline the important issues facing each country as they compete with each other globally. Of great importance are technologies such as quantum computing, electric vehicles, military, and global trade that China would like to dominate. The China topics are being included on the ArmchairTechInvestor ArmchairPolitician.US blog sites.

This book will outline the details of U.S. foreign policy, particularly as they are directed toward defeating ISIS, developing Middle East coalitions to confront Iran and their Hezbollah, and Houthis proxies in Lebanon, Syria and Yemen. We will also examine U.S. objectives relative to domestic economic and defense policies, and regulation in area such as the environment, energy and the economy. This book and the associated blog are structured in a way that this could be the second of several books that will look objectively at U.S. political issues.

International relations are also important parts of this book. The Europeans are going through their problems, particularly in handling millions of people immigrating into the EU with virtually no vetting of the immigrants. They face weakened defenses in view of the aggressive international ambitions of China and the Russians in the Balkans, Ukraine and elsewhere. Trump seems to be having some success in getting the NATO countries to meet their agreements to spend 2% of their GDP on defense. This could help improve their readiness, with Germany in particular being in need of improved defenses. So far unaddressed by the U.S. are the global political, economic, and military ambitions China is addressing by the development of its One Belt, One Road (OBOR) Initiative and the relations China is developing with about 70 countries.

ArmchairTechInvestor.Com Opinion and Objective

ArmchairTechInvestor's objective is to examine media coverage of Trump, analyze Trump's political objectives and results, then scrutinize the realities of the performance of the U.S. economy and the U.S. Government globally. Of particular interest is how the U.S. will meet the Chinese OBOR Initiative and technology developments' global threat over the next 20 years. We have been publishing our ArmchairTechInvestor blog since late 2017.

INTRODUCTION

Obama Legacy Issues, Recent U.S. International Issues, Trump State of the Union Address-2018-Achievements-2017, Plans-2018, ABC Response to State of the Union Address, Trump Has Addressed Significant U.S. Weaknesses, Worldwide Threats, China vs. U.S.-2018 Book Overview

Obama Legacy Issues

President Obama signed an Iran Nuclear Agreement. Because Iran is Shiite, this alienated Sunni U.S. partners in the Middle East, including Afghanistan, Iraq, Saudi Arabia, United Arab Emirates (UAE) and about another 45 Sunni Arab partners. The Obama administration tried to develop a dialogue with Iran, but failed, as is evident from the violently anti-America attitude of Ayatollah Ali Khamenei, the leader of Iran. A significant Obama mistake was the Iran Nuclear Agreement. It freed up substantial Iranian assets that are being used to finance their terrorist activities, estranged the U.S. from Israel, and Middle East countries that include Saudi Arabia. Iran is working with North Korea, and unless North Korea can be stopped, it is likely that both countries will end up with shared nuclear and missile launch capabilities.

Obama also caused the relationship with Israel to deteriorate. Trump has restored the U.S. relationship with one of the strongest democracies in the world. The fight to preserve democracy is strongly of conflict with China and Russia that feel threatened by the freedoms afforded to the citizens of countries such as the U.S., countries in Europe, South Korea, Japan and India, which could be all be very strong allies of the U.S.

Obama managed what he turned into a historically weak U.S. economy from 2009 to 2016. In the defense area. Obama substantially reduced U.S. military readiness, and drastically reduced troop levels in the Middle East. Separately, he failed to address aggressive regional expansion by Iran, Russia, China and ISIS. He failed to address the unwillingness of some countries to meet their NATO defense expenditure commitments.

He ignored the porous U.S. borders that have contributed to drugs and gangs. He promoted immigration without proper vetting from the Middle East. Also, the relationships with Israel and Middle Eastern countries such a Saudi Arabia and other Sunni countries deteriorated. The U.S. and Saudi Arabia have organized about 50 of these countries, mostly Sunni Muslim countries, to combat terrorism. Many of these countries, including Saudi Arabia, are now working with Israel.

Obama came into power at the low point of the 2007-2009 recession. Normally following a recession, the economy would accelerate rapidly for several years, and then slow down, with the result typically having been a growth rate that averaged over 3%. Obama only managed to achieve an all-time low economic growth rate of 2% over his eight years is office. The Obama administration had an anti-banking attitude, probably because his administration blamed the financial industry companies for the 2007-2009 recession, particularly the banks. He adopted the Dodd-Frank regulations, which slowed bank lending significantly. This was accompanied by an anti-business attitude that was characterized by a significant number of new regulations on businesses

Trump State of the Union Address-2018-Achievements-2017, Plans-2018

- Wants to Make America Great for all Americans;
- Has dealt with hurricanes, floods and fires;
- 200,000 new manufacturing jobs were created;
- Wages are rising;
- Lowest unemployment rates have been achieved;
  - o African American unemployment is at lowest ever; and
  - o Hispanic unemployment is also at the lowest ever;
- Small business confidence is strong;
- The stock market strong;
- Workers 401K retirement programs are up;
- About the third largest tax cuts and reforms in history have been achieved;
- Middle class and small business in particular are benefitting;
- Family tax deductions have been doubled to $24,000;
- The child tax credit has been doubled;

- The Obamacare individual healthcare mandate has been eliminated;
- Trump slashed the business tax rate to 21% to make U.S. businesses competitive worldwide;
- Small business has had a 20% tax reduction increase;
- So far there have been 3 million tax cut bonuses;
- $350 billion is being returned to the U.S. by Apple and 20,000 U.S workers will be added;
- Exxon is making a $50 billion investment in U.S.;
- American flag pride will be encouraged;
- In God We Trust will also be encouraged;
- The police, military and veterans will be supported;
- The child who put flags on 40,000 graves of soldiers was recognized;
- Standing for the National Anthem will be encouraged;
- Choice in healthcare will be pursued;
- The Veterans Administration Accountability Act reforms the VA;
  - o 1,500 people who didn't perform are gone; and
  - o Veterans need to be taken care of;
- Federal workers who fail need to be removed;
- Regulation removal is being pursued;
- The war on energy and clean coal has been ended;
- Detroit is revving up its engines;
  - o Chrysler is moving a major plant from Mexico to Michigan;
  - o Toyota and Mazda will build a plant in Alabama;
  - o All of the auto companies are coming back and new plants will be everywhere, according to Trump;
  - o The U.S. is where the action is;
- We are becoming an exporter of energy to the world;
- The FDA is approving medical devices more quickly;
- Experimental technology should be made available for the terminally ill;
- The U.S. must reduce the price of prescription drugs;
  - o They cost less internationally;
  - o This is a top priority; and
  - o Lower prices will occur;
- The U.S. faces unfair trade practices;
  - o Trade deals must be reciprocal;

- o There will be new trade deals;
- o Intellectual property will be protected; and
- o Enforcement will be strong;
- Infrastructure issues;
  - o $1.5 trillion is needed for infrastructure over 10 years;
  - o State & Local involvement is needed;
  - o Private investment will be encouraged;
  - o A 1-2 year approval process needs to be developed;
  - o Roads, bridges, highways, waterways, and railways need to be improved;
- Workforce development and job training are needed;
  - o Vocational schools are needed;
- Prison reform is needed;
  - o Second chances should be given to prisoners;
  - o Avoid development of terrorists;
- Illegal immigrant communities cause problems;
  - o There are losses of lives caused by illegal immigrants;
  - o They are competing for U.S. citizen's jobs;
  - o There is a need to close loopholes;
- U.S. Immigration and Customs Enforcement (ICE) activities help with the problem;
  - o U.S. citizens need to be protected;
  - o The U.S. needs to defend them; and
  - o Americans are dreamers too;
- A needed immigration reform package has four pillars. The package needs to be detailed, and a fair compromise needs to be negotiated with the Democrats;
  - o There needs to be a path to citizenship for 1.8 million illegal immigrants;
  - o There needs to be education and work requirements plus good citizenship over 12 years;
  - o The U,S. needs to secure the border fully;
    - ♣ A wall is needed;
    - ♣ More border patrol people are required;
    - ♣ Catch and release needs to be ended;
      - • It is dangerous;
- The visa lottery needs to be ended and immigration must;
  - o Be merit based;

- o   Those approved must love and respect the U.S.;
- o   They must be skilled; and
- o   They must work;
- The U.S. needs to end chain migration;
  - o   Distant relatives should not be allowed to enter;
  - o   Spouses and minor children should be allowed;
- U.S. Opioid and drug addiction needs to be addressed;
  - o   The sources of U.S. opioids need to be restricted, including those coming from China via the U.S. mail system;
  - o   The U.S. needs to be tougher on dealers;
  - o   Treatment needs to be provided;
- Terrorists need to be pursued;
- Countries that could be a threat include;
  - o   China; and
  - o   Russia;
- Unmatched military power is needed;
  - o   Sequestration needs to be ended;
  - o   The U.S. needs to modernize and rebuild defenses;
- The U.S. needs to extinguish ISIS;
  - o   Close to 100% of their territory in Iraq, Syria and elsewhere has been recaptured;
  - o   The U.S. needs to continue the fight;
- Unlawful enemy combatants are a U.S. problem;
  - o   They need to be treated like terrorists;
  - o   Many are let go;
  - o   The U.S. needs to keep Guantanamo open;
- In Afghanistan;
  - o   We have new rules of engagement;
  - o   We don't tell our plans publically;
- The U.N. has been unfair;
- With regard to Israel;
  - o   Jerusalem is the capital;
- $20 billion of U.S. aid is being sent;
  - o   It will go only to friends;
- Iran policy;
  - o   Stand with Iranian people in their quest for freedom; and
  - o   The Nuclear Pact is flawed;
- With regard to Cuba and Venezuela;

- o   We need to put sanctions on dictatorships;
- North Korea issues;
  - o   Nuclear missiles are a risk to U.S.; and
  - o   They are a threat to America and our allies;
- We need to protect our citizens;
  - o   Talents such as music need to be nurtured;
  - o   Science and discovery are important personal qualities;
  - o   They are Making America Great again;
- Rediscovering America again will be the theme for 2018.

ABC Response to State of the Union Address

TRUMP CLAIM 3: "We are now an exporter of energy to the world."

ABC TAKE: Mostly spin

According to ABC: Continuing a longstanding trend, energy exports did tick up slightly during the first 10 months of the Trump administration, from 11.5 quadrillion BTU (standard unit of measurement) in January to October 2016 to 14.6 quadrillion BTU in January to October 2017. But the U.S. has exported energy, from crude oil to natural gas to coal, for a long time.

ArmcairTechInvestor Response: The increase in U.S. energy was more than an uptick. Exports increased by 27% in 2017. The increases are probably largely from liquefied natural gas (LNG) from shale, which Trump has supported, and from coal, for which China is the largest importer, and which Trump has also supported.

TRUMP CLAIM 5: "Working with the Senate, we are appointing judges who will interpret the Constitution as written, including a great new Supreme Court justice, and more circuit court judges than any new administration in the history of our country."

ABC TAKE: True

ABC WHY: The Senate confirmed 12 of Trump's circuit court nominees in his first year in office -- far more than his recent predecessors.

ArmcairTechInvestor Response: In this case, ABC got it right.

TRUMP CLAIM 6: "The coalition to defeat ISIS has liberated very close to 100 percent of the territory just recently held by these killers in Iraq and in Syria and in other locations as well."

ABC TAKE: True

ABC WHY: The State Department reported in December, 2017 that ISIS had lost 98 percent of the territory it once held specifically in Iraq and Syria.

ArmcairTechInvestor Response: The Trump claim is close to being true. The reality is that 50% of the 98% that has been liberated occurred during the first 11 months of the Trump administration. Giving authority to military troops on the ground, a change from the Obama administration, was an important element in this success. However, the battle against ISIS has expanded geographically to the Philippines and other places in Asia, plus West Africa. Terrorist cells also remain in Syria and Iraq and have increased in Afghanistan during 2018. The efforts to defeat ISIS must continue.

TRUMP CLAIM 7: "Under the current broken system, a single immigrant can bring in virtually unlimited numbers of distant relatives. Under our plan, we focus on the immediate family by limiting sponsorships to spouses and minor children. This vital reform is necessary, not just for our economy, but for our security and our future."

ABC TAKE: False

ABC WHY: Citizens and green card holders can petition for immediate family, not an unlimited number of family members.

ArmcairTechInvestor Response: The ABC response of false is misleading or incorrect. It is our understanding that anyone who gets a green card can petition to bring in their family, who in turn get green cards and can bring in their relatives. There are 4 million such persons waiting for entry into the U.S.

Additionally, ABC said the green card holders can petition for a spouse, minor child, or unmarried son or daughter, to also become a permanent resident. And, refugees or asylum seekers can apply for a spouse or minor child to also obtain their refugee or asylum status. Still, after applying, there is a long waiting list for all applicants besides a spouse, parent or minor child. As of November 2017, nearly 4 million people are waiting to get off the list, according to the State Department. Once someone gets to the front of the line, he or she must pass the required background checks and meet the other requirements for admission.

TRUMP CLAIM 8: "For decades, open borders have allowed drugs and gangs to pour into our most vulnerable communities. They have allowed millions of low-wage workers to compete for jobs and wages against the poorest Americans. Most tragically, they have caused the loss of many innocent lives."

ABC TAKE: Mostly spin

ABC WHY: A 2016 report by the National Academies of Sciences, Engineering and Medicine, found that the impact of immigration on the wages of native-born workers overall is very small.

ArmcairTechInvestor Response: The 2016 report mentioned by ABC only talks about jobs. There is no doubt that illegal immigrants are important to industries such as agriculture, but there is no reason such immigrants cannot be allowed to enter legally. There is no doubt that gangs such as MS-13, from El Salvador, have used illegal immigrants to build its gangs in most of the U.S. states, and has tens of thousands of current members. They also prey on immigrant children to build their gangs.

According to the Trump White House:
- On average, the Department of Homeland Security (DHS) apprehends over 1100 people a day crossing the border illegally, with December, 2017 marking the eighth month in a row of an increase in apprehensions at the border. That is a rate of almost 400,000 per year;
- DHS refuses entry to 7 known or suspected terrorists every day, 50 every week, 2,500 every year. Although the terrorists are under

1% of the apprehensions, the numbers are disturbing because of the amount of havoc one terrorist can reap;

- Roughly 628,000 aliens overstayed their visa in Fiscal Year 2016 alone;
  - o Canadian visa holders were the largest number of visa violators;
- As of May 2016, there were 950,062 aliens with final orders of removals on ICE's national docket;
  - o Some Democrats are trying to abolish ICE despite it being an immigration enforcement unit of U.S. laws;
- Officials apprehended 8,000 family units in December, 2017. This is almost 100,000 family units per year;
- There was a 306% increase in unaccompanied alien children detained at the border since April, 2017. Most will be released after no more than 20 days;
- Officials apprehended over 4,000 unaccompanied alien children (UACs) in December, 2017. This is almost 50,000 children per year; and,
- 95% of family units and unaccompanied children who are released pending a hearing never show up at the hearing.

Putting in a southern border wall will eliminate many of the hundreds of thousands of illegal immigrants per year, including terrorists, gang members, and illegal drug traffickers. The above facts are not mostly spin, as claimed by ABC.

TRUMP CLAIM 9: "In recent weeks, two terrorist attacks in New York were made possible by the visa lottery and chain migration. In the age of terrorism, these programs present risks we can just no longer afford. It is time to reform these outdated immigration rules and, finally, bring our immigration system into the 21st century."

ABC TAKE: Mostly spin

ABC WHY: Both men entered the country legally through the two programs President Trump mentioned and were not radicalized until years after they arrived in the U.S.

ArmchairTechInvestor Response: The ABC response does not address the real problems of the visa program and chain migration. Radicalization is only one of the risks of not vetting immigrants and orienting the visa program to those who will be self-sufficient and contribute to the U.S. by being good citizens. The ABC response of mostly spin is incorrect.

TRUMP CLAIM 10: "Last year, Congress also passed, and I signed, the landmark VA Accountability Act. Since its passage, my administration has already removed more than 1,500 VA employees who failed to give our veterans the care they deserve."

ABC TAKE: Mostly spin

ABC WHY: The law was enacted in June, by that time 500 of the 1,500 Veterans Affairs employees removed from their jobs for poor performance had already been fired under a previous system.

ArmchairTechInvestor Response

There is no doubt that the VA has provided miserable support for veterans, including under the past administration. Trump is a strong supporter of the military and U.S. veterans. For ABC to call his statement "mostly spin" implies that Trump is not a supporter of the VA, and ignores the fact that, even though it took Trump six months to pass the VA Accountability Act, he was a strong advocate for change from the moment he became President, which is when the first 500 VA employees were removed.

TRUMP CLAIM 11: "Last year, the FDA approved more new and generic drugs and medical devices than ever before in our history."

ABC TAKE: True

ABC WHY: The FDA approved 1,027 generic drugs in fiscal year 2017, a "record number," according to Commissioner Dr. Scott Gottlieb.

ABC said: "The agency's Center for Drug Evaluation and Research also approved 46 so-called novel drugs, the highest number in at least a decade, and a record 95 "novel" devices in 2017. New drugs included cancer therapies and medications to treat infectious diseases and neurological disorders."

ArmchairTechInvestor Response:

ABC is acknowledging that Trump is making a large impact on the Food and Drug Administration (FDA). In addition to the results being achieved, it remains to be seen if drug prices can be reduced, particularly by FDA support for generics.

TRUMP CLAIM 12: "We slashed the business tax rate from 35 percent all the way down to 21 percent, so American companies can compete and win against anyone else, anywhere in the world. These changes alone are estimated to increase average family income by more than $4,000."

ABC TAKE: It's complicated

WHY: It's a bold prediction, based on economic estimates that are far from uniform.

ArmchairTechInvestor Response:

ABC says that the tax reductions are complicated, and economic estimates vary. Those statements are misleading. The average corporate tax rate around the world is 23%, and at a 35% tax rate, U.S. corporations were at a disadvantage. With the corporate tax rate at 21%, companies will, in general, be able to compete more effectively internationally. The tax changes will also allow the return of trillions of dollars U.S. companies have been holding offshore to avoid taxes. That has changed, and a significant amount of this money will likely come back to the U.S.

The improvements in income for families will come from increased income from companies that pass on part of their tax reductions to their employees. Also, there will be reductions in taxes for families. Additionally, there are possible increases in family income because of economic growth, which could reach 3% in 2018 and 2019, and the possibility that growth could thereafter be above 2.5% of GDP. Those economic increases could raise wages, which have recently gone from about 2.5%

increases during the Obama administration, to the 2.9% level reached in January 2018.

As of mid-2018, wages were growing more rapidly, but the media is pointing out that they are being offset by inflation increases. This is misleading. The Fed is trying to reverse zero interest rate Obama policies, and get the inflation rate up to 2%, which seems to be occurring.

Trump Has Addressed Significant U.S. Weaknesses

The Trump administration has seven main focuses as a result of the Obama administrations policies. They are:

- Improving the U.S. economy, including job growth and manufacturing through corporate tax reductions, and repatriating offshore corporate cash;
- Rebuilding U.S. defenses, including upgrading the U.S. Navy, and Air Force readiness;
- Reengaging in the Middle East, particularly with Saudi Arabia and other Sunni Muslim countries;
- Addressing terrorism, drugs and gang violence by strengthening U.S. borders and immigration policies;
  o   Confronting Iran, Russia, ISIS and China;
- Improving NATO defenses;
- Improving the efficiency of the United Nations; and,
- Developing a stronger U.S. relationship with Israel.

Trump is focused on achieving historical U.S. economic growth rates of 3% by:

- Reducing taxes, and regulations;
- Bringing back jobs that have been lost, particularly because of the trade deficit; and,
- U.S. companies, such as Apple, Google and other large tech companies leaving the U.S.

He has substantially increased the defense budget to restore U.S. readiness. This could take as long as 10 years. He has developed strong relationships with Saudi Arabia, and its Arab partner countries to confront Iranian and

Russian expansion in the Middle East. A strong relationship with India is being developed. Trump has rebuilt relationships with Afghanistan, Iraq, and the Kurds to aggressively go after ISIS, and in the first eleven months of his presidency has reduced the territory they occupy by 50%. The Trump administration has addressed some of the shortcomings of NATO, including the substantial failures of many members in not meeting their commitments to spend two percent of their GDP on defense. The head of NATO is addressing this shortcoming, and several countries have also agreed to meet their two percent obligations. The most egregious underperformer is Germany, which certainly has the resources to spend two percent of GDP on defense, and has not yet agreed to meet their commitment to NATO.

This second book objective includes looking at Chinese policies as they affect current and possible future relationships. This requires looking at the nuances of U.S. domestic and international relationships as they affect the **China vs. U.S. 2018** theme. It also means looking at Chinese domestic and international policies in a current and possible futures context.

ArmchairTechInvestor Opinion

One important achievement has been to begin closing U.S. borders to Mexico, which will be helpful in controlling drug supplies, drug cartels, and other criminals in illegally attempt to enter the U.S. from Mexico and Latin America. An important Trump victory was the Supreme Court blocking attempts to overturn lower courts trying to block the Trump administration's plans to increase the vetting of immigrants from the Middle East and elsewhere. However, the race will be a long one in these areas, particularly because of Democratic obstructionism in the House and Senate. This is characterized by the approval ratings of Nancy Pelosi and Chuck Schumer, both of which have been in the twenties.

On the positive side, the stock market is hitting all time highs, the defense budget, which was approved in February, 2018 has been approved by the House, the Senate and Trump. Iran, Russia and China are being confronted where the U.S. has differences, and the relationships with Russia and China are being strengthened where we have common interests. And, the U.S. has substantially strengthened its relationships with Israel and Sunni Arab countries, many of whom now have relationships with Israel.

The U.S. objectives will be to describe the complex politics of many situations worldwide, including the motivations for many countries and other organizations such as Hamas, Hezbollah and ISIS, develop U.S. policies and solutions to those problems. These situations and issues will be described on a regional basis that includes the Middle East, Asia, Europe, North America (Canada and Mexico) and Africa. These objectives will be discussed in the context of the U.S.-China 2018 relationship.

Worldwide Threats

Worldwide Threats Outlined In Senate Intelligence Committee Hearing-The Threats Are Widespread

*The threats from ISIS will continue to be challenging, despite widespread defeats in Syria and Iraq. They include:

- They are engaged in an Insurgency in Afghanistan;
- The U.S. needs to continue to hit them with airstrikes;
- Their funding will continue and needs to be addressed;
- Their flow of fighters needs to be confronted;
- In Iraq and Syria, ISIS is regrouping in ungoverned portions of the countries;
- ISIS is extending its global presence to Asia and other regions;
- It continues to champion its cause;
- Their engaging in international attacks will continue to be a threat; and,
- They will continue to encourage sympathizers to attack in their home countries.

Al Qaeda continues to be a major actor in global terrorism. Its long-term intent is to attack the U.S. and U.S. interests abroad.

Transnational organized crime will continue to be a problem, including:

- Drugs;
- Human trafficking;
- Depleting U.S. national resources; and
- Siphon money from governments in the global economy.

Regional threats include:

South Asia

- Afghanistan:
  - o Kabul is bearing the brunt of a Taliban led insurgency;
  - o Other issues are:
    - ♣ Their security forces face unsteady performance; and
    - ♣ With help Afghanistan will probably retain control of most major population centers.
- Pakistan, which has a very close relationship with China:
  - o Provides terrorist safe havens for attacks in Afghanistan and India, including on U.S. interests;
  - o The Pakistan military is unlikely to have a lasting effect on restraining terrorists;
  - o It will maintain its terrorist ties and restrict its cooperation with the U.S.; and
  - o It will continue its strong ties to China, including the building of a harbor as part of the One Belt, One Road Initiative.
- India is likely to become an increasingly strong U.S. partner, and offers an offset to some of China's ambitions.
- Russia will continue its assertive foreign policies to shape outcomes. These include:
  - o More authoritarian activities to maintain control and offset challenges to Putin's rule;
  - o Promote Russian influence and propaganda efforts that are:
    - ♣ Cheap;
    - ♣ Low risk;
    - ♣ Plausible deniability; and
    - ♣ Proven to be effective at sowing division.
  - o Russia will continue using:
    - ♣ Propaganda;
    - ♣ Social media;
    - ♣ False flag personas and sympathetic spokesmen to exacerbate social and political divisions in the U.S.; and
    - ♣ 2018 midterm U.S. elections are a target.
  - o Russia and China share many common goals with the most powerful one being their dictatorships. This gives both of

them an overarching goal of defeating the U.S., the most powerful democracy in the world, in any way they can.

Middle East and North Africa

- In the region, the issues will continue to be:
  - o Political turmoil:
    - ♣ Economic fragility will be a problem;
- Civil and proxy wars will continue using:
  - o Hezbollah in Syria and Lebanon; and
  - o The Houthis in Yemen.
- Iran is the most prominent state sponsor of terrorism. And it will:
  - o Expand its regional influence;
  - o Use the regional fight against ISIS to:
    - ♣ Solidify partnerships;
    - ♣ Transform battlefield gains into political security and economic agreements;
  - o Develop military forces that threaten U.S. forces and its allies;
  - o Continue to develop the largest ballistic missile force in the Middle East;
  - o Use the Islamic Revolutionary Guard Corps that may be a risk to U.S. naval and allied naval operations in the region;
  - o Continue provocative behavior in Northern Israel that:
    - ♣ Has the Potential for escalation into a war with Israel.
  - o The Lebanese Hezbollah activities include:
    - ♣ Support of Iran;
    - ♣ Thousands of fighters to Syria; and
    - ♣ Directs other militant groups, promoting regional instability.
- Turkey will seek to thwart Kurdish ambitions:
  - o Their incursion into Northern Syria is complicating counter ISIS activities in the region, which Increases the risk to U.S. forces; and
  - o Turkey is developing closer ties to Russia and China;
- In Syria, unrest and fighting will continue in 2018:
  - o Some areas will be recaptured by Syria, Russia and Iran and violence will decrease in some areas;
- Iraq will see a lengthy period of turmoil and conflict;

- Iran has used ISIS to deepen its influence in military and security elements and political arms of Iraq;
- In the Yemen war:
  o Because of the Iranian backed Houthis and Saudi Arabia coalition:
    ♣ A tragic humanitarian crisis will worsen:
      • 70% of 20M people need assistance

Europe

- In Europe, the center of gravity is shifting to France:
  o President Macron is more assertive in addressing European and global challenges; and
- German elections reinforce Germany's weakness;
- Efforts by some governments in Central and Eastern Europe to undermine judicial independence and parliamentary oversight and increase control over the media are weakening the rule of law;
  o Provides opportunity for democratic declines and offers opportunities for Russian and Chinese influence; and
  o Latvia elections have encountered meddling by Russia.

U.S. problems:

- Failure to properly address long-term fiscal situation has increased national debt to $20 trillion and growing. This is:
  o Unsustainable; and a
  o Dire threat to economic and national security;
  o Needs to be addressed before crisis occurs that threatens U.S. national security;
- Need tech communications:
  o Internet of Things (IoT) causes large cybersecurity problems.

*Worldwide Threats Hearing, Senate Intelligence Committee, Dan Coates-Director of National Intelligence, February 14, 2018

China-Space Military

There will be threats in space. Russia and China will continue to expand space-based reconnaissance. These include:

- Communications and navigation systems, including:
    o Broaden the applications they use;
    o Increase the number of systems; and
    o Broaden their breadth of capabilities.
- Counter space weapons will mature. They will include:
    o Anti-satellite weapons; and
    o Efforts to reduce U.S. effectiveness and advantages in space.

China Foreign Policy-East Asia

- North Korea is an Increasing threat to the U.S.:
    o It may not be willing to negotiate its missiles and nuclear weapons away;
    o They are considered critical to its security;
    o It seeks to end Seoul's reliance on Washington;
    o It wants to eventually dominate the Korean Peninsula;
    o There will be additional missile tests in 2018;
    o North Korea will do an atmospheric nuclear test over the Pacific;
    o It is a direct threat to the U.S.; and
    o Provides conventional threats to South Korea, Japan and Guam.
- China:
    o Will seek to expand its influence and shape events and outcomes globally;
    o Other Chinese threats include:
        ♣ Firm stands it will continue to take on claims to East China Sea and South China Sea;
        ♣ It will continue to reaffirm its relationship with Taiwan; and
        ♣ It will continue to develop its One Belt, One Road initiative to:
            • Expand its trade, investment, and partnership reach to geostrategic locations across Asia, Africa and the Pacific;

o   It provides an important possible avenue to denuclearizing the Korean Peninsula.

ArmchairTechInvestor Opinion

The Senate Intelligence Committee hearings provided a good summary of some of the threats facing the U.S., but there are many other threats that we will address in China vs. U.S. 2018.

China vs. U.S.-2018 Book Overview

There are two objectives of the ArmchairTechInvestor blog, which is the impetus for this book. The first is to examine recently changed China policy. They want to dominate seven areas that have been identified. To meet their policy objectives, plus substantially improve the efficiency of the Communist Party, they will need to become or be a worldwide leader in adopting and developing new technologies., Second is to examine the objectives of the Trump presidency, describe the obstacles it faces world-wide, and report objectively on the results that are being achieved by the Trump administration.

With regard to President Trump, he is modifying his campaign promises as he meets the realities of foreign governments and entities such as ISIS. We expect him to stick to his basic themes, such as immigration reform, supporting Israel, developing U.S. job growth through bringing back jobs that are being exported, building U.S. infrastructure, and putting in lower corporate and personal tax rates to stimulate economic growth.

The over 20% increases in the major stock market indexes, such as the Dow Jones index, the S&P 500 index and Nasdaq, indicate that Wall Street believes President Trump will be successful in improving economic growth through increasing corporate profitability, increasing individual jobs, and growing personal after-tax disposable income. Very strong business confidence, and consumer confidence are important elements of the strong economic and stock market results.

The Trump administration has expressed opposition to the Iran Nuclear Agreement. After investigating Iran's compliance, in view of its missile launch developments, and expanding regional terrorism, the U.S. has declared Iran to be in non-compliance with the Agreement. Sanctions on Iran have been imposed by the Trump administration.

Iran is increasing its influence in Iraq, Syria, Yemen, Lebanon and elsewhere, The Trump administration is aggressively opposing regional hegemony by fighting ISIS, Iran, and Russia. This fight is also being pursued by developing relationships with Saudi Arabia, and other Sunni Arab countries. The U.S. is also financially supporting Egypt, Jordan, Pakistan, Lebanon and Israel. Under Trump's new guidelines, the relationships with Pakistan, because of its support for terrorists in Afghanistan, and Lebanon, because the role of Hezbollah in the country, could be reduced or eliminated.

CHAPTER 1

China vs. U.S-Economy, Regulation, Territorial Ambitions-Trade, Xi Reorganization, One Belt, Growth, Jobs, U.S. Immigration, Chinese International, China vs. U.S.-Trade, Trans Pacific Partnership, Nafta, Visas, WTO, U.S. Investment, Currency, U.S. Trade Deficit and Jobs

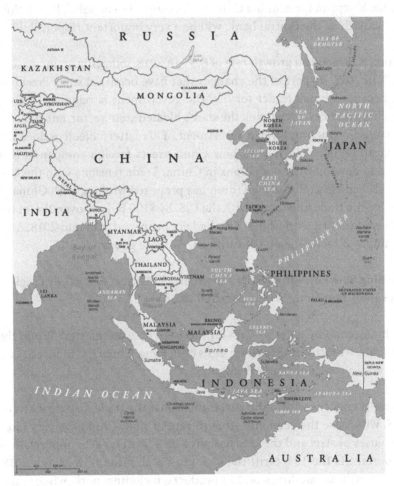

Image: China to Australia Map
Image Source: Getty Images

Economy-China

Xi Jinping has become China's President for life. This occurred in early 2018. This could bring profound changes to the way China is operated. The management of the Chinese economy is one case in point. Liu He, who is a Harvard graduate, has assumed leadership of the economy, including the financial system and the industrial sector, over which Xi Jinping previously presided. In October 2017, Mr. Liu produced an economic blueprint for running China's economy, "Xi Thought". Regulation, particularly of the central bank, will be a very important responsibility.

China is targeting a growth rate of 6.5% in 2018, following an increase of 6.9% in 2017. As part of the changes that have occurred since President Xi became China's leader for life, the government is reigning in risky lending practices, revamping the state's bloated state sector, and has also espoused attracting foreign investment. This latter objective does not seem to be likely, in view of how China treats foreign companies that want to develop their operations in China. Trade tensions with the U.S. are also an issue. President Trump has proposed working with China to reduce the trade imbalance with the U.S. by $100 billion, over 25% of the U.S. trade deficit with China. This had not happened as of mid-2018. And, Trump was racheting up the tariffs on Chinese goods.

*Beijing Sees Growth of 6.5% This Year, Wall Street Journal, by Lingling Wei and Chun Hong Wong, March 5, 2018

China's economy grew by 6.8% in the March, 2018 quarter. While the economy was strong, there were signs of slowing. China has reduced taxes on certain companies by $38 billion.

There is concern within the government that the trade dispute with the U.S. will cause the economic growth rate to slow. China has very large surpluses of steel and the U.S. has put a 25% tariff on U.S. imports. Less important is the 10% tariff the U.S. put on aluminum in March 2018. In turn, China put duties on 128 products, including: pork; wine; seamless steel pipes; and subsequently, soybeans and cars. Many of these are targeted at states where Trump has strong political support. The U.S. has suggested that trade with China needs to be reduced by about $100 billion. In April 2018, China suggest that trade talks with the U.S. be held in Beijing. Short-term growth in China is also being impacted by efforts to closing smokestack industries to reduce adverse health impacts, and reducing the availability of debt for such companies.

To forestall a possible growth rate slowdown, China has reduced bank reserve requirements to increase business lending. When the changes took effect on April 25, 2018, they were expected in result in about $200 billion of funds being available for such loans.

China Moves to Forestall Growth Slowdown, Wall Street Journal, by Lingling Wei, April 18, 2018

China Unemployment

The unemployment rate in China declined slightly to a record low of 3.89% in the first quarter of 2018 from 3.90% in the fourth quarter of 2017. The unemployment rate in China averaged 4.11% from 2002 through 2017.

China Provinces Map

Image: China Provinces Map
Image Source: Getty Images

China Labor Force

The World Bank estimates that the labor force in China grew from 639.943 million in 1990 to 785.368 million in 2017 a 0.76% growth rate. China's population reached 1,390.08 million people in Dec 2017. Monthly Earnings of China stood at 824.40 USD in Dec 2016. The country's Labor Force Participation Rate dropped to 68.93 % in Dec 2017.

China Productivity

*China is able to achieve economic growth of over 6.5% despite a work force growth rate of under 1% because its high productivity and a labor force participation rate of 69%. China's labor productivity improved by 6.85 in Dec

2017, compared with a growth of 6.49 % in the previous year. China's Labor Productivity Growth data is updated yearly, available from Dec 1953 to Dec 2017, averaging at 7.45 %. The data reached an all-time high of 15.12 % in Dec 1970 and a record low of -26.45 % in Dec 1961. CEIC calculates labor productivity growth from the annual real GDP Index and annual employment. The Ministry of Human Resources and Social Security provides employment statistics. Employment excludes Foreign Nationals working within the country. *https://www.ceicdata.com/en/indicator/china/labour-productivity-growth

Economy-Growth and U.S. Trade

China's growth rate is targeted by the government at about 6.5% in 2018. Substantial reorganization of the economy is occurring. Risky lending practices are being addressed. There is trade tension with the U.S. based upon tariffs the U.S. has adopted on steel and aluminum. Ignored in these discussions are often the tariffs China places on imported goods, such as a 25% tariff on foreign manufactured automobiles. Also ignored are restrictions China places on goods it considers to be vital to its national defense. This is allowed by the WTO under obsolete designations given to China in the early 2000s.

Energy-China

*China is replacing coal with LNG. This resulted in a substantial increase in LNG imports from the U.S. in 2017. This has caused LNG prices in Asia to surpass their level in 2014. China plans to increase the level of LNG usage from 7% of its energy mix to 10% by 2020. China imports 56 million tons of LNG per year. That is slated to rise by about one-third to 74 million tons in 2020.

*China Draws Gas Out of Global Market, Wall Street Journal, By Sarah McFarlane and Nathaniel Taplin, January 24, 2018

Banking and Insurance Regulation

The banking and insurance commissions will be merged. This will set the stage to address deep-seated risks to the banking system and the economy. The central bank will set overall rules for the banking and insurance industries. Oversight of individual firms will be left to the new commission. The head of this commission will be Liu He, a close confidant of President Ji, and his top economic advisor. This should lead to capital markets reforms that include reducing debt levels, and reducing the risk of financial products, such as derivatives. Also included is pricing authority and antimonopoly enforcement from other departments as well as product safety, including food and drugs.

China-Territorial Ambitions-Political Influence, Military Influence and Trade

While the U.S. is emphasizing its policy of negotiating bilateral trade agreements, China is doing just the opposite. It has developed a trade agreement, called the Regional Comprehensive Economic Partnership with 16 countries making up 39% of global GDP. China is the main trade competitor of the U.S. on the global stage. It has an ambitious project called the One Belt, One Road Network that will connect 60 countries to China economically, and as joint investors. These types of activities can result in relationships that go far beyond trade and can involve joint investment, political and military relationships.

Political and State Organizations-Xi Reorganization and Economy-China

China's Economy Is Likely to Become More Market Oriented, Particularly for State-Owned Businesses

Regulation, particularly of the central bank, will be a very important responsibility. The banks are likely to push back against controls on risky lending and investment practices that add debt to the financial system.

The objective will be to put the Chinese economy on a sounder footing. This will likely be accompanied by market-based changes. State-owned companies will need to begin to make a return on their investments.

According to Barry Naughton, a China expert at UC San Diego, Mr. Liu, has a good relationship with Xi Jinping, but for him to be successful, he will need to maintain that relationship.

*Trusted Xi Ally Set to Guide China Economy, Wall Street Journal, by Lingling Wei, February 27, 2018

ArmchairTechInvestor Opinion

The elevation of Xi Jinping to President of China for life could have profound implications for Chinese policy. Leaders such as Mr. Liu for the economy, and others for different sectors, are likely to allow these new leaders to take on more responsibility.

Moving to a more market-based economy could assist China in making Chinese government companies less of a risk to the economy, and aid their ability to deal with other companies. It may also become a tool that the U.S. can use to assist it in resisting Chinese subsidies of its companies that have increased the U.S. trade deficit with China.

Additional Chinese Objectives-Land Management, Anti-Corruption and Veterans Affairs

Additionally, in prospect are to:

- Create of a new ministry to manage land, ocean and other resources;
- Intensify an anti-corruption crackdown; and
- Add a new veterans affairs ministry.

Office of International Development

An office of international development cooperation has been created, under which the One Belt, One Road Trade Network will fall. The office is described as providing foreign aid, but its objectives are far broader and include political and military influence, building an extensive array of jointly owned facilities with the host nation, and extending China's global presence.

U.S. Trade Deficits

The U.S. Faces Many Trade Barriers: How Can Fair Trade Be Achieved?

The U.S. had a $752.5 trade deficit in goods in 2016. There are trade barriers imposed by foreign countries that are not possible in the U.S. These contributed to the trade deficit. The largest trade deficits in 2016 were with China, $347 billion, and the European Union, $146.8 billion. According to an article by Wilbur Ross, the U.S. Secretary of Commerce, in the Wall Street Journal, China's tariffs on 20 of 22 goods are higher than those in the U.S. The European Union (EU) has higher tariffs than the U.S. in 17 of the 22 categories. An example is that the EU has a 10% tariff on imported automobiles, while the U.S. has a tariff of 2.5%. The EU ships four times as many automobiles to the U.S. as are exported by the U.S. to the EU. China, which is the world's largest automobile market, imposes a 25% tariff on vehicles, and larger tariffs on luxury vehicles. This is probably a large factor in U.S. automobile manufacturers setting up operations in China. Also, China requires that foreign manufacturers set up joint ventures with Chinese companies. While the details are not clear about vehicles, Chinese regulations often put intellectual property at risk.

In addition to tariffs, there are many other non-tariff barriers. Both the EU and China have trade barriers that include:

- Onerous regulations for certification or registration of products;
- Unscientific sanitary rules for agricultural products;
- Requirements that companies build local factories;
- And, forced technology transfers.

Both China and the EU help finance their exports through:

- Grants, Low-cost loans;
- Energy subsidies;
- and Special value-added tax refunds and, below-market real estate sales and leases.
- There are also other export product subsidies.

Trade and Trade Barriers-China

The U.S. faces many barriers to fair trade imposed by foreign countries. The largest culprit is China, with whom the U.S. has the largest trade deficit. The Chinese trade barriers include:

- Providing knowledge to Chinese auto manufacturers, in particular, but also other Chinese companies, of future government policies;
- Forcing technology transfers to local Chinese companies by requiring foreign companies to form joint ventures with Chinese companies; and
- Imposing tariffs, such as those that cause foreign manufactured autos to be very expensive.
  - o   To avoid the joint ownership requirement, Tesla is starting a manufacturing plant in Singapore, and will pay a 20% tariff on vehicles sold in China. These unfair trade practices are being used to allow Chinese companies to dominate the future electric car industry. China may ban the sale of internal combustion vehicles in China as early as 2030.

U.S.-China Trade Policies: China Manipulates It's Currency While It Ostensibly Encourages Worldwide Free Trade

There are areas where the Chinese yuan trades outside of China, including in Hong Kong. The Chinese buy the yuan in those markets to keep its value close the level China is targeting in its currency manipulation efforts. The yuan gained 1.1% against the U.S. dollar in 2016. Federal Reserve rate increases, that could total about 1% in 2018, will put some pressure on the yuan. One of the issues China faces is the forward value of the yuan. The yuan was down 3.2% versus the dollar, in forward trading, at the end of 2016. Such a decline would make Chinese imports less expensive, and could contribute to increases in the U.S. trade deficit with China.

China Policies-Currency-Yuan

*China's manipulation of its currency, the yuan, is one way to disadvantage the U.S. and other countries that trade with them. In May 2018, the decline in the yuan was near its weakest level in the last two months, and was down 1.1% compared with the U.S. dollar. However, other currencies have declined more against the dollar, with the Japanese yen down 3.5% and the euro down 1.9%. The supposition is that upcoming U.S.-China trade negotiations have caused China to prop up its currency, relative to a basket of other currencies, before the meetings, in view of Trump's presidential campaign position that China is causing its currency to be undervalued.

*Yuan Weakness Revives Manipulation Debate, Wall Street Journal, by Saumya Vaishhampayan, May 5, 2018

China's Trade Policies: Automobiles Show the Difficulties the U.S. Faces in Reducing the Trade Deficit with China

U.S. Automobile companies are effectively banned from competing in China. U.S. Automobiles are taxed at a rate of 25%, that effectively makes U.S. produced automobiles uncompetitive in China. There are also Chinese policies that are anticompetitive, even for companies that want to establish manufacturing plants in China.

The industrial sector, in the past, accounted for the largest part of China's GDP, followed by agriculture. In 2013 the service sector became the largest contributor to GDP.

China joined the World Trade Organization (WTO) in 2001. However, the old system, the Catalogue for Guiding Foreign Investment in Industries remains in place. The Catalogue, revised most recently in 2015, divides China's economy into four categories for foreign investment purposes: prohibited; restricted; permitted; and, encouraged.

Encouraged industries, make up about 75% of the Catalogue, but automobiles are an example of how China protects certain local companies. China views automobiles as a strategic industry, because it is important to China's development of high tech manufacturing. In addition to the 25% tariff on imported automobiles, any company wishing to manufacture cars in China must work with a Chinese joint venture partner. This requirement can lead to those joint venture companies stealing the intellectual property of their partners. China has said it may ease auto industry regulations within 8 years.

Sales of imported cars are 4%, of the 24.4 million vehicles produced in 2016, about the same as 15 years earlier.

ArmchairTechInvestor Opinion

Since Chinese automobiles are not an important factor in the U.S. trade deficit with China of $347 billion in 2016, any import taxes on Chinese goods would need to be applied to other goods manufactured in China. The trade deficit with China is a part of overall U.S. policies with China. In addition to import tariffs, and restrictions on U.S. investment in China, including the transfer of U.S. intellectual property to Chinese companies, the issues with China are many, with some of them being:

- Chinese manipulation of their currency to increase U.S. imports;
- The buildup of Chinese artificial islands in the South China Seas;
- Taiwan, and the issues of a one-China Policy; and,
- China's relationship with North Korea, and their unwillingness to confront their nuclear ambitions.

China's Unfair Trade Practices Are Evident In Their Electric Car Regulations: What Can The U.S. Do?

***The U.S. has been examining unfair trade practices that China uses to increase U.S. exports from China, reduce U.S. imports, and steal U.S. technology, among other issues. They have announced government regulations of the auto industry that will require vehicle makers to meet government requirements that certain percentages of the autos sold be electric, in a yearly quota mandate, with non-electric autos eventually being eliminated.

China Trade Barriers-Electric Vehicles

The automobile companies that wish to sell autos in China must accelerate electric automobile sales by 2019. There is a global push worldwide to build electric automobiles, so it is not surprising that China wishes to accelerate their use, particularly with the air pollution problems in the country. The UK and France intend to sell only electric vehicles by 2040. India plans to sell only electric vehicles by 2030. The issues are what China requires of foreign automobile manufacturers that are unfair trade practices. China may eliminate the sale of internal combustion engine vehicles in China by 2030.

In April 2017, the preliminary electric automobile plans for China were announced, but Chinese automobile manufacturers, many of them government owned, had been previously made aware of the plans, giving them a competitive advantage. This was a clear unfair trade practice given to Chinese auto manufacturers.

Based upon the preliminary plans, Ford, Renault-Nissan, and Volkswagen have all set up new electric car joint ventures with local companies, as required by the Chinese government. China is focusing on dominating the electric car industry, and these required joint ventures are a way for local Chinese companies to steal foreign car manufacturer technology.

The Chinese electric car plan involves yearly quota increases in pure-electric, plug-in hybrids, and fuel cell cars. The key requirement is for each company is to reach electric car production levels equal to 12% of all of their Chinese car sales in 2020. Many of the car companies have said that this is an aggressive schedule. China has said that it will eventually require that all cars sold in China be electric, but has not set a date. An immediate issue for the auto manufacturers is to find a market for the electric vehicles they are required to produce. The electric cars today can go about 300 miles before they need a recharge. The infrastructure for local car recharging, and recharging while on longer trips, will take time to develop, and gaining consumer acceptance of the requirements will also take time to develop.

***China Speeds Push for Electric Vehicles,** Wall Street Journal, by Yoko Kubota and Trefor Moss, Sept. 28, 2017

ArmchairTechInvestor Opinion

One of the issues is that China has severe trade restrictions that disadvantage foreign car manufacturers; They favor Chinese companies with advance notice of their plans; Foreign vehicle manufacturers must set up joint manufacturing operations with local companies, forcing the foreign companies to transfer their electric car manufacturing technology to Chinese companies; and, there are tariffs on foreign imports that force companies to manufacture electric cars in China, if they want to participate in the China market, thus reducing auto imports.

**An example of these tariffs is: A Jeep Wrangler could cost $30,000 more in China than in the U.S. This situation illustrates an area of increasing friction between the two countries. The Rubicon model of the Wrangler has a suggested retail price of $40,530 in the U.S. In China, the same vehicle should cost a buyer a lofty $71,000. This occurs because of taxes that Beijing charges on cars, minivans and sport utility vehicles that are made outside of China.

China's Taxes on Imported Cars Feed Trade Tensions With U.S., New York Times, By Keith Bradsher, March 20, 2017

An important element that is occurring is the push by China to dominate electric car manufacturing through the unfair trade practices they use to dominate local Chinese markets, and prepare for Chinese company domination of the global market. The world is going toward electric vehicles; and, U.S. companies such as Tesla, and the U.S. car manufacturers will need to develop electric cars that can sell worldwide, but at the same time many of the U.S. companies are forced to develop Chinese operations that will reduce jobs that could exist in the U.S.

U.S. Trade Deficit and Jobs

Autos are an Important Component. The four largest U.S. trade deficits, in 2016, were with China, ($347 billion), Japan ($69 billion), Germany ($65 billion), and Mexico ($63 billion).

President Trump stated in a meeting that 70,000 factories have closed since China joined the WTO (World Trade Organization) in 2001. Since the U.S. joined Nafta (North American Free Trade Agreement) in 1994, one third of U.S. manufacturing jobs have been lost. This statement is correct. U.S. manufacturing jobs in 1994 were 18.3 million, and they dropped to 12.3 million in 2016, a one-third decline.

Trade Deficits and Jobs-U.S.

70,000 U.S. factories have closed since China joined the World Trade Organization in 2001, according to President Trump. China has many trade barriers, including the theft of intellectual property, the requirement that those setting up manufacturing plants in China have a Chinese partner, and the designating some industries as vital to national defense. A similar pattern of U.S. job losses has occurred since Mexico joined Nafta in 1994.

U.S. Manufacturing Job Declines

The Largest Trade Deficits are with Mexico, Germany, Japan and China.

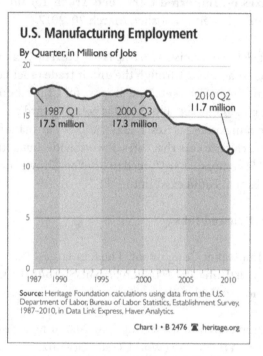

Image: U.S. Manufacturing Job Declines
Source: Heritage Foundation

The U.S. imported $78 billion of cars and auto parts from Mexico in 2015. The U.S. trade deficit with Mexico was $58 billion that year. The U.S. had auto imports of about $31 billion from Japan.

U.S. trade data show that in the 10 months ended in October 2016, automotive vehicle and parts imports from Mexico totaled $89.6 billion. The next largest import nations were Canada with $54 billion and Japan, was

$44 billion. Germany is much lower, but has large auto parts production in Mexico that show up in the U.S.-Mexico import data.

While vehicles were the main imports from Canada and Japan, more than half, $46.8 billion of the auto imports from Mexico were vehicle parts in that 10-month period. U.S. government data show that car parts imports into the U.S. nearly doubled in the past five years through 2016.

According to President Trump, Toyota, as well as 3 German companies, are planning new automobile manufacturing plants in Mexico. They were threatened with a new 35% border taxes, which appeared to be in about the 20% range in Congress, but such taxes have not been implemented by the Congress. The Nafta trade negotiations with Mexico and Canada will likely determine whether there can be agreement among the three countries as to how to treat the vehicle import market.

ArmchairTechInvestor Opinion

Much of the U.S. Auto Trade Deficit Is with Mexico and Germany, Which President Trump is Aggressively Moving to Address.

China dwarfs the trade deficits for the next three deficit countries, whose deficits total $197 billion, or 57% of that with China.

In addition to Mexico, Japan and Germany sell many vehicles in the U.S, and have big U.S. manufacturing plants in the U.S., with luxury vehicle manufacturing being important.

Japan

President Trump has warned Japan's Toyota it could be subject to a "big border tax" if it builds its Corolla cars for the U.S. market at a planned factory in Mexico.

According to a Forbes opinion article in 2012, More than 682,000 U.S. jobs are generated by the Japanese-branded automobile companies' production facilities, Additionally, more than 678,000 U.S. jobs are generated by the Japanese-branded automobile companies' dealer network. As one of the largest job creators in the country, the Japanese auto industry should be looked at with a breath of fresh air.

In 2012, Japanese auto manufacturers produced 3.3 million units in the U.S. providing a total compensation for U.S. jobs that exceeded $85 billion annually.

This compares with the current $69 trade deficit with Japan. Additionally, Softbank recently announced a $50 billion investment it plans to make, with could generate 50,000 U.S. jobs. However, President Trump is trying to stop future Japanese production in Mexico.

Germany

German carmakers employ about 33,000 workers in the United States and German automotive suppliers about 77,000 more. Trump criticized German carmakers, such as BMW, Daimler and Volkswagen for failing to produce more cars on U.S. soil.

"I would tell BMW that if you are building a factory in Mexico and plan to sell cars to the U.S., without a 35 percent tax, then you can forget that," Trump said. This is unlikely to be implemented by the Trump administration.

BMW executive Peter Schwarzenbauer told reporters the company was sticking to plans to invest about $1 billion in a new plant in Mexico, which is due to go into production in 2019, and create at least 1,500 jobs.

While investing in Mexico, German carmakers have quadrupled light vehicle production in the United States over the past seven years, to 850,000 units. More than half of these are exported from the U.S., Germany's VDA automotive industry association said. A border tax would not impact the sales of these U.S. manufactured vehicles, except to the extent that U.S. imported parts from Mexico increase in cost.

BMW

A BMW spokeswoman said a planned plant in the central Mexican city of San Luis Potosi would build the BMW 3 Series beginning in 2019, with the output intended for the world market. The plant would be an addition to existing 3 Series production facilities in Germany and China.

In June 2016, BMW broke ground on the plant, pledging to invest $2.2 billion in Mexico by 2019, for an annual production rate of 150,000 cars.

Audi

In 2016, VW's Audi division inaugurated a $1.3 billion production facility, with 150,000 vehicles production capacity, near Puebla, Mexico. Audi said it would build electric and petrol Q5 SUVs in Mexico.

The border tax was a major issue in Congress, with the House favoring it, and many in the Senate opposed. It was eliminated in the tax bills in early 2018.

Mexico and Germany are the major countries with which the U.S. must deal in trying to turn around U.S. vehicle manufacturing jobs.

Trade Policies: What are the Global Connections Between U.S. Jobs and Eliminating Trade Deficits?

President Trump had a meeting with manufacturing CEOs in 2017, and Rex Tillerson, the then Secretary of State, and Department of Homeland Security Secretary John Kelly met with Mexican Foreign Minister Luis Videgaray.

A CNN Article in 2016 featured "Trump's trade talk is 'bluster'

Trade likely sped up the shift, but many experts say it was inevitable. It's unlikely many manufacturing jobs will ever return, even if Trump's walls get built.

"Trump's talk on trade is bluster," says economist Charles Ballard of Michigan State University. "Even if you did [what Trump says], you wouldn't reverse the technology, which is a very big part of the picture."

ArmchairTechInvestor Opinion

The issues are tax reductions and manufacturing job creation. The quote of Charles Ballard only refers to a wall being built, not U.S. corporate tax deductions, which will be the most important element of President Trumps' manufacturing and other job growth efforts. There is also the issue of the introduction of robots in production. However, the issue is whether more U.S. manufacturing jobs can be created, not whether they can return to prior levels. The escalating Trump tariff threats with China and the EU could increase U.S. jobs.

U.S. Trade-Asia-Trans Pacific Partnership (TPP)

Trump Has Scuttled The TransPacific Partnership (TPP). Will The U.S. Lose Because Of This Policy?

The U.S. withdrew from the Trans Pacific Trade Partnership (TPP). The TPP was the 12-nation trade deal that included the United States, Japan, Mexico, Canada, Australia, New Zealand, Vietnam, Peru, Chile, Malaysia, Singapore, and Brunei. It was never ratified by the Congress. Trump's America First theme, and the cancellation of the TPP, has led many in Asia to view the U.S. as anti-trade, and China as pro-trade. However, the U.S. has negotiations underway with many of these countries, plus the Nafta trade agreement with Canada and Mexico. The main uncertainty is whether the U.S. can negotiate a bi-lateral agreement with Japan, which prefers to have the U.S. join the TPP.

President Trump's trip to Asia in early November 2017, was supposed to be about the possible de-nuclearization of the Korean Peninsula. However, an important element of the trip was to make it clear that Trump wants to follow-up on the U.S. withdrawal from the TPP by arranging bilateral trade agreements with the countries in Asia. Had the U.S. done this 15 years ago with China, instead of relying on the World Trade Organization to police the compliance of countries with its edicts, including China, the trade situation with China might be quite different today.

*An advantage of an agreement, such as the TPP, includes preferential terms for member countries, that can reduce tariffs from what they might otherwise be. The TPP group of countries represents 16% of global GDP. However, countries other than the U.S. would be only 35% of TPP. Japan is 16% of the GDP of the original 12 countries. And, Mexico and Canada, with whom the U.S. is negotiating a Nafta agreement, together are 9% of the GDP. The other 8 countries total only 10% of the GDP of the original 12 countries.

Not being a member of TPP could be negative for U.S. farming interests. For example, in July 2017, Japan imposed a 50% tariff on U.S. frozen beef. Australia's tariff cost is 27.5% because of their membership in TPP. Japan has also signed an agreement with the European Union to import their farm products. It is working on a similar agreement with Canada, whose pork producers are taking market share from the U.S.

**There are many barriers to the U.S. rejoining the TPP. The other eleven countries have already reached an Agreement, forming TPP-11. Once 6 countries ratify the agreement, it will become active. That could occur about first quarter, 2019. Until the Agreement is ratified, the U.S. will not be able to join it. 20 provisions in the original agreement, some of which were important to the U.S., were eliminated. These would need to be restored, and other concessions given to the U.S. to make this a better deal that the original agreement. To add additional benefits for the U.S. and get all 11 countries to agree to add the U.S. as a new member could be very difficult.

While the U.S. is emphasizing its policy of negotiating bilateral trade agreements, China is doing just the opposite. It has developed a trade agreement, called the Regional Comprehensive Economic Partnership with 16 countries making up 39% of global GDP. China is the main trade competitor of the U.S. on the global stage. It has an ambitious project called the One Belt, One Road (OBOR) Initiative that will connect about 70 countries to China economically, as joint investors, and perhaps also politically and as defense partners. These types of activities can result in relationships that go far beyond trade and can involve joint investment, political and military relationships.

*Trump's Pacific Trade Tear, Wall Street Journal Editorial, November 11, 2017

**Re-Entry to Trade Deal Won't Be Cheap, Wall Street Journal, by Bob Davis, April 16, 2018

ArmchairTechInvestor Opinion

It may turn out the renegotiating Nafta with Mexico and Canada will work out to the benefit of the U.S. mainly by requiring and verifying certain levels of U.S. content in automobiles imported into the U.S. It is much less certain that this will be the case for the U.S. withdrawal from the TPP. There are benefits in developing relationships with countries in Asia, beyond just the trade aspect of those relationships. Having the TPP as one element of a relationship with a country can be very beneficial overall.

If the U.S. wants to be a player in Asia, it will need to be viewed as a reliable long-term partner. Being a democracy that can change policy, as administrations change, does not bode well for forging lasting partnerships. That is the main issue for the U.S. in developing lasting foreign policy relationships, including trade relationships. It is no wonder that results occur such as how disadvantaged the U.S. is in its trading relationship with China. They know who they are, and where they are going, and can therefore take a very long-term view in executing their plans.

U.S. Trade-North America-Nafta

The Nafta Negotiations Show That Mexico Is Violating The Agreement In The Auto Industry. Autos Are A Big Trade Problem, And China Is An Important Contributor To The Problem

The auto industry is an important reason for the $63 billion trade deficit that the U.S. has with Mexico. In the auto industry, manufacturers have integrated supply chains of parts used in manufacturing vehicles. Cars made in the three countries can cross the borders duty free, if 62.5% of the content is made in a Nafta country. The U.S. wants to raise that percentage to 85%, with a minimum of 50% of the content being made in the U.S. The U.S. is trying to get the auto manufacturers to return their plants from Mexico to the U.S. An alternative way to address that issue is to require that 50% of the content of an auto be produced in the U.S.

An important issue that the U.S. is pressing is verification that 62.5% of the content of a car manufactured in Mexico comes from one of the three Nafta signatories. The U.S. allegation is the auto supply chain in northern Mexico uses components, particularly from China, that are not identified as foreign components. The U.S. is moving to have the suppliers document rigorously that their components are made by the Nafta countries. In addition, the auto manufacturers in Mexico must, for several dozen components used in engines and transmissions, use only Nafta manufactured parts.

There is a tracing list used to identify the origin of automobile parts. The U.S. would like to see it expanded. Of particular interest are steel, leather and fabric used in the manufacturing of seat cushions. Components that are alleged to come from China include steel and other metals, hardware and electronic components.

The downside case is that companies will start manufacturing vehicles in China where the import duty is only 2.5%. The U.S. duty of 2.5% compares to the 25% tariff that China imposes on foreign manufactured cars that are sold into China. This tariff injustice is being addressed by Trump.

ArmchairTechInvestor Opinion

The U.S. Trade deficits with Mexico and China, when examined, expose some of the unfair trade practices that China and Mexico use against the U.S. The inequity of the current Nafta trade pact illustrates some of the ways the U.S. is disadvantaged by the pact, with the most egregious being the manufacturing of autos in Mexico that are imported into the U.S.

The most blatant disparity that the U.S. faces with China is the 25% import duty China charges for foreign imports compared to the 2.5% tariff that the U.S. charges. The benefit of Nafta to Mexico and Canada is that they can avoid possible higher U.S. import tariffs by fairly meeting the Nafta domestic manufacturing requirements.

President Trump is to be praised for his willingness to challenge the Nafta and Transpacific Partnership (TPP) benefits to the U.S., particularly with respect to their U.S. job development issues.

China-Visa EB-5 Investment Program

This is a program to encourage foreign investments, particularly real estate, in the U.S. There are limits on the number of investors by country. There is a backlog of EB-5 investors, with China having the most potential investors. In China the backlog is 10 years for this very popular program.

The real estate industry is a primary beneficiary of this program. The investors need to make their investments in advance. With the 10-year backlog in some cases, some of the real estate companies would like to repay the investments before the Visa holders get to the U.S. This would create a problem for the Visa holder. Under the current program, they would lose their Visa if their investment was returned. This can easily happen in the real estate industry, where investment properties are often sold in less than 10 years. A redeployment provision is being implemented that allows a Visa EB-5 applicant to reinvest the money and remain eligible.

The program can be attractive to municipalities and redevelopment companies. However, criticism of the program comes from the complaints that the program favors investments in higher income less risky neighborhoods. There are developers that are targeting tier two and three real estate markets. These markets are attractive to homeowners that want to improve their lifestyle in an economical neighborhood. This favors neighborhoods that are under developed, but can be improved by proper property selection and knowledgeable property improvement investments and marketing.

ArmchairTechInvestor Opinion

The program came up for renewal by Congress in December 2017. There are proponents of the program that would like to see the minimum investment increased and more of the investments made in rural and disadvantaged communities. There are other improvements that could provide assurances that the programs meet the objectives of creating 10 or more jobs, and improving the opportunities in disadvantaged communities.

This is an example of a Visa program that, if designed properly, can aid the development of real estate markets that are in need of being upgraded while providing attractive possible investment returns, and using foreign investors who wish to come to the U.S. to make those investments. This could promote U.S. job growth. If each of the investors created 10 jobs, this would add 100,000 jobs per year in the U.S.

U.S.-China Trade-World Trade Organization (WTO)

The WTO was established to facilitate worldwide trade and has 164 members. China became a member in 2001. At that time China was categorized as an emerging country. Today, they are clearly no longer in that category, but still have protections accorded to such countries. President Trump has taken the position that the WTO is lethargic in addressing current issues. Trump has articulated issues that do not cover the whole range of free trade abuses, particularly by China. His stated issues are:

- A disputed settlement process;
    o He has criticized the body's dispute settlement process and asserted the right to ignore rulings that it believes violate U.S. sovereignty;
- Institute penalties for dumping;
    o China, has steel and aluminum industries that are state-sponsored. China sits on a massive supply of these goods, and its trading partners have accused it of undercutting prices.
- Improve the dispute mechanism system;
    o The WTO has been criticized by member nations for being slow to resolve disputes, a problem the organization has acknowledged. A dispute between the EU and China resolved last year took seven years to litigate. Failure to come to timely decisions allows potentially illegal trade practices to continue for years, critics say. Trump could press the WTO to add resources to the dispute process, and to put time limits on decisions.

Additional WTO issues with regard to China are:

- Intellectual property theft, with no legal means of addressing the issues;
- Non-tariff barriers and subsidies have proliferated;

- Loans are given by state-owned banks on easy terms with low interest rates
- Use is made of the 2008 Anti-Monopoly Law to force companies that have substantial market share possibilities to transfer of intellectual property to enter the China market.

All of the above abuses violate WTO agreements, but companies that press their case at the WTO are being threatened with denial of access to the China market if they file an action at the WTO.

The WTO's agreements are outdated, and lawsuits can take a very long time.

*Tackling China's Protectionism, Wall Street Journal Editorial, March 20, 2018

ArmchairTechInvestor Opinion

The U.S. needs to match on a targeted basis many of the trade barriers that exist in other countries. The restrictions and aid to Chinese companies cannot always be matched by the U.S. to aid U.S. companies.

In the case of import tariffs, if the industry is vital to national defense, the President can impose import tariffs that match the import tariffs of China and other countries. Trump has imposed tariffs of 25% on steel and 10% tariffs on aluminum during the second week of March 2018.

The U.S. does not support export products by financings or other financial means. It is unlikely that the U.S. will attempt to meet these financial subsidies, with the trade deficit continuing to reflect these barriers to fair trade. The U.S. will not force foreign companies to set up joint ventures, or attempt to steal intellectual property, both of which China does.

With so many obstacles to trade by the EU, and especially by China, as slow and lethargic as the WTO is, it is probably the only place where many of the U.S. trade grievances can be addressed. The alternative for the U.S. is to adopt unilateral domestic sovereignty policies.

Chinese Investment-U.S.

Chinese Companies Continue To Increase Investment in U.S. Manufacturing Plants, But Their Size is Dwarfed by the Trade Deficit

The Chinese trade deficit with the U.S. has at least two dimensions:

- The import of low-cost Chinese goods. This is somewhat being offset by Chinese companies setting up U.S. manufacturing operations. However, the size of these investments is dwarfed by the $367 billion trade deficit we have with China; Also,
- The U.S. has lost over 60,000 factories since China joined the WTO in 2001.

ArmchairTechInvestor Opinion

China has been encouraging worldwide trade, while it manipulates its currency at home. The U.S. has publicly criticized China's trade policies, saying it has violated the World Trade Organization (WTO) trade rules, and has promised to be harsh on enforcement.

The U.S. can take steps to enforce the WTO rules, implement sanctions, and take other unspecified steps in response to trade violations by China. A CFIUS program exists that can Block China's investment deals based upon national security issues. Such Chinese investments in the U.S. tripled in 2016 to $45.6 billion. The possible unfriendly Qualcomm acquisition by Broadcom, a Singapore company, is also a way that China can infiltrate the U.S. Also, currency manipulation could be designated as an unfair trade practice.

China Policies-Currency-Yuan

*China's manipulation of its currency, the yuan, is one way to disadvantage the U.S. and other countries that trade with them. In May 2018, the decline in the yuan was near its weakest level in the last two months, and was down 1.1% compared with the U.S. dollar. However, other currencies have declined more against the dollar, with the Japanese yen down 3.5% and the euro down 1.9%. The supposition is that upcoming U.S.-China trade negotiations have caused China to prop up its currency, relative to a basket of other currencies, before the meetings, in view of Trump's presidential campaign position that China is causing its currency to be undervalued.

*Yuan Weakness Revives Manipulation Debate, Wall Street Journal, by Saumya Vaishhampayan, May 5, 2018

China's trade surplus numbers grew 4.2% in January and February 2016. China has $3 trillion of Forex (Foreign Exchange) reserves. They Increased in February 2016 by $7 billion. This unusual outcome occurred despite a Chinese need to support their currency, because of the economic weakness and skepticism at home. China should have been buying their currency, and reducing their Forex reserves. It is possible China is using derivatives to support its currency. They could be offering to buy their currency later at a higher price, to discourage shorting of the currency. However, this may only serve to delay any downward pressure on the yuan until later.

Other efforts to Prop up the yuan involve:

- They are battling capital outflows;
  o Controls are being put on Chinese companies seeking to invest abroad;
- Restrictions are being put on the conversion of the yuan into other currencies; and
- A crackdown is being put on underground banks seeking to move capital offshore, such as through the use of bitcoins.

A U.S. increase in interest rates that is underway will likely weaken the yuan. Because of economic issues, China is not likely to raise own interest rates.

Interestingly, China did not face a leadership struggle in 2016. Quite to the contrary, the existing leadership strengthened its position of power.

Chinese companies inflate import values to avoid tight controls on moving capital offshore.

CHAPTER 2

China's One Belt, One Road Trade Initiative

One Belt, One Road Initiative Map

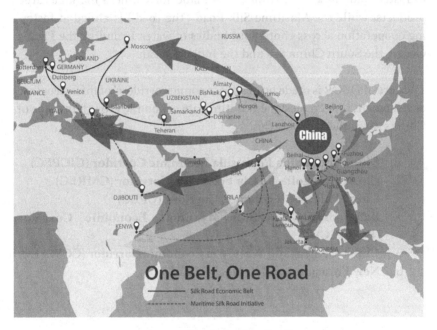

Image: One Belt, One Road
Image Source: Getty Images

China One Belt, One Road (OBOR)

What is OBOR?

The One Belt, One Road (OBOR) is a Chinese-backed plan of interconnected infrastructure projects stretching across over 60 countries from Western Europe to Southeast Asia. Initially unveiled in September 2013, OBOR is the focal point of China's plans for economic development, both of the countries surrounding China's Western provinces and its surrounding countries. Cost estimates have ranged from $US4-8 trillion, with funding from existing and new Chinese financial institutions, including the newly established Asia Infrastructure Investment Bank (the AIIB)

OBOR comprises 'the Silk Road Economic Belt' ('the belt'), which will include integrated infrastructure projects across Asia and Europe intended to foster trade links and stimulate demand for Chinese manufactured products, while the Maritime Silk Road ('the road') is aimed at fostering cooperation across contiguous bodies of water, including the Pacific Ocean, the South China Sea and the Indian Ocean.

The core of OBOR is made up of six 'economic corridors' of infrastructure development that are designed to stimulate economic growth in some of China's surrounding countries.

1. **China-Indochina Peninsula Economic Corridor (CICPEC)**
2. **China-Mongolia-Russia Economic Corridor (CMREC)**
3. **China Pakistan-Economic Corridor (CPEC)**
4. **Bangladesh-China-India-Myanmar Economic Corridor (BCIMEC)**
5. **China-Central and West Asia Economic Corridor (CCWAEC)**
6. **New Eurasian Land Bridge (NELB)**

Six OBOR Initiative Corridors

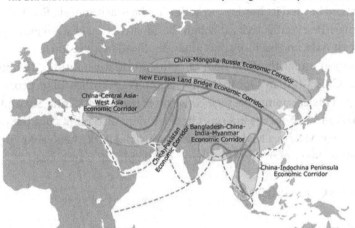

The Belt and Road Initiative: Six Economic Corridors Spanning Asia, Europe and Africa

Image: 6 OBOR Initiative Corridors
Image Source: Hong Kong Trade Development Council (HKTDC)

China

**"Vision and Actions on Jointly Building Silk Road Economic Belt and 21st Century Maritime Silk Road is the blueprint of China's connectivity strategy. As far as Southeast Asia is concerned, the two most important aspects of the document are the 21st Century Maritime Silk Road and the China-Indochina Peninsula Economic Corridor. Moreover, it emphasizes construction of ports, port cooperation, land-water transportation channels and multimodal transport system. This arrangement also includes Lancang-Mekong River navigation."

*"The Chinese government's initial 2013 OBOR Initiative vision dared to imagine a network covering 65 countries with 4.4 billion people and aggregate economic value to $21 trillion or 29 per cent of global GDP. The Asian Development Bank estimated that to bring it to reality, Asia would need to invest about $26 trillion between 2016 and 2030 in order to maintain growth momentum. For ASEAN infrastructure alone, the investment would need to be about $3.2 trillion."

The white paper on **Development of China's Transport** provides an official account of China's connectivity strategy. The first element is to build
a comprehensive transport network within the China and construct links
that extend beyond its borders. In addition, the Maritime Silk Road will address maritime connectivity through the construction of strategic ports in
Southeast Asia, and building port alliances. Similarly, a vision for maritime
cooperation under the One Belt, One Road Initiative outlines the building the China-Indian Ocean-Africa-Mediterranean Sea Blue Economic
Passage. This economic passage constitutes the South China Sea and the
coastal states in Southeast Asia. The document also points out the progress made in Malaysia Malacca Seaside Industrial Park, the Kyaukpyu port
and SEZ in Myanmar, and the Sihanoukville SEZ in Cambodia.

Maritime Connectivity

Though many Southeast Asian nations have agreed to participate in the
OBOR Initiative, there are a wide range of security and strategic challenges to the maritime connectivity plan. In fact, the disputes over the
South China Sea Islands remain the most complicated issue. Therefore,
China's foreign policy towards Southeast Asian nations is aimed at enhancing mutual trust and cooperation with these countries to strengthen
cooperation in various fields.

Of all the issues, enhancing maritime security cooperation with the
Southeast Asian countries will be a priority for China. Additionally, maritime connectivity will have strategic implications in the Indo-Pacific
region. These developments in the South China Sea, and China's connectivity projects undertaken in the Malaysian Peninsula along the Strait
of Malacca, will inevitably raise India's concerns. In South Asia, development of Hambantota port in Sri Lanka and Gwadar port in Pakistan
have been fuelling tensions in the Indian Ocean region. Subsequently,
the strategic importance of the Andaman & Nicobar Islands will increase
for India's security and maintenance of peace and stability in the region.

ASEAN Countries-Maritime Partnerships

Chinese President Xi Jinping's speech at the People's Representative
Council of Indonesia in October 2013 proposed a maritime partnership

between China and the ASEAN countries to build the 21st Century Maritime Silk Road. In addition to maritime connectivity, China is working on China-Laos, China-Vietnam, China-Malaysia and China-Thailand railway projects as well. Also, China is developing China-Laos, China-Vietnam and China-Myanmar cross-border economic cooperation zones. The China-Thailand rail line going through Laos will be part of an ambitious China-Singapore rail link. In this regard, the beginning of the construction of the East Coast Rail Link project began in Malaysia in August 2017, is very important.

In fact, the coastal states in Southeast Asia such as Vietnam, Cambodia, the Philippines, Thailand, Malaysia, Myanmar, Brunei, Singapore and Indonesia and the only landlocked country Laos would take part in the BRI to build highways, railways and sea ports to realize the China-Indochina Peninsula Economic Corridor and the 21st Century Maritime Silk Road. However, Myanmar, Thailand, Cambodia, Malaysia and Vietnam would provide nodes connecting the Belt and Road. The Belt stands for the continental sections of the Silk Road while the Road is the maritime domain of the Silk Road. For example, the development of the China-Indochina Peninsula Economic Corridor would connect the inland cities to the seaports in the coastal areas. Thus, the Belt and Road are complementary to each other. Therefore, infrastructure development points in the direction of building land-and-sea transportation channels for supporting and sustaining major inland cities along the Belt and port cities which constitute the Road. The China-Indochina Peninsula Economic Corridor would constitute international transport routes connecting core cities along the Belt and Road and industrial parks.

*China's Connectivity Strategy in Southeast Asia, Science, Technology and Security Forum, Dr. Puyam Rakesh Singh, August 18, 2017

China is providing financing in the form of high interest loans. China is being accused by many of using the loans to put many small countries in default, and to thereby take over the projects that they have financed.

**According to Wikipedia there are numerous difficulties being faced by the One Belt, One Road project. They include:"

- **Nepal - $2.5 billion:** $2.5 billion Budhi Gandaki Hydro Electric Dam Project was canceled by Nepal in November 2017 for the violation of bidding rules.
- **Hungary:** European Union is investigating Hungary-Serbia high-speed railway project build by Chinese contractors for the violation of bidding rules.
- **Myanmar - $3 billion:** $3 billion refinery contract to China was terminated after financing issues.
- **Pakistan - $22.3 billion:** $10 billion Karachi rail project and $260 million Gwadar airport were stalled and $12 billion Diamer-Bhasha Dam in Gilgit-Baltistan was cancelled due to ownership stake.
- **Thailand - $15 billion:** High-speed railway was cancelled in 2016 for not subcontracting sufficient work to Thai companies.
- **Tanzania - $11 billion:** Bagamoyo Port was stalled due to financing issues.
- **Sri Lanka - $1.5 billion:** Hambantota Port led to Sri Lanka running into financial problems due to the high interest rate of loan given by Chinese, leading to assets transfer to China.
- **Asia, Africa, and the Middle East projects:** BMI Research database of Asia, Africa and the Middle East shows many projects are too vague and some are planned up to 30 years in the future."

**One Belt, One Road, Wikipedia, May 18, 2018

***"China's ambitious push to build a modern-day Silk Road through Asia and Europe has suffered a number of rebuffs in recent weeks after Pakistan, Myanmar and Nepal cancelled put on hold a number of major infrastructure projects funded by Chinese investment."

***"**Why Greece is banking on China's modern-day Silk Road to help its economic recovery,** South China Morning Post, By Catherine Wong, December 26, 2017

With many of the projects being port developments, these joint ventures with the countries could allow China to expand their naval presence throughout Asia, Africa and the Middle East.

ArmchairTechInvestor Opinion

We believe the OBOR project is an effort by China to use its substantial infrastructure building expertise, and abundant financial resources, as a way to extend its influence politically, economically and militarily to surrounding countries is Asia, Africa and the Middle East. Most threatening to the U.S. is the increased maritime military threat.

The U.S. is likely to be involved in the project through the participation of U.S. companies. Technology developments and petroleum projects are the most likely areas of substantial involvement by the U.S. companies.

China-Military Expansion

Three Examples of China Using Its One Belt, One Road Network Initiative To Project An Increase In Military Power Are In Sri Lanka, Pakistan And Djibouti

China-Military

China has been working on enhancing connectivity with the Southeast Asian nations under the framework of the Silk Road Economic Belt and the 21st Century Maritime Silk Road. This initiative is also known as the Belt and Road Initiative (BRI), and will provide a new impetus to regional and global connectivity. China's connectivity strategy seems to be closely aligned with its military modernization, to ensure maritime security along the key sea-lanes. As Beijing's aspiration to become a maritime power has been articulated, it will be difficult for China to overlook the strategic significance of the South China Sea and the Indian Ocean. It is inevitable that the development of transport infrastructure for connectivity between China and Southeast Asian countries will have strategic implications across the Western Pacific Ocean and the Indian Ocean.

*One can profess that China's One Belt, One Road (OBOR) trade network, covering over 60 countries, is for humanitarian purposes and will assist the countries on the network in improving their economic opportunities. The network connects with about 65 percent of the world's population and over 30% of its GDP. China's role is to finance infrastructure development in the countries. China goes into the countries and provides high interest loans that many of the countries can't afford. If they default, China can then take over the facilities, and establish a permanent presence within those countries. This can also have the effect of the country not being able to arrange outside financing, making them even more reliant on China.

With regard to loans having been made by China, If repayments are not made, the country begins a long-term period where their foreign policy choices will be constrained. Sri Lanka is an example of what can occur. A new government in Sri Lanka had a desire to develop closer relations with India and the U.S. They were constrained by a previous debt for equity swap with China that resulted in China getting a 99-year lease on a very strategically important port at Hambantota, Sri Lanka. The loan that was made was not a financially sound investment and resulted in Sri Lanka defaulting on the loan, with tragic consequences to the country.

* **China's Belt and Road Initiative is Being Blamed for Sri Lanka's Hambantota Port Problems. But the Real Story is Rather Different,** Silk Road Briefing, April 23, 2018

**Large government-backed loans to foreign countries come with social and political strings attached. The Washington Post reports that China's ZTE Corporation "sold technology and provided training to monitor mobile phones and Internet activity." Today, Chinese tech giant Huawei is partnering with the government of Kenya to construct "safe cities" that leverage thousands of surveillance cameras feeding data into a public security cloud "to keep an eye on what is going on generally" according to the company's promotional materials. Not all elements of China's domestic surveillance regime are exportable, but as the "New Digital Silk Road" takes shape, the public and online spaces of countries along it will become less free.

China's vast foreign investment program comes at a sharp cost to human rights and good governance, Foreign Policy, By Richard Fontaine and Daniel Kliman, May 16, 2018

***According to the Washington Post's, By Bill Gertz, "China is constructing its second overseas military base in Pakistan as part of a push for greater power projection capabilities along strategic sea routes. The facility will be built at Jiwani, a port close to the Iranian border on the Gulf of Oman, according to two people familiar with deal."

Djibouti is a different situation. China already has a base there and has plans to expand that base into a regional military supply port.

Some Pentagon officials regard the Djibouti base, and the future second base at Jiwani, as part of efforts to control oil shipping in and out of the Persian Gulf and the Red Sea. Both Chinese bases are located near strategic chokepoints-Djibouti near the Bab el Mandeb on the Red Sea and Jiwani close to the Strait of Hormuz on the Persian Gulf.

"Djibouti's government will embrace greater Chinese involvement in the nation's ports and sees no reasons for U.S. concern that its strategic interests may be threatened", Finance Minister Ilyas Dawaleh said.

Djibouti is located on a global shipping crossroads that links the Red Sea and Suez Canal, Djibouti has become increasingly important to regional and world powers. Djibouti is almost the size of the state of Massachusetts. The largest U.S. military base in Africa is situated there and China's first such overseas facility, which was inaugurated in August 2017, is also in the Doraleh area.

The Horn of Africa country is embroiled in a dispute with DP World Ltd. over the running of the Doraleh Container Terminal and has struck a deal to boost cargo trade with a company working with Chinese state-owned enterprises. It would be "ridiculous" to imagine that China could restrict or deny U.S. access to Doraleh as a result of the deal, Dawaleh said in a phone interview.

"Djibouti's development needs all its friends and strategic partners," he said. "At the same time, no one can dictate to us who we should deal with."

U.S. Africa Command General Thomas Waldhauser warned that a Chinese takeover of Doraleh could have "significant" consequences if there were restrictions on the U.S.'s ability to use the facility.

***Beijing is using commercial bridgeheads to give its warships staying power in the Indian Ocean,** Foreign Affairs, By Keith Johnson and Dan De Luce, April 17, 2018

ArmchairTechInvestor Opinion

China may be providing benefits to some of the countries on their OBOR network. Others are likely to be unable to meet their debt payments to China, and China will extract a substantial price for such defaults. Many of these defaults will result in China essentially owing the assets in the partner country.

Estimates put China's total Belt and Road-related construction and investment at more than $340 billion from 2014 to 2017. The total project cost is estimated to be from $4 trillion to $8 trillion dollars, so it appears that as much as 8% of the total cost of the project has already been made by China. The size of the project represents an enormous financial commitment, even for China.

China's plans call for the Jiwani base in Pakistan to be a joint naval and air facility for Chinese forces, located a short distance up the coast from the Chinese-built commercial port facility at Gwadar. Both Gwadar and Jiwani are part of Pakistan's western Baluchistan province. There is social unrest in that province, and China has a commitment from Pakistan to provide a 15,000 person military guard to protect the Gwadar Port area. It is reported that most of the people living in the area are Chinese.

China is a tough negotiator and will extract a significant price, if there is a default on their debt. As happened in Sri Lanka, this can include the conversion of their debt to equity in a project, with China essentially owning the project.

The Americas

*The sea routes of the One Belt, One Road (OROR) trade initiative can reach North America and South America by connection with the Panama Canal. Panama provides maritime access through the Panama Canal from the Pacific Ocean to the Atlantic Ocean, and connections to Canada,

Mexico and the U.S. in North America. It also provides access to Central America and South American economically important countries such as Argentina and Brazil.

Panama has been working on an expansion of the Panama Canal to accommodate today's largest ships. This 9-year and $5 billion project went into operation in June, 2016. It added new locks at both its Atlantic and Pacific access points facilitating the passage of vessels carrying up to 13,000 containers.

The largest percentage of the ships passing through to the canal are going through the Canal. They constituted almost one-third of the traffic in 2016. An additional 25% of the traffic was from the U.S. east coast to the East Coasts of Central and South America. Much of this traffic originated in West Asia before passing through the Suez Canal.

"The expanded Panama Canal is expected to have a significant impact on the freight flow between Asia, the US and Central and South America, becoming an increasingly attractive alternative to the ports on either of the US coasts for any Asian traders looking to distribute across Latin America, especially if they are targeting the Colombian or Venezuelan markets."

*The Belt and Road Initiative: Country Profiles, Hong Kong Trade Development Council, May 17, 2018

For 2016, Panama received foreign direct investment (FDI) totaling $3.6 billion, with China contributing some $37 million. As of the end of 2016, China's total FDI commitments to Panama exceeded $268 million, a considerable rise from 2007's total of $55 million. In the case of Hong Kong, it had a total FDI commitment to Panama of $33 million in 2016, making it the country's sixth largest Asian investor, after Taiwan, South Korea, Singapore, Japan and mainland China.

*The Belt and Road Initiative: Country Profiles, Hong Kong Trade Development Council, May 17, 2018

Africa

China's Interest In Africa Has Been Heightened By A Thirst For Oil, But It's Shifting To Building Its One Belt, One Road Network

Below is an analysis of some of the major efforts China is undertaking in Africa to advance its One Belt, One Road (OBOR) Initiative.

Djibouti

*Djibouti is not a new effort for China in Africa. China already has a base there and has plans to expand that base into a regional military supply port.

Some Pentagon officials regard the Djibouti base, and the future second base at Jiwani, as part of efforts to control oil shipping in and out of the Persian Gulf and the Red Sea. Both Chinese bases are located near strategic chokepoints-Djibouti near the Bab el Mandeb on the Red Sea and Jiwani close to the Strait of Hormuz on the Persian Gulf.

Africa-Asia OBOR Road and Maritime Loops

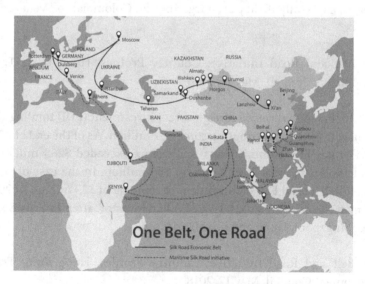

Image: Africa-Asia OBOR Road and Maritime Loops
Image Source: Getty Images

"Djibouti's government will embrace greater Chinese involvement in the nation's ports and sees no reasons for U.S. concern that its strategic interests may be threatened", Finance Minister Ilyas Dawaleh said.

Because Djibouti is located on a global shipping crossroads that links the Red Sea and Suez Canal, Djibouti has become increasingly important to regional and world powers. Djibouti is almost the size of the state of Massachusetts. The largest U.S. military base in Africa is situated there and China's first such overseas facility, which was inaugurated in August 2017, is also in the Doraleh area.

The Horn of Africa country is embroiled in a dispute with DP World Ltd. over the running of the Doraleh Container Terminal and has struck a deal to boost cargo trade with a company working with Chinese state-owned enterprises. It would be "ridiculous" to imagine that China could restrict or deny U.S. access to Doraleh as a result of the deal, Dawaleh said in a phone interview.

"Djibouti's development needs all its friends and strategic partners," he said. "At the same time, no one can dictate to us who we should deal with."

U.S. Africa Command General Thomas Waldhauser warned that a Chinese takeover of Doraleh could have "significant" consequences if there were restrictions on the U.S.'s ability to use the facility.

*Beijing is using commercial bridgeheads to give its warships staying power in the Indian Ocean. Foreign Affairs, By Keith Johnson and Dan De Luce, April 17, 2018

Ethiopia

Ethiopia is a Northeastern African country in the Horn of Africa. It is landlocked and borders Djibouti on the east. With a population of over 90 years, it is the second largest African country, with only Nigeria being larger. The country is underdeveloped, and has a small GDP per person.

China has been Ethiopia's largest trading partner over the last 10 years. Cumulative foreign direct investment (FDI) from China increased more than tenfold from $109 million in 2007 to $1,130 million in 2015. In one year's time, the amount increased to over $2 billion in 2016. Chinese FDI is pivotal in infrastructure development, telecommunications, energy and manufacturing. Ethiopia completed it first freeway in 2014, aided by China. China has a very strong rail development capability, and provided funding for the Addis Ababa rail project. China has also aided Ethiopia in developing industrial parks.

**"The Belt and Road Initiative could advance Ethiopia's development as well as that of other African countries, Ambassador Tekeda Alemu, Ethiopia's permanent representative to the United Nations, said in May, 2017. The initiative offers opportunities for participating countries to mobilize resources and speed up development, Alemu said in an interview with Chinese media in his office in New York."

**Belt and Road has promise for Ethiopia, Africa: envoy

By Hong Xiao and Wang Linyan, China Daily USA, May 11, 2017

Madagascar

Madagascar is an island country in the Indian Ocean and is about 250 miles from the east coast of Southern Africa. Madagascar has bilateral investment agreements with seven countries including China.

U.S. has signed the African Growth and Opportunity Act (AGOA), which expanded the product scope for duty-free exports to the U.S., based on an existing Generalized System of Preferences (GSP).

Africa Map

Image: Africa Map
Image Source: Getty Images

***"In March 2017, China and Madagascar signed a memorandum of understanding (MOU) to jointly advance the One Belt, One Road Initiative, as well as bilateral agreements in economic co-operation, trade and infrastructure construction. Total trade between Madagascar and China increased by 8.6% to $1.25 billion in 2017. According to China's Ministry of Commerce, China's cumulative FDI in Madagascar was $297.6 million in 2016, compared to $25.4 million in 2011."

***China welcomes Madagascar to join Belt and Road construction**

Source: Xinhua March 27, 2017-03-27, Editor: Huaxia

Morocco

Morocco is considered to be well diversified in the region. It is estimated that the Moroccan economy grew by 4.2% in 2017. Real GDP growth is expected to reach 3% in 2018. The country considers itself to be a regional hub in Africa. The country has initiated a program to increase its competiveness.

The U.S. has a free trade agreement. Other free trade agreements include the European Union (EU), European Free Trade Association and the Pan-Arab Free Trade Area (PAFTA), which consists of 17 Arab member countries.

****"Chinese Foreign Minister Wang Yi and Moroccan Minister of Foreign Affairs and International Cooperation Nasser Bourita on Friday signed a Memorandum of Understanding (MOU) on joint construction of the Belt and Road." Additionally, Mr. Bourita indicated "Morocco welcomes Chinese companies to expand markets in Africa and the Arab states by making use of his country's geographical advantages. Bourita also said "Morocco supports China's efforts to safeguard its sovereignty, territorial integrity and legitimate maritime interests." This could preclude Morocco from challenging China's claims in the Indian Ocean, including those China claims that are challenged by India.

**** **China, Morocco sign MOU on Belt and Road**

Source: Xinhua|, November 17, 2017, Editor: Mengjie

South Africa

South Africa has a population of over 50 million people. It also had a relatively high per-capital income of $5,018 in 2016. It sits at the southern tip of Africa and considers itself to be the gateway to Africa. The China OBON Initiative has challenged that assumption by largely bypassing South Africa in implementing its African leg of the maritime portion of the network.

South Africa has a stagnant economy and grew by only 0.3% in 2016. South Africa has challenges that include poverty, inequality and unemployment. South Africa's largest export market is China, which accounted for 9% of its exports in 2016. China supplies imports totaling 18% of South Africa's imports. South Africa's large trading partners include the U.S. The U.S. African Growth and Opportunities Act (AGOA) allows about 7,000 kinds of South African products to be exported to the U.S., with attractive quotas and duty-free treatment, until 2025.

According to *UNCTAD*, inflow foreign direct investment (FDI) in South Africa was $2.3 billion in 2016, an increase from $1.7 billion in 2015, about a 35% increase. South Africa is a member of the COMESA-EAC-SADC Tripartite Free Trade Area. This free trade area includes the three largest regional economic communities (RECs) in Africa:

- The Common Market for Eastern and Southern Africa (COMESA);
- The East African Community (EAC); and,
- The Southern African Development Community (SADC),

This creates an integrated market with a combined population of about 600 million people and a total GDP of about $1 trillion. This agreement is tentative, and will come into force when it is ratified by the 26 member states.

South Africa became the fifth member of the prestigious BRIC Summit in April 2011. The other four members are China, India, Russia and Brazil. Being a member of BRIC was supposed to allow South African businesses to gain improved access to a group which includes over 40% of the world's population and 17% of the global trade. After the seventh BRIC Summit in 2015, the New Development Bank was established with an initial authorized capital of $100 billion. The fund's objective is to support infrastructure and sustainable development projects in emerging economies.

*****"China's Belt and Road Initiative (BRI) delivers a final blow to South Africa's foreign policy claim to be the gateway to the African continent. As China boosts its preferred Silk Road partners, it leaves South Africa at a loss for its very own foreign policy identity—and opens up a murkier future for the African continent."

After China unveiled its OBOR Initiative in 2014, it started to pursue its Africa agenda without going through South Africa. China made clear its growing relationship with other African states that included Kenya, Tanzania, Djibouti, Ethiopia and other emerging partners in East Africa.

China insisted on including it OBOR Initiative in different forums, especially BRICS and the Forum on China–Africa Cooperation (FOCAC). In these forums there was no coordinated African effort to limit China's influence in continent-wide development. China seems to be looking at expanding BRICs to include countries such as Kenya and Egypt or, alternatively to focus more on its OBOR Initiative and less on the aims of BRICs.

*****South Africa's dilemma in the Belt and Road Initiative: Losing Africa for China?, Friedrich-Ebert-Stiftung, by Tamara Naidoo, February 26, 2018

Tunisia

China's energy needs were the genesis of its interest in North African countries. Beginning in 2017, China became more interested in Tunisia in conjunction with its OBOR Initiative following projects in Algeria and Egypt that ran into difficulties, triggered by lower oil prices. Algeria had problems with permits and was frustrated that 40,000 imported Chinese labors were being used instead of local laborers being hired. Projects in Egypt have also been unsuccessful.

******"Talks were launched in 2015 with the goal of better integrating the Tunisian market into the EU. In this sense, Tunisia functions as an ideal middleman for a China interested in controlling physical passageways between North Africa and Europe as part of the One Belt, One Road initiative. China is apparently interested in Tunisia's Bizerte port, which offers easy access to Europe and is located at a critical hub of fiber optic submarine network cables.

China's interest in Tunisia is mutually beneficial. With national inflation expected to reach between 9% and 12%, crippling IMF and government imposed austerity measures and a devalued dinar and high unemployment, Tunisia's economy needs help. In a 2016 survey, Afrobarometer found that 47% of Tunisians believe China's economic assistance is helping to meet Tunisia's needs."

******Tunisia hopes boost in Chinese investment can ease economic woes, Al-Monitor, Sarah Souli, March 19, 2018

China-Indochina Peninsula Economic Corridor-Vietnam, Laos, Myanmar Thailand, Cambodia

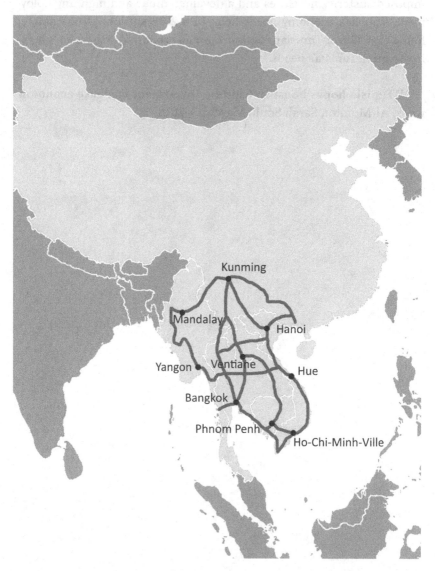

Image: China-Indochina Peninsula Economic Corridor
Image Source: Sebastien Goulard, Cooperans

The Indochina Peninsula Economic Corridor starts in Kunming, China and has two corridors that run south from China through Vietnam, Laos, Thailand and Cambodia. There is also a western corridor that runs west in China from Kunming, to Myanmar and then south to link up with an East-West Corridor that goes through Thailand and Laos. In the south, there is also a second east-west corridor that links up with the north-south corridors.

Vietnam

*"Under the OBOR Initiative, China plans to enhance cooperation with Vietnam to gain access to Haiphong port for the landlocked southwestern region of China. It has been constructing a new standard gauge rail line connecting Kunming and Hekou in its Yunnan Province. Hekou and Lao Cai are border towns on the two sides of the China-Vietnam border. To extend this rail line further to Haiphong port in Vietnam, the two sides have begun negotiations for construction of Lao Cai-Hanoi-Haiphong rail line. Yuxi, a town about 55 miles to the south of Kunming is the point of intersection for the China-Vietnam and China-Laos railways."

*China's Connectivity Strategy in Southeast Asia, Science, Technology and Security Forum, Dr. Puyam Rakesh Singh, August 18, 2017

**"Vietnam is the sixth largest economy in the 10-member ASEAN bloc, trailing the Philippines yet followed by Myanmar. Its service, industry and agriculture sectors account for, respectively, 44%, 39% and 17% of GDP. Major industry and service sectors of the country include manufacturing, mining, construction, real estate and finance.

There were anti-Chinese riots in 2014, which damaged foreign-invested factories. The Vietnamese government undertook a series of remedial measures, including tax breaks and land rent exemption, to compensate the affected companies. Security conditions were reportedly enhanced that has improved foreign investors' confidence has gradually improved, with investors remaining positive on Vietnam's business environment and economic potential.

Vietnam's top export markets in 2016 were the U.S., China and Japan. Major imported items in 2016 consisted of machinery, equipment and parts, and electronics, computers and accessories. A large part of Vietnam's imported capital goods is related to export assembly. China is the largest source of Vietnam's imports, followed by Korea and Japan.

***Vietnam, considered a key part of the maritime component of China's ambitious OBOR Initiative, is a land full of opportunity. In particular, there has been a focus on Northern Vietnam's Haiphong Port, with plans to complete a major facilities upgrade by the end of 2017. Haiphong is a key element along two of the proposed trade corridors. One is along a route connecting Nam Ninh, Lang Son, Hanoi and Haiphong, while the second connects Kunming, Lao Cai, Hanoi and Haiphong. "These proposals would see Vietnam playing an enhanced role in transporting goods produced in the Chinese mainland, while opening the local consumer market to external suppliers. Improved links are also expected to help develop Vietnam's own industrial base."

The Belt and Road Initiative: Country Profiles, Hong Kong Trade Development Council, May 17, 2018

***China's One Belt One Road Initiative, WHAT IS BELT AND ROAD INITIATIVE?, Medium, By Markus Patrick Chan, September 9, 2017

Laos

As part of the plan to make Laos a land-linked state, construction work on the China-Laos railway project began in December 2016. The rail line stretching about 257 miles will connect Boten on the Chinese border to Vientiane on Thailand's border. China-Laos railway would play a key role in bridging the transport infrastructure gap to build China-Singapore railway, which is a part of the Trans-Asian Railway network. This line will connect Vientiane and Nong Khai across the Mekong River to connect Thailand to China's rail network via Laos.

**"Laos is the only landlocked ASEAN country, bordering Myanmar, Thailand, Vietnam and Cambodia, as well as China. With GDP growth averaged about 7.7% over the past decade, Laos is one of the fastest growing economies in ASEAN. The economy of Laos is heavily reliant on the mining and hydropower sectors."

Thailand, China and Vietnam are the largest trading partners of Laos. Laos has entered free trade agreements with China, India, Japan, Korea, Australia and New Zealand under the ASEAN agreement. Laos has signed bilateral investment agreements with 25 countries, including China, Japan, Korea and UK. It has also concluded a bilateral trade agreement with the U,S., which includes some investment requirements.

China's OBOR railroad with ASEAN linking China's border to Vientiane has started. Construction in Laos has progressed to more than 10 per cent of the project. Daochinda Siharath, deputy director of the Lao National Railway State Enterprise and deputy general manager of the Laos-China Railway Co, said that the Laos section of the China-Laos-Thailand railway is about 13.5 per cent built after construction began in January, 2017. The five-year project runs until December 2021, It has an estimated total cost of $5.9 billion. Laos owns 30% of the company while China is owns the rest. The Export-Import Bank of China is the main source of loans for the project, in which debt financing accounts for 60 per cent of the total cost.

*"The Chinese government's initial 2013 OBOR Initiative vision dared to imagine a network covering 65 countries with 4.4 billion people and aggregate economic value to $21 trillion or 29 per cent of global GDP. The Asian Development Bank estimated that to bring it to reality, Asia would need to invest about $26 trillion between 2016 and 2030 in order to maintain growth momentum. For ASEAN infrastructure alone, the investment would need to be about $3.2 trillion."

Myanmar

In Myanmar, China is planning to build a deep-sea port and special economic zone in Kyaukpyu. Interestingly, China has been discussing the feasibility of building the Kyaukpyu port since the 1990s. Moreover, the two sides signed an agreement for the joint development of Ayeyawady River Corridor in May 1997. Under the Western Development Programme, Yunnan Province began to lobby for construction of international passages linking Yunnan and the Southeast Asian countries. China and

Myanmar had signed MOUs on rail and road corridor projects. The proposed Ruili-Kyaukpyu road and rail corridor will help China to secure a shorter route to the Bay of Bengal. However, the railway project has been cancelled while negotiations have been going on for the China-Myanmar Economic Corridor. Nevertheless, the energy pipelines and Kyaukpyu deep-sea port and Kyaukpyu Special Economic Zone (SEZ) in Rakhine state of Myanmar will definitely enhance China's presence in the Bay of Bengal.

Thailand

July 11, 2017, Thailand approved the first phase of a high-speed railway that will connect Yunnan Province of China and Bangkok. The project is part of the ambitious China-Singapore railway. In December 2014, the two sides signed the MOU to build rail lines connecting Nong Khai, Bangkok and Rayong in Thailand. Interestingly, the railway line connecting the border town of Boten and Vientiane in Laos will connect with the high-speed railway projects in China and Thailand.

*"Thailand is the second largest economy in the 10-nation ASEAN, following Indonesia. Service is the largest sector of the economy with a GDP share of 55%, followed by 36% in industry, with agriculture constituting 9% of GDP. Major sectors include electronics, car making, transport, storage, communication, tourism, finance and real estate."

Thailand is a very important electronics manufacturer. The largest exports are computers and parts, automobiles and parts, machinery and equipment. The most important imports are crude oil, parts of electronics and electrical appliances, chemicals, automobiles and parts.

Thailand's top three trading partners were China, Japan and the U.S. in the first half of 2017. Thailand is a member of ASEAN, which has an agreement with China to establish the China-ASEAN Free Trade Area (CAFTA), and over 90% of the products traded between China and Thailand are now tariff-free. In November 2015, ASEAN and China concluded an improved agreement on CAFTA that projected that bilateral trade would increase to $1,000 billion, from about $480 billion in 2014. The improved CAFTA deal also covers technological cooperation.

*****Thailand has plans to build a 540-mile railroad link to its border to connect with the Laos-China railway, which is under construction and will go to the eastern ports and industrial zones of the EEC.

Thailand said a $44 billion plan to add infrastructure and upgrade industry on its eastern seaboard can link up with China's OBOR Initiative. The $44 billion EEC project is planned to turn Thailand's Eastern provinces into a trade and industry hub creating as much as 100,000 jobs a year by 2020. The majority of the jobs will be in the manufacturing and service industries.

"The EEC plan covers Rayong, Chachoengsao and Chonburi provinces. Under the project, Thailand will aim to take on Singapore's dominance in aircraft maintenance, repair and overhaul as part of a $5.7 billion upgrade of U-Tapao International Airport. The Thai government has given approval for a 138 mile high speed train project worth $6.25 billion to link three airports as part of the development of its eastern economic corridor (EEC)."

A high-speed China-Thailand railroad under OBOR is under construction and will be the first high-speed railway in Thailand. The railroad will connect Thailand to Laos and Kunming in China. Submarine cables will connect Bangkok with Hong Kong and mainland China. This extensive connectivity is expected to boost tourism and attract investment.

****Thailand To Integrate The EEC With China's One Belt One Road Initiative, The Thai government intends to connect the Eastern Economic Corridor (EEC) to China's One Belt One Road (OBOR), Thailand Business News, By Olivier Languepin, March 2, 2018

Cambodia

Cambodia is also a key partner of the BRI. China has invested in the construction of Phnom Penh Autonomous Port on the Mekong River and Sihanoukville Special Economic Zone (SEZ). In addition, China has expressed interest in building railways to connect Cambodia with other neighboring ASEAN states.

China's Connectivity Strategy in Southeast Asia, Science, Technology and Security Forum, Dr. Puyam Rakesh Singh, August 18, 2017

*Cambodia is part of the China-ASEAN Free Trade Area (CAFTA).

Foreign direct investment in Cambodia reached $16.7 billion in 2016, with projects mainly in the sectors of banking and finance, manufacturing, real estate, agriculture, tourism, energy, transport and telecom.

*****"Cambodia has been an enthusiastic supporter of China's Belt and Road Initiative (BRI) and has made significant in-roads linking its own development to Chinese expansion; however, with the influx of Chinese capital, Cambodia will find itself drawn further into the sphere of China's economic and strategic influence."

Cambodia has become an attractive country for Chinese foreign direct investment. It offers political stability, low labor costs, easy market access, and a strategic location in Southeast Asia that have all led to a very large increase in Chinese money.

"During Xi Jinping's 2016 visit, China signed 31 economic agreements, including $237 million in soft loan deals with Cambodia. Xi also pledged to push for Chinese investment in Cambodian infrastructure and cancelled roughly $89 million in Cambodian debt."

Despite having a rapidly growing economy, Cambodia has infrastructure problems that include:

- Electricity;
- Rural road transport; and,
- Water sanitation.

With few other financial alternatives sizeable enough to cover Cambodia's infrastructure needs, the promise of a large, no-strings-attached loan makes China's OBOR proposal difficult to resist.

"Participation in the OBOR Initiative, brings with it access to the enormous infrastructure funding of Chinese-led financial institutions, such as the Asian Infrastructure Investment Bank, the Export-Import Bank of China, the China Development Bank, and the Silk Road Fund."

China is the largest foreign investor in Cambodia's energy sector, with more than $7.5 billion of total investments in hydropower plants. Cambodia and China have agreed on several hydropower dam projects. Kemchay Dam was constructed with Chinese assistance and possesses an electrical capacity of 194 megawatts, enough to cover a very large area of the country.

"The biggest hydropower dam, Lower Sesan II Hydropower Plant, will generate up to 400 megawatts per hour once operational, providing enough power to radically transform Cambodia's energy infrastructure."

China also offers developmental assistance on Cambodia's transportation infrastructure, including bridges, highways, railways, and ports.

China has also helped Cambodia to upgrade its deepwater Sihanouk Autonomous Port, which could contribute to expand China's growing influence and expansion in the Indian Ocean.

The Chinese investments involve economic and strategic risk to Cambodia. With an increasing number of plants to generate electricity, some of China's projects do not meet international standards, which have resulted in adverse impacts on local livelihoods and the ecosystem.

"Nearly 5,000 families are likely to be evicted from their villages when the dam's reservoir fills, and the dam may block key fish migration routes, which would threaten loss of most of the fisheries resource that many people depend on. Deals between China and Cambodia have met with additional criticism over major land concessions, the disregard of human rights, and the extent of control over Cambodian development given to Chinese contractors."

China is Cambodia's largest creditor. As their debt grows, it may increase beyond their ability to pay it, and Cambodia may find itself in a similar scenario to Sri Lanka in which state property is used as equity to pay their Chinese creditors.

The China relationship may have the following negative effects:

- Lock this small state securely under China's growing strategic sphere of influence;
- Cause Cambodian foreign policy to prioritize short-term benefits in a way that privileges Chinese political and diplomatic interests at the expense of ASEAN counterparts and other regional powers;
- Prejudice negatively Cambodia and their partners territorial claims on the South China Sea; and
- Cause concerns that China's growing political and economic leverage over Cambodia will bring a future of Cambodian foreign policy as no more than an extension of Chinese regional influence.

*****Money talks: China's belt and road initiative in Cambodia, Global Risk Insights, by Qi Lin, January 7, 2018

Russia-Mongolia-China Road Corridor

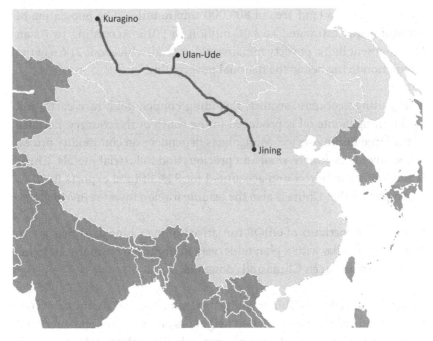

Image: Russia-Mongolia-China Road Corridor
Image Source: Sebastien Goulard, Cooperans

***The Russia-Mongolia-China Road Corridor runs from Tianjin in China north through Mongolia to Ulan Ude in Russia. The corridor is supposed to open in 2018. This is the development of a central railway corridor, organizing transit trucking activities on the Tianjin-Ulaan Baatar-Ulan-Ude route and paving a road along this route. "Chinese Foreign Minister Wang Yi, said construction of a transport corridor linking the three countries helps support economic development, and encourages Mongolia's participation in international affairs."

***Russia-Mongolia-China Road Corridor to be Ready in 2018**

Silk Road Briefing, September 8, 2017

Mongolia

*"Mongolia has a land area of 600,000 square miles. The population of Mongolia was estimated at 3.06 million in 2015. According to Asian Development Bank, poverty remains widespread, with about 21.6% of the population living below the national poverty line."

The leading economic sectors, including copper, gold, rare earth and coal mining. Some oil is produced in the south of the country. Because of the large mining sector, Mongolia is dependent on commodity prices, especially for cashmere wool and precious and industrial metals. China is the leading importer and accounted for 84% of total exports in 2015. It is reported that China is also the leading foreign investor in Mongolia.

**One of the corridors of OBOR Initiative linking China to Russia passes though Mongolia, with a plan underway to improve communication infrastructure between China and Mongolia.

Mongolia, unveiled its "steppe route" program. Planned are the construction of road links between its two neighbors and the development of the power grid. This national program must then be integrated into OBOR Initiative, as announced by the two countries several times.

"Thanks to the OBOR initiative, Mongolia hopes to reduce its dependence on extraction, diversify its economy and develop its industrial sector. Better integration into regional transport networks would enable Mongolia to increase its exports. Although the steppe route means greater integration with China. Mongolia also hopes that the new silk roads will diversify its economic partners, and attract European investors.

Mongolia, a new link in the Belt and Road initiative, OBOReurope, April 10, 2017

The Russia-Mongolia-China Road Corridor runs from Tianjin in China north through Mongolia to Ulan Ude in Russia. The corridor is supposed to open in 2018. This is the development of a central railway corridor, organizing transit trucking activities on the Tianjin-Ulaan Baatar-Ulan-Ude route and paving a road along this route. "Chinese Foreign Minister

Wang Yi, said construction of a transport corridor linking the three countries helps support economic development, and encourages Mongolia's participation in international affairs."

***Russia-Mongolia-China Road Corridor to be Ready in 2018

Silk Road Briefing, September 8, 2017

China Pakistan-Economic Corridor

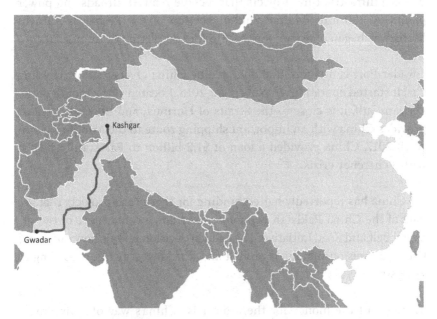

Image: China Pakistan-Economic Corridor
Image Source: Sebastien Goulard, Cooperans

Pakistan

*"Pakistan is part of the southern region of the Asian continent that is known as South Asia. It is located on the crossroads of Asia and the Middle East, bordering China in its north-most area, India in the east and Iran and Afghanistan in the west. Pakistan is the world's sixth most populous country with about 200 million people. It is the second largest economy in South Asia after India."

Pakistan is a member of the South Asian Association for Regional Cooperation (SAARC), Pakistan is also a member of the South Asia Free Trade Area (SAFTA). Pakistan is one of the member states of Central Asia Regional Economic Cooperation (CAREC) and Economic Cooperation Organization (ECO). Importantly Pakistan has signed a bilateral a trade agreement with China, and agreements with Malaysia and Sri Lanka that also have ports financed and managed by China.

The China-Pakistan economic corridor is being established to develop modern infrastructure projects that include roads, railroads and power plants. A 250-mile Multan-Sukkur section of the Peshawar-Karachi Motorway began construction in 2016 for completion in August 2019.

Gwadar Port is financed and operated by China Overseas Port Holding Co., It started operations in November 2016. Located at the mouth of the Persian Gulf, it is close to the Straits of Hormuz, and the Gwadar Port provides China with an important shipping route to the Middle East. In April 2017, China provided a loan of $1.2 billion to Pakistan to help it with a currency crisis.

***"China has reportedly halted funding for three road projects that are part of the China-Pakistan Economic Corridor, a centerpiece of the so-called Belt and Road initiative. The sudden decision reveals how unilateral Chinese decision-making is on Belt and Road investments, according to analysts.

Turning off the money for the project is "China's way of conveying a diplomatic yet strong message to the Pakistanis: We will pay, but only on our terms," the European Foundation for South Asian Studies, an Amsterdam-based think tank, said in a note, describing the situation as "a temporary punitive step to affirm control."

This is another example of the risk that Sri Lanka learned about when it couldn't make payments on the Chinese loans that financed its port project and led to China essentially owing the port. The same thing has happened to Pakistan's Gwadar Port. Pakistan has no control of it.

China's One Belt One Road Initiative is likely to end up being a way for China to expand its territorial presence in Asia, Africa, the Middle East and even Europe.

***Pakistan learns the downside of taking infrastructure money from China,** China giveth, and China taketh away. CNBC Asia-Pacific, Nyshka Chandran, December 12, 2017

Bangladesh-China-India-Myanmar Economic Corridor

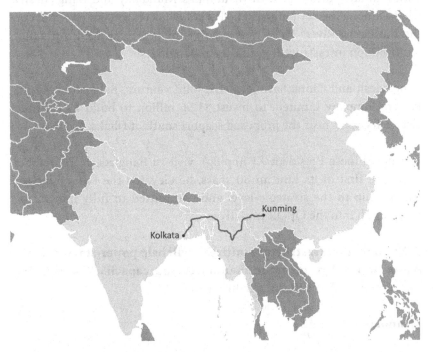

Image: Bangladesh-China-India-Myanmar Economic Corridor
Image Source: Sebastien Goulard, Cooperans

Bangladesh

The BCIM economic corridor: Prospects and challenges, Observer Research Foundation, K. YHOME, February 10, 2017

**"Bangladesh is the third most-populated country in South Asia (after India and Pakistan). It shares borders with India to the north, west and east, and overlooks the Bay of Bengal to the south. It has two existing major ports, the Port of Chittagong and the Port of Payra that should be converted to deep-sea ports by 2025.

***"China intends to set up economic corridors in alliance with other countries – with one covering Bangladesh, India and Myanmar (i.e. the BCIM Economic Corridor). The Corridor will link India's Kolkata with China's Kunming, with Myanmar's Mandalay and Bangladesh's Dhaka among the key points." The Port of Dhaka is a major river **port** on the Buriganga River. The Chinese government has pledged to finance multi-billion infrastructure projects in Bangladesh.

Bangladesh and China have formed a joint venture, Bangladesh-China Power Company Limited, to invest $1.56 billion to build a coal-fired electricity plant near the proposed seaport south of Dhaka.

During Chinese President Xi Jinping's visit to Bangladesh in October 2016, the first of its kind in 30 years, he elevated the two countries' partnership to the strategic level and committed to fully integrating Bangladesh into the OBOR Initiative.

*****Xi Jinping's infrastructure initiative will help power-starved South Asian nation fire up more manufacturing capacity**, South China Morning Post, April 10, 2017, Sidney Leng

Myanmar

Myanmar, being very small, is the seventh largest economy of the 10-member ASEAN bloc. It has a large service sector which accounts for about 46% of GDP. Industry and agriculture respectively account for 28% and 26% of GDP. Major sectors include agricultural processing, manufacturing, construction and transportation.

Myanmar's GDP is forecast to expand by 7.7% in FY 2017/18 and 8% in FY 2018/19 on the back of improved global commodity prices and stronger demand from trading partners. Cumulative FDI into Myanmar had reached $62.6 billion as of July 2017, with the Chinese mainland, Singapore and Hong Kong being the main sources.

****The Bangladesh-China-India-Myanmar (BCIM) OBOR Economic Corridor is the economic link connecting the Ganges River of India, the Ayerwaddy River of Myanmar, and the Mekong River of Indo-China. It is the lead bridge connecting the Pacific Ocean and the Indian Ocean. It is a market focus point for China, South and South East Asia. Therefore, building of the BCIM Economic Corridor could serve the common interests of the sub-regional countries' economic and social development."

The maritime route connecting Myanmar to India is a transport loop, which aims to provide maritime access of goods from Kolkata, via Myanmar's port of Sittwe, to Paletwa by inland water transport along the Myanmar River, Kaladan, and back via highway to Mizoram in northeast India.

****"One Belt-One Road Initiative and MYANMAR" Connectivity: Synergy Issue and Potentialities, Global New Light of Myanmar, Than Zaw, March 11, 2018

The Bangladesh-China-India-Myanmar Economic Corridor (BCIM-EC) starts in Kunming in Southwestern China, goes west through Myanmar and India, through Bangladesh, and then ends up in Kolkata, India.

In a major development in realizing the BCIM-EC, the first meeting of the BCIM-EC joint study group was held in December 2013 in Kunming, thus officially setting up the mechanism to promote cooperation. The current government in New Delhi under Prime Minister Narendra Modi, in the past has continued with the same enthusiasm of the Manmohan Singh government in acknowledging the progress made in promoting cooperation under the BCIM-EC framework. However there are political issues about China surrounding India in the Indian Ocean.

This area is seen as:

- "The meeting point of the three markets of China, Southeast Asia and South Asia and thereby connecting two major markets of China and India and even the whole of Asia.
- Second, even as the sub-region suffers from poor infrastructure, its rich natural resources promise huge potential for large-scale development; and
- Third, the sub-region is isolated from global markets and is characterized by relative poverty; and,
- Lastly, all the four countries have actively participated in regional and sub-regional organizations with the aim to integrate into the global economy.

Eastern India may derive substantial economic benefits from the BCIM-EC, as might Bangladesh, Myanmar and the Kunming area of China.

There are design issues that begin with the actual route, include land issues such as dams, and environmental issues, that need to be addressed.

India

*****These developments in India's neighborhood would enhance competition for access to markets and resources between China and India. As China also strengthens maritime security and military cooperation with these countries, security dynamics in the region will be an area of concern. Most importantly, China's increasing influence in South and Southeast Asia under the framework of BRI has wide-ranging strategic implications in the Indo-Pacific region. As China aspires to become a maritime power and enhance its naval presence in the Indian Ocean, rivalry in the region would require new security mechanisms to deal with the changing power dynamics. The failure will give birth to security dilemma and periodic tensions.

**"India's exports expanded by 9.9% year-on-year (YOY) to $191.3 billion in the first eight months of 2017, while imports grew 27.2% YOY to $288.8 billion in the same period. India's major export markets included the

UAE, the U.S. and Hong Kong. Major import sources were China, the UAE, Saudi Arabia, Switzerland and the U.S."

The Belt and Road Initiative: Country Profiles, Hong Kong Trade Development Council, May 17, 2018

India's technology services sector is a very important export source. A Make in India initiative was launched in September 2014 to make India into a world-class manufacturing hub through attracting foreign direct investment (FDI). India recorded an FDI inflow of $100 billion between October 2014 and June 2017, up 64%. As of June 2017, India's cumulative inward FDI amounted to $342 billion. Mauritius was the largest FDI source for India, followed by Singapore and Japan Cumulative FDI from Chinese mainland amounted to $1.7 billion respectively.

China intends to set up economic corridors with many countries in the region, including the Bangladesh-China-India-Myanmar (BCIM) Economic Corridor, which was jointly proposed by China and India in 2013.

India has concluded several free trade agreements (FTAs) with countries and regions including Afghanistan, Bhutan, Ecuador, Singapore, Malaysia, Sri Lanka, Nepal, Korea, Chile, Japan, Africa, the ASEAN and the MERCOSUR (Brazil, Argentina, Uruguay and Paraguay). India also engages in the Agreement of South Asia Free Trade Area (SAFTA), and the Asia Pacific Trade Agreement (APTA). Currently, India is negotiating FTAs with Australia, Canada, Egypt, Indonesia, Israel, New Zealand, Thailand, the Gulf Cooperation Council (GCC) and the EU.

China's promotion and financing of its OBOR initiative is creating strains with India. An increase in tensions between these regional heavyweights is not an outcome China advertises.

*****"A quadrilateral meeting was held between senior officials from the United States, Japan, India, and Australia on the future of a 'free and open Indo-Pacific.' India's participation in the dialogue is yet another signal that China's method of implementing the OBOR is driving a wedge between China and India and creating an opportunity for the United States to strengthen its ties with New Delhi."

One result of China's initiative is that the Indian Ocean part of the Initiative threatens to surround India. So far this has not occurred.

Beijing's handling of territorial disputes in the era of OBOR has increased tensions in the region. The OBOR vision statement claims "Principles of Peaceful Coexistence" which include a "mutual respect for each other's sovereignty." Contrary to this principle, China has escalated sovereignty disputes by pressing territorial claims against its neighbors.

In the South China Sea, China has challenged Vietnamese claims by moving a state-owned oilrig into disputed waters and constructed airstrips suitable for military aircraft, and other military installations, on disputed features in the Spratly Islands.

On the Doklam Plateau in 2017, China challenged Bhutan's sovereignty by attempting to extend a road into disputed territory. This led to a military standoff with India, Bhutan's protector. These actions directly contradict the OBOR vision statement and send a signal to China's neighbors that it will aggressively use its power to assert claims over disputed territories. Neighboring states are now forced to consider how China's OBOR investments may be leveraged to strengthen its position on competing territorial claims.

China's OBOR Initiatives are challenging India's territorial claims in Kashmir. The China-Pakistan Economic Corridor goes through territory in Kashmir that Pakistan controls and India claims. India believes that China has abandoned its neutral stance and sided with Pakistan. "China's failure to address Indian concerns was the initial cause of New Delhi's reluctance to join the One Belt, One Road Initiative. China's unilateral implementation of its vision for the OBOR Initiative over Indian objections has increased bilateral tensions.

India has additional concerns in the Indian Ocean. "China has invested in port facilities in states surrounding India including Pakistan, Myanmar and Sri Lanka. Investment in these ports has given rise to the "string of pearls" theory, which speculates that China will leverage these facilities for military use. When viewed on a map, these maritime investments represent the encirclement of India at sea. Chinese docked attack submarines at a Chinese-constructed port in Sri Lanka. This indicates a militarization of these OBOR-related investments in India's island neighbor. Naval encirclement is a significant security concern as India depends upon sea transport for about 90 percent of its international trade.

********"India is also concerned about shifting regional security alignments because of Chinese investments in its land and sea neighbors. Indian Foreign Secretary Jaishankar commented on New Delhi's concerns about the potential consequences of the BRI in March 2016: The interactive dynamic between strategic interests and connectivity initiatives ... is on particular display in our continent... We cannot be impervious to the reality that others may see connectivity as an exercise in hardwiring that influences choices" they make.

India pundits have expressed concerns that countries such as Sri Lanka will get trapped in debt and servitude to China, as they did. Sri Lanka's debt default resulted in China getting control of a deep-water port at Hambantota for 99 years in a debt for equity swap. In this exchange, the PRC gained a potential "pearl" to add to its string. Sri Lanka has actually renewed ties with India due to concerns about undue Chinese influence stemming from its debt. "If future trends align with the projections of OBOR critics, the PRC could parlay economic investment into puppet states that encircle India on land and sea. Unfortunately, if other potential puppet states turn toward India instead, it could still result in increased tensions as Chinese debtors become more entangled with India."

India signed a bilateral logistics exchange memorandum of agreement (LEMOA) with the United States in 2016, which granted reciprocal logistics access to military bases. With Japan, India has increased security cooperation by selecting Japan as a permanent participant in the traditionally U.S.-Indian Malabar security exercise in 2015. These actions signal an active effort by New Delhi to address its security concerns with China by keeping friendly military powers engaged in the region.

India has also sought to increase its economic relationships with democratic regional powers to promote its own vision for connectivity development. Indian Prime Minister Modi has unveiled the Asia-Africa Growth Corridor (AAGC), a connectivity initiative conceived by India and Japan and seen as a potential counter to the OBOR Initiative. "If India chooses deepened cooperation with democratic powers in the wake of the initial "quad" meeting, it will be another sign of the ever-increasing tensions between New Delhi and Beijing due to the OBOR. More troubling, the 'quad' meeting portends a trend toward military and economic polarization in Asia.

******China's Belt and Road Initiative Is Stoking Tensions with India,** The National Interest, Mitchell J. Hays, November 16, 2017

Azerbaijan

*"Azerbaijan is one of the most convenient routes from Northeast Europe to Central Asia and the Middle East. Situated on the shores of the Caspian Sea in Southwestern Asia, it shares borders with Russia, Georgia, Armenia, Turkey and Iran. It has the biggest port on the Caspian Sea (Baku International Sea Trade Port), Azerbaijan is a logistics hub for the Caspian region".

*The Belt and Road Initiative: Country Profiles,** Hong Kong Trade Development Council, May 17, 2018

**Azerbaijan is ideally situated to be an important part of China's OBOR Initiative. It has a modern port at Baku and is an ideal partner for a land route through the North that goes through Barda its capital in the old days. The shortest way to approach West Asia from China is via Baku, the current capital of Azerbaijan. China is the manufacturer of the world's fastest and most luxurious trains. A railroad track is already operational from Aktau and Turkmenbashi, transporting goods to the New Baku International Sea Trade Port and then westward to Turkey and Europe.

Barda, about 150 miles west of Baku, was a trading hub on the ancient overland Silk Road. The China-Central Asia-West Asia Economic Corridor is a land-based substitute for these two traditional routes.

"Azerbaijan is an ideal partner for construction of the Belt for three reasons:

- The Azerbaijan-located Caspian rim area is becoming a new joint zone of East Asian, European and Russian economic interest;

- Azerbaijan is the forerunner in the rejuvenation of the ancient Silk Road in terms of re-development multiple large-scale transnational transport systems; and
- Azerbaijan bears similarities with China, which contribute to mutually beneficial cooperation."

Azerbaijan and China need to identify specific areas of cooperation.

**Azerbaijan forms a key link in the Silk Road chain, By Malik Ayub Sumbal, China Daily Europe January 20, 2017

***"Azerbaijan is a major supporter of the Transport Corridor Europe-Caucasus-Asia project, initiated by the EU and considered the backbone of the Silk Road.

The Baku-Tbilisi-Kars railway has been dubbed the Iron Silk Road.

China has initiated the Silk Road Fund, for which the Asian Infrastructure Investment Bank will allocate very large sums for the construction of these international corridors. "According to estimates, the trans-Caspian route could be transporting around 300,000-400,000 containers by 2020, bringing in hundreds of millions of dollars."

***Relations between China and Azerbaijan are growing fast and Azerbaijan has great potential to become a valuable partner in the Silk Road project - one of the great initiatives of the 21st century.

Malik Ayub Sumbal is the Editor in Chief of Eurasia Media Network and The Caspian Times., China Daily European Weekly, January 20, 2017

Bhutan

*"Bhutan, with the smallest population in South Asia, is a small, landlocked Himalayan kingdom set in between China to the north and India to the south. Bhutan has forged a close relationship with India, with its robust GDP growth driven primarily by selling hydropower to India in recent years. Indeed, about 90% of Bhutan's exports go to India, which mainly composed of hydropower and base metals. As to imports, about

80% are sourced from India, including fuel and machinery. Other import sources include France, Japan, Singapore and China.

Bhutan has a weak relationship with China, and is being bypassed by China's OBOR Initiative.

Brunei

Brunei is located on the north coast of the island of Borneo, facing the South China Sea and surrounded by East Malaysia. Its economy is heavily resource-dependent, with the oil and gas sector accounting for some 60% of GDP and more than 90% of its export and fiscal receipts. Despite having the smallest population in ASEAN, Brunei's per-capita income is the second highest in ASEAN after Singapore.

Brunei is a member of the ASEAN Economic Community (AEC), Brunei has entered free trade agreements (FTAs) with China, Korea, India, Australia and New Zealand under the ASEAN context. A bilateral FTA with Japan was also entered into. Also, Brunei has participated in the negotiation of the Regional Comprehensive Economic Partnership (RCEP), and the Comprehensive and Progressive Agreement for Trans-Pacific Partnership (CPTPP).

On a tiny island of Muara Besar, off Brunei's northern tip on the South China Sea, thousands of Chinese workers are building a refinery and petrochemical complex, along with a bridge connecting it to the capital, Bandar Seri Begawan. It is a $3.4 billion complex, and is run by China's Hengyi Group. When completed, it will be Brunei's largest-ever foreign investment project, and comes at a time when the oil-dependent country badly needs it. The Muara Besar project is expected to provide over 10,000 jobs, but claims that thousands of Chinese workers have been shipped in to build the complex has angered some local residents.

"Brunei is an important country along the 21st century Maritime Silk Road," China's Ambassador to Brunei Yang Jian said at the opening ceremony in February 2017 for a joint venture, running Brunei's largest container terminal.

*****As Western banks leave, China adds Brunei to new silk road,
Reuters, By Praveen Menon, March 4, 2018

Maldives

Maldives is a small island country in the Indian Ocean, about 620 miles
southwest of Sri Lanka. A middle-income country with a small population
inhabiting some 200 of its 1,000 islands, Maldives relies on its tourism
and fishery sectors for economic growth. Maldives is one of the countries
along China's Maritime Silk Road under the OBOR Initiative.

*"China provided financial aid, and assisted with the construction of
China-Maldives Friendship Bridge, which will increase connectivity between the islands in Maldives. The project was started in 2015 and is
scheduled to be complete in August 2018. In addition to inviting Chinese
airlines to land in Maldives, the government is building a new runway at
the Velana International Airport with Chinese loans and infrastructural
assistance, which was expected to be completed in mid-2018".

***The Maldives has and autocratic president, Abdulla Yameen. "If he
cracks down on the opposition to consolidate power ahead of another
election, analysts and diplomats warn that the small nation's troubles
could provoke a larger crisis that draws in China and India, which have
long competed for influence in the Indian Ocean region".

"Mohamed Nasheed, the opposition leader, has largely lived in exile since
his term as the country's first democratically elected president ended in
a 'coup of sorts' in 2012. He expressed fears that an expansionist China
is propping up Mr. Yameen to lock the country into a 'debt trap', a term
that refers to China's taking over of infrastructure projects when a country cannot pay back its loans, such as the recent takeover of a port in Sri
Lanka."

Indian officials have expressed concern about the situation, but have had a
weak response. Indian influence in the Maldives has declined since 2012,
when it did not stand firmly behind Mr. Nasheed, who had been an ally,
as he was removed from office. Anand Kumar, a fellow at the Institute
for Defense Studies and Analyses in New Delhi, said "although India

was clearly alarmed about losing influence to the Chinese in the Indian Ocean, it had struggled to respond".

***Maldives Crisis Could Stir Trouble Between China and India,** New York Times, By Mujib Mashal, February. 14, 2018

The China-Central Asia-West Asia Economic Corridor, Kazakhstan, Kyrgyzstan, Tajikistan, Uzbekistan, Turkmenistan, Iran and Turkey

The China-Central Asia-West Asia Economic Corridor

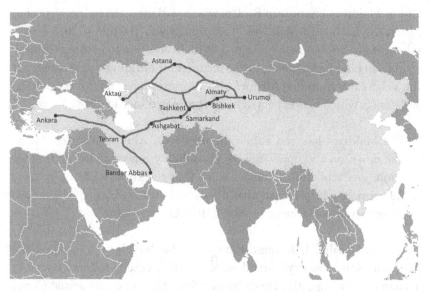

Image: China-Central Asia-West Asia Economic Corridor
Image Source: Sebastien Goulard, Cooperans

This is one of the main axes of the new Silk Road; it connects the Chinese province of Xinjiang to the Mediterranean Sea, through Kazakhstan, Kyrgyzstan, Tajikistan, Uzbekistan, Turkmenistan, Iran and Turkey. It follows the ancient Silk Route. This initiative is completed by bilateral cooperation agreements between China and Central Asia states. This corridor aims to better connect all the regional economies to China but also to Europe and thus offers a new intercontinental communication network that will open up Central Asian states.

This corridor requires the construction of numerous transportation and energy infrastructures from the Middle East to China. It is supplemented by various measures aiming at increasing trade among all states involved in the OBOR.

Kazakhstan

*"Kazakhstan is an important world energy supplier due to its significant reserves of oil natural gas and coal. It is estimated that proven reserves in Kazakhstan account for some 3% of world oil reserves, 1% of world gas reserves and 4% of the world coal reserve. It is also endowed with some other mineral deposits like chrome, lead, tungsten, copper, zinc, iron and gold."

***A visit by Chinese Premier Li Keqiang led to economic deals totaling $14 billion. This was followed by China officials announcing that Kazakhstan would launch more than 20 joint projects with Chinese companies, focusing on priority sectors in the Kazakh manufacturing industry, such as mining, oil and gas, construction, chemical and light industry, and transport. "In March 2015, the two countries signed a series of cooperation agreements worth of $23.6 billion, on closer co-operations in various sectors such as railway, electricity, nuclear energy and agriculture."

An oil-and-gas development project in Aktyubinsk region of Kazakhstan involved oil pipelines being built to allow direct oil exports to China, including the pipeline running from Kazakhstan's Caspian shore to Xinjiang of China. Major participants in the projects include the China National Petroleum Corporation and the Kazakh oil company KazMunayGas.

****Kazakhstan needs to find alternates for growth, by diversifying and innovating, itself instead of relying solely on natural resources. The OBOR Initiative provides an opportunity for Kazakhstan to attract Chinese money and technologies, and become one of the largest transit hubs in Eurasia.

****Practitioners' perspectives, Kazakhstan and the Belt and Road, GRATA Law Firm, Shaimerden Chikanayev, April 27, 2017

Kyrgyzstan

"Kyrgyzstan is a mountainous country located at the crossroads of Asian cultures. Its economy relies heavily on the exploitation and export of gold, mercury, natural gas and uranium, along with agricultural products such as cotton, meat, tobacco, wool and grapes. Due to its mountainous landscape, livestock farming dominates its agricultural economy, while aluminum production represents the bulk of its industrial production. Meanwhile, the service sector, including banking and tourism, has become an increasingly important growth driver."

Business ties are improving. Bilateral trade is also looking better, with

Russia being the largest trading partner, followed by China. "There are now more than 250 Chinese companies registered in Kyrgyzstan, including Zhongda China Petrol Company and Zijin Mining Group, and covering various industries such as mining, trading, construction, telecommunications, agriculture and metallurgy."

At a meeting in May, 2017, the Kyrgyz President praised the OBOR Initiative. According to the head of the foreign policy department of the Kyrgyz president's office, Aizada Subakozhoeva, Atambayev "noted the importance of expanding fiber-optic communication lines from China to Europe via Kyrgyzstan, e-commerce, and the creation of logistics centers. The project of construction of the China-Kyrgyzstan-Uzbekistan railway was noted as promising."

Central Asia, especially Kazakhstan, may be a bridge between markets but are there benefits beyond transit fees? As Fallon pointed out in her *RFE/RL* interview, "China's investment in [rail links and connectivity] could be beneficial for connecting these various economies. But some are concerned that the trains will just go through Central Asia and bring these goods to Europe and not really help Central Asian economies as much."

*****Majlis Podcast: What Does China's One Belt, One Road Project Mean For Central Asia?, OBORwatch, December 6, 2016

*****What's Next for the Belt and Road in Central Asia?, Three regional presidents attended the Belt and Road Forum in Beijing last weekend. By Catherine Putz, May 17, 2017

Tajikistan

*Tajikistan is the poorest country in per-capita GDP among the Central Asia countries. Surrounded by Afghanistan, China, Kyrgyzstan and Uzbekistan, Tajikistan is a landlocked mountainous country, with 90% of its country being mountainous. Tajikistan has close ties with Russia and is highly dependent on remittances coming from Russia. About half of its working-age males are working abroad, mostly in Russia. In 2014, the total volume of remittances amounted to $3.9 billion, nearly 50% of the country's GDP.

*****"Tajikistan's trade with China has been increasing. The value of bilateral trade increased from $0.5 billion in 2007 to more than $2.5 billion in 2014. Meanwhile, Chinese enterprises have been staffing more infrastructure projects in Tajikistan, including the Sahelistan Tunnel and Tajik-Uzbek Highway, as well as various resources extraction projects."

Because of its geographical location and its isolated location, the government is focused on the development of transport infrastructure. Tajikistan has 14 bilateral and 12 multilateral agreements in place, has transport operations to 33 countries worldwide, and has a bilateral agreement on international road transport to China.

China's OBOR Initiative opens up significant opportunities for the region's carriers. It also gives them access to the sea. The OBOR development is also consistent with an important Tajikistan government strategic development initiative, which is to put an end to transport isolation and to transform Tajikistan into a transit country.

*****Tajikistan – transport leader reveals how TIR in China will open up vast opportunities" for the region, IRU, September 5, 2017

Uzbekistan

Uzbekistan Is very focused on the cultivation and processing of cotton, fruits, vegetables and grain (wheat, rice and corn)." Uzbekistan, is also a world leader in terms of its gas, coal and uranium resources, while also said to have more than 1,800 different mineral reserves." It has population of over 30 million. It is the most populous country in Central Asia, accounting for 45% of the total population. This, however, has not led to the formation of a lucrative consumer market, despite the country enjoying average GDP growth of more than 8% per annum over the past decade.

Uzbekistan uses the Latvian seaport of Riga and also has some of the shortest overland routes connecting Europe and Asia.

******"Uzbekistan is located at the heart of Transport Corridor Europe–Caucasus–Asia (TRACECA) and three of the six Central Asia Regional Economic Cooperation (CAREC) corridors. Dating back to Soviet times, rail and road transport have been the country's key and cheapest means of transport. According to current estimates, some 95% of cargo travelling through or to Uzbekistan still travels by road or rail."

Uzbekistan was a key participant in the ancient Silk Road hundreds of years ago. When the OBOR Initiative was first raised by President Xi Jinping in 2013 the country responded to China's initiative immediately, and signed agreements with the Chinese government, including investment and infrastructure construction for the Initiative.

Uzbek President Shavkat Mirziyoyev stated: "We believe participating in the OBOR Initiative meets the priority of our five-year development strategy for Uzbekistan 2017 – 2021."

********Belt and Road a 'great opportunity': Uzbek official**

China Daily, By Ren Qi, December 12, 2017

Turkmenistan

*Situated in the southwest of Central Asia and bordering Kazakhstan to the northwest and Uzbekistan to the north and east, Turkmenistan has budget surpluses resulting from the development of energy sources and commodities such as oil, natural gas and cotton. It has extremely large gas deposits underneath the Karakum Desert (which occupies 70% of the land area of Turkmenistan) gas is the core of Turkmenistan's economy. These gas sources include the Galkynysh gas field, which has the second-largest volume of gas in the world after the South Pars field in the Persian Gulf.

It's the Year of the Dog in China but here in Ashgabat, this year's slogan is: "Turkmenistan is the heart of the Great Silk Road". This, like much else in Turkmenistan, has been decreed by its strongman President Gurbanguly Berdimuhamedow. He has declared the nation to be a linchpin of central Asia's new era of prosperity and promise. To illustrate its commitment, a container and ferry seaport has opened on the Caspian Sea, linking Turkmenistan with Azerbaijan, Kazakhstan, and Russia. There are also plans for a superhighway to Turkey, and more natural gas and oil exports.

***"Looked at from Turkmenistan, the motivation behind the OBOR Initiative includes promoting rapid economic development in China's sprawling western Xinjiang province to contain its large, restive, Turkic language-speaking and Muslim Uyghur population. Many Uyghurs live in Turkmenistan, where the language spoken is close to their own." Whatever the precise interpretations of China's motives, Turkmenistan has climbed on board the OBOR Initiative.

***Turkmenistan dreaming: Gurbanguly Berdimuhamedow's big bet on Belt and Road, Financial Review, by Andrew Clark, April 27, 2018

Iran

*******Iran is on the China-Central-West Asia (CCAWA) Economic Corridor of the OBOR Initiative. Chinese President Xi visited Iran in January 2016 and the two dictatorship countries agreed to increase bilateral trade by more than tenfold to $600 billion in the next decade. Areas of cooperation include energy, trade and industry. Iran is located in

Southern Asia bordering the Persian Gulf, the Caspian Sea and the Gulf of Oman. It has an attractive opportunity to serve as a gateway to a regional market of 400 million people that includes Afghanistan, Iraq, Russia and Turkey, and the Central Asian countries. The OBOR Initiative is primarily intended to promote land and sea connectivity with countries along its key routes. However, the International North-South Transport Corridor (INSTC), which was established by Iran, India, and Russia in 2000, plans to connect the Indian Ocean and Persian Gulf to the Caspian Sea via Iran, and onward to northern Europe via St. Petersburg, Russia. As a multimodal transport corridor, INSTC will make Iran a key link in connecting the three founding members and 11 other state members.

China has become Iran's top trading partner. Chinese companies have gradually replaced those in the EU and the U.S. following nuclear sanctions. In 2016 trade with China reached $31.2 billion, and grew to $18.1 billion in the first half of 2017. China became the largest crude oil export market of Iran in 2017, followed by India. Additionally, Chinese companies China National Petroleum Corporation (CNPC) and the Sinopec Group, have won major oil exploration contracts in Iran. In 2021, another recent example of Iran-China co-operation can be found in the $4.8 billion South Pars contract to develop the largest natural gas field in the world. Iran's other key trading partners include Turkey, Korea and the UAE. Iran is proposing trading agreements with a number of countries including Malaysia, Pakistan, Turkey, India and the Eurasian Economic Union (EEU).

"Chinese businesses involved in Iranian developments are worth at least $33 billion as of June 2017 according to Beijing's Commerce Ministry", part of China's OBOR Initiative. "In September 2017, China provided a $10 billion credit line to five Iranian banks financing water, energy and transport projects, and in March the two countries inked a $700 million deal allowing China to build a train line that links the port of Bushehr to the rest of Iran's railway network."

*******China stands to gain in Iran after US quits nuclear deal**, AFP, Julien Girault, May 17, 2018

Turkey

*Turkey has been going through mounting geopolitical tensions with neighboring countries. It has also had high inflation because of a weak lira, which is casting doubt on its growth prospects. Despite these problems, government-sponsored credit guarantees have restored confidence in the Turkish economy. Its economy grew at a 5.1% annual rate in the six months through June 2017, and was expected to grow by 5.3% in the year 2017.

But given further recovery of the global economy and solid gains in industrial production and investment, the Turkish economy is forecast to see 4.0% growth in 2018. This is despite its geopolitical problems.

*******The relationship between Turkey and China is turning into one of a strong friendship. Turkey's sour relationships with NATO, the EU and Germany are driving it into the arms of China. Also Turkish President Recep Tayyip Erdogan's human rights abuses, and use of the electoral process to essentially create a dictatorship are ignored by China. The Turkish Foreign Minister promised to eliminate any anti-Chinese media reports and stated "we see China's security as our security". Turkey and China are developing shared interests. This is an example of China befriending countries that are looking for alternatives to the West.

"The friendship has, to a substantial extent, already been struck. Beijing purchased a stake in Turk Telekom, a company that has been allegedly used by the Turkish government to spy on Turkish citizens and regime opponents. High-speed rail, ports and other infrastructure projects have all been lined up. The OBOR will also assist Ankara in promoting its construction industry in Central Asia, where Turkish firms have been operating since the 1990s."

*******Why is Turkey so eager to be led down the Belt and Road?, East Asia Forum, Nicol Brodie, October 28, 2017

China's One Belt, One Road Initiative And Asia Is A Crucial Trade Route Starting Point, Part 3, Indonesia, Malaysia, Nepal, New Zealand, Philippines, Singapore, South Korea,

Sri Lanka, Timor-Leste

Below are summaries of the OBOR initiatives in the countries covered in the Asia Part 3 Regions.

Indonesia

"Indonesia is the largest economy in the 10-nation ASEAN followed by Thailand. Service and industry are Indonesia's main economic drivers, accounting for 46% and 40% of GDP respectively, with the remaining 14% attributable to agriculture. Major sectors include manufacturing (tobacco, food and beverages, transport equipment and machinery), mining, construction, transport and communication, finance and real estate."

Indonesia's major trading partners include China, Japan, Singapore and the U.S.

Chinese enterprises are actively participating in Indonesian infrastructure projects. A Sino-Indonesian joint venture was formed in 2016 to build the 142km high-speed railway between Jakarta and Bandung. CAMC Engineering Company is participating in the re-development of container facilities on Batam Island, a free trade zone of Indonesia just to the south of Singapore.

Indonesia has an ambitious infrastructure-building plan, and President Joko Widodo in May, 2017 attended an international forum in Beijing to promote the One Belt, One Road (OBOR) Initiative.

****"Chinese Premier Li Keqiang has said his country wants to work closely with Indonesia to better link its Belt and Road Initiative to the South-east Asian nation's development strategy. Xinhua news agency quoted Mr Li as saying: 'The economies of the two countries are highly complementary and the potential for economic and trade cooperation is huge.' He added that China attaches great importance to developing ties with Indonesia."

****China wants closer ties with Indonesia, says Premier Li Keqiang, The Straits Times, Feb 9, 2018. Goh Sui Noi

Malaysia

*Malaysia's economy expanded by 4.2% in 2016, slowing from 5% in 2015. The IMF expects GDP growth at around 5.4% in 2017. Major Malaysian exports include electronics and electrical products (E&E), palm oil and palm oil-based products and refined petroleum products. Major export markets include Singapore, China, the U.S., EU and Japan."

Malaysia's major imports were intermediate goods and capital goods, including electronics, machinery and petroleum products. The major imports came from China, Singapore, EU, Japan, and the U.S.

*****"The Belt and Road Forum (BRF) held in Beijing in May 2017, yielded a total of nine memorandums of understandings (MOUs) and agreements signed between Malaysian and Chinese companies. Among the major projects under the initiative is the Malaysia-China Kuantan Industrial Park in Pahang, Melaka Gateway, East Coast Rail Link and Xiamen University Malaysia."

******These agreements were mostly trade based and boasted a total value of $7.22 billion or RM31.26 billion. Prime Minister Datuk Seri Najib Razak met with his Chinese counterpart President Xi Jinping in May, 2017. "Najib said the 'One Belt One Road Initiative' would derive massive benefits to Malaysia in terms of excellent infrastructure, connectivity, social facilities, better living standards and abundant business opportunities."

A digital free trade zone was set up by Alibaba Group Holding Ltd (Alibaba Group), is expected to begin at the end of 2019.

"In Malaysia the effect has also been observed as OBOR-related projects such as the Melaka Gateway deep-sea port have faced heavy criticism in regards to its necessity, contract awards and funding."

******China's Belt and Road: What's in it for Malaysia? The Borneo Post, September 3, 2017, Sunday Rachel Lau

China's One Belt, One Road Initiative And Asia Is A Crucial Trade Route Starting Point, Part 4, Mongolia, Nepal, New Zealand, Philippines, and Singapore

Below are summaries of the OBOR initiatives in the countries covered in the Asia Part 4 Regions.

Nepal

* "Nepal is a landlocked Himalayan country sandwiched between China and India. It maintains close relations with the two countries, especially with regard to infrastructure investment. Its hilly topography, however, poses a significant challenge to the improvement of transportation facilities within the country."

In September 2015, after Nepal adopted a constitution that was received angrily by India, It imposed a five-month-long trade blockade on Nepal. The blockade proved to be a turning point for China, pushing Nepal closer to its neighbor.

****"Faced with crippling shortages of fuel, cooking gas, and even medicine, the then coalition government led by nationalist communist leader Khadga Prasad Sharma Oli signed agreements with Beijing to secure sea access via Chinese ports and to import petroleum products from China, breaking India's monopoly over Nepal's fuel supplies and access to seaports."

****Nepal joins China's 'One Belt, One Road' initiative, possibly alarming India, South China Morning Post, October 10, 2017

New Zealand

*"New Zealand is largely a service-based economy, with its services sector accounting for almost 72% of the country's GDP, and the industry and agriculture sectors taking up GDP shares of about 20% and 8% respectively. Major economic sectors include real estate services, professional, scientific and technical services, manufacturing and retail trade and accommodation."

New Zealand has many free trade agreements (FTAs). It has bilateral FTAs with Australia, China, ASEAN, Singapore, Malaysia, Korea and Thailand. It is also a member of the Trans-Pacific Strategic Economic Partnership with Brunei, Chile, Singapore and New Zealand. The Trans-Pacific Partnership (TPP) Is trade deal that has not yet been approved by its members. Major pending FTAs are with Russia-Belarus-Kazakhstan, India and the EU.

*****New Zealand is wary of the Chinese objectives with regard to their OBOR Initiative, despite having signed a MOU with China. "In a statement, Foreign Affairs Minister Gerry Brownlee said Kiwi officials were still working with their Chinese counterparts on a detailed work plan, to be completed within the next 18 months. As a government, we are refining how we will engage with the Initiative. Brownlee said New Zealand's approach to Belt and Road would 'be consistent with our track record as an advocate for open, rules-based trading systems'."

*****What does China's Belt and Road mean for NZ?, Newsroom, Sam Sachdeva, July 21, 2017

Philippines

*The Philippine economy is expected to have growth of 6.6% in 2017, led by strong domestic demand and a recovery in exports.

President Rodrigo Duterte remains popular after a year in office. Underlining his policy is opening the door to closer economic cooperation with China.

"Infrastructure development has become a top priority, with a list of mega infrastructure projects amounting to $160 billion in the pipeline. Infrastructure spending is ambitiously targeted to increase from less than 2% of GDP in 2016 to 5% by 2017, then further expanding to 7% by 2019. Infrastructure investment is expected to be a major economic driver over the next few years."

******China's President Xi met with President Duterte in November 2017. Both sides committed to cooperate in infrastructure construction, agriculture, investment and other areas aligned with the OBOR Initiative and with the Philippines' development strategy. The Philippines has entered into over 10 bilateral co-operation agreements with China.

********Nomura: Philippines a winner, but also most at risk, under China's 'Belt and Road'** By Ian Nicolas Cigaral (philstar.com), April 17, 2018

Singapore

*"Singapore's services sector contributes some 70% of the country's GDP with the sectors of wholesale & retail trade, business services and finance & insurance being the prime drivers. The industrial sector takes up almost the remaining GDP share, as agriculture contributes to less than 1% of GDP. Construction, electronics, biomedical, petroleum and petrochemicals are the key industry sectors, while precision engineering is also gaining impetus as a driver too."

*******The top export markets for Singapore were the Chinese mainland first, Hong Kong second, Malaysia, Indonesia and the U.S. Although, many of the trade corridors under the OBOR initiative will bypass Singapore, China's OBOR Initiative will be a focal point in its relationship with Singapore, Prime Minister Lee Hsien Loong has said. Mr Lee said Singapore and China have identified four major areas of cooperation: infrastructure connectivity, financial connectivity, joint collaboration to help other OBOR countries, and offer of services to resolve cross-border commercial disputes. Singapore is a global financial center and one of the largest offshore yuan centers in the world.

Also, many Chinese companies use Singapore as a base of operations in the region.

*******Belt and Road Initiative a focal point for Singapore's ties with China, The Straits Times, By Danson Cheong, April 8, 2018

China's One Belt, One Road Initiative And Asia Is A Crucial Trade Route Starting Point, Part 5, South Korea, Sri Lanka,

Tajikistan, and Thailand

Below are summaries of the OBOR initiatives in the countries covered in the Asia Part 5 Regions.

South Korea

*The South Korean economy grew by 3.1% in 2017, following a 2.9% expansion in the previous year. Korea is very dependent on trade, with total foreign trade accounting for about 80% of the country's GDP. China was Korea's largest export partner 2017, and accounted for about 25% of total exports. Other major export destinations were the U.S., 12%, and Vietnam 8%. Major sources of imports to Korea were China, 20%, Japan, 12% and the U.S., 11%.

**The tensions between North Korea, and South Korea and the U.S. have slowed any benefit South Korea might get from China's OBOR Initiative. So far, China's Initiative has focused on investments, particularly infrastructure projects, in Central and Southeast Asia, Africa, and Europe. "However, the Chinese government's Vision and Action Plan also foresees the provision of economic opportunities to regions in Northeast Asia. Specifically, three northern Chinese provinces — Liaoning, Jilin, and Heilongjiang — are positioned to become part of a Northeast Asian economic zone that could link Russia, Mongolia, and possibly even the Korean Peninsula."

South Korea has developed its own Eurasia Initiative (EAI). EAI is also based on economic cooperation in Eurasia through infrastructure projects, such as the trans-Korean railway, that ultimately hope to promote peace to the Korean Peninsula. By doing so, South Korea could also access train routes over the Eurasian landmass, reducing the logistics costs of its exports to Europe by up to 30%. This initiative could also benefit North Korea, should a unified Korean Peninsula come about.

The OBOR Initiative makes no mention of South Korea or North Korea. By creating new access to the Eurasian market, South Korea hopes to create an improved economy, while becoming less dependent on trade with China and the United States. At the same time, the initiative foresees possible North Korean economic integration into the region, which might trigger changes for South Korea.

***"Comparing the outlook of the two initiatives for the peninsula, it seems that they cannot coexist at this state without creating further tensions in the region. If China does not include South Korea in its initiative, but approaches North Korea for trade, then relations between Seoul and Beijing might deteriorate. Likewise, China will not be too pleased if the South pushes forward with an initiative that diminishes China's economic grip on the peninsula."

****One Belt, One Road, One Korea?,** Together, China's Belt and Road and South Korea's Eurasia Initiative could help pave the path to peace on the peninsula., The Diplomat, By Maximilian Römer, February 10, 2018

Sri Lanka

Sri Lanka's economy is growing at about a 4.5% rate. Sri Lanka is a mid-sized country in South Asia in terms of GDP and population. The services sector is about 60% of the Sri Lankan economy. Information technology, financial services, tourism and telecommunications are the main growth engines. The industry sector accounts for about 26% of GDP.

In July 2017, the Sri Lanka Ports Authority (SLPA) and China Merchants Port Holdings (CMP) signed an agreement under which the joint venture majority-owned by the CMP, which will invest up to $1.12 billion, will handle the commercial operations of the Chinese-built Hambantota Port on a 99-year lease, with the port expected to play a strategic role in the OBOR Initiative.

In 2016, Sri Lanka granted China the permission to build its flag-ship Colombo Port City under the Megapolis initiative. Huawei has also invested significantly in Sri Lanka and teamed up with the major Sri Lankan telecom operators. Sri Lanka defaulted on its Hambantota Port project, and China traded debt for equity and basically owns the project for 99 years.

Sri Lanka has abundant potential as an investment destination, especially its location in the middle of the Indian Ocean. It is adjacent to one of the busiest sea-lanes in the world and in the middle of the OBOR region. Its opportunity should be leveraged carefully by policy makers. "The clumsy foreign policy misjudgments of early 2015 must be carefully rectified and left behind. While the OBOR opens up enormous possibilities, Sri Lanka is also in a position to exploit its strategic location in the centre of the rapidly expanding South Asian economies."

***One Belt One Road – A Unique Opportunity For Sri Lanka**, by Dr Palitha Kohona, February 10, 2018

Timor-Leste

*Located on the eastern half of Timor Island in Southeast Asia, Timor-Leste lies close to Indonesia and about 375 miles away from Australia. Timor-Leste's economy is very dependent on its offshore oil and gas resources. They generate more than 90% of the country's revenue. A public-private partnership has been established to build a new seaport at Tibar Bay, west of the capital Dili, with an expected investment of about $490 million. Construction began in June 2017. "The new port is planned to handle the commercial cargo operations of the existing Port of Dili, which is highly congested with limited expansion possibilities."

**Zhang Ping, special envoy and also vice chairman of the Standing Committee of the National People's Congress of China said that China is willing to continuously make efforts with Timer-Leste to strengthen the alignment of their development strategies, actively engage in cooperation based on the OBOR Initiative and constantly push ahead a comprehensive partnership. Timor-Leste's new President Francisco Guterres Lu-Olo said that his country supports and actively participates in the OBOR construction. Lu-Olo also said that Timor-Leste is willing to further strengthen its cooperation with China in various fields and constantly enhance relations between the two countries.

Europe

China's One Belt, One Road Initiative And The Balkans Are Seaport Links Between Asia And Europe- Albania, Bosnia and Herzegovina, Bulgaria, Croatia, Greece, Macedonia, Montenegro, Romania, Serbia and Slovenia

Below are summaries of the OBOR initiatives in the countries covered in the Balkans Region.

Albania

*"Albania is a small country in Southeast Europe, located across from Italy (less than 45 miles from the Italian coast) and bordering Montenegro to the northwest, Kosovo to the northeast, Macedonia to the east and Greece to the south and southeast. With a coastline on the Adriatic Sea to the west and on the Ionian Sea to the southwest, Albania is strategically placed at the center of a natural crossroad in Europe."

*The Belt and Road Initiative: Country Profiles**, Hong Kong Trade Development Council, May 17, 2018

**"China would like to take an active part in Albanian major infrastructural and energy projects such as roads, hydro-electric power stations and economic development zones, and strengthen cooperation on cultural and people-to-people exchanges, film-making, education and tourism, the Chinese vice premier said."

****China, Albania agree to expand cooperation under Belt and Road, 16+1 framework,** Xinhua|, Yameni, April 18, 2017

Bosnia & Herzegovina

Bosnia and Herzegovina (B&H) shares borders with Croatia, Serbia and Montenegro in Southern Europe. A number of agreements between the EU and B&H have been concluded, including the Stabilization and Association Agreement (SAA), which became effective on June 1, 2015. In addition to the SAA, B&H has signed the Central European Free Trade Agreement (CEFTA) with Albania, Kosovo, Macedonia, Moldova, Montenegro and Serbia. It has also signed free trade accords with Turkey and joined the European Free Trade Association, (EFTA), a common market that includes Switzerland, Norway, Iceland and Liechtenstein.

***Gen. Chang Wanquan said that Bosnia and Herzegovina is a trusted friend of China in Central and Eastern Europe. In recent years, mutual political trust between the two countries has been deepened, and exchanges and cooperation have been steadily advanced in various fields. Marina Pendes, the Defense Minister of B&H, said that the two countries and two militaries have profound friendship. Bosnia and Herzegovina firmly adheres to the One-China policy and firmly believes that the Belt and Road Initiative will benefit countries and people along the way and of the world as a whole.

***Chinese defense minister meets with Bosnia and Herzegovina counterpart, China Military, Editor: Yao Jianing, May 17, 2017

Bulgaria

""Bulgaria has a strategic location at the center of the Balkans and Southeast Europe, and the main roads of Europe to the Middle East and Asia pass through it. Ease of transportation is provided by five Pan-European corridors (IV, VII, VIII, IX and X), four major airports (Sofia, Plovdiv, Bourgas and Varna), two of the largest ports on the Black Sea (Varna and Bourgas) and numerous other ports along the Danube River."

Bulgaria could become a bridge for Chinese cargo and open the "New Silk Road"(One Belt One Road Initiative) to Central and Western Europe, said Transport Minister Ivaylo Moskovski in response to a question on the Trans-Caspian transport corridor, reports Bgnes.

****"A meeting in early 2018 was attended by representatives of Georgia, Azerbaijan and Kazakhstan (rail and sea carriers, logistics companies). For the purpose of acquainting with the opportunities of the Bulgarian ports, visits to ferryboat complex Varna, port of Varna and port of Burgas (Port Bulgaria West and BMF Port) were organized within the meeting. In order to develop the cooperation with the participants in the project, representatives of BDZ - Freight Transport EOOD took part in various initiatives, within which the potential of the Trans-Caspian International Transport Route was presented."

******Bulgaria can Open the "New Silk Road" to Central and Western Europe**, Novinite.com, April 29, 2018

Croatia

*Croatia is located in Southeast Europe, and is bordered by Italy, Slovenia, Hungary, Serbia, Bosnia and Herzegovina and Montenegro. "With three major Pan-European corridors (X, V and VII) crossing through it, Croatia provides one of the shortest routes linking Western Europe with Asia, Eastern Europe and the Mediterranean. This advantageous geo-strategic position, coupled with lower operating costs compared to the majority of other EU members, has made Croatia increasingly attractive as an investment destination in Europe."

Pragmatic Croatian-Chinese cooperation has been considerably strengthened, Chinese Ambassador Hu Zhaoming said.

****"Over the past 25 years, the mutual understanding of the two peoples has deepened greatly. Pragmatic cooperation between Croatia and China has gained in strength and last year our trade volume reached $1.2 billion, which means that it grew over 30 times in the past 25 years," Hu said, adding that "our relations are at a new starting point, facing new historical opportunities. Although the two countries have established a comprehensive cooperative partnership, the ambassador noted that bilateral cooperation lags behind China's cooperation with Croatia's neighbors.

******China, Croatia could enhance ties under Belt and Road Initiative: ambassador,** Xinhua|, Yang Yi, September 15, 2017

Greece

*****In 2016, the Chinese state-owned firm COSCO Shipping completed the acquisition of a 51% stake in Piraeus Port, Greece, one of the biggest ports in Europe. "Greece, a key point along the route of the ancient Silk Road, will once again serve as the hub connecting Asia, Europe and Africa, according to the Greek Ambassador, Leonidas Rokanas. 'Eventually, Piraeus will become the main entry point for Chinese exports to southern, eastern and central Europe,' Rokanas told the South China Morning Post. To use a Chinese metaphor, Piraeus will form the 'head of the dragon' of the so-called land-sea express route, leading to the heart of Europe through Greece."

For Greece, the deal could represent a major boost for its recovery following the debt crisis that started in 2009, and racked its economy. The port sale has ushered in a flurry of Chinese investments totaling $1.6 billion from companies including mobile giants Huawei and ZTE, the China Machinery Engineering Corporation as well as State Grid, Shenhua Group and Sinovel in the energy sector.

For China, the deal represents an important element of the OBOR Initiative as some 50 per cent of China's GDP and around 90 per cent of the EU's external trade depends on shipping. "The land-sea express passage connecting southeast and central Europe to China via Piraeus ... has further upgraded the significance of Piraeus," said the Greek envoy.

Greece has already taken concrete steps towards making the Port of Piraeus the entry point for an extended railway network into inland Europe. Greek Prime Minister Alexis Tsiaris expressed the intent of Greece to upgrade the railway connection between Piraeus and Serbia's capital Belgrade.

In September, Greece signed an agreement with Bulgaria on the construction of a high-speed railway network, named "Sea2Sea", that will connect three ports in Greece, Thessaloniki, Kavalla, Alexandropoulos, with three Bulgarian ports, Burgas and Varna on the Black Sea and Ruse on the Danube, Europe's second-longest river.

*****Why Greece is banking on China's modern-day Silk Road to help its economic recovery,** South China Morning Post, By Catherine Wong, December 26, 2017

Macedonia

"Macedonia is a landlocked and mountainous country in Southeast Europe. One of the least developed of the Yugoslav republics to gain independence in 1991, Macedonia remains one of the poorest economies in Europe. However, given its considerable economic reforms, Macedonia was ranked 10th in the World Bank's annual Ease of Doing Business Report 2016. Macedonia's sea transport relies mainly on ports in neighboring countries, such as Port of Thessaloniki in Greece and Port of Durres in Albania, through road and rail links."

The infrastructural projects built with Chinese aid are extremely important for the region of Central and Eastern Europe, but we also need educational, scientific and cultural connection, Macedonian President Gorge Ivanovo admits.

******"China once again comes close to the position it had two centuries ago, and that is to be the biggest economy in the world. As a result of this progress, China has made a huge step forward in many other fields," Macedonian President Ivanovo says, pointing out that the countries from Central and Eastern Europe can benefit especially from the Chinese accomplishments in the area of technology and innovation."

******"One Belt, One Road" initiative brings more than infrastructure to Central and Eastern Europe,** Xinhua|, Editor, Mu Unequal, October 8, 2017

Montenegro

*"Montenegro is situated at the center of the Balkan Peninsula in Southern Europe. Its southern coastline lies on the Adriatic Sea, while borders are shared with Albania, Serbia, Bosnia-Herzegovina and Croatia. With access to the Mediterranean Sea, and having the Port of Bar as its most important south Adriatic port, Montenegro serves as a link between

Southern Europe and Africa, the Middle East, India, Russia and Asia."
Montenegro has free trade agreements with the EU, the European Free
Trade Association (EFTA), the Central European countries (CEFTA) and
Russia.

President Aleksandra Vučić said that Serbia is in the midst of a physical
transformation that Vučić has promised his compatriots will end their
isolation and open the door to the European Union. To turn his "passion"
into reality, the Serbian president is relying not just on Europe, but on an
old ally farther east, China.

*******For China, its investments are both economic and political. The
Balkans form an important corridor along Beijing's OBOR Initiative and
also promise to further China's influence in European politics. Chinese
shipping giant Cosco has acquired a controlling stake in Greece's Piraeus
port, the country's largest. The Chinese have already turned it into one of
the world's top 50 ports in terms of container volume.

That was only the first step. China wants to transform Piraeus into a
European beachhead. For Europe-bound Chinese ships, which usually
travel through the Suez Canal before heading to a northern port such
as Rotterdam or Hamburg, Piraeus' relative proximity makes is a more
attractive option, if the Balkans can be provided with modern roads and
rails on which the freight can travel.

*********Beijing's Balkan backdoor**, Politico, By Matthew Karnitschnig,
July 13, 2017

Romania

*"Romania is located at the intersection of the EU, the Balkans and the
former Soviet countries, Romania is crossed by three important Pan-
European transportation corridors. As a major crossroad for international
economic exchange in Europe, the country's leading seaport, Constanta,
is the biggest and busiest in the entire Black Sea region, capable of hosting
vessels of more than 150,000 tons."

Romania has abundant high quality natural resources. They include mineral deposits such as oil and gas, as well as highly fertile agricultural land. In recent years, investment has been made in energy, machinery, healthcare and transport, which should help Romania achieve its EU 2020 targets, particularly in R&D spending and improvements in energy efficiency.

********"Romania can develop an energy center and can become one of China's long-term economic partners in the energy field. Romania has a huge processing capacity of 5 million tons in good, competitive refineries and this should be an asset to put on the table for Silk Road development. Romania was the first country to exploit petroleum by training petroleum engineers and building one of the first refineries, and it has not lost this knowledge and expertise."

"OBOR is the project of the century because it has many stakeholders and will produce manifold effects on the countries involved. There are also a large number of challenges that lie ahead for the Chinese institutions in charge of this project," believes Liviu Muresan, president of EURISC, a Bucharest-based think tank that has been working with Chinese academics, researchers, and China-based think tanks for many years.

Romania has expertise in critical infrastructures, ranging from the maritime field to space. Space is a key enabler for critical infrastructure that coordinates systems on Earth, and the field is usually approached through joint projects because one country cannot manage all the risks. EURISC has introduced the critical infrastructure dimension in the OBOR Initiative during discussions with Chinese partners, think-tanks, and the China National Petroleum Corporation.

"Expertise in resilience and critical infrastructure is something few organizations possess. The Shanghai Institute for International Studies, an influential Chinese think tank both in China and abroad, considered EURISC's contribution on "Critical Infrastructure Perspective on the Belt and Road Initiative and its Opportunities and Challenges" to be a useful conceptual approach for research and cooperation within the 16+1 initiative and OBOR Initiative."

*********The Impact of China's One Belt, One Road on Romania, Geopolitical Monitor, By Marcela Ganea, December 19, 2016

Serbia

*"Serbia is a landlocked country situated in the centre of the Balkan Peninsula in Southeast Europe. As a viable platform for customs-free exports to a market of almost 800 million people, Serbia enjoys free trade with the EU. It is also the only country outside of the Commonwealth of Independent States (CIS) that has a free trade agreement (FTA) with Russia. In January 2014, Serbia officially commenced EU membership negotiations (with full membership expected in 2020)."

********"President Xi Jinping of China chose an industrial town on the Danube River to announce that Serbia was at the center of a $900 billion OBOR infrastructure initiative. Standing on the grounds of a Communist-era steel plant in Smederevo, about 28 miles east of Belgrade, the capital, Mr. Xi promised to pour money into roads and railways to create a transport corridor for Chinese goods to flow to West European markets. Called the New Silk Road, the route would run from China to Germany, via the port of Piraeus in Greece, passing through the Balkans."

During Mr. Xi's state visit, he said China would bring more jobs, improve living standards and lift the country's economic growth. More important, by opening its economy to China, Serbia cemented Beijing's support against European Union pressure to recognize Kosovo's independence.

Some in China have questioned the economic viability of Beijing's investment spree. And outside of China, some fear that China's ambitions would keep the authoritarian leaders of countries like Serbia in power and leave the nations deep in debt and stuck with environmentally flawed projects.

Now, China's ambitions in the Balkan region have set up a potential clash with the European Union's plans, with countries like Serbia placing themselves in the middle.

********As China Moves In, Serbia Reaps Benefits, With Strings Attached, New York Times, By Barbara Surk, Sept. 9, 2017

Slovenia

*Slovenia borders Italy, Austria, Croatia and Hungary. It stretches across the Alps, the Dinaric Alps and the Pannonian Plain to the Mediterranean. "Slovenia, has a superb geographical position at the heart of the region. Intersected by traditional trade and transport routes, Slovenia is the location of choice for international companies. The two Pan-European transport corridors intersect at the Slovenian capital, Ljubljana. Shipping to Slovenia's only cargo port, Port of Koper, means gaining 7 to 10 days for ships arriving from Asia compared with sailing to Europe's northern ports."

Slovenia's key industries include logistics and distribution, automotive, chemicals and pharmaceuticals, electrical engineering and electronics, machinery, metalworking and wood-processing.

Slovenian Prime Minister Miro Cerar had a meeting with the Prime Minister of the People's Republic of China, Li Keqiang that focused on deepening economic cooperation, the opportunities offered by the 16+1 initiative, and Slovenia's role in the Silk Road Economic Belt and 21st Century Maritime Silk Road initiative, which it formally joined in November, 2017.

*********"The Slovenian PM placed particular emphasis during the meeting on a number of highly promising areas, such as cooperation in the civil aviation sector, the introduction of direct flights between Slovenia and China and investment in airport capacities, the automotive and high-tech industries, and science. Agriculture and tourism are two other promising sectors. The number of Chinese tourists visiting Slovenia and Europe has grown significantly in recent times, and further growth is anticipated."

*********PM at summit of Central and Eastern European countries and China, Government of the Republic of Slovenia, November 29, 2017

China's One Belt, One Road Initiative And Europe Is Destination For Links From Asia- European Region 1-Austria, Belarus, Czech Republic, Estonia, Hungary and Latvia

Below are summaries of the OBOR initiatives in the countries covered in European Region 1.

Austria

*Austria has a population of about 9 million. It is a landlocked country in the middle of Europe. It borders Germany, the Czech Republic, Slovakia, Hungary, Slovenia, Italy, Switzerland and Liechtenstein. Austria is known for its political and economic stability, and is one of the richest countries in the world, having a per-capita GDP of more than $47,000.

*The Belt and Road Initiative: Country Profiles, Hong Kong Trade Development Council, May 17, 2018

**"According to the Central Bank of Austria, China's total stock of FDI in Austria amounted to $773 million as of the end of 2017, a considerable increase on the $163 million recorded in 2009. With an Austrian FDI level of $3 billion as of the end of 2017, Hong Kong, however, was the largest Asian investor in the country overall."

**"The China-proposed Belt and Road Initiative opens up opportunities for Austria and China to boost cooperation, Austrian Chancellor Sebastian Kurz told Xinhua. "I see transport, energy and telecommunications, sustainable technologies, rural development, financial services and e-commerce as attractive areas with special expertise" for bilateral cooperation within the framework of the Belt and Road Initiative, Kurz said."

**Belt and Road Initiative spells opportunities for Austria-China cooperation, Xinhua, April 7, 2018

Belarus

*"Belarus is a landlocked nation. It borders Russia, Latvia, Lithuania, Poland and Ukraine. Due to its strategic location, it is an important trade and transport route in Eurasia. The country's transportation infrastructure consists of a broad network of motorways, railways and air routes. The thoroughfares crossing the country – including two Pan-European corridors (II and IX) – are the most important component of the European transportation system."

Belarus is a founding member of the Eurasian Economic Union (EAEU). It is not only as a gateway to the other signatories, Russia, Kazakhstan, Armenia and Kyrgyzstan, but also to the whole regional market. Each year over 100 million tons of European cargo cross Belarus. Russia and the EU receive 90% of the cargo.

***"Belarus is implementing over 30 investment projects financed by Chinese loans, worth about $6bn. The Great Stone Industrial Park is the largest of them. Lukashenka insists that only high-tech companies with guaranteed sales markets should become residents of the park. Currently, eight residents are registered within the park, including China Merchants Group, Huawei, and ZTE. An imbalance in Belarusian-Chinese trade, however, is raising concern within the Belarusian government. In 2016 it exceeded $2.5bn."

***Belarus and One Belt, One Road, alternative oil, SCTO, Belarus state press digest, May 20, 2017

Czech Republic

*The inroads that China and Hong Kong are making in improving their trade are nowhere more evident than in the Czech Republic. "Hong Kong's total exports to the Czech Republic surged by 27% to $826 million in the first eleven months of 2017, while its imports from the Czech Republic grew by 14% to $180 million", with the trade deficit expanding dramatically.

****The Czech president, Miloš Zeman, a populist who was re-elected earlier in 2018. He is on record calling Xi his "young friend", and Belt and Road "the most remarkable initiative in modern human history". The following are some details of China's involvement in the Czech Republic:

- In 2014, the Czech government proclaimed that the country would aspire to become "China's gateway to Europe";
  - o It broke entirely with the pro-democracy principles;
- By 2015, Zeman had named as his honorary adviser Ye Jianming, the chairman of a Chinese mega-company: CEFC, which had arrived in the Czech Republic promising billions of dollars of investments;
- CEFC embarked on a buying spree:
  - o Travel services;
  - o An airline company;
  - o A brewery;
  - o A football club; and
  - o A media group. I
  - o It also lost no time hiring scores of former Czech elected officials, who often double as advisers at various ministries, or indeed within the presidential castle.
    - ♣ CEFC's main investments in the Czech Republic weren't economic, they were about buying up the loyalty of Czech officials.
    - ♣ As time passed, actual investments remained negligible. The few deals that did materialize were mostly real estate acquisitions.
- In March, 2018, Ye suddenly ran into trouble in Beijing.
  - o News broke that he'd been arrested and come under investigation for financial irregularities.
  - o Prior to that, in November, 2017, the head of CEFC's non-profit arm, the former Hong Kong politician Patrick Ho, was arrested in New York and accused of bribing presidents and government ministers in Africa.
- The result was that the heavily indebted CEFC would effectively be taken over by the Chinese state, together with its Czech acquisitions.
  - o So much for the hopes that the company would save the Czech economy as a private investor.
- Debates have ensued about the wisdom of tying the country's future to mysterious Chinese entities and to the Communist regime in Beijing;

- Some of the metaphors Chinese media have attached to the Belt and Road project are revealing. They often call it "globalization 2.0", or the "New World Order".
  - What that vocabulary struggles to mask is that the whole endeavor is driven far more by politics than by markets.
- Other problems are:
  - Deals are negotiated at state-to-state diplomatic summits;
  - Open tenders are shunned;
  - Contracts are awarded by political fiat;
  - Ostensibly commercial companies put former politicians on their payrolls by the dozen;
- As it turns out, CEFC's main investments in the Czech Republic weren't economic, they were about buying up the loyalty of Czech officials. What China has to show for itself in my country is hardly innovation. Rather, it has brought us a new take on age-old crony capitalism.

****China's gift to Europe is a new version of crony capitalism, The Guardian, Martin Hala, April 20, 2018

Estonia

*Estonia as can be seen is the closest point of access to China in terms of rail connectivity. However, its not just China that OBOR connects. The South-East Rail section, when completed, will add countries such as Vietnam, Thailand, and Myanmar to that list, although there are serious infrastructure problems in linking these markets to China's high-speed network.

*****"Among the three Baltic States, Estonia has the highest per-capita GDP. The Estonian economy largely relies on the sectors related to forestry, while its energy sector is based on oil shale. Estonia's transportation abilities are enabling it to develop into an increasingly important logistics hub moving goods, knowledge and people in the east-west direction. Situated on a busy trading route between East and West, Estonia operates nearly 30 well-developed ports. Among them, the state-owned port of Tallinn is the largest."

China's OBOR Initiative reaches the markets of the EU by concentrating on Estonia and its infrastructure and logistics initiatives. Estonia, with a population of just 1.2 million, is among the smallest countries in the EU. China's strategy has been to target Estonia as the nearest full EU member, and to take advantage of and help develop Estonia's 'smart' IT driven interconnectivity.

Estonia has effectively become the world's first 'digital state' where nearly all interactions between the government and its citizens are now online. This gives foreign nationals, with Estonian e-residency, access to the EU but without having to leave their homes. The current 10,000 e-residents are planned to grow to 10 million by 2025 and increase its services revenue. Speeding up the entire delivery and excise process and adding a digital layer of security, is a perfect match for China and the EU's needs. This is one reason that Alibaba is interested in partnering with Estonian companies.

*****China Eyes Estonia as Smartest and Nearest Port for EU Access, Silk Road Briefing, July 20, 2017

Hungary

*"Hungary has been a member of the EU since May 2004, and it has adopted the EU's common external trade policy and measures. A number of Chinese mainland-origin products are subject to EU's anti-dumping duties, including bicycles, bicycle parts, ceramic tiles, ceramic tableware and kitchenware, fasteners, ironing boards and solar glass, which are of interest to Hong Kong exporters".

******"The centerpiece of China's OBOR initiative in Eastern Europe is a planned 220 mile high-speed Chinese-funded railway connecting Budapest, Hungary to Belgrade, the Serbian capital. In 2013 it was described by commentators as China's "express lane" to Europe. The $3 billion investment is set to be the first part of a much larger rail route linking the Chinese-run Greek port of Piraeus with Europe's heartland.

The Belgrade-Budapest railway has encountered EU delays and contractual problems. Work on the Serbian portion of the line should have begun in November, 2017. But progress on the Hungarian part, which started in 2015, has stalled. This largely comes down to European Union rules. Serbia is only a prospective member of the EU and only has to abide by a looser set of rules.

******China's Relationship With Hungary Is Being Tested As The EU And Russia Apply Pressure**, David Hutt, September 5, 2017

Latvia

Located between Lithuania and Estonia, Latvia provides a strategic location for business operations targeting developed economies of the EU as well as the emerging markets to its east. Latvia is also a natural gateway between the EU and Russia, and the other former Soviet states.

*"Latvia is the transport and logistics hub of the region, with three major, ice-free international ports –namely Riga, Ventspils and Liepāja – closely linked to the country's well-developed rail, road and pipeline infrastructure. Meanwhile, Riga International Airport is the largest airport, serving about two-thirds of all flights in the region, whereas Ventspils is the busiest port."

*******"In May 2018, several officials from Beijing showed particular interest in the Port of Riga. It was an opportunity for the Freeport of Riga Authority to present the Port of Riga as an effective transit hub for the transportation of Chinese container cargoes and as a good place for Chinese investment. The representatives of the city of Beijing were informed of the potential investment and cooperation opportunities in the Port of Riga.

*******Riga Port has the potential to become a significant transit hub for the New Silk Road**, Embassy of the Republic of Latvia, June 4, 2018

China's One Belt, One Road Initiative And Europe Is Destination For Links From Asia- European Region 2- **Lithuania, Maldives, Moldova, Poland, Russia, Slovakia, and Ukraine**

Below are summaries of the OBOR initiatives in the countries covered in European Region 2.

Lithuania

*"Lithuania is bound by Latvia to the north and Poland to the south. Lithuania is the largest country among the Baltic States in terms of population, territory and economy. It is located at the intersection of three very large markets of almost 800 million consumers in total. Lithuania provides access to the Western markets of the EU and Scandinavia, and the Eastern markets of Russia and the other former Soviet states."

Tensions between Russia and Lithuania have been increasing since the Ukrainian Crisis began in 2013. However, economic co-operation between China and Lithuania has been deepening. There is the 16+1 formula promoting regional co-operation between Central and Eastern Europe and China, plus the expressed interest of Chinese participation in the Rail-Baltic project. This project could enhance regional cooperation, and bring Chinese-Lithuanian relations to a higher level. The EU-backed railway will connect Lithuania with the other Baltic States, Finland and Poland.

Lithuania is improving its maritime access as a way of boosting its economy. The port of Klaipeda, which is a company owned by Lithuania, brings 6% of GDP. The OBOR Initiative is developing four modes of improvement.

"The port is well located, and can serve Scandinavia, Eastern Europe and Great Britain, using the very dense network of container lines connections. Currently Klaipeda serves 42 million tons of goods annually. This fact places it on the third place among the ports of this part of the Baltic Sea, behind the large Russian ports of Primorsk and Ust-Luga. The average annual increase in port operation efficiency is 6.4%".

**The construction of infrastructure for LNG handling is in progress. Creating a transshipment center for railway transport in both directions for goods transported between China and Europe is also being considered, which will allow loading of goods directed to the Chinese market.

Klaipeda is just starting cooperation under the OBOR Initiative. The contractor of the high quality terminals, which are currently being built, is a single company, named Company Investment Limited.

**Lithuania's investments within the framework of 'One Belt One Route' projects, Coordinating Secretariat for Maritime Issues, "16 + 1", October 26, 2017

Moldova

*Moldova is located in Southeastern Europe and is north of the Balkan Peninsula. Moldova is landlocked Moldova is located between Romania and Ukraine. "Its favorable location and good transportation infrastructure provides easy access to the EU and the former Soviet countries. The longest Pan-European Corridor IX (connecting Helsinki in Finland and Alexandroupoli in Greece) crosses Moldova from north to south, while the Corridor VII (connecting Passau-Germany with the Black Sea) passes through the Giurgiulesti Port on the Danube River."

Historically, Moldova's largest industries have been manufacturing, agriculture and food processing, textiles, apparel and footwear. However, Information, Communication Technology (ICT), medicine, automotive and renewable energy are emerging growth sectors, with many foreign investors entering the market.

Moldova is a member of the Central European Free Trade Agreement (CEFTA), which includes Albania, Bosnia and Herzegovina, Kosovo, Macedonia, Montenegro and Serbia. Also, in June 2014, Moldova and the EU signed an Association Agreement (AA). The AA introduces a preferential trade regime. the Deep and Comprehensive Free Trade Area (DCFTA), which sets up a free-trade area between Moldova and the EU.

****If China can reach an OBOR deal with Moldova, it could set an example in the region. China has invested heavily in the country since the late 2000s, including agreeing a $1 billion loan in 2009. The former Soviet Union's second-smallest state, by area, after Armenia, is anxious about getting foreign funds. In 2016, it had a gross domestic product of $6.75

billion and a GDP per capita of $1,900, according to World Bank figures. The corresponding numbers for China were $11.2 trillion and $8,123.

Moldova exported $14.5 million worth of goods – mostly wine and furniture – to China in 2016, while the value of its imports from the world's second-largest economy, including electrical machinery, plastics, rubber and chemical products, totaled $394 million. This is another example of the very large trade deficits that countries such as Moldova run with China.

In addition to free-trade negotiations, representatives from China National Nuclear Power Company, and their Moldovan counterparts have held talks to boost cooperation in the energy sector.

****Can a China-Moldova free-trade deal give Beijing a foothold in Eastern Europe?, South China Morning Post, Liu Zhen, December 29, 2017

Poland

*Poland is a member of the European Union (EU), and its trade relations with the Chinese mainland are affected by EU's common external trade policy and measures. Under a new structure, tariff preferences are removed for imports into the EU from countries where per-capita income has exceeded $4,000 for four years in a row. As a result, the number of countries that enjoy preferential access to EU markets was reduced from 176 to fewer than 80 markets.

"While the Chinese mainland remains a beneficiary, many of its exports such as toys, electrical equipment, footwear, textiles, wooden articles, and watches and clocks have already been "graduated" from the preferential treatment. A number of Chinese mainland-origin products are subject to EU's anti-dumping duties, including bicycles, bicycle parts, ceramic tiles, ceramic tableware and kitchenware, fasteners, ironing boards and solar glass."

The author argues that at the moment cooperation with China neither poses a serious political threat per se, nor represents a source of sustainable economic growth in the region.

*****The underlying problems of Sino-Polish cooperation remain the same. In other words:

- The trade deficit has been growing steadily; while,
- The most needed greenfield investments have been minimal;
- The importance of China for the region is still marginal in comparison to Western Europe;
- Cooperation should be continued but it should focus more on areas that would actually be profitable for the CEE economies in the longer perspective, bearing in mind each economies' comparative advantage:
  o e.g. food processing or the aviation industry in Poland.
- When it comes to long-term risks, the biggest threat might come from potential Chinese acquisitions of European know-how in sensitive sectors, such as high-tech or telecommunications;
  o This way, Central and Eastern European (CEE) countries should cooperate closer with the rest of EU in order to pressure Beijing to open up its domestic market, while closely monitoring Chinese investments in Europe in sensitive sectors.

*****China, Poland, and the Belt and Road Initiative - the Future of Chinese Engagement in Central and Eastern Europe, Geopolitica, Alicja Bachulska, December 12, 2017

Russia & Ukraine

New Eurasia Land Bridge Economic Corridor

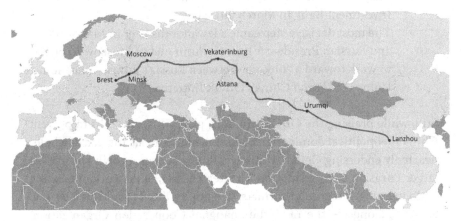

Image: New Eurasia Land Bridge Economic Corridor
Image Source: Sebastien Goulard, Cooperans

*"To stimulate investment with an aim to diversify its economy, the Russian government is providing a wide array of incentives for investors developing new product, technology in the energy efficiency, nuclear engineering, space technology, medicine and IT industries. Other key sectors for development include pharmaceutical and medical, real estate, innovations and technology, infrastructure, aluminum, iron and steel, lead, platinum-group metals, precious metals, nickel, copper, zinc, coal, telecommunications, transportation, agriculture and food and gas."

The Ukraine crisis made Russia embrace the OBOR Initiative by:

- Beginning confrontation with the West and Russia's deteriorating economy due to U.S.-led sanctions and falling oil prices left Moscow little choice.
- Without Ukraine, the second-largest post-Soviet economy and a market of about 44 million people, Moscow's hopes to create an integrated bloc that would be on par with the European Union and other centers of global economic power were essentially dashed.

- Lacking a market of sufficient size to create its own viable geo-economic area, Russia was left with the only option of moving into another nation's economic orbit.
- Russia joined the China-controlled Asian Infrastructure Investment Bank in March 2015; but
- The most decisive step came a few months later in May, when Xi and Russian President Vladimir Putin met in Moscow to pledge to work toward a "link-up" between Russia's Eurasian Economic Union (EEU) and China's OBOR Initiative.

Still, while praising the OBOR Initiative plan, Moscow seeks to prevent China's geopolitical domination of continental Eurasia. Instead of wholeheartedly endorsing China's Initiative, Russia pushes its own vision of "a larger Eurasian partnership" or "Greater Eurasia," a network of existing and emerging integration formats." Beijing's OBOR would be just one element, alongside the EEU, the Shanghai Cooperation Organization, the Association of Southeast Asian Nations and potentially even the EU.

Putin's Silk Road gamble, The Washington Post, By Artyom Lukin. February 8, 2018

Slovakia

*Slovakia is uniquely situated in the heart of the Europe, between East and West, and between Poland, Hungary, Austria, the Czech Republic and Ukraine. The country has an inland hub. "It connects Europe with China over three transit corridors, the Trans-Siberian transit (Slovakia-Manchuria), the Kazakh transit (Slovakia-Alashankou) and the Trans-Caspian transit (Slovakia-Alashankou via Azerbaijan and Georgia). This location has enabled Chinese manufacturers to ship parts and components directly by rail in about 12 days to factories in Slovakia for processing near their final European market."

*"With its strong industrial base, Slovakia's economy has become one of the fastest-growing in the EU. It has had an average annual GDP growth of 1.9% since its adoption of the euro in 2009. It is the best-performing EU member in the 16+1 format (co-operation between 16 CEE countries and China)".

Slovakia has had an economic concentration on export-led development. It has aggressively developed export-oriented manufacturing, especially in the automotive and electronics industries. It has also become strong shared services centers (SSCs) and business process outsourcing centers (BPOs).

******To further develop bilateral relations, China needs to take into account the public discourse of target countries. The importance of understanding other cultures and domestic settings is not a new concept in Chinese political philosophy. Recently, Zhao Lei, a professor at the Chinese Central Party School, recognized the need to use other countries' domestic media outlets to spread a positive image of China.

******"To generate soft power, China will likely deploy narratives tailored to the specific perceptions of target audiences. Beijing already relies on controversial means to control media narratives, namely buying foreign media outlets. In 2015, it came to light that China Radio International (a state-owned radio broadcaster) was covertly backing at least 33 foreign radio stations that broadcasted positive news of China".

********Do the Central European media show caution towards China?**, Matej Šimalčík, East Asia Forum, Institute of Asian Studies, February 14, 2018

Ukraine

*"Ukraine sits at the crossroads of Eastern Europe and Russia. Aside from a heavy reliance on commodities such as coal and steel and industries like transport equipment manufacturing, Ukraine's resources and economic strengths include rich agricultural land, a strong scientific establishment and significant mineral reserves."

WTO membership in 2008 has brought Ukraine significant benefits, including access to steel and textiles to the EU. Recently, the EU has surpassed Russia to become Ukraine's most important trading partner.

*******"Despite the 2014 Ukrainian revolution and the subsequent Russian annexation of Crimea, the Association Agreement with the EU, including a Deep and Comprehensive Free Trade Area, aims to deepen political and economic relations between the EU and Ukraine, and to pave the path to gradually integrate the country with the EU's Internal Market."

*******As Trump Is Distracted, The Chinese Are Moving In On Ukraine. Newsweek, By Nolan Peterson, December 12, 2017

Middle East

China's One Belt, One Road Initiative And The Middle East Is A Crossroads, Part 1, Afghanistan, Armenia, Bahrain, Egypt, Georgia, Iraq, Israel, Jordan, Kuwait, Lebanon, Oman, Palestine, Qater, Saudi Arabia, Syria, United Arab Emirates, and Yemen

Below are summaries of the OBOR initiatives in the countries covered in the Middle East Part 1.

Afghanistan

*In May 2016, Afghanistan signed a Memorandum of Understanding (MOU) with China on the One Belt, One Road (OBOR) Initiative. The aim is to foster cooperation that includes policy coordination, infrastructure development, trade and investments. Projects implemented include a cargo railway connecting China to Northern Afghanistan and a direct flight between Kabul and Urumqi. China has committed to invest $100 million in OBOR projects in Afghanistan.

In August, 2017, the U.S. implemented a new Afghanistan policy, which adds 4,000 U.S. troops to facilitate the efforts, directed at terrorists and criminal networks while expanding the use of unmanned aircraft and special operations teams.

China is Afghanistan's third largest trading partner, with bilateral trade estimated to have been over $1 billion in 2015. Afghanistan is in the middle of some very large OBOR investments being made by China. There is a China-Pakistan Economic Corridor in which China is investing $46 billion. China is making a very large commitment to Pakistan. With militants using Pakistan as a sanctuary to attack Afghanistan, some uncertainty is introduced into how the investments China is making in Afghanistan will tie into the larger OBOR plans for the area. China and the U.S. should be partners in Afghanistan, as both need a peaceful country and a stable government.

*China's Belt and Road Meets Trump's Afghanistan Plan

Could China play the good cop while the U.S. plays the bad cop?

The Diplomat, By Yu Fu, December 21, 2017

Armenia

**Armenia borders Iran and Turkey in the Middle East, and is at the cross-roads between Asia and Europe. It has mountainous terrain and is rich in minerals that include aluminum, iron, gold and silver. As a way station on the original Silk Road, Armenia has planned a new rail link to Iran and a new North-South highway which will allow goods to be transferred from Armenia's southern border to Georgia and beyond to Black Sea ports that include Batumi and Poti in Georgia.

Armenia is a small country with a GDP of about $10.6 billion. It has not been formally invited to join the OBOR Initiative. "There is no formal invitation to the country," says Hrant Abajyan, Armenia's trade representative to China in Beijing.

Armenia states that it is convinced that the Initiative will be important in developing relations between participants, and that "it can and must be an *integral and indivisible part of this initiative."

**Making sense of Belt and Road – The Belt and Road country: Armenia

EUROMONEY, By: Chris Wright, September 26, 2017

Bahrain

***Bahrain is an island country in the Persian Gulf. It is connected to Saudi Arabia by the 15-mile-long King Fahd Causeway. It is the smallest country among the six-member *Gulf Co-operation Council (GCC)*. More than 50% of the people in Bahraini are expatriates, including Indians, Pakistanis, Bangladeshis and Filipinos. Bahrain has signed free trade agreements with the US, Singapore and the European Free Trade Association.

Bahrain has a double taxation agreement with China. Many Chinese enterprises have set up businesses in Bahrain. They include the Bank of China, the China Harbour Engineering Company and Huawei. Huawei, which may be banned in the U.S. because of possible spying by the Chinese government, opened its first Middle East IT tech center in 2012. Mainland China company Chinamex partnered with Bahrain's Diyar Al Muharraq and built Dragon City, a retail and wholesale mall development modeled on the UAE's successful Dragon Mart. Dragon City began operations in December 2015.

The six member-countries of the GCC (Bahrain, Kuwait, Oman, Qatar, Saudi Arabia and the UAE) are considered an important trade region and was the EU's fourth-largest export market in 2016.

**"According to Bahrain's Minister for Transportation and Telecommunications Kamal bin Ahmed Mohammed, the ambitious multi-trillion-dollar Belt and Road Initiative (BRI) by China could become a great opportunity for the Gulf nations.

The Gulf region, which is a central location of the BRI, is a prime market for China and vice versa."

*****China's 'One Belt, One Road' is a 'win-win' for GCC – Bahrain Minister**, GulfInsider, May 13, 2018

Egypt

Egypt's GDP growth rate was 4.3% in 2016, and reached 5.4% in the March quarter of 2018. The Suez Canal is a vital shipping lane that connects the Mediterranean Sea with the Red Sea. To double the shipping capacity of the Canal, the Egyptian government started the Suez Canal Corridor Area Project (SCCAP) in August 2014. The project will include industrial and technology parks in addition to the new Canal sector. Revenue is projected to increase to $15 billion in 2023 from $5.3 billion in 2015. with the SCCAP expected to spur foreign investment and create jobs.

****Egypt should be able to serve as the hub for OBOR Initiative into the Middle East and Africa. With Egypt viewed by China as one of the five most attractive countries for mergers and acquisitions potential, their relationship has been elevated to a "strategic partnership". There is now a growing new commercial relationship between them.

New elements in attracting Chinese capital are new standards that define and require that developments be green. The definition of green is being developed by China to suit its own needs.

******Greening the belt and road: opportunities for Egypt**, Middle East Institute, By Deborah Lehr and Yasser Elnaggar January 23, 2018

Georgia

*****Georgia is well situated to be an important participant in the OBOR Initiative. It is located at the eastern part of the Black Sea. Russia is north and northeast and to the south are Armenia and Turkey. Georgia is a logistics and transshipment corridor to the Caucasus mountains and Central Asia. 60% of all types of its overland international freight are in transit. Infrastructure upgrades are underway at the major seaports of Batumi and Poti. There are several other planned projects, as well as the construction of a deep-sea port at Anaklia. This port will accommodate larger vessels. All of these projects should strengthen the country's logistical importance.

Former Georgian President had a disastrous plan to build skyscrapers that would house 500,000 residents. The city of the future is today an array of tetrapods that form a breakwater for the Anaklia Black Sea Deep Water Port, which Georgia hopes will be a key link on China's OBOR initiative.

This is the foundation for the Anaklia Black Sea Deep Water Port, Georgia's bid to become a key link in China's sprawling Belt and Road Initiative. The bid to construct the $2.5 billion port was expect to go to Chinese investors, but instead went to a group of Americans and

Georgians. A key factor was that of the jobs going to Chinese workers, an estimated 6,400 jobs will go to Georgians, easing the 12.5% unemployment rate. In Pakistan, the Chinese port development there resulted in the jobs going to the Chinese.

The South Caucasus offers the West an attractive alternative to other OBOR trade routes. Georgia is more geopolitically palatable than Iran. Tbilisi, where the port is located ranks favorably in global indices measuring corruption and ease of doing business. Also, Georgia signed a Deep and Comprehensive Free Trade Agreement with the EU that became effective in 2016 allowing Georgia to serve as a logistics hub with the EU. China followed suit with a bilateral free trade agreement that came into effect on January 1, 2018.

Georgia became directly involved in OBOR 2016 when it joined the Asian Infrastructure Investment Bank (AIIB), a $100 billion fund designed to finance Belt and Road projects. Georgia has signed an agreement under which the bank will provide $114 million to build the Batumi Bypass Road, a new highway to connect Georgia's outlying areas through a series of mountain tunnels.

Georgia seems to have avoided the pitfall of having China build and manage its most important port project and instead can manage its three ports as a integrated program, with the larger vessels going to the Anaklia port.

*****With Port Project, Georgia Seeks Place on China's Belt and Road. Georgian infrastructure remains underdeveloped, which could leave Anaklia disconnected, Eurasianet, Bradley Jardine, February 21, 2018

China's One Belt, One Road Initiative And The Middle East Is A Crossroads, Part 2, Iran, Iraq, Israel, Jordan, Kuwait And Lebanon

Below are summaries of the OBOR initiatives in the countries covered in the Middle East Part 2.

Iraq

*Iraq has the world's fourth largest proven oil reserves, which puts it in a favorable position because of China's thirst for oil. Iraq's oil output has increased following its gaining strength follow the U.S.-led invasion in 2003. Iraq mainly exports crude oil to India, China, the U.S. and South Korea, and imports food, medicines and manufactured items from Turkey, China, Syria and the U.S.

Iraq has established four free zones to promote trade through advantageous customs incentives. Chinese companies are among the largest foreign investors in Iraq's oil sector, with PetroChina, Sinopec and China National Offshore Oil Company (CNOOC) involved in development of many of the country's oil projects.

Iraq borders on the Persian Gulf. At present, Iraq is not listed as a participant of the OBOR Initiative. However, the country is one of the principal suppliers of oil to China. Bilateral trade between the two countries has been increasing steadily. Given that Iraq's southern (Saudi Arabia), northern (Turkey) and eastern (Iran) neighbors are all slated to be participants of the OBOR Initiative, it is unclear to what extent Iraq might benefit from the Initiative at the expense of its neighbors.

Israel

*Israel grew GNP by 4% in 2016 and by 3.3% in 2017. Israel is considered to be one of the most advanced countries in the Middle East and is a high-tech powerhouse. Despite the fact that Israel is a democracy, China might find it advantageous to develop businesses that use their technology and geographic location.

***Many international high-tech companies have opened up branches as well as research and development centers in Israel. They include Microsoft, IBM, Cisco and Motorola. There have been a number of acquisitions of Israeli technological companies by U,S, firms such as Google, IBM and Facebook. Major transactions span various high-tech sectors, including software, mobile application and digital advertising. Such acquisitions could be of interest to Chinese companies.

"Israel is actively promoting cooperation with China and other parties under the Belt and Road Initiative, welcoming Chinese enterprises to participate in various infrastructure projects in Israel. Israel is attempting to add sea ports and new railroad networks. China Harbour is building a new port next to Ashdod's existing one, and the Shanghai International Port Group (SIPG) has won a 25-year license to operate another deep-sea private port planned in Haifa. It is reported that Israel would like China to participate in the building of a railroad connection between the ports in Eilat and Ashdod, connecting the Red Sea to the Mediterranean Sea."

***China and Israel to enhance trade cooperation through the "One Belt, One Road" Initiative,** ChinaGoAbroad, May 25, 2018

Jordan

*Jordan's economy is about 67% services, 30% industry and 3% agriculture. The major export markets are 50% Arab countries. Exports to the U.S. are almost 20% of the total, and Jordan's currency is pegged to the U.S. dollar.

"Jordan has signed free trade agreements (FTAs) with the US, Canada, Turkey, MERCOSUR (which includes Argentina, Brazil, Paraguay and Uruguay), Egypt, Morocco, Tunisia (the Agadir Agreement), the *EFTA* states (which includes: Switzerland, Norway, Iceland and Liechtenstein), and Singapore. Jordan is a member of the Pan Arab Free-Trade Area (PAFTA) Treaty, with members including: Egypt, United Arab Emirates (UAE), Bahrain, Jordon, Tunisia, Saudi Arabia, Sudan, Syria, Iraq, Oman, Palestine, Qatar, Kuwait, Lebanon, Libya, Morocco, and Yemen."

****Chinese Ambassador to Jordan Pan Weifang spoke during a press conference in Amman. "AMMAN — Jordan and China are holding talks regarding the signing of a memorandum of understanding (MOU) on cooperation, as part of China's One Belt, One Road initiative, according to the Chinese ambassador. A multibillion land and maritime project, the One Belt One Road project aims to connect China to the rest of the world, including Jordan."

"Following the signing of the MOU, we will witness increased cooperation and projects between the two sides in various areas," Chinese ambassador to Jordan, Pan Weifang, said at a press conference in November, 2017."

****China's One Belt, One Road initiative to benefit Jordan — ambassador, The Jordan Times, By Mohammad Ghazal, November13, 2017

Kuwait

*Kuwait participates in the *China-GCC Free Trade Agreement* negotiations. The oil sector plays a dominant role in the Kuwaiti economy, with the country estimated to own roughly 6% of the world's oil reserves. Oil exports account for over 90% of Kuwaiti government revenues and 50% of nominal GDP. Kuwait's major export markets include India, Saudi Arabia, China, Iraq and the UAE."

*****Kuwait's Silk City and the five-island developments are a key project in the One Belt One Road initiative. Kuwait is expecting to spend over $100 billion to build one of the world's longest causeways to their northern area. "The plan is to reinvigorate the ancient Silk Road trade route by establishing a major free trade zone linking the Gulf to central Asia and Europe. The 36-kilometre (22-mile) bridge, three-quarters of it over water, will cut the driving time between Kuwait City and Subbiya to 20-25 minutes from 90 minutes now. It is already nearly three-quarters completed. A $3 billion 5,000-megawatt power plant has already been built in Subbiya."

*****Kuwait's Silk City project expected to top $100B, Daily Sabah, March 8, 2017

*****"Mr. Jiang Zengwei said Kuwait and China have signed several cooperation agreements, which have further laid the foundations for promoting mutually beneficial growth. "China is today one of the Kuwait's most important trading partners and an important source of crude oil from Kuwait. Bilateral trade was $12 billion in 2017, recording a year-on-year growth of 28%."

*****Kuwait's Silk City is key project in China's One Belt One Road initiative, AME info, March 22, 2018

Lebanon

*Lebanon is at the eastern end of the Mediterranean Sea. Syria is to the north, and Israel is to the south.

Ravaged by civil wars over the years 1975-1990, Lebanon has seen its debt balloon to 150% of GDP as it went through reconstruction. The government has been divided, but has seen the influence of Hezbollah increase.

"Lebanon has expressed a keen interest in China's Belt and Road Initiative, seeing itself as a gateway to the Arab world. Al-Fayhaa Union of Municipalities, a union of three municipalities in Lebanon, signed an agreement with the Silk Road Chamber of International Commerce (SRCIC) in November 2017 for an active role in the OBOR."

******The Union of Tripoli's municipalities was hailed for joining the SRCICI, pointing to the "special importance of Tripoli and its huge potentials not only for Lebanon but for the whole region which enables it to enhance trade with China."

During the signing it was stated "we will not spare any effort in boosting Tripoli's standing and its openness on Chinese markets and such an alliance will prepare it to become a special hub for cooperation with China within the Belt and Road initiative."

Important to success will be "the strategic location of Tripoli and its seaport on the Mediterranean and its human resources and infrastructure including the airport and railroads and logistic services it provides."

********Lebanon's Tripoli keen for active role in Belt and Road initiative**, Xinhua, November 11, 2017

China's One Belt, One Road Initiative And The Middle East Is A Crossroads, Part 3, Oman, Pakistan Palestine, Qatar, Saudi Arabia And Syria

Below are summaries of the OBOR initiatives in the countries covered in the Middle East Part 3.

Oman

*Oman is located "in the Gulf of Oman, the Arabian Sea and the Strait of Hormuz, a major transit point for crude oil and a trade route connecting the Middle East, India, Africa and Europe. Oman ranks the fourth out of the six members in the Gulf Co-operation Council (GCC) by population, after Saudi Arabia, the UAE and Kuwait." The deep-sea SOHAR Port is "located at the centre of global trade routes between Europe and Asia, making it an ideal business location."

*The Belt and Road Initiative: Country Profiles, Hong Kong Trade Development Council, May 17, 2018

"New Chinese investments are working to transform a small fishing village in Oman into the country's new industrial center, according to a new report by Reuters. The city receiving all of the industrial attention is located 345 miles south of Muscat. The project promises an overall surge in Chinese investment in the country if it shows any indications of a success."

**Oman is central to China's OBOR Initiative, with oil being a prime driver, at least for the next few years. However, longer term, China could ban fossil fuel cars in China, with them being replaced by electric vehicles. This could happen by about 2030.

**Oman To Become A Key Part Of China's Silk Road, Oilprice.com, By Zainab Calcuttawala, September 7, 2017

Palestine

* "Palestine is located on the eastern coast of the Mediterranean Sea. It comprises two non contiguous areas – the Gaza Strip and the West Bank. Gaza, the smaller of the two, is bordered by Egypt and Israel, while the West Bank is surrounded by Jordan and Israel."

The overall unemployment rate in Gaza was 44% while that in West Bank was lower at 18% in 2017."

Palestinian president Mahmoud Abbas visited China in July 2017. Four agreements were signed including promoting tourist destinations and economic cooperation. Also, "China will support the building of Palestine's Tarqomia Industrial Zone, west of Israeli city Hebron."

****China's peace initiative for the Israeli-Palestinian conflict was announced on July 31, 2017. Few new ideas were included in the plan, and this was not the first time China has proposed a plan, with the last one being in 2013. This proposal is even more vague. It omits Palestinian demands to establish an independent Palestinian state that enjoys full sovereignty, as well acknowledging Israel's right to exist while addressing its legitimate security concerns.

"The 2017 proposal is the first to be made in the context of the One Belt, One Road (OBOR) vision. This vision has unprecedentedly advanced China's interest in the Middle East, and its stake in regional stability has grown significantly. Concomitantly, OBOR provides China with unprecedented means to influence regional processes in ways that it finds acceptable under its "business first" approach to the Middle East. As for similarities, both proposals are finely balanced in their requirements from the involved parties."

****China Has a New Middle East Peace Plan, What's new in Beijing's latest proposal and what does it tell us about China's views and intentions concerning the region?, The Diplomat, By Yoram Evron, August 14, 2017

Qatar

*Qatar is one of the wealthiest countries in the world in terms of GDP per capita. Qatar's economy is highly dependent on oil and gas, which accounts for over 50% of GDP, 85% of export earnings, and 70% of government revenues. The government has been making efforts to diversify the economy into a sustainable long-term income model. This includes investments in the petrochemical sector, promotion of business tourism, and financial sector improvements.

*"Qatar's real GDP growth expanded by 2.5% YOY in Q1 2017 on the strength of its non-oil sector. The country is projected to expand by 3.4% in 2017 due to massive infrastructure investment and further economic diversification."

Oil and gas rich Qatar is viewed as an important staging point for the OBOR Initiative. China is the world's leading buyer of oil and gas.

*****"Professor Wang Yiwei of the People's University in China believes that even though Chinese investments will not be directly affected by the current conflict, the growing instability in the region could still have a negative impact on China's economic cooperation with the Gulf States."

Bahrain, Saudi Arabia, Egypt and the United Arab Emirates have severed diplomatic ties with Qatar. They accused Qatar of supporting terrorist groups and of interfering in other states' internal affairs. Libya also severed ties, as did Yemen, the Maldives and Mauritania.

"Despite some temporary problems, China has nothing to worry [about the present row]," Bian Yongzu, an expert at Chungyang Financial Research Center said."

***** **How Qatar Row Could Impact China's One Belt, One Road Project**

Sputnik International, Aleksey Nikolskyi, August 6, 2017

Saudi Arabia

*"Saudi Arabia is part of the Greater Arab Free Trade Area Agreement (GAFTA). Under the GAFTA, the country enjoys free trade with Algeria, Bahrain, Egypt, Iraq, Kuwait, Lebanon, Libya, Morocco, Oman, Palestine, Qatar, Sudan, Syria, Tunisia, the UAE and Yemen. As member of the GCC, Saudi Arabia also has free trade agreements (FTAs) with Singapore, New Zealand and the European Free Trade Association (EFTA) comprising Switzerland, Norway, Iceland, and the Principality of Liechtenstein."

There are negotiations underway on the establishment of FTAs with the EU, Japan, China, India, Pakistan, Turkey, Australia, Korea and the Group of Mercosur (Brazil, Argentina, Uruguay Paraguay, and Venezuela).

******China's "One Belt and One Road" initiative is expected to make "creative" contributions to helping Saudi Arabia realize its "Saudi Vision 2030" plan, Saudi Ambassador to China Turki Bin Mohamed Al-Mady said. To diversify its heavily oil-dependent economy, Saudi Arabia announced a "Saudi Vision 2030" growth strategy in 2016, which includes privatizing some state-owned companies."

Chinese President Xi Jinping visited Saudi Arabia in January 2016. Both countries agreed to form a comprehensive strategic partnership. The areas of cooperation could include technology, security and defense, which would be addressed in separate agreements.

"Saudi Arabia was one of the first countries to respond positively to the [Belt and Road] initiative," he said. "In terms of strategic location, Saudi Arabia serves as the central hub connecting three continents - Asia, Africa and Europe, and has been an important part of the initiative."

Al-Mady said that he hopes Saudi Arabia can play a more central and positive role in promoting the initiative to strengthen the in-depth integration of the initiative and the "Saudi Vision 2030."

******Belt, Road initiative will help Saudi Arabia realize 2030 vision, ambassador says, ChinaGoAbroad, Xinhua, May 25, 2018

Syria

*"Syria is a Middle East country at the eastern end of the Mediterranean Sea, bordered by Iraq, Israel, Jordan, Lebanon and Turkey. Damascus is the capital, while Aleppo is the largest city. Syria has a young population, with more than 50% of its citizens aged below 25."

Sanctions were imposed on Syria by the U.S., the EU, the Arab League, Turkey and Canada. Since then Syria has traded heavily with Iraq. Most Chinese companies have discontinued their operations, but indicated in 2017 that they looked forward to reconstruction projects following the war in Syria. The China Petrochemical Corporation and China National Petroleum Corporation have previously invested in Syria's hydrocarbon sector.

*******"By working through what is still the internationally recognized government of Syria, Beijing will be able to claim that it has avoided taking sides in a civil war (now nearly over) but is now engaging with a sovereign state...While relying on Middle Eastern oil supplies, China has traditionally avoided diplomatic entanglements there, so this support for

Assad marks a shift in regional diplomacy that Chinese diplomats will undoubtedly try to conceal behind the language of non-intervention."

*******Is China coming into Syria for its "One Belt, One Road"?

Informed Comment, By Neil Thompson, January 1, 2018

China's One Belt, One Road Initiative And The Middle East Is A Crossroads, Part 4, Turkey, United Arab Emirates, And Yemen

Below are summaries of the OBOR initiatives in the countries covered in the Middle East Part 4.

United Arab Emirates

The United Arab Emirates (UAE) is heavily on the oil-related sectors. It is trying to diversify in several ways. It has an $81.7 billion plan to promote a knowledge-based economy, which will include investments in education, health, energy, transportation, water and the space industry. It is already diversified to the extent that slightly less than 70% of its GDP is non-oil related, with the objective being to take that to as high as 80% by 2021. The plan also includes tripling the labor force in the "knowledge economy" by 2021.

"China's investment in the UAE has been growing in recent years, with cumulative FDI rising from $764.3 million in 2010 to $4.6 billion in 2015." In May 2017, UAE Minister of State Sultan Ahmed Al-Jaber commented that the UAE strongly supports China's OBOR Initiative. "Foreseeing a 50% growth by 2040 in the energy demand in Belt and Road countries, he noted that both China and the UAE have made strategic co-investments in the energy sector. For example, China National Petroleum Corp. (CNPC) and China CEFC Energy Co., have recently taken a minority share in the UAE's onshore oil reserves."

On the regional level, The UAE is trading with Arab nations through the *Greater* Arab Free Trade Area Agreement (GAFTA). Under the GAFTA, the UAE has free trade with Algeria, Bahrain, Egypt, Iraq,

Kuwait, Lebanon, Libya, Morocco, Oman, Palestine, Qatar, Saudi Arabia, Sudan, Syria, Tunisia and Yemen.

****Chinese contractors have become increasingly active in local construction projects and Chinese visitors continue to increase according to consultants JLL. According to JLL, the UAE plays a crucial role in China's proposed OBOR Initiative.

Dubai is a key city in this strategy, and a gateway to stable markets, especially in Africa. Currently about 60 percent of Chinese exports to regional markets are channeled through the UAE. JLL pointed to a number of significant Chinese investments in the UAE – such as in Abu Dhabi Industrial Park and Dubai Food Park – as signs of growing Chinese economic involvement in the country.

******Chinese economic influence in the UAE growing, says JLL**

The UAE is a significant part of the country's $124 billion 'one belt, one road' initiative

Asian Business, By Bernd Debusmann Jr, February 7, 2018

*****Another indication of the involvement of China in the UAE is an MOU that has been signed with the Shanghai Stock Exchange with Dhabi Global Market (ADGM) to establish a Belt and Road Exchange," Richard Teng, chief executive of ADGM's Financial Services Regulatory Authority, told CNBC.

"The joint exchange is poised to support businesses and investors along the Belt and Road. This Beijing-backed scheme plans to link the world's second-largest economy to the west via a vast land and maritime infrastructure network across Eurasia."

******China and UAE move a step closer to opening a 'Belt and Road Exchange',** CNBC, Sam Meredith, April 24, 2018

Yemen

*"Yemen sits at the southwest tip of the Arabian Peninsula, between Oman to the east and Saudi Arabia to the north. It overlooks the Bab al-Mandab Strait where the Red Sea joins the Gulf of Aden. It has been locked in a complex civil war since 2015, with the rebel Houthi group fighting against the Yemen government backed by a Saudi-led coalition, the Islamic State and Al-Qaeda. The prolonged civil war has led to famines and humanitarian crises in the country."

The Houthi group, backed by Iran, is fighting against the Yemen government backed by a Saudi-led coalition, the Islamic State and Al-Qaeda.

Yemen is a small oil-producing country, not a part of OPEC. It is one of the world's poorest countries, and has a young population. "Yemen allows foreign oil companies to exploit its oil fields in light of their capital and technology resources. Prior to the civil war in 2015, the oil sector accounted for 65% of its fiscal revenue and one-quarter of its GDP. Yemen's oil exports had been suspended since early 2015, but were resumed in 2017. "International oil companies in Yemen, such as Austria's OMV are also looking to resume oil production in south Yemen in 2018."

*****'Yemen is facing an acute humanitarian crisis after nearly three years of civil war, with more than 10,000 deaths and three-quarters of the country's population in dire need of humanitarian assistance.' China has not been a leader in Yemen, but has supplied humanitarian role, largely driven by China's close relationship with Saudi Arabia.

"As Yemen's major trade partner, China has an outsized economic presence in the country and can play a significant economic role in Yemen's postwar reconstruction through its OBOR Initiative."

*****China and Yemen's Forgotten War, US Institute of Peace, By I-wei Jennifer Chang, January 16, 2018

CHAPTER 3

Trump Budget, Economic Assumptions, Budget Strategy, Tax Reductions, Immigration, Entitlement Programs, Household Debt, Debt: U.S. National Debt And Fed Portfolio Balances, Deficit, and Government Funding and the Debt Ceiling

Trump Budget

The Trump Budget is an outline of the discretionary spending priorities over the next four years. Not included are the personal and corporate tax reductions, which were passed in December 2017. In 2018, budget initiatives will require a 60-vote threshold compared to the 51 votes require in the Senate in 2017. This will likely require bills to be bipartisan in 2018 and beyond. One area where there might be bipartisan support is infrastructure spending. Support for the U.S. military already has bipartisan support.

Federal $300 billion Spending Deal Signed By Trump, Ending A Government Shutdown And Implementing A Two Year Budget Deal: Will The Deficit Balloon?

On February 8, 2017, a $300 billion budget deal became law. Shortly thereafter, Trump introduced his detailed fiscal 2019 budget forecast that did not include the details of the $300 billion budget deal. The 2019 budget forecast has been analyzed, and the differences of the two budgets have been highlighted. The main issue is that Trump will not be able to reduce non-defense spending to offset the increases in defense spending. Also, the tax cuts and inflation will need to grow corporate and individual taxes by over 6% per year over the next 10 years to meet the budget forecasts.

The details are that the deal would raise the spending caps by about $300 billion through 2019. The limit on military spending would be increased by $80 billion in the 2018 fiscal year and $85 billion in 2019. The limit on non-defense spending would increase by $63 billion in 2018 and by

$68 billion in fiscal 2019. The budget does have in it the personal tax reductions, the corporate tax reductions, including the reduction in the corporate rate to 21%.

Included in the budget are an increase in defense spending by $44 billion in 2018 and an identical $44 billion increase in fiscal 2019. The spending bill has defense spending at a total of $165 billion over the two years. Therefore, the budget understates the deficit because of the increase in defense spending by $77 billion in fiscal 2019.

The limit on non-defense spending adds $131 billion to spending in 2018 and 2019. The budget shows an increase of $42 billion for non-defense spending for the two years. Thus, the budget understates the deficit for non-defense spending by $89 billion by 2019. The total increase in the deficit for the second year, fiscal 2019, is $166 billion. The budget shows a deficit of $984 billion in 2019, but the $350 billion spending increase takes the deficit to $1,150 billion in 2019. If the budget deficit increases by $166 billion per year for 10 years, besides the $1.5 trillion the tax cuts added to the deficit, the $350 billion spending increase adds about $1.66 trillion to the 10-year deficit.

ArmchairTechInvestor Opinion

The U.S. budget deficit is out of control. The Democrats have forced Trump to increase non-defense spending by just about the amount of defense spending, jettisoning his plan to reduce government waste. The Trump budget shows a deficit of $445 billion in fiscal 2028. To get to that level, non-defense spending would need to decline by $200 billion per year, instead of the $89 billion per year increase in 2019. Thus the deficit could be $290 billion higher because of the inability to achieve lower non-defense spending, even if non-defense spending stays flat after 2019. The deficit was $665 billion in fiscal 2017. Higher non-defense spending could take the deficit to $755 billion in 2018, even if Trump is able to achieve his projected economic growth rate of 3% over the 10-year period to fiscal 2028.

Despite the tax reductions, Trump is forecasting that individual income tax receipts will increase from $1,660 billion in 2018 to $3.070 billion in 2028, a 6.34% compound growth rate. For this to occur, a 3.0% GDP growth rate would probably need to be accompanied by a 3.4% average inflation rate through 2028.

Corporate tax receipts are projected to go from $218 billion in fiscal 2018, after a $79 billion reduction from 2017, resulting from the corporate tax reductions, to $413 billion in 2028. This is a 6.6% compound increase over the 10 years from 2018. This again implies a very strong economy and over a 3% inflation rate.

The saving grace for Trump could be a 3% growth in the economy that pushes the inflation rate above 3%. Non-defense spending would need to stay flat after 2019, which does not seem likely. Those events are required to have the deficit grow from $665 billion in 2017 to about $735 billion in 2028, a 0.9% growth rate. Instead, It appears likely that the deficit will continue to balloon.

The Congress Passed A Budget That Was For Two Years Through Fiscal 2019. But, It Did Not Include The Details Of The Trump Budge That Was Subsequently Released.

President Trump outlined his tax plan on September 27, 2017. This provided an outline for what a House version of the bill might look like. The suggested corporate tax rate is set at 20%, but it turned out to be 21%. There are small business owners that use corporate entities that allow them to use pass through accounting, and report the results on their personal tax returns, instead of having to file corporate tax returns. This tax rate has been suggested to be 25%, but the final bill gave them a 20% tax reduction.

President Trump believes that the corporate and small business tax reductions will increase the economy's growth rate from about a low 2% of GDP under the 8 years of the Obama administration, to above 3%, and more in line with historical growth rates. This would increase jobs, but the jobs market was tight in early 2018. Job growth would add to corporate and personal income growth, and in turn, cause Federal income tax income receipts to grow. This would reduce the impact of the tax reductions, and perhaps even reduce the deficit.

It had been suggested that the personal income tax brackets be reduced from seven to three, with perhaps a fourth tax bracket included to assure that the highest income earners are perhaps held to no income tax reductions, as is being advocated by the Democrats. The hope was that this might draw in some Democrats to support the bill, especially in the Senate, where three defections among the Republicans, such as John McCain, Lisa Murkowski, Rand Paul and Susan Collins seemed possible.

ArmchairTechInvestor Opinion

The 2019 budget was completed in 2018. The Congress, and particularly the Senate, have been inept at getting through legislation passed by the House. However, there was an unexpected breakthrough that allowed the tax cuts to be passed. There are several hundred House passed bills that have not been addressed by the Senate, with Democratic obstructionism, led by Senator Schumer, being an important factor.

Budget Strategy

The basic strategy with regard to spending is to increase defense expenditures, increase infrastructure spending, build a border wall, and reduce spending for departments and other government entities, where possible.

Trump Budget Strategy: Target 10% or More Budget Reductions for Most Departments, and the EPA, While Increasing Defense and Border Security Expenditures.

ArmchairTechInvestor Opinion

The Trump Budget for 2018 was an outline of the discretionary spending priorities over the next four years. Not included were the personal and corporate tax reductions, infrastructure spending initiatives, and spending in excess of the $4.5 billion in the budget for a Southern border wall, all of which might increase the deficit. Those spending cuts for the various government agencies and departments will not materialize until a least fiscal 2020, but it is helpful to understand Trump's objectives from his original fiscal 2018 budget.

Government Spending: If Trump Can Stimulate the U.S. Growth Rate, Tax Increases Could Help Reduce the Deficit, Subject to the Impact of Tax Reductions.

- Spending on Social Security, unemployment, and labor was estimated to be about 36% of all outlays in 2017. This was greater than average when compared to budgets from other years. (Average proportion = 35%);
- Medicare and general health spending was estimated to be about 28% of all outlays in 2017. This is one of the highest proportions spent when compared to budgets from other years. (Average proportion = 14%);
- Spending on national defense was estimated to be about 15% of all outlays that year. This was less than average when compared to budgets from other years. (Average proportion = 22%);
- As for spending on net interest, the government estimated it would dedicate about 7% of all its outlays that year to paying down its accumulated debt. This is less than average when compared to budgets from other years. (Average proportion = 8%); and
- All other programs (agriculture, energy, commerce and housing credit, community and regional development, etc.) in 2017 were estimated to make up approximately 14% of national spending.

Total Spending was forecasted to be $4,089 billion in fiscal 2017. Social Security was expected to be 967 billion, or 23.7% of the spending budget, and a 4.7& increase from fiscal 2016. Medicare was estimated to be $602 million, or 14.7%, and a 2.2% increase from fiscal 2016, while Medicaid was $377 billion, or 9.2% of the budget, and a 2.7% increase from fiscal 2016. Other mandatory spending was $529 billion, or 14.3% of expenditures. With defense being $583 billion, or 15.8%, that left only $581 billion, or 15.8% of discretionary spending that could be reduced through budget cuts.

ArmchairTechInvestor Opinion

Hypothetically, a 10% reduction in discretionary spending could save $58 billion. Increasing the real growth of GDP to 3.0%, and increasing the inflation rate to 3% could generate over 6% growth of U.S. taxes, before the Trump tax cuts. Social Security increases could be covered, and Medicare and Medicaid could decline about 2-3% each as a percentage of U.S. government spending.

U.S. Immigration

Immigration-Visa Program

The Visa Program Is Vital To Improving The U.S. Job Market, And The EB-5 Program Is Important To The Real Estate Market.

Trump's ambition is to improve the immigration system to bring in immigrants that are beneficial to the U.S. This is a broad objective. Trump has cut the number of immigrants in half to 45,000 for the 2018 and implemented a temporary ban on 11 countries to be sure the U.S. has a system to properly vet them. The Visa system involves many more people, and one portion of it is the Visa EB-5 program. It allows 10,000 people per year to come in as investors that invest at least $500,000 in the U.S and create at least10 jobs.

Immigration-The Wall

The Trump administration is in the process of evaluating 8 prototype walls, and has $4.5 billion of spending in the 2017 budget for a Southern border wall. In the Dreamer negotiations, Trump is asking for $25 billion of funding for border security, but it was not included in the spending extension through fiscal 2018.

The border wall that President Trump has promised will take several years to build and will not be entirely a physical wall. Only 115 of the 2,000 miles in Texas are fenced. Getting land rights from the owners will be time consuming.

Trump Border Security: The Wall Is Unlikely To Be All-Physical. Many Technical and Procedural Issues Exist

The actual "wall" is expected to be a combination of a physical wall, border agent increases, technology, and aerial surveillance.

The budget was expected to increase by $4 billion, with 5,000 being added to the border patrol, and 10,000 Immigration and Customs Enforcement (ICE} agents being added, including a increase in those at the jails when violent criminals are released, including in sanctuary cities. The physical construction of the wall may face the 60-vole threshold in the U.S. Senate, but much of it might be done under currently in-place legislation.

As part of discussions with Mexico, the amount of aid to Mexico is being identified. The U.S. plans to provide $135 million of aid to Mexico in 2018. Trade, including Nafta, is an issue that is being addressed in bilateral negotiations with Mexico and Canada.

With regard to the physical wall, only 115 of the 2,000 miles in Texas are fenced. Most borderland is privately held, so this will be an issue. It may require that eminent domain be invoked. A wall along the Rio Grande requires a Mexican-U.S. commission approval. Flooding and satisfying Indian tribes are also issues. In 2006, Congress approved the Secure Fence Act that approved a 700-mile fence.

In 2016, 220,000 of the 400,000 immigrants detained were from Latin America, and were characterized as fleeing violence and poverty. The order returns undocumented immigrants to their country of origin. They would be processed in Mexico, before being returned home.

The Wall Street Journal has estimated that there are about 8 million un-documented immigrants in the workforce. The guidelines are broad, and could include those with misdemeanors, such as having an expired visa, or driving with an expired license, if a misdemeanor has been committed. Of 65,000 deportations in 2016, 90% were convicted criminals, and 2,000 were affiliated with gangs.

Will farmers, food companies, and builders face staff shortages? The Trump Administration has stated that it will deport criminal aliens, those who pose national security and public-safety threats, drug traffickers, and other "bad guys". The 750,000 so-called "dreamers", those undocumented immigrant children born in the U.S., will not be allowed to stay, unless the Congress can act to allow them to remain in the U.S.

Immigration-Travel Ban

Trump Orders 90-Day Temporary Travel Ban Order for 6 Countries.
The Trump Administration has issued what appear to be legal travel restrictions. The liberal 9th Circuit Court overturned the order. If was overturned with Neil Gorsuch on the Supreme Court. However, the Supreme Court is likely to further consider the order.

The 90-day temporary ban was ordered by the President. The Executive Branch has the authority, under the direction of the President, to conduct such activities. 300 refugees are being investigated for terrorism activities. 6 countries are covered, Libya, Syria, Iran, Sudan, Yemen and Somalia. Three are state sponsors of terrorism, and 3 have lost control of their countries, and 3 provide safe havens for terrorists. None provide reliable vetting, and extreme vetting is being required. Iraq has been removed from the list, and is coordinating with the U.S. Those with green cards, valid visas as of Jan 27, 2017, or are U.S. citizens, are exempted from the order.

Immigration Policy-What Is the Real Story in Sweden?

Sweden

President Trump was criticized by the liberal media for his remarks on the Swedish immigration problems, which he attributed to a Fox news report. The details emerged, and the liberal media was nowhere to be seen.

The Swedish Situation

275,000 asylum seekers entered Sweden from 2014-2016. This is more per capita than any other European country. In 2015, 80%, lacked passport or other identification, and the majority came from Muslim nations. According to Jimmie Akkeson, the chairman of the Sweden Democrats, the largest party opposing the socialists:

- Islam has become Sweden's second largest religion;

- 300 Swedish citizens, with immigrant backgrounds, have gone to fight for ISIS, and are starting to return, while being welcomed by the socialists;
- The first large scale Islamic inspired attack was in December, 2010 in Stockholm;
- Anti-Semitism has risen;
- The number of sex crimes has nearly doubled over the last two years;
- Women feel increasingly unsafe;
- Unemployment is large in the Muslim sections;
  o   The government is incurring large costs in subsidizing these communities; and,
- The opposition party is growing rapidly in popularity, and may beat the socialists in the next election.

Economic Growth

President Trump has the objective of achieving an economic growth rate of 3% or more of GDP. The objective is to stimulate growth by tax reductions, increased labor utilization, and productivity increases. It appears that the growth rate should remain in the area of 3% in 2018.

Economy-Inflation

The Fed Has Been Trying To Get The Inflation Rate Up To 2%. Do We Now Need To Worry About High Inflation?

Since the Trump Presidency started in January 2017, the Fed has been concerned about the inflation rate being below their targeted 2% rate. The economy has been strong, reaching a 2.5% growth rate in 2017. And, Trump is projecting that the economy, because of the tax cuts, deregulation, and job creation, will average 3.0% over the next ten years. Higher inflation seems to be in prospect.

The consumer price index (CPI) rose a seasonally adjusted 0.5% in January 2018. For the 12 months through January, the CPI grew at a 2.1% pace. A jump in gasoline prices contributed to the increase. When stripped of food and energy costs, the core CPI was up only 1.82%. The overall inflation environment does seem to be firming early in 2018 as U.S. unemployment is reaching record low levels of 4.1% and worldwide economic growth is pushing commodity prices higher.

Another fundamental inflation index, the producer price index (PPI), measures the inflation rate of goods sold to consumers, businesses and other entities such as governments. The core PPI rose 0.4% in January, 2018, and was up by 2.5% for the last 12 months ending in January. The PPI itself was up by 2.7% for the 12-month period. Energy price increases contributed to the PPI increase.

ArmchairTechInvestor Opinion

We expect the U.S. economy to grow by over 3% in a 2018, driven by corporate and personal tax reductions, and deregulation. We expect worker wage increases to be strong in 2018, driven by unemployment rates that could go below 4.0%. Commodity prices should continue to increase, driven by worldwide economic growth. Growth in the U.S. could be over 3% of GDP. All of those factors lead us to expect that the PPI for core prices should go over 3% in 2018, and the core CPI should reach at least a 2.5% rate for the year.

Household Income-U.S.

Household income has shown no growth over the last eighteen years. It has started to grow over the last two years, and reached a new record in the June quarter of 2017.

Household Debt-U.S.

Household Debt Remains Low: However, Fed Funds Rate Increases Could Create An Issue

Household debt, including rapidly growing student loans, has surpassed the peak in 2008, at the beginning of the housing induced recession, and reached $12.73 trillion. Delinquencies are low, and the backdrop bodes well for consumer spending participation in a growing economy.

Mortgage balances totaled $8.63 trillion, 67.8% of total loans, and grew at about a 6.8% annual rate in Q1 2017. There was only a 1.7% 90-day delinquency rate for mortgages. The housing market has been strong, but interest rates are over 4% in early 2018, compared to under 3.5% in the second half of 2016. With Fed rate increases scheduled that could take these rates over 4.5%, mortgage costs could begin to negatively impact the housing market.

Student loans have been widely discussed. They have grown rapidly, and in 2017 were at $1.34 trillion, 10.5% of total household debt, and grew by about 10.0% annually in Q1 2017. 11.0% of student loans are 90-days overdue or delinquent.

Auto loans were $1.167 billion at the end of Q1 2017, 9.2% of total debt. Auto loan defaults of 90-days or more were 3.8%. The automobile industry has not been doing well recently, with inventories increasing, and sales slowing.

Credit card balances were $764 billion, only about 6% of total loans, and declined by about 7.9% in the first quarter. They do not appear to an economic issue.

ArmchairTechInvestor Opinion

The economy was weak in the first quarter of 2017, with an increase of only 0.7%. However, lower inventories were a big factor in the shortfall, and 2.5% growth for the year 2017 occurred. Trump policies are targeting job growth in the U.S. and 3% economic growth. The unemployment rate will need to go under 4.0% in 2018, to continue job growth. However, there are many individuals and students that have stopped looking for work, and the real unemployment rate is at least 3% higher.

Jobs and Productivity

Reported job growth is nearing full employment. However, if those who have stopped looking for a job were included, the unemployment rate would be about 3% higher. Since 2004, productivity growth has been at the lowest level since World War II.

Unemployment Rate

The unemployment rate includes only those who have looked for work in the last four weeks. The employed includes anyone who has worked one hour or more in the last week. Excluded from the labor force are those who have given up looking for work. For those working, there is no recognition given to whether those working are working full time. Under Obamacare, employers are not required to provide insurance, if an employee works 29 hours or less. This has reduced full time employment.

Tax Reductions

Trump was successful in reducing the corporate tax rate to 21%. The number of personal tax brackets was left at 7, and personal tax reductions were enacted. The presumption is that tax cuts will stimulate the growth rate of the economy, and allow offshore corporate cash to be repatriated to the U.S.

The 2017 Trump Tax Bill Provided Large Corporate Tax Reductions of $125 Billion And About $50 Billion Of Middle Class Tax Reductions

The corporate tax reduction passed by the Congress in late 2017 will take effect on January 1, 2018, not in 2019 as proposed by the Senate.

After Trump first suggested a 15% corporate tax rate, and then 20%, a rate of 21% was included in the bill. Having a higher tax rate helped meet the requirement that the bill not raise the deficit at the end of the 10-year forecast period. It also made U.S. businesses competitive worldwide, with the worldwide corporate tax rate averaging 23%.

Important to the success of the tax bill is increasing economic growth to over 3%. However, offsetting the prospects are actions by the Fed during the Obama years that kept interest rates at 0%. Also, the economy was stimulated by injecting money into the economy by building up Fed portfolio holdings to a record $4.5 trillion. The Fed will be raising interest rates, perhaps as many as 4 times in 2018. By early 2018, it had also begun to slowly sell its portfolio holdings. Both of these initiatives are likely to slow economic growth, and make it more difficult to reach 3% or higher economic growth.

Capital investment was weak during the Obama administration. It is argued that the corporate tax reductions will put more capital in the hands of businesses, and will have a "supply side" effect that will stimulate capital investment.

Included in the final tax bill was the corporate alternative minimum tax. Included also was a provision that allows capital equipment purchases to be immediately deducted. The bill included interest rate caps based upon EBITDA for the first four years, and then it shifts to a less attractive cap based upon EBIT. Private equity companies are still allowed to treat "carried interest" as a capital gain.

The bill simplifies the tax code by eliminating some deductions, reducing others, such as the deduction of state income taxes, state property taxes and home mortgage interest deductions. Offsetting the reduction in deductions is an increase in the individual and family personal deductions, with the family deductions going from $12,000 to $24,000.

The bill included a provision that eliminated the Obama healthcare requirement that everyone must have healthcare insurance or pay a tax. This eliminates the taxes from people not wanting healthcare coverage, but required to pay a penalty. This may be offset by somewhat higher support for insurance companies providing Obamacare coverage.

Not included in the bill was the border adjustment tax that would have taxed imports, exempted exports, and raised about $1 trillion in taxes over 10 years.

ArmchairTechInvestor Opinion

Passing the Tax Reform Bill was a challenge. The Republicans succeeded despite having only a very narrow Senate majority. They tried to get some Democrats to support the tax bill, but all voted no. Another hurdle was the almost universally negative press. President Trump sold tax reform and worked with the Congress to pass it.

The Trump belief is that getting the growth of the economy to over 3% of GDP will generate enough tax revenues to offset the tax reductions. Whether this works will be an interesting observation in 2018 and 2019.

Corporate taxes in fiscal 2017 were $297 billion, or 8.96% of collections. The overall corporate tax rate should have been about 35%. The tax bill that passed in December 2017 lowered that rate to 21%. If corporate taxes grow 5% in 2018, without the tax reduction, with the tax reduction corporate tax receipts should be about $187 billion in 2018, a 37% or $125 billion decline.

The Democrats had argued that the tax bill was aimed at benefitting the wealthy. This is far from accurate. According to the nonpartisan Joint Committee on Taxation, in 2019, 48% of households will receive tax reductions of greater than $500. There are 100 million households in the U.S. If the taxes paid by all households averaged $500 per household, the tax bill would involve $50 billion of household tax reductions in 2019.

The House Tax Cut Plan Could Fulfill Trump's Objectives Of Reducing Taxes And Growing The U.S. Economy

The tax reduction bill from the House has mostly delivered on the Trump tax plan. The corporate tax rate was reduced to 21% instead of the 15% Trump wanted, which makes U.S. corporations slightly lower than the 23% average of foreign corporations. This tax rate was made permanent, which was an important achievement. How this would work out with respect repatriating U.S. corporate profits that are offshore will remain to be seen, but it should be helpful. Companies that are subchapter S corporations or limited liability companies, and the owners report income on their personal returns, will have a 20% tax reduction. Both of these tax reductions should help in generating jobs and perhaps grow the U.S. economy at over a 3% growth rate. Also aiding corporations is the immediate expensing of new equipment purchases by U.S. businesses, and allowing small businesses to write off loan interest payments.

On the personal tax side, 401(k) plans and IRA plans, which are very popular retirement savings plans, were retained in their present form. The family standard deduction was doubled from $12,000 to $24,000, as expected. In taxing the wealthy, the Republicans bowed to the Democrats and kept the highest tax rate at 39.6%, for individuals over $500,000 per year, and married couples making over $1 million per year. With this change to the original plan, there are three additional tax brackets of 12%, 25% and 35%. The 12% bracket for the lowest income earners was increased from 10% in Trump's recommended plan. The 12% tax bracket will apply up to $45,000 for individuals, and up to $90,000 for married couples. The 25% tax bracket will apply up to $200,000 for individuals and up to $260,000 for married couples. Above these levels, the 35% tax bracket applies up to $500,000 for individuals, and up to $1 million for married couples.

One of the most controversial changes will be to reduce mortgage tax reductions from a $1,000,000 mortgage, the current cap, to mortgages of $500,000. This will only apply to new mortgages.

Another controversial change was the elimination of tax deductibility for state income taxes. In 2016 the highest tax states were:

- California 13.3%;
- Oregon 9.9%;
- Minnesota 9.85%;
- Iowa 8.98%;
- New Jersey 8.97%;
- Vermont 8.95%;
- District of Columbia 8.95%; and
- New York 8.82%

Also included was a limit of $10,000 being put on state and local property taxes. The alternative tax credit was repealed, but a new family tax credit was created.

ArmchairTechInvestor Opinion

The House Tax Reduction Bill balances most of the tradeoffs between tax reduction, a simpler code, and tax deductions. The corporate changes were about as expected, and should be strong enough to make possible the Trump goal of 3% economic growth in 2018 and into the foreseeable future.

A one-time tax was levied on the offshore profits of U.S. companies. This could allow as much as $1.5 trillion of offshore profits to come back to the U.S. This would certainly provide new capital for U.S. domestic investment in addition to corporate stock buy-backs.

The individual tax revisions did not substantially simplify the tax code, and make it much easier for individuals to do and file their own tax returns. The alternative minimum tax was retained. Some individuals will have more money to spend on consumption, including durables.

The unknowns are whether the tax reductions will stimulate inflation and economic growth, offsetting the initially reduced government taxes. Also uncertain is whether increased growth can eliminate some of the increased government.

Entitlement Programs

Trump Budget-Social Security, Medicare, Medicaid & Obamacare Repeal-The Issues Are Serious

The Trump Budget is supposedly a balance one at the end of 10 years, but the revenue growth numbers are unrealistic. It appears that a 3% GDP growth rate is assumed, without the personal and corporate tax deductions that are supposed to drive the higher GDP growth rate.

The personal and business tax reductions are irrelevant to what happens to Social Security, Medicare, and Medicaid

Medicaid is a particularly large program because there are no revenue sources, such as there are for Social Security and Medicare, to offset the costs. It was forecasted to be $378 billion in 2017, and grow at a 3.2% compound growth rate to $524 billion in 2028. With a 5.0% growth rate of GDP, it goes from 2.0% of GDP to 1.7% of GDP. The presumption seems to be that Medicaid will grow at about a 1% growth rate, assuming that medical costs only grow at the 2.3% inflation rate that is forecast.

Social Security is forecasted to go bankrupt in about 20 years. However this is misleading. Social Security is a pay as you go program, and as long as Congress is willing to fund the difference between Social Security payroll receipts and Social Security Payments, the program should continue. In 2017 Social Security payments were forecasted to be $946 billion, or 4.9% of GDP.

Social Security payroll receipts were forecasted to be $857 billion in 2017. This is $89 billion less than payments in 2017. Receipts are expected to grow to $1,379 billion in 2018, with the payment shortfall increasing to $346 billion. Receipts go from 4.5% of GDP in 2017 to 4.4% of GDP in 2027. In 2017, the compound growth rate of receipts was expected to be 4.9%, about what was expected to be the growth rate of GDP at that time. This implies that payroll payments will grow at about the rate of GDP. This does not seem to be an unreasonable assumption.

The other large program we are examining is Medicare. Medicare payments show the same pattern as Social Security, which is what one would expect. Medicare payments were expected go from $593 billion in 2017 to $1,168 billion in fiscal 2018, a 7.0% growth rate, compared to a 6.2% growth rate for Social Security payments. Medicare payments were expected to grow from 3.1% of GDP in 2017 to 3.8% of GDP in 2028.

Medicare payroll receipts go from $258 billions, or 1.3% of GDP in fiscal 2017 to $427 billion, or 1.4% of GDP in 2028, a 5.2% compound growth rate, only slightly more than the forecasted 5.0% compound growth rate of GDP. The Medicare deficit was expected to go from $335 billion in 2017, about 3.8 times the deficit of Social Security, to $471 billion in 2028, about 1.4 times the Social Security shortfall.

ArmchairTechInvestor Opinion

The Medicare and Social Security programs are definitely problems. The problem in 10 years is that the number of retired persons will grow much more rapidly than employment, which generates Social Security and Medicare payments. Because of this the deficit for Social Security will be 1.2% of GDP, compared to only 0.4% of GDP in 2017. The deficit for Medicare is even more of a problem. The Medicare deficit grows from

0.7% of GDP in 2017 to 2.4% of GDP in 2027. The increase in the Social Security and Medicare deficits are forecasted to grow by 2.5% of GDP. This is almost equivalent to the amount of defense expenditures, and will crowd out discretionary spending, if it is not addressed by adjusting payroll taxes upward, or setting later Social Security or Medicare qualification ages.

Deficit

With the current deficit at 104% of GDP, and with the long-term average being 62%, the size of the US deficit is an issue. For the next 10 years, it appears unlikely that the U.S. can run surpluses that might reduce the debt percentage of GDP because of tax reductions, the military buildup, infrastructure spending, the border wall and other possible spending initiatives such as healthcare. It is also questionable whether substantial reductions of other government spending can be enacted, because of probable Democratic filibusters in the Senate.

What Are the Deficit Issues? The Trump Policies Are Unlikely to Reduce a Currently Very High Deficit Level.

To address the budget deficit, the first element is understanding the budget deficit as a percentage of GDP. A corporate analogy is a company looking at its debt as a percentage of revenues. However, the drawback is that the Government does not make a profit. In 2010, the deficit reached a high 9.8%, as the Government went through supporting U.S. companies, such as the large banks, and the auto companies. In 2015, the deficit as a percentage of GDP was down to 2.4%.

A second way of looking at the deficit on a current basis is as a percentage of GDP. As GDP grows, the deficit percentage of GDP may grow or decline. If the Trump policies produce over 3% GDP growth, and the debt grows at less than 3%, the debt as a percentage of GDP will decline.

Government Debt to GDP in the United States averaged 61.94 percent from 1940 until 2015, reaching an all time high of 121.70 percent in 1946 and a record low of 31.70 percent in 1974. The United States recorded a government debt equivalent to 104.17 percent of the country's Gross Domestic Product in 2015.

ArmchairTechInvestor Opinion

With the deficit at 104% of GDP at the end of 2015 and growing, and the long-term average being at 62%, the size of the U.S. deficit is an issue. For the next 4 years, it appears unlikely that we can run surpluses that might reduce the debt percentage because of the military buildup, infrastructure spending, the border wall, additional non-defense, and other possible spending initiatives.

Government Funding and the Debt Ceiling

When the U.S. government spends, it needs to issue debt to fund the spending. The Congress passes debt ceilings that must be raised periodically. Two alternatives are to eliminate debt ceilings entirely, or tie debt ceilings to spending increases so that they are automatically increased when budgets are passed. Both of these possibilities are being considered by the Trump administration.

The Debt Ceiling Is A Continuing Political Issue: Would It Be Better To Repeal The Debt Ceiling?

*The Washington Post reported that President Trump and Senator Schumer had a verbal agreement to permanently remove the debt ceiling, and at the same time provide funding for hurricane relief. An agreement was targeted for December 8, 2017, and any agreement would need to be confirmed by the Congress. The possible agreement is a slap in the face to Republicans, and the debt ceiling deadlines are continuing thorns in the side of those in Congress, because of the political infighting they engender.

It is reported that Vice President Pence is open to changes he considers in line with the "Gephardt Rule", a parliamentary rule making it easier to tie raising the debt ceiling with Congress passing a budget. The rule is named after former House majority leader Richard A. Gephardt (D-Mo.).

This could be another way to get around continually having to raise the debt ceiling separately.

Article 1 of the Constitution sets up Congress's powers, giving it the authority to write and pass legislation and appropriate government money. Because the U.S. government spends money in excess of tax and fee receipts, it must borrow to fund the deficit. If the borrowing exceeds the debt ceiling, the debt ceiling must be raised. This happens very often. These votes are often politicized and can cause uncertainty in the financial markets.

Treasury Secretary Steven Mnuchin has suggested scrapping the existing debt-limit process and replacing it with one that automatically lifts the borrowing limit every time Congress appropriates future spending.

*Trump, Schumer agree to pursue plan to repeal the debt ceiling, Washington Post, By Damian Paletta and Ashley Parker September 7, 2017

ArmchairTechInvestor Opinion

Having a debt ceiling that needs to be raised periodically is attractive to conservatives. This gives them an opportunity to publicize the fact that the government continues to increase the national debt, with the risks that carries for future economic growth and for future generations.

President Trump became frustrated at the inaction of the Congress in passing his agenda legislation, and the discussion with Senator Schumer postponed the delays that the hurricanes and the debt ceiling approval would cause the Congress.

A Government Shutdown Was Avoided: Who Won?

A government shutdown has been avoided through the bipartisan passing of a funding bill that keeps the government open through the end fiscal 2017 in September. The bill includes some spending increases wanted by the Trump administration, but leaves many of their initiatives to be decided when the fiscal 2018 bill is adopted.

The biggest wins for the Trump Administration were:

- $15 billion of extra funding for defense programs and combat operations in Afghanistan, Iraq and Syria. A small chunk of that money;
  - o $2.5 billion, is restricted until Trump sends Congress a plan for how to defeat the Islamic State; and
- $1.5 billion is to be used only for surveillance, plus repair to existing barriers.

There are a number of other programs that are either supported only by the Democrats or are bipartisan. They include:

- Almost $296 to support Puerto Rico's Medicaid program;
- Over $1 billion for health insurance for mine workers; This was a bipartisan addition;
- $8.1 billion in disaster relief for states hit hard by floods, wildfires and other disasters; This was a bipartisan addition;
- $2 billion in additional funding for medical research; This was a Democratic addition;
- $1.65 billion for Pell grants for needy college students;
- $990 million for global famine-relief efforts;
- $68 million to reimburse New York and Florida law enforcement agencies for the costs of helping the Secret Service protect Trump and his family;
- $407 million in additional wildfire funds;
- $100 million more to fight opioid addiction;
- $130 million in additional funds for substance abuse and mental health;
- $30 million more for grants to help states fund mental health programs for low-income residents; and
- A provision to prevent the Department of Justice from spending any money to interfere with state medical marijuana laws.

The Democrats stopped the defunding of Planned Parenthood. Included in the bill was continued funding to support insurance companies offering low-cost insurance to low-income Americans under Obamacare.

There are many requests by the Trump Administration that will be issues in crafting the fiscal 2018 funding bill. They include:

- Trump's request for $1.4 billion to begin construction of a wall on the U.S.-Mexico border;
- Trump's request to cut non-defense spending by $18 billion;
- Extra funding to hire more Immigration and Customs Enforcement agents;
- Restricting "sanctuary cities" from receiving Federal grants; and
- Dodd-Frank regulation of the financial industry.

ArmchairTechInvestor Opinion

The funding bill was the first bipartisan bill during the Trump Administration. It also ended the Obama administrations requirement that any defense spending be accompanied by an equal non-defense spending increase. Trump has threatened a government shutdown in September, presumably if he is displeased with how the Democrats negotiate the fiscal 2018 spending bill. Trump's tax cuts, climate change plans, defenses plans, particularly the fights against ISIS, North Korea, and Iran, and government spending cuts will likely be the main issues.

Federal Reserve

The Federal Reserve is tasked with stimulating economic growth, and achieving a reasonable inflation rate, which is currently targeted at 2%. In April 2018, it is suggesting that at least 3 increases in the Federal funds rate will occur in 2018. It also has $4.5 billion of securities it acquired during the Obama years. It plans to sell those slowly in 2018. Both of these objectives will reduce the money supply, and presumably slow the economic growth rate.

The Federal Reserve Plans To Continue Increasing Interest Rates, And Sell Portfolio Securities: If They Do It GDP Growth Could Slow

The Federal Reserve (Fed) has traditionally controlled economic growth and inflation by controlling the growth of M1, the money supply. The larger the growth of the money supply, bank lending and corporate borrowing should increase, and businesses should invest to grow their businesses. This prescription has not worked for the last 8 years under the Obama administration. Obama inherited a recession recovery period. The Fed kept interest rates at near 0%, and the U.S. still had one of the weakest recovery periods in recent history. GDP growth averaged 2%, and appears likely to remain at or above the 2.5% rate in 2017 for the next year or two.

The Fed target for interest rates is 0.75% to 1%. If the economy remains strong, which seems to mean 2% growth in GDP, the Fed is likely to raise interest rates at least three times in 2018, leaving interest rates on short-term government bonds at 1.75% to 2.0% at the end of 2018. The most noticeable effect will likely be to increase home mortgages rates from about 4% at the end of 2017, to about 5% at the end of 2018.

The Fed is slowly selling some of its securities, which will have the effect of reducing the money supply, and thereby slowing the economy. The level of the currency in circulation has increased from about $800 million eight years ago to about $1.5 billion today. The Fed has about a $4.5 trillion level of securities it owns as of the end of 2017, including about $1.8 billion of mortgage-backed securities. This level of securities owned has increased from about $500 million in 2008. It appears that a normal level of securities owned by the Fed could be 10% to 20% of GDP. The U.S. GDP was $18.56 trillion in 2016. Thus the Fed had securities that were about 23% of GDP, which was on the high side. The Fed started slowly selling some of its securities near the end of 2017.

The Fed looks at the effect of an interest rate increase on foreign countries. Their economies look strong internationally, so Fed rate increases should not have much of an effect in 2018.

Countries with trade surpluses with the U.S. will benefit from increased Fed rates. Japan had $1.09 trillion U.S. securities, and China had $1.06 trillion in 2017.

U.S. Debt as a Percentage of GDP

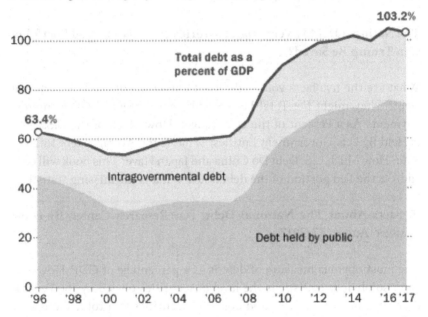

Debt now exceeds gross domestic product

Debt as a percentage of GDP, fiscal 1996-present

Source: TreasuryDirect (U.S. Department of the Treasury, Bureau of the Fiscal Service); "The Debt Limit: History and Recent Increases" (Congressional Research Service, RL31967); Bureau of Economic Analysis; Pew Research Center estimates.

PEW RESEARCH CENTER

Image: Debt Now Exceeds Gross Domestic Product
Image Source: Pew Research Center

ArmchairTechInvestor Opinion

The objectives of the Trump administration are to stimulate growth to over 3% by stimulating job growth, by reducing our trade deficit, particularly with Germany, Mexico, Japan and China, and bringing jobs back to the U.S. Other measures designed to increase growth in the U.S. include:

Tax reductions, Infrastructure spending, and repatriating foreign dollars of U.S. companies.

The Fed increases in interest rates, and the sale of their securities, could reduce the U.S. GDP growth rate, and make it more difficult for Trump to meet his 3% growth rate objective.

The National Debt Is Very High Historically, As Is The Fed Portfolio: Can Trump Be Saved?

What are the five facts you might like to know about the U.S. National Debt? They might be: Total Debt; Debt As a Percent of GDP; Interest Payments As a Percent of the U.S. Budget; How Much of the U.S. Debt Is Held By U.S. Government Entities; What Is the Average Debt Interest Rate? How Much U.S. Debt Do China and Japan Have? This book will only address the Fed portion of the debt issue. What is the missing statistic?

*****5 Facts About The National Debt,** Pew Research Center, By Drew Desilver, August 17, 2017

The most obvious measure of debt is as a percentage of GDP. However, a not so obvious statistic is the level of securities owned by the Federal Reserve. The Fed has acquired portfolio securities that total about $4.5 trillion dollars in 2017. The Fed has begun the process of cutting its balance sheet, which grew from about $1 trillion to $4.5 trillion in five years. The large increase is the result of an aggressive bond-buying stimulus program. Trump is now facing the problems created by the Obama administration. The Fed program was implemented to keep interest rates low and support a collapsed housing market. Since December 2015, the Fed has gradually raised the benchmark fed funds rate from near zero, amid a somewhat improved labor market and flat U.S. economic growth. But, its large portfolio of Treasury bonds and mortgage-backed securities has remained in place.

The economy at a level where the Fed is trying to raise interest rates, keep the inflation rate above 2%, and sell its portfolio securities. How can this black magic occur, since, selling Fed securities from its portfolio will have the effect of taking money out of the money supply, and therefore making economic development more difficult. This should endanger the Trump administration goal of over 3% growth, while growth was at 2.5% in 2017.

ArmchairTechInvestor Opinion

The Fed is in a balancing act between trying to the keep inflation rate at 2% or higher, raise the Federal funds rate, and beginning to reduce the large Fed securities portfolio (beginning in September, 2017) acquired to improve a historically weak economy averaging only a 2% growth rate, after a severe economic recession in 2008-09. All of these issues do not even begin to address the large Federal deficit, and the ballooning Federal debt.

A Trump miracle is needed, particularly because of the lack of support he is getting from the Republican House and Senate, and the alternative being a big spending Democratic Party that has already proven that the U.S. government is not a panacea. Private enterprise might provide a better solution, particularly if tax reductions and corporate profits repatriation can be achieved. The Congress is believed to be broken, with approval ratings for Paul Ryan and Charles Schumer under 30% in 2017.

The U.S. Dollar Has Declined By 5% Since The Peak Achieved After The Trump Election: This Should Be Helpful In Reducing The Trade Deficit

President Trump's election, and the euphoria about his tax cuts, bringing jobs back to the U.S., and undertaking to improve our crumbling infrastructure, caused the U.S. dollar to improve about 5% and reach new highs in December, 2016.

The Federal Reserve increased interest rates by 0.25% on December 14, 2016. The dollar fluctuated, but dropped about 2.5% by the time the Fed raised rates by another 0.25% on March 15, 2017. The drop in the dollar is a little surprising, since increasing the rate on U.S. government rates should attract capital to the U.S., and increase the value of the dollar. The dollar typically declines after Fed rate increases, but these declines are probably a reflection of future expectations, not the rate increase itself.

ArmchairTechInvestor Opinion

The election of President Trump caused the Democrats to attempt to obstruct President Trump's agenda of job and economic growth, regulatory reform, healthcare reform, increased defense spending, and the reduction of the size of government. It has promoted getting a special prosecutor to see if a crime was committed with respect to the Russians, or the firing of James Comey, the ex-FBI director. It seems unlikely that an obstruction crime was not committed, which should come out at some point.

From an economic standpoint, the decline of the dollar, if it remains low, should be helpful in improving the U.S. foreign trade imbalance. And, it might help in job creation.

CHAPTER 4

Chinese Local Investment Objectives, Economy, Capital Investment, Consumer Investment, Chinese Companies, Financial Markets

Chinese Tech Companies:
Alibaba
Anbang
Baidu
Broadcom
Huawei
Tencent Holdings
Xiaomi
Zejiang Geely-Daimler-Volvo
ZTE

China Uses Restrictions Banned By The World Trade Organization to Restrict Competitive Tech Company Access To The China Market.

Chinese tech companies are heavily favored in accessing the China market. The restrictions on foreign competitors vary by sector, but the most onerous restrictions are on providing Internet access to their databases or Internet search services. Only three Chinese companies, Alibaba Group Holding, Baidu and Tencent Holdings, are allowed to directly access the Internet.

Alibaba

*Alibaba Group Holding is one of three companies, including Tencent Holdings, and Baidu that dominate e-commerce, social media, and mobile payments. With China moving toward what could be mostly an all-electric automobile market by 2030, providing a variety of subscription services to vehicles is viewed as an extremely large market opportunity in China, but also perhaps elsewhere. For example, Renault is forecasting

that it could achieve a fivefold increase in revenues by 2023 as a result of its ability to sell automobiles on Alibaba's platform.

China is encouraging Chinese companies to list their stocks in China. However, there are Chinese stock market listing requirements that make this difficult for companies that are listed on the New York Stock Exchange, or other foreign exchanges. If they are listed elsewhere, they are not eligible for listing in China. Chinese regulators are looking at using American Depository Receipts (ADRs) as a way of getting around this dilemma. Alibaba uses these ADRs for its U.S. listing. Alibaba may be able to raise capital in China less expensively, but stock listed in China will not be convertible into its U.S. ADRs. That probably makes it inevitable that over time there will be two listing prices for Alibaba's stock.

*Alibaba Looks to go Home, Wall Street Journal, by Julie Steinberg and Liza Lin, March 17, 2018

Anbang

**Anbang is essentially a bankrupt very large insurance company that tried to act like a money manager in the guise of being an insurance company. Its distress is comparable to the failure of AIG in the U.S. The interesting aspect of Anbang is that the Chinese financial regulator is running the company and looking to use successful companies, such as Alibaba and TenCent Holdings, to bail out Anbang in return for being allowed to provide additional financial services beyond mobile services, which together they dominate. This is a risk that existing shareholders of Alibaba and Tencent Holdings may be required to take in return for China tight control being loosened on financial services sectors that are not openly competitive.

**Beijing Could Recruit Help to Clean Up Anbang's Mess, Wall Street Journal, by Jacky Wong, February 21, 2018

Baidu

***Baidu is one of three companies, including Tencent Holdings, and Alibaba Group Holding, that dominate e-commerce, social media, and mobile payments in Chins. In particular it provides search and mapping services. With China moving toward what could be mostly an all-electric automobile market by 2030, providing a variety of subscription services to vehicles is viewed as an extremely large market opportunity in China, but also perhaps elsewhere.

***China's Tech Giants Take to the Road,** Wall Street Journal, by Trefor Moss and Liza Lin, March 19, 2018

Broadcom

Broadcom is a very large semiconductor company based in Shanghai. It attempted a hostile takeover of Qualcomm, which has an impressive portfolio of intellectual property patents. The U.S. rejected the attempted acquisition on the grounds that such an acquisition could jeopardize national security and the development of 5G Internet technology in the U.S. 5G will become crucial for developing advanced services such as artificial intelligence.

Huawei

****Huawei is a Chinese telecommunications equipment manufacturer. It is the world's largest wireless equipment manufacturer and the third largest smartphone maker. The company is making an investment in the United Kingdom. The UK has set up a facility, run by Huawei to examine the intricacies of their own equipment. U.S. politicians have expressed concern that the company's equipment can be used to gather intelligence for China or even disable U.S. equipment. Even equipment in other countries might also be used for spying on the U.S. or network control purposes. The U.S. is a member of the "Five Eyes" intelligence-sharing partnership that also includes Britain, Canada, Australia and New Zealand. These countries could be vulnerable to Huawei equipment security risks.

The House and Senate have each introduced bills to address the Huawei risk. Huawei counters that it is an employee-owned company and is respected in 170 countries around the world.

Canada's Parliament is debating cybersecurity risks. South Korea's largest carrier's CEO called Huawei a "concern". Australia ruled out Huawei for its Solomon Island undersea cable deployment despite the fact that Huawei is an advisor to it on its development of a 5G wireless network.

******Huawei's Breadth Raises Concern**, Wall Street Journal, by David George-Cosh, February 24, 2018

*****Caution Over Huawei Grows,** Wall Street Journal, By Dan Strumph and Paul Vieira, March 21, 2018

Tencent Holdings

******Tencent Holdings is a Chinese Internet company. Because the Chinese Internet is very tightly controlled by the Chinese government, Tencent Holdings is in a very enviable position. One important capability is their ability to provide GPS mapping services. Driverless vehicles could be an extremely important application. Vehicle manufactures will need to use an Internet company to provide driverless vehicle services. Its Hong Kong-listed stock has doubled in 2017.

Tencent Holdings has made a number of attractive investments. One example is an investment in Tongcheng-Elong Holdings. The company is considering an IPO that could give it a valuation of several billion dollars. It runs Internet portals that provide online China and international travel services.

********Tencent-Backed Travel Company Is Cruising Toward IPO**, Wall Street Journal, By Julie Steinberg and Liza Lin, March 10, 2018

Xiaomi

*******Xiaomi, is one of the largest cellphone makers in the China, and has a $46 billion market capitalization. It has high quality cellphones that rival Apple in looks, but are inexpensive. It is planning an IPO that could have a valuation of $100 billion or more. Xiaomi is essentially an Internet company. Its China market share was 12% in 2017 and its shipments grew 50% to 96 million units. However, the company is risky and subject to the vagaries of hardware development companies with low margins. On revenues of $15.2 billion, it had profits of about $1 billion. By contrast Apple had a market capitalization of about $900 billion in early 2018. In China, non-Internet companies are generally banned from using GPS for self-driving vehicles and existing providers such as Xiaomi are very much in demand to provide future services for self-driving electric vehicles.

*******Hot Xiaomi Carries Big Risks, Wall Street Journal, by Li Yuan, March 17, 2018

********Beijing Dials Up Pressure on Xiaomi, Wall Street Journal, Stella Yifan Xie, March 2, 2018

Zejiang Geely-Daimler-Volvo

Geely has become the premier Chinese vehicle manufacturer by connecting with Western automaker technology. The journey began with Geely introducing a Chinese manufactured automobile at a Detroit auto show in 2006. The automobile was roundly criticized, particularly for its poor quality. Geely went to Ford to buy Volvo, and with Volvo doing poorly in 2010, it was bought from Ford for $1.8 billion, a fraction of what Ford had paid for it. The road forward for Geely was a risky one, but relying on the manufacturing expertise of Volvo in Sweden, the design vision of a seasoned Western car designer, it has had increasing success both worldwide and in China. China is going toward all-electric vehicles, and Volvo plans to have 90% of its vehicles electric or hybrid by 2020. It has manufacturing plants in China and Europe and has a U.S. plant that will open in the U.S. in 2018.

ZTE and Huawei are two Chinese companies that pose a threat to the U.S. broadband communications networks. ZTE has become the fourth largest cellphone supplier in the U.S. The UK banned the use of ZTE equipment because of concerns that China could force the company to infiltrate the UK's broadband communications infrastructure. China essentially requires Chinese companies that wish to do business in China to pledge allegiance to China. This can result in those companies being used to spy on countries where they do business. This is the equivalent of the U.S. requiring Apple to spy on behalf of the U.S. government, which they would not do. The reverse is true in that Apple would be required to support Chinese government objectives, if it were to do business in China.

The technological war with China has begun. It remains to be seen whether U.S. companies can do business in China without giving away their technology to China.

ZTE

In the case of the U.S. companies such as ZTE and Huawei are finally being restricted because the business they do in the U.S. could provide a threat to U.S. security.

CHAPTER 5

U.S. Tech Companies:
Alphabet (Google)
Amazon
Apple
Boeing
Daimler
Facebook
IBM
Lockheed Martin
Microsoft
Qualcomm
Tesla

U.S. and other foreign tech companies are severely restricted in accessing the China market. The restrictions vary by sector, but the most onerous restrictions are on providing Internet access to their databases and search services to their customers.

China Has Semiconductor Fund Plans Underway To Try And Beat The U.S. In The Future Race For Semiconductor Technology Superiority

In 2013, Chinese government officials invaded the Beijing and Shanghai offices of Qualcomm. After a 15-month investigation, regulators saddled the company with a $975 million fine. In addition to the fine, Qualcomm:

- Was branded a monopoly;
- Was forced to reduce prices;
- Had to move more of its technical manufacturing to China;
- And, help boost the technological abilities of Chinese companies.

By 2018, a growing number of American companies "have complained that China has pressured them into sharing their technology in similar ways".

The U.S. is finally standing up to an aggressive China by confronting large Chinese companies that are trying to enter the U.S. market, and could threaten U.S. security. Qualcomm, a worldwide leader in semiconductor technology, was threatened by an unfriendly takeover by Broadcom, a Singapore-based company. The U.S. blocked the acquisition on national security grounds. There were several concerns. The acquisition of Qualcomm could have reduced U.S. superiority in semiconductors. It could also have reduced the U.S. lead in next generation 5G broadband networks. Qualcomm has a large business in China, and China has threatened to block Qualcomm has made an offer to acquire NXP Semiconductors, an important part of its growth strategy. The acquisition has been stalled by an antitrust review. In early May, 2018, "Chinese officials said that Qualcomm will have to make more concessions to compensate for the market power it would enjoy after completing the deal, without providing details."

China has used the national security threat issue as a way to protect Chinese companies. China is still considered to be an emerging country under the World Trade Organization rules, showing how antiquated is the WTO.

*Qualcomm May Be Collateral Damage in a U.S.-China Trade War

New York Times, By Ana Swanson and Alexandra Stevenson, April 18, 2018

**China announced plans to significantly improve the competitiveness of its state and Chinese semiconductor companies when it launched a $21.8 billion semiconductor development fund in 2014. A U.S. Trade Representative's report on March 22, 2018 declared the 2014 fund as an effort by government agencies and state-owned companies to meet Chinese national strategic objectives.

China has also announced a new fund that could total about $47.4 billion. Important semiconductor industry sectors it will support are likely to include microprocessors and graphic processors. The objective is to reduce China's dependence on foreign semiconductor products from companies such as Qualcomm, IBM and Nvidia.

China Plans Fund to Boost Semiconductors, Wall Street Journal, By Yoko Kubota, May 5, 2015

Alphabet (Google)

Google is blocked in China, and unlike Apple, it has not been able to limit the download of apps sufficiently to be able to enter the Chinese Internet search market.

*Why Google Quit China—and Why It's Heading Back, The Atlantic, by Kavin Waddell, January 19, 2016

Amazon

Online Internet retailers in China are not allowed to sell directly. This requires Amazon to go through a complicated process that severely limits its capabilities in China, compared with the big three allowed Chinese company Internet providers.

Amazon has warned, "Our Chinese and Indian businesses and operations may be unable to continue to operate if we or our affiliates are unable to access sufficient funding or if China enforces contractual relationships with respect to the management and control of such businesses." The company added that if its international activities were found to be in violation of any existing or future laws in China or India or if interpretations of those laws and regulations were to change, it would lead to fines, license revocation and or a complete shutdown of operations.

In China, the Amazon website is operated by local companies owned by Chinese nationals in order to meet ownership and licensing requirements.

*Amazon Warns of Ending India and China Operations Due to Complicated Laws,** International Business Times. By Jerin Mathew, November 3, 2014

Apple

Apple did well in the December quarter of 2017, increasing revenues by 11% in the Asia-Pacific region, but is losing market share in the huge smartphone markets in China, India and other Asian countries. Taking significant market share is Xiaomi. Which has inexpensive smartphones, and feature rich smartphones that compete with Apple's X. The X sells for about $1,000.

Xiaomi, often called the Apple of Asia, has a smartphone, the Redmi Note 4. In China, that sells for about $200 and competes with the Apple X. Xiaomi's market share was 19% in 2017, compared to 3% in 2015. Apple's market share in China was about 8% in 2017, down from 13% in 2015.

The typical smartphone in India, for example, sells for about $200, and is not subsidized by the wireless carrier, as in the U.S. These smartphones may have batteries that are sensitive to power fluctuations, and often have features, such as cameras, that are unique to the Indian market.

Asian Rivals Put Apple Under Pressure, Wall Street Journal, by Newley Purnell, March 2, 2018

China is issuing demanding cybersecurity requirements. It is requiring that all cloud data be located on servers in China, including encryption keys. Apple has said that the keys will be stored in a secure location, will retain control of them, and hasn't put in any backdoors. However, Chinese seizure is always a possibility, or it could require that Apple give them specific keys. The U.S. Congress is very concerned about these keys being stored in China

This could make the data vulnerable to Chinese surveillance. Apple also removed 700 apps that allow users to bypass Internet restrictions. Other restrictions include censoring content, and having to set up joint ventures with Chinese companies. Chinese companies assemble most smartphones.

**Apple's Cook Plays Along With China, Wall Street Journal, by Yoko Kubota, February 27, 2018

***Apple Puts iCloud Keys in China, Wall Street Journal, by Robert McMillan and Tripp Mickle, February 26, 2018

Boeing

Boeing is an extremely large commercial plane producer. It is also an import resource to NASA in pursuing a commercially competitive space vehicle program, including using very powerful space launch systems that can compete with Space-X, which is looking to launch a system that might reach Mars in 2017.

China and Russia are modernizing their nuclear forces, and there is growing risk from North Korea.

*The first phase of a U.S. land-based missile program replacement for the Minuteman 3, deployed in silos in the Great Plains, is underway. The first phase is a $700 million design phase, and Boeing and Northrop have been selected to compete for this business. It will include 600 land-based missiles, of which 400 will be deployed, and 200 will be used for testing.

*Nuclear Missile Overhaul Falls to Small Pool of Contractors

Wall Street Journal, By Doug Cameron, August 27, 2017

Daimler

Daimler has said it plans to begin assembling Mercedes-Benz vehicles in 2018 from a $1 billion facility shared with Renault-Nissan (RENA.PA) (7201.T) in Aguascalientes in Mexico. In February, 2018, Li Shufu, the chairman of Chinese automaker Geely, bought Daimler stock, worth $9 billion. Geely will not own the stake. (GELYF) It will be held by an investment vehicle known as Tenaclou3 Prospect Investment Ltd., according to the filing. In 2010, Geely purchased Volvo from Ford for $1.8 billion, a fraction of the $6.4 billion that Ford had paid for Volvo in 1999. The purpose of the Geely investment in Daimler is not clear, but because Geely is working to improve the quality of its vehicles, particularly in the luxury vehicle area, that is very likely a reason.

*China Humiliates Another Western Company, Wall Street Journal, by Michael Auslin, February 21, 2018

Facebook

In December, 2017, Facebook had 2.13 billion active users, a 15% year-to-year increase. It had revenues of $40.7 billion in 2017. It is extremely profitable, with pre-tax margins of about 50%.

Facebook is facing significant scrutiny because of the hacking that allowed 50 million of their customer's data being used for political purposes without their knowledge. It also faces issues in Asia that included it being banned in the Chinese market.

*Russian interference in the 2016 presidential election is also an Issue. Russians bought ads that were targeted at creating social divisions in the U.S. Facebook generates about $40 billion of annual revenues from ads that are narrowly targeted at specific audiences.

*Tone-Deaf: Facebook's Russia Bungle, Wall Street Journal, By Deepa Seethharaman, Robert McMillian and Georgia Wells, April 3, 2018

**Facebook and the Tools of Uprising, Wall Street Journal, by Christopher Mims, February 20, 2018

IBM

U.S. companies such as Tesla, Apple and IBM will, through their foreign subsidiaries in China, meaningfully assist China in their global trade ambitions. It is a brilliant scheme to use unfair trade practices to promote Chinese trade, economic and political influence in the region from

Europe to Asia and Africa, and use U.S. companies such as Tesla and IBM to do it.

* Staying up with China in quantum computing, and trying to get to a 100-qubit quantum computer will likely be the next military frontier for the U.S. Countries such as China, Russia, the U.K., the European Union, and Australia are in a race to develop quantum computers, as are companies such as Intel, IBM, Microsoft and Alphabet (Google). The winners of the race will be able to obsolete existing cybersecurity technologies and systems.

China is apparently the leader in quantum computer research. In mid-2017, it launched the first satellite capable of transmitting quantum data. It is building the world's largest quantum computing facility. Its focus is on code breaking, and supporting its military with quantum navigation systems for stealth submarines. It appears to be getting close to getting a 40-qubit quantum computer prototype.

*The Computer That Could Rule the World, Wall Street Journal, by Arthur Herman, October 27, 2017

Lockheed Martin

*The first phase of a U.S. land-based missile program replacement for the Minuteman 3, deployed in silos in the Great Plains, is underway. The first phase is a $700 million design phase, and Boeing and Northrop have been selected to compete for this business. It will include 600 land-based missiles, of which 400 will be deployed, and 200 will be used for testing.

Some have estimated that the total cost could be as high as $500 billion over the next 20 years, which is about 5% of the Defense Department budget. A decision is expected in 2020 to determine the general contractor for the Ground-Based Strategic Development (GBSD) program, including the ICBMs, new communications systems, and a refurbishment of the launch silos. Aerojet Rocketdyne Inc. has announced it is building the rocket motors for Northrop.

*Lockheed Pursues Longer Jet Pack, Wall Street Journal, March 10, 2018, by Doug Cameron, March 10, 2018

Microsoft

Microsoft is at the center of an email data storage lawsuit that an appeals court has ruled on, and warrants cannot be enforce on getting access to data that is stored exclusively on foreign servers. The case, as of early 2018, is at the Supreme Court. The companies want to protect user data, and in some cases, the public authorities in some case are seeking access to that data. In the case of data in China, the authorities often have full unrestricted access to that data.

Companies such as Microsoft and Alphabet (Google) claim that if their customer data were not protected, they would be in the middle between U.S. law and the foreign country data privacy requirements. U.S. dominance of the $250 billion cloud computing industry is claimed to be at stake.

In the case in question, the data is stored on a database in Ireland, to which Microsoft has full access in the U.S. The case revolves around an antiquated 1986 U.S. law, the Stored Communications Act. The law is not a fit for today's large-scale cross-border data storage environment. The current law needs to be interpreted until the Congress can revise it.

Google and other tech companies are supporting Microsoft.

*Justices to Hear Microsoft Case on Email Storage, Wall Street Journal, By Brent Kendall and Nicole Hong, February 27, 2018

**Justices Grapple With Microsoft Case, Wall Street Journal, by Brent Kendall and Nicole Hong, February 26, 2018

Companies have a choice of where they store their data. If U.S. law does not apply to data stored outside the U.S., then the tech companies can find a place to store U.S. data that would be immune to access by U.S. authorities.

***Microsoft's Legal Cloud Cover,** Wall Street Journal. Editorial, February 27, 2018

Qualcomm

Qualcomm is a worldwide leader in semiconductors used in cellphones and wireless communications networks. Qualcomm has developed 5G wireless networks that are used throughout the world. It was in a hostile takeover situation that could have resulted in a Singapore company, Broadcom, taking over the 5G networks being developed in the U.S. These networks will significantly improve the performance of artificial intelligence networks. The two risks are that:

- China could have been in control of the networks that are used to deliver artificial intelligence in the U.S., and are very important to military systems; and,
- China might have used Chinese companies, including Huawei, the second largest supplier of 5G networks worldwide, to infiltrate the U.S. broadband communications networks;
  - o Chinese companies have sworn allegiances to China, or they wouldn't be allowed to operate in China. This presumable applies to Broadcom.

The Treasury department blocked the Broadcom acquisition of Qualcomm.

In November 2017, a new bill was introduced in the U.S. Congress entitled the Foreign Investment Review Modernization Act. The Committee on Foreign Investment In the United States (CFIUS) has the responsibility to review foreign investment in the U.S. There are continued attempts by China to invest in U.S. technology. The most recent controversy surrounds Broadcom's hostile bid to take over Qualcomm. One issue is whether Broadcom might do something to Qualcomm that would make the U.S. dependent on a Chinese company, Huawei, a very large Qualcomm rival, for its communications networks, particularly the next generation 5G networks in the U.S. These networks will bring significant new capabilities for applications, such as artificial intelligence (AI).

The new bill comes amid increasing scrutiny of defense threats under the Trump administration, as the U.S. government has blocked several investments from China, including the high-profile proposed acquisition of Lattice Semiconductor Corp by Chinese state-backed Canyon Bridge Capital Partners.

*For Qualcomm, Yet More Fights Are on the Card. Wall Street Journal, by Ted Greenwald, March 20, 2018

**Treasury's Qualcomm Reversal, Wall Street Journal, Editorial, March 6, 2018

***The Qualcomm Question, Wall Street Journal, Editorial, March 5, 2018

Tesla

Tesla has substantial electric car intellectual property, including wireless car batteries, which it will protect by building an electric car manufacturing plant in Shanghai, thereby avoiding Chinese companies stealing their technology.

China does not allow foreign companies in China to set up manufacturing plants anywhere except in "free trade zones". One of those free trade zones is Shanghai, where Tesla will locate its plant. There are also ten more such free trade zones throughout China.

China uses unfair trade practices, such as requiring foreign manufacturers to have a Chinese partner, or pay a 25% import duty, if the car is manufactured outside of China. Tesla seems to be unwilling to give away its technology to a Chinese company partner, and perhaps give away 50% of the local Chinese market to them.

Batteries, which are a significant portion of the cost of an electric car, will undoubtedly be able to be imported to the Shanghai plant. This will protect Tesla's electric car battery technology. Tesla will also be able to benefit from the low cost of Chinese manufacturing, by being in Shanghai. This plant will be able to ship to Asian and European markets from this plant, and enjoy the low cost of Chinese manufacturing plants.

It will also benefit from the low cost of automobile parts manufactured in China for its export markets outside of China.

*Tesla Plugs In Own China Plant, Wall Street Journal, Tim Higgins, Trefor Moss and Eva Dou, October 23, 2017

China Faces Restrictions On Investing In U.S. Tech Companies: Will U.S. National Defense Be Strengthened?

In November 2017, a new bill was introduced in the U.S. Congress entitled the Foreign Investment Review Modernization Act. The Committee on Foreign Investment In the United States (CFIUS) has the responsibility to review foreign investment in the U.S. There are continued attempts by China to invest in U.S. technology. The most recent controversy surrounds Broadcom's hostile bid to take over Qualcomm, a worldwide leader in semiconductors used in cellphones and wireless communications networks. One issue is whether Broadcom might do something to Qualcomm that would make the U.S. dependent on a Chinese company, Huawei, a very large Qualcomm rival, for its communications networks, particularly the next generation 5G networks in the U.S. These networks will bring significant new capabilities for applications, such as artificial intelligence (AI).

The new bill comes amid increasing scrutiny of defense threats under the Trump administration, as the U.S. government has blocked several investments from China, including the high-profile proposed acquisition of Lattice Semiconductor Corp by Chinese state-backed Canyon Bridge Capital Partners. Trump has also introduced a 25% tariff on steel imports, and a 10% tariff on aluminum, on the basis that U.S. manufacturing of these products in vital for U.S. national defense.

The new bill also updates the CFIUS definition of "critical technologies" to include emerging technologies that could be essential for maintaining the U.S. technological advantage over countries that pose threats. China is likely to be the most important country affected by the changes.

The bill defines "critical technology" as "technology, components, or technology items that are essential or could be essential to national security," and including "emerging technologies that could be essential for maintaining or increasing the technological advantage of the United States over countries of special concern with respect to national security, or gaining such an advantage over such countries in areas where such an advantage may not currently exist." "Presumably this category includes artificial intelligence, robotics, aerospace, etc., and could be far reaching," wrote Rob Hunter, partner at Baker & McKenzie LLP in a note, "To be sure, CFIUS can already reach investments in this category where the foreign acquirer takes 'control.' However, some investments that might not amount to 'control' would also be captured where the buyer would have access to non-public information held by a critical technology company."

ArmchairTechInvestor Opinion

China has ambitions to become the worldwide leader in defense, and defense technologies. The U.S. is beginning to fully realize the dimensions of this threat to the U.S. The first year of the Trump presidency has begun to plan for and confront these threats. A defense technology war, particularly with China and Russia, has begun.

CHAPTER 6

Chinese and U.S. Defenses, Army, Navy, Air Force, Nuclear Weapons, Missiles And Space

Defense Budget-China, Russia and the U.S.

Worldwide threats to the U.S. are increasing from China, Russia, ISIS, Iran and North Korea. President Trump has achieved defense spending increases for fiscal 2018 that will only begin to restore the U.S. defenses to the level they were at in 2009. It will take a decade or more of defense spending increases to restore U.S. military capabilities.

China Has The Second Largest Defense Budget After The U.S.: An 8% Increase Is Expected For 2018

*China's defense budget is expected to reach $173 billion in 2018, compared to $716 billion expected for the U.S. in 2019. 2018's defense budget comes to about 1.3% of China's 2017 GDP of $12.4 trillion. Analysts don't consider China's publicly announced defense spending to be entirely accurate, since defense equipment projects account for a significant amount of "off book" expenditures.

China's defense budget is so large now that double-digit annual percentage increases are no longer necessary, said military commentator Song Zhongping.

New funds are going mainly to raise living standards for service members, increase training and prepare for potential crises on the Korean Peninsula, the border with India or in the South China Sea or Taiwan Strait, Song said.

China is nearing completion of a reduction of its military forces by 300,000, taking the total to 2 million and still has the largest military in the world.

Shanghai military expert Ni Lexiong said China was seeking to avoid a full-on arms race based on quantity of weapons, choosing instead to invest in high-tech systems and training. China's range of weapons is impressive. They have:

- A second aircraft carrier they are about to launch;
- Stealth fighters they are integrating into their air force;
- An array of advanced missiles that are long-range and able to attack sea and air targets;
- China's navy has been training on the Liaoning aircraft carrier, which was bought from Ukraine and heavily refurbished.
- In April, 2017, it launched a 50,000-ton carrier built entirely on its own, based on the Ukrainian model.
- An improved Type 093B Shang class nuclear-powered attack submarine equipped with anti-ship missiles is considered only slightly inferior to the U.S. Navy's mainstay Los Angeles class boats;
- The Type 055 guided-missile destroyers are at the forefront of China's naval technology;
  - o Such vessels stand to alter the balance of power in the Indo-Pacific, where the U.S. Navy has long been dominant, and regional rivals such as Japan and India are stepping up their presence.
  - o Most navy ships already have anti-ship cruise missiles, with longer ranges than those of their U.S. counterparts.
- China has begun equipping combat units with its J-20 stealth fighter jet,
  - o This is China's answer to fifth-generation jets such as the U.S. F-22 and F-35;
- China's missile technology is also impressive;
  - o The DF-21D is built to take out an aircraft carrier; and
  - o A new air-to-air missile has a range of 249 miles that could attack U.S. air assets, such as early warning aircraft, and refueling tankers crucial to U.S. Air Force operations.

All three of China's sea forces, the navy, coast guard and maritime militia, are the largest of their types by number of ships, allowing them to "maintain presence and influence in vital seas," according to Andrew

S. Erickson of the U.S. Naval War College's China Maritime Studies Institute.

Rivals such as the U.S., Japan and India should be less anxious at the moderate rate of budget growth, although they "won't feel happy" to see rapid enhancements in China's air, naval, missile and anti-satellite capabilities, said Ni, a professor at Shanghai University of Political Science and Law.

*No. 2 spender China to boost defense spending in 2018

Associated Press, By Christopher Bodeen, Mar 5, 2018

ArmchairTechInvestor Opinion

China has a wide range of both defensive and offensive weapons systems. Their navy is predicated on having a large number of smaller ships. The U.S. is moving its navy in that direction. The U.S. has a huge superiority in aircraft carriers, which serves the U.S. well in operating in Asia, and somewhat offsets China's land-based aircraft presence.

The U.S. is also far superior in its space-based weapons systems being developed by NASA, and a range of commercial competitors, such as Space-X. U.S. space technology allows the Space Station to be accessed, and Space-X has plans for a Mars mission that it hopes will be developed by 2024.

Space-based weapons systems will become an important element of future U.S. defense capabilities.

U.S.-Defense Budget

The Defense Department Budget Is Too Low: When Can U.S. Military Capabilities Be Restored?

Despite the increases in the Department of Defense (DOD) budget, additional increases are needed. The Obama budget in 2012 projected military increases to $661 billion in 2018. In 2011, the 2011 Budget Control Act was enacted and mandated across-the-board tax cuts known as sequestration. This happened just as the worldwide threats to the U.S. were growing.

Russia and China have become more belligerent. Russia has annexed the Crimea, fomented revolt in the Ukraine, and rapidly scaled up its activities in Syria in support of Assad, and threatened U.S. planes there.

Additional Threats To U.S.

North Korea is rapidly developing nuclear weapons, and aggressively moving to develop an ICBM that can reach the U.S. Despite signing the Iran Nuclear Agreement, Iran has been aggressively expanding its influence in the Middle East, including supporting the terrorist proxies Hezbollah in Lebanon and Syria, Hamas in the West Bank, and the Houthis in Yemen. It is also working with Russia in support of Assad in Syria. The Taliban is resurgent in Afghanistan. ISIS has been very aggressive in Syria and Iraq, but is now losing there but is much more aggressive in recruiting terrorists in Europe, and to a certain extent, the U.S. It has recently expanded its activities in Asia, including The Philippines. North Korea, Russia and China are all expanding their cyber terror activities. That is a very brief summary of the increased threat facing the U.S.

According to a Wall Street Journal Opinion piece by Dick Cheney, and Congresswoman Liz Cheney, there are very serious deficiencies in all of the areas of the U.S. military. The army is outmanned, with only 58-brigade combat teams battle ready. The Navy is at its weakest level in modern times, and fewer than 50% of the Navy's aircraft are able to fly because of parts and maintenance issues. The Air Force is at its smallest level ever, and less than half of its planes are combat ready. The Marine Corps is very undermanned and equipped.

The 2018 budget Increases DOD's budget authority by $52 billion above the current 2017 level of $587 billion, to $635 billion. This comes after 5 years of significant underinvestment in defense, and is still below the $661 billion forecasted for fiscal 2018 before sequestration.

ArmchairTechInvestor Opinion

The 2018 defense budget is a modest beginning on rebuilding the U.S. military. We have outlined below the needs of the U.S. Navy, and the Army, Air Force and Marine needs will be similarly analyzed.

The U.S. faces a range of defense challenges, including China, ISIS, Iran, Russia, and North Korea. President Trump has indicated that defense spending will increase, with nuclear weapons, fighter aircraft, and the U.S. Navy having been mentioned.

A good way to look at defense spending is as a percentage of Gross Domestic Product (GDP). In FY 2017, total U.S. government spending for defense (including military defense, veterans' affairs, and foreign policy) was budgeted to be $853.6 billion. This was forecasted to be 4.4% of GDP. Military spending was budgeted at $617.0 billion, Veterans spending was budgeted at $180.8 billion, and foreign policy and foreign aid spending was budgeted at $55.8 billion.

Defense spending stood at 6.8% of GDP at the height of the Reagan defense buildup. But, beginning even before the breakup of the Soviet Union, it began a decline, reaching below 6 percent in 1990, below 4 percent in 1996 and bottoming out at 3.5 percent of GDP in 2001, about half the level of 1985. But 9/11, the terrorist attack on iconic U.S. buildings in 2001, changed that, and defense spending began a substantial increase in two stages. First, it increased to 4.6 percent by 2005 for the invasion of Iraq, and then to 5.0 percent in 2008 for the "surge" in Iraq. Spending increased further to 5.7 percent in 2011 with the stepped-up effort in Afghanistan. Defense spending is expected to decline to 3.8 percent GDP by 2020.

U.S. Defense-Nuclear Weapons-China, Russia and the U.S.

Two initiatives being pursued by the Trump administration are:

- To upgrade U.S. missile systems, including the Minuteman system, and nuclear systems such as our nuclear submarines;
- And, upgrade U.S. missile defense systems. In early March 2018, Russia announced a new missile capability that they claim makes their nuclear missiles undetectable by U.S. missile defense systems.

This appears to have been posturing by Russia prior to the reelection of Putin.

Two Nuclear Issues Are Upgrading U.S Current Nuclear Missile And Missile Defense Systems

Two initiatives being pursued by the Trump administration are:

- To upgrade our missile systems, including the Minuteman system, and nuclear systems such as our nuclear submarines; and,
- Upgrade U.S. missile defense systems;
  o In early 2018, President Putin of Russia made the statement that Russia has nuclear missiles that can evade U.S. missile defense systems;
- With regard to the missile defense systems, there are two needs that are required. The U.S. needs to be able to track and destroy:
  o Missiles that are medium range or shorter; and
  o Long range ballistic missiles that are launched into space, and need to be destroyed either before or after they go into space.

Systems such as the Aegis Missile Defense at sea, and the Terminal High Altitude Area Defense (THAAD) on land, are the two systems the may be able to destroy missiles that don't go into space.

An older missile defense system is the Groundbased Midcourse Defense (GMD) system, that has a success rate of nine of seventeen intercepts in trials, That said, a test conducted May 30, 2017 of a simulated ICBM aimed at the West Coast destroyed the mock warhead, but no more tests are planned until late in 2018. Work is underway in Congress to upgrade this to a more integrated system.

North Korea's testing of intercontinental ballistic missiles comes as the U.S. still has reliability issues with its homeland missile defense system. There is no guarantee it will destroy any incoming nuclear warhead from North Korea. The ground-based interceptors in Alaska and California, have been tested, but, U.S. government agencies have critiqued the test as not being realistic, said John Park, director of the Korea Working Group at the Harvard Kennedy School.

The Minuteman III was tested May 3, 2017 near Lompoc, CA. It is an important element of U.S. defense strategy: a fleet of intercontinental ballistic missiles capable of destroying any location on Earth with a nuclear blast in 30 minutes or less. Although the flight test proved the Minuteman is still capable of performing its mission, major components of the missile and the control centers used to launch them are obsolete and have become increasingly expensive to maintain.

At the same time, Russia and China are upgrading their nuclear capabilities. Pakistan, India and Israel continue to build new nuclear weapons and delivery systems. Air Force officials worry increasingly about the Minuteman's ability to penetrate adversaries' future missile defense systems.

The Pentagon has begun work to replace the Minuteman fleet with a new generation of missiles and launch control centers, but the plan would cost of $85 billion. Two defense firms will be awarded three-year contracts for $359 million each in 2017, with a test flight program scheduled for launch in the mid-2020s.

ArmchairTechInvestor Opinion

The ICBM missile defense system of the U.S. appears to be unreliable, despite a successful missile intercept in 2017. The neglect of this system is a remnant of the Obama administration letting U.S. military defenses decline significantly. The Minuteman missile system needs to be upgraded to allow it to be successful in evading missile defense systems of others. Similar upgrades are needed for ship missile launch systems. The threat from North Korea is real, and the U.S. needs substantial improvements in its offensive and defensive missile systems.

Defense-Missile Program

Improvements to the U.S. missile programs, including submarine, aircraft, and the ground-based Minuteman 3 missile system are long overdue, particularly in view of the increasing threat from Russia and North Korea. The first phase, the initial design, is underway and Boeing and Northrop have been selected to compete for this phase.

U.S. Selects Possible Contractors For $85 Billion Missile Program: Boeing & Northrop Selected

*The first phase of a U.S. land-based missile program replacement for the Minuteman 3, deployed in silos in the Great Plains, is underway. The first phase is a $700 million design phase, and Boeing and Northrop have been selected to compete for this business. It will include 600 land-based missiles, of which 400 will be deployed, and 200 will be used for testing.

The replacement comes at a time when China and Russia are modernizing their nuclear forces, and there is growing risk from North Korea, which has demonstrated an ICBM that might be able to reach the U.S., and in 2017 detonated successfully a Hydrogen bomb that they will attempt to put on the ICBM missile tip.

Lockheed Martin was eliminated from what is expected to be an $85 billion program. Some have estimated that the total cost could be as high as $500 billion over the next 20 years, which is about 5% of the Defense Department budget. A decision is expected in 2020 to determine the general contractor for the Ground-Based Strategic Development (GBSD) program, including the ICBMs, new communications systems, and a refurbishment of the launch silos. Aerojet Rocketdyne Inc. has announced it is building the rocket motors for Northrop.

After languishing for years due to budget cuts under the Obama administration, the GBSD program has finally been instituted as one leg of the triad of nuclear missiles, which include submarine launched missiles, and aircraft launched nuclear missiles.

This program will compete for defense dollars with contracts for new naval vessels, such as aircraft carriers, and jet fighters.

*Nuclear Missile Overhaul Falls to Small Pool of Contractors

Wall Street Journal, By Doug Cameron, August 27, 2017

ArmchairTechInvestor Opinion

The U.S. is overdue in modernizing its triad of nuclear weapons systems. The Minuteman 3 system was being designed in 1963, when Brad Peery worked on the design of a 3rd order control system for the Minuteman while he was at TRW Space Technology Labs. The defense buildup needs to continue after the Trump Presidency, since it will take at least 20 years to upgrade all of the U.S. military capabilities.

Defense-Air Force

Trump Is Trying To Restore Air Force Readiness: Will He Be Successful?

The Air Force is at its smallest level ever, and less than half of its planes are combat ready. Obama seriously depleted the capabilities of the U.S. military, including the Air Force. While Trump is attempting to restore our military capabilities, it will take some time to restore the Air Force's readiness.

According to Maj. Gen. Jim Martin, the Air Force budget director, the budget addresses critical shortfalls while building a larger, more capable and more lethal Air Force.

Addressing readiness deficiencies, the budget funds, among other elements:

- Flying hours to executable levels and weapons system sustainment to near capacity;
- Two additional F-16 training squadrons and ensures advance weapons schools and combat exercises are fully funded to restore full-spectrum readiness long-term;
- The Intercontinental Ballistic Missile Program;
- The space procurement strategy;
- The nuclear enterprise;
- Munitions to support ongoing operations; and
- Replenishing current inventories.

Delaying modernization has become a trend in recent years, allowing potential adversaries to narrow the capability gap. This budget addresses modernization by:

- Advancing recapitalization of the current fighter and tanker fleets by procuring 46 F-35A Lightning and 15 KC-46 Pegasus aircraft;
- Continuing modernization efforts for the 4th and 5th generation aircraft;
- Continuing efforts from fiscal 2017 to maximize munitions production capacity to sustain global precision attack capabilities.

The fiscal 2018 Air Force space investment budget request addresses the development of resilient capabilities and architectures to negate or defeat threats. Space investment elements include:

- Funding:
  - o   The Space-Based Infrared System;
  - o   The Space Modernization Initiative;
  - o   Tech Maturation; and
  - o   Cyber Security;
- Modernization of protected satellite communications and development and fielding of space battle management command and control.

The research, development, test and evaluation investments saw notable growth this in 2017, and are designed to pay significant future dividends through game-changing technologies that, when fielded, will increase lethality and provide the joint force a technological advantage.

The F-35 is the core next generation aircraft program, and will replace several existing Air Force planes. The Air Force is putting much of its aircraft eggs in this basket.

ArmchairTechInvestor Opinion

The increased Air Force budget is a step along a path that should take about five years to restore the Air Force to full readiness. It should run into little opposition in getting basic approval from the Congress.

Defense-Air Force-U.S.

The U.S. Air Force is at its smallest level ever, and its readiness is seriously depleted. Aircraft modernization is underway. Space modernization is also being undertaken. The F-35 will replace several existing aircraft programs. Readiness deficiencies are being addressed, and flying hours are being increased.

Defense-Navy-U.S.

It is planned to increase the Naval fleet from 275 to 350 ships, but this will take additional resources. The 2018 budget adds 8 additional ships. The Navy would like to add one additional carrier to the current eleven. It is likely that the Navy will become more mobile in response to the current threats, particularly from Russia and China, which are also increasing their Navies.

The Trump Naval Buildup Is About To Begin: What Will Be Its Direction?

In 2017, President Trump has promised to expand the current Naval fleet from 275 to 350, which is near the 355 that the Navy Department was recommending. The U.S. is on the way to 308 ships, but building up to 350, or more, will likely require significant additional shipbuilding resources. However, the numbers can be reached in different ways. Our current program is built around carriers. Another possibility is to add ships that create a more mobile Navy, which may be better suited to the current threats we face, particularly from Russia and China.

Trump's 2018 budget includes 8 additional ships, which are likely to be small surface ships. The U.S. has 11 aircraft carriers, and, although it will take at least a decade, the Navy would like to add one more to the fleet. To reach a 350 ship level will take decades, which will be complicated by ship retirements. The U.S. has a substantial competitive advantage, particularly when confronting China, in submarines.

The Navy would add 16 more large surface combatants built by both General Dynamics and Huntington Ingalls, four more amphibious warfare ships, and 18 more attack submarines from Huntington Ingalls and

General Dynamics Electric Boat. The plan also calls for three more combat logistics force ships, three more expeditionary support base ships, and two more command and support ships.

Indicative of other Navy difficulties, are longer that desired deployments, and maintenance requirements that include not being able to deploy a carrier to the Persian Gulf because of long-deferred of maintenance.

Sen. John McCain, R-Ariz., is the chairman of the Armed Services Committed. In a January, 2017 white paper, he proposed procuring 59 ships by 2022, including five fast-attack submarines, five fleet oilers, three destroyers, two amphibious ships, two afloat forward staging bases, two undersea surveillance ships, two survey ships, two patrol ships, one aircraft carrier and one new small surface combatant.

McCain also advocated abandoning the Littoral Combat Ship in favor of speeding up the procurement of the next small surface combatant, a true frigate to replace the LCS. Under McCain's timeline, the Navy would buy only the bare minimum of littoral combat ships to "serve as a bridge" for when the new small surface combatants begin arriving in 2022, about seven years ahead of the current plan.

McCain also said the Navy should focus investment on undersea warfare, where the U.S. has an advantage, and should procure two to three manned submarines per year in 2020, and four per year starting in 2021, to give industry time to ramp up to meet the government's need.

ArmchairTechInvestor Opinion

On June 3, 2017 President Trump nominated Richard Spencer to be Secretary of the Navy, after his prior nominee withdrew in February. This did not allow a coherent Naval policy to be developed and presented in time for the fiscal 2019 discussions in February, 2018. However, this book has outlined what we believe will be the issues. The bottom line is that the Navy is likely to be rebuilt in ways that will allow The U.S. to effectively confront Iran in the Persian Gulf, China in the South China Seas and the Indian Ocean, and Russia worldwide, while substantially expanding the U.S. submarine fleet.

Defense-Space-NASA And SpaceX

NASA

SpaceX and other space companies are competing against NASA. These satellite launch systems are smaller than some being developed by NASA. Lockheed Martin and Boeing are the primary contractors on NASA's SLS/Orion satellites. They include a very powerful Space Launch System rocket, which is being developed by Boeing for NASA.

NASA vs. SpaceX

SpaceX is successfully competing against NASA using reusable rockets. It has launched a spacecraft to the Space Station. SpaceX has executed successful launches of its reusable Falcon 9 space launch system. Falcon 9 engines are reused by landing them on an ocean platform. Its spacecraft are also recovered after reentry. Twenty-four launches were scheduled for 2017, but 18 were completed. launches could grow to 52 in 2019, or one per week. SpaceX has announced a new launch system, BFM that is planned to send a payload to Mars by 2024. This is a much larger launch system than the Falcon 9.

SpaceX Continues Its Space Successes: However, Other Companies And Countries Will Be Competing

In 2017, SpaceX executed many successful launches of its reusable Falcon 9 space launch system. The first was from the east coast, and successfully put a Bulgarian telecommunications satellite in orbit. Its engines, which were being reused, were successfully recovered by landing them on an ocean platform.

The second launch was two days later from the west coast. It involved putting into orbit 10 Iridium satellites. Iridium has an existing data and voice satellite system that will be replaced by 75 satellites, with six more SpaceX launches planned to deploy and replace the existing satellite system. Iridium is a $3 billion satellite system, and the largest, SpaceX customer. Again, the launch vehicle was reused, and also the engines were recovered by landing them successfully on an ocean platform.

SpaceX is projecting that by successfully recovering launch engines and space capsules, it will significantly reduce the costs of its space launches. Their plan is for as many as 52 launches in 2019, following the 18 launches in 2017. It is unclear whether launch costs are coming down as much as expected.

India and China Space Programs

India and China are also planning their own space launches for others. They are both expected to be competitors of SpaceX. India expects to spend $6 billion on its space program over the next 5 years, launching over 25 satellites. In May, India launched its "South Asia Satellite", which Sri Lanka, Afghanistan, and Nepal can use at no cost. India has very low manufacturing costs. Competition with China is a prime focus of the Indian satellite program. India has satellite ground stations in Indonesia, Brunei, and Mauritius. It is also building a satellite ground station in Vietnam. The Indian network can also be used for military purposes, including monitoring activities in the South China Sea, which China is attempting to dominate. China has strenuously objected to India's activities.

China Space Program

China offered to build telecommunications satellites for Afghanistan, Sri Lanka and Nepal, where India is offering free use of their satellites. China is developing a trading network called One Belt, One Road. It is an ambitious project that includes a traditional land-base trading route from China to Europe. It also includes satellite expenditures that are expected to be about four times those of India.

India Space Program

India is also offering its technology to the private sector. It is planning to sell its small launch rocket, the PSLV, to a joint venture. It is also planning to license production of its larger GSLV rockets to local industrial firms.

U.S. Space Program

The U.S. space program is about $40 billion per year, and appears to be about six times that of China. In addition to SpaceX, other competitors in this arena are Richard Branson's One-Web Ltd., China-based startups One-Space and ExPace. Astrome Technologies, an Indian start-up company plans to launch 150 satellites to provide wireless communications to difficult-to-reach locations. In 2017, Team Indus, a Bangalore-based Indian company, planned to launch a moon-lander in a Google Lunar XPrize competition.

The Trump budget for NASA is $16.9 billion, down about 12% from the current 2017 budget of $19.2 billion. Lockheed Martin and Boeing are the primary contractors on NASA's SLS/Orion satellites. They include a very powerful Space Launch System rocket, which is being developed by Boeing. SpaceX has said that they will develop even more powerful launchers, but they are not close to being ready. These NASA launches should be manned flights to the moon and Mars. The total cost is expected to be about $1.6 billion for the first vehicle, with yearly expenses running about $300 million. The first unmanned launch is scheduled for September, 2018. It now appears the first launch could be manned, and might be in 2019. This could cut out two years of development, as the first manned launch was scheduled for 2021. One SLS/Orion launch per year is scheduled.

SpaceX, and NASA budget cuts, appear to be putting pressure on NASA to reduce the costs of the SLS/Orion. Lockheed and Boeing are already talking about 50% cost cuts in the future.

ArmchairTechInvestor Opinion

Renewed space competition is underway, and Elon Musk's SpaceX appears to be a leader in the race. However some large competitors could emerge, many of them driven by Indian space launch capabilities. Space is an important frontier that is drawing many participants. It is also important to the U.S. from a defense standpoint, particularly with North Korea developing nuclear weapons, and ICBMs capable of delivering them to the U.S., or putting them into orbit.

NASA vs. SpaceX

SpaceX is exposing NASA's Development Weaknesses

SpaceX, the private rocket company being funded by Elon Musk, is developing reusable launch vehicles and space capsules for space flight. Missions include flying in earth orbit, as well as traveling to the moon and Mars. Landing the launch vehicles and recovering them, and recovering the space capsules, could substantially reduce the cost of space travel. SpaceX is planning both flights with crews or passengers, and cargo flights.

On March 30, 2017. A successful SpaceX Falcon 9 launch occurred that reused launchers from a previous flight for the first time. By reusing launchers, their cost is expected to drop by about 10% in the next few years, and long-term by as much as 30%.

Jeff Bezos, the founder of Amazon, is working through Blue Origin LLC with SpaceX to get customers for their launches. It currently takes 4 months to relaunch a rocket, and the objective is to eventually bring that down to several days or less. According to the Wall Street Journal, launch revenue is expected to be about $2.2 billion by 2020. Jeff Bezos has said he will sell $1 billion of his Amazon stock per year to help fund this development. These launches are expected to be substantially less expensive than NASA's launch of its Orion satellites.

ArmchairTechInvestor Opinion

The moon and Mars space launch program will accelerate will the competition between SpaceX and NASA. SpaceX is developing a commercial operation that will include both project and space ride operations. Having the marketing operations of Blue Origin could reduce SpaceX launch times to 1 per day compared to 1 per year for NASA. SpaceX is projecting profitability before 10 years, while NASA has no plans for profitability. Eventually SpaceX may be able to land astronauts on the moon, as NASA plans to do. The differences between these governmental and private space programs could be a good example of the cost savings that can be achieved by private operations compared to governmental programs.

SpaceX Continues To Challenge And Supplement The Work Of NASA. A Whole New Era Of Space Travel Is Underway.

Elon Musk's SpaceX continues to make significant progress in developing a reusable space launch system. NASA is also moving to develop a much more powerful launch vehicle, and to reduce the cost of space system purchases. A successful SpaceX launch in late 2017 moved their program forward. Used in the launch was a refurbished cargo capsule. The capsule was filled with materials for the Space Station. This launch followed a successful launch two months earlier that resulted in the launch vehicle being vertically landed so that it can be reused also.

One of the difficulties in recovering the cargo capsule is damage that is done to the heat shield when the capsule reenters the atmosphere. A new heat shield was used in a 2017 launch, and it will be interesting to see what happens when this capsule is recovered after it completes its mission to deliver materials to the Space Station. Another issue is protecting the capsule from water damage when new parachutes guide the capsule into the ocean. An ocean landing is a friendly landing place because it absorbs the capsule impact by being more resilient to the impact, but presents a challenge in protecting the capsule from water damage caused by possible leaks.

ArmchairTechInvestor Opinion

The U.S. needs to dominate outer space for a variety of reasons. The most important issue is raised by the North Korean missile threat. One threat is the possibility that an orbital missile might be used to disable the U.S. electrical network. Of course, there is also the issue of North Korea trying to launch a nuclear missile at the U.S.

NASA finally seems to be developing reusable and more powerful launch systems, after having to rely on the Russians to resupply the Space Station. Space travel by individuals could happen in the near future.

The Challenge For SpaceX Will Be To Make Its Falcon 9 Spacecraft Safe Enough To Carry Astronauts For NASA in 2018-Will It Happen?

SpaceX is all about reusable space vehicles. On December 15, 2017, it launched a flight for NASA to resupply the international Space Station. The space vehicle included a reused Falcon 9 booster rocket, the first launch for a reusable vehicle for the U.S. government. There has been some skepticism about the reliability of reused space launch systems. The U.S. military also seems inclined to employ reused space launch vehicles.

The recent results have been positive for SpaceX. However, they have plans to send astronauts into space in 2018. NASA has safety and reliability requirements. The risks include blastoff risks, possible radiation dangers, and splashdown uncertainties.

Boeing also has a contract with NASA to send astronauts to and from the Space Station, but also has its own issues. Their manned vehicle, the CST-100 Starliner, has had excess weight, and vibrations during launch problems. Boeing does have other possibilities. They can fly astronauts on their Atlas V rockets, which have a longer and better safety record than the SpaceX Falcon 9. They also believe the Starliner will be a safe and robust vehicle that will meet all NASA mandatory safety requirements, and will be the lowest risk system available to NASA.

SpaceX is using a very different spacecraft design that allows them to reuse their launch vehicles and space capsules. However there have been some reliability issues for an internal fuel tank. Elon Musk is the owner of SpaceX. His team is redesigning the internal fuel tank, and needs to demonstrate the reliability of an internal helium tank that they plan to use.

*SpaceX Launch Reuses Booster For NASA Flight, Wall Street Journal, by Andy Pasztor, December 15, 1017

ArmchairTechInvestor Opinion

SpaceX is revolutionizing the space launch industry. Their ability to use space launch vehicles and space capsules that have been recaptured and reused potentially allows them to launch space vehicles at a very rapid rate, and significantly reduce the cost per launch. 2018 will be a pivotal year for them. They will need to demonstrate that reused vehicles can reliably transport astronauts to and from space.

Boeing and others will have the ability to reliably transport astronauts into and out of space. On December 17, 2017, The U.S. used a Russian Soyuz space capsule to deliver 3 astronauts to and from the Space Station. It will be important for SpaceX to demonstrate that they can deliver astronauts into and out of space safely and at a lower cost. Space X also plans to deliver astronauts to Mars as early as 2024. It takes a giant launch vehicle to reach Mars. If they are successful in meeting that time schedule, they are likely to be the first company to send astronauts to Mars, and should beat the others by years.

SpaceX Continues Innovate By Announcing Plans For A Mars Flight By 2024: Who Can Compete?

SpaceX has continued its success with its Falcon 9 space launch system, launched 18 launch vehicles in 2017. It has a strong customer base, including one with NASA to deliver supplies to the Space Station.

*Elon Musk unveiled plans for a giant new Big Fucking Rocket (BFR) that could be used to launch a Mars vehicle by as early as 2022, or 2024. This could be as much as 10 years earlier than planned by any other company or country. It will be the biggest rocket ever built, with a capsule larger than a superjumbo airliner. This would be a fleet of extremely powerful rockets and spacecraft. The market is commercial satellite operators. Musk plans to use cash flow from current operations to finance his Mars ambitions. The Falcon 9 is operating successfully. The company's Falcon Heavy is four years late. Both of these systems will be replaced by the BFR. Also, a manned Dragon capsule has not yet flown and is just as late as the Falcon Heavy. Outside experts have estimate the cost of the Mars mission at $10 billion. SpaceX's current customers are commercial customers and the Pentagon.

The Falcon 9 has a payload of 5 tons. By comparison, the Heavy has a planned payload of 30 tons, and the BFR is planned to carry 150 tons. Musk said that he was "fairly confident" that in 2024 as many as four BFRs could be launched, with two of them carrying crews. The SFR would be capable of carrying passengers to Mars. Such a round trip is estimated by Musk to take six to twelve months. A previous estimate is that it could cost a person $200,000 to go to Mars.

***Musk's Mars Shot: To Red Planet by 2024**, Wall Street Journal, by Andy Pasztor, September 29, 2017

ArmchairTechInvestor Opinion

Space X continues its impressive success with its Falcon 9 reusable rocket system. It has very aggressive plans for its massive BFR rocket system that could make a trip to Mars possible by at least 2024. The BFR could also replace both the Falcon 9 and the Heavy, but there are significant financial risks to the strategy because of the huge payloads the BFR would carry, and the issue of finding customers needing that much capacity.

CHAPTER 7

Foreign Policy-Europe, Russia, the Balkans, Ukraine, NATO and the United Nations

Foreign Policy-European Union (EU)

Russia and Turkey are fomenting discord in the Balkans. The Balkan countries are looking to a reluctant EU to help them. The U.S. is also an alternative, but the U.N. has a history of bringing peace in the region. Should none of these entities step up to provide assistance, the countries could turn to Turkey and Russia.

Another EU issue is the U.S. withdrawing from the Iran Nuclear Agreement. They are looking for ways to keep the Agreement alive without having U.S. participation.

The European Union And The Balkans' Defense Are Shared Issues With The U.S. Will The U.S. Step Up?

The European Union (EU) has many defense issues that could draw the U.S. into a conflict because of the U.S. guarantees to defend NATO countries against attack. There are other issues, such as immigration, that can affect the U.S. because of the ease of flying from Europe to the U.S. with European passports.

Politicians in Poland and Hungary are at odds with the EU. The Hungarian Prime Minister, Viktor Orban, said that the biggest opponents are not the opposition parties to his reelection, but Brussels and Berlin, because of the EU requirement that EU countries open their borders to immigrants. Those two countries and the Czech Republic have refused to comply with an EU court decision requiring the taking in of refugees.

Another issue that differs between the EU and the U.S. is free trade. The EU is in favor of what they call free trade, and are negotiating with New

Zealand and Australia. The U.S. has issues with the EU over barriers they have erected to disadvantage U.S. company exports.

There are issues between the EU and Russia over attempts by Turkey and Russia to exert influence, and possibly even try to acquire, countries in the Balkans, Serbia and Albania through their proxies in those countries. Russia is supporting the Serbian government to acquire large portions of Bosnia populated by Serbs. Turkey's support could aid Albania in acquiring heavily Albanian Kosovo and Macedonia where an Albanian minority would like to reunite with Albania. EU membership is being sought by Serbia, Macedonia, Montenegro, Kosovo and Bosnia to thwart the aggressive regional ambitions of Russia and Turkey. With the UK withdrawing from the EU, the EU seems reluctant to add new members with their own territorial issues. For the EU to be a solution, the U.S. will need to step up to help save the Balkans.

ArmchairTechInvestor Opinion

The countries of the EU have not met their own defense needs, nor contributed meaningfully to the defeat of ISIS in the Middle East. In addition, Turkey and Russia are threatening to foment the land acquisition ambitions of Balkan countries. The UN has traditionally played a role in stabilizing the region, but the countries are now turning to the U.S., if the EU will not extend a helping hand to them. The other alternative is for them to rely on Russia and Turkey.

Foreign Policy-Russia

Russia's main policy can be defined simply. Their actions include: Undermining democracies; Taking advantage of ethnic and religious tensions; and, developing new locations for gathering intelligence, and projecting military influence. Assisting Russia could be the negative reaction to U.S.-Russian sanctions and possible Trump campaign collusion, that are being investigated by the U.S,, Russian involvement has been shown in the U.S. in election in 2016. Even if collusion is not shown by the special investigator or the Congress, this has been detrimental to the U.S. because of the diversion of attention from many pressing world events.

Russia And Chechnya Have Reached A Fragile Truce: Will The Ambitions Of The Chechnyan Leader Fracture The Peace?

*Chechnya has been a thorn in the side of Russia. The autonomous region is under the leadership of a Russian appointed leader, after years of fighting for independence from Russia. That leader, Ramzan Kadyrov, is now angling to become a leader of the worldwide Muslim movement to impose Sharia law that governs as an integrated church-state, with strict laws, as it is doing in Chechnya. Kadyrov has recently built his Muslim following by denouncing the situation in Myanmar, where Muslims are being herded into next-door neighbor Bangladesh.

After a decade of unsuccessfully fighting for independence, the Chechnya autonomous region is now firmly under the control of its Russian-appointed leader, Ramzan Kadyrov, although separatist groups continue low-level guerrilla attacks. Chechnya is oil rich. The region has been relatively stable under Mr. Kadyrov. However, his government has been accused of human rights violations, including kidnappings and torture, and controlling the media. He has been pro-Moscow, and appears to have a strong relationship with Vladimir Putin, although some of his policies and politics are anathema to that relationship.

Oil-rich Chechnya has enjoyed a period of relative stability under Mr. Kadyrov. But critics have accused the pro-Moscow leader and his government of suppressing media and other freedoms, as well as human rights violations including kidnappings and torture. He is a Sunni leader that has espoused a softness that allows him to attract millions from the Sufi religious order, and even Shiites. He is said to be an ambitious person that sees himself a broad Muslim leader that also promotes Russia. As a Russian political leader, Kadyrov provides Russia with access to regional Islamic meetings.

*Chechnya Leader Seeks Global Muslim Role**, Wall Street Journal, By Yaroslav Trofimov, September 21, 2017

ArmchairTechInvestor Opinion

Ramzan Kadyrov, as a Muslim leader chosen by Putin to lead Chechnya, has vaulted himself into a position as a possible Muslim leader with broad appeal. His ruthless leadership and promoting of Sharia law make him an unacceptable partner of Western democracies. He is also giving Russia access to the Muslim religion, and his policies have been reconciled with those of Russia. Kadyrov could become a Muslim leader to be reckoned with by the U.S., if he can broaden his appeal within the Muslim world. His policies are often at odds with those of Russia, and he is seen by some as a leader who might eclipse Putin in governing Russia. However, given Putin's ruthless ambitions, that seems to be unlikely.

Russia Is Taking Advantage Of U.S. Policy Lapses, And Is Expanding Its Global Influence

Russia's main policy can be defined simply. Their actions include:

- Undermining democracies;
- Taking advantage of ethnic and religious tensions; and,
- Developing new locations for gathering intelligence, and projecting military influence.

President Obama's foreign policy lapses created many problems. The vacuum he left in Iraq and Syria has been beneficial for many parties. ISIS moved in and established caliphates in Mosel, Iraq and Raqqa, Syria, and took control of large parts of both countries. Syria went through its own civil war, with various militant groups fighting Bashar Al-Assad, and his Syrian dictatorship.

The U.S. was largely on the sidelines. Obama wanted to overthrow Assad, but couldn't find a strategy to make that happen. Obama drew a red line over Assad's use of chemical weapons, but he failed to respond when Assad used chemical weapons in late 2015 in the Syrian town of Sarmeen and Idlib Province. This is just one chemical weapons attack account from Syria. Russia and Iran stepped in and supported Assad, and his power has improved immensely, with ISIS being substantially defeated, and Iran on its way to developing a military supply route from Iran to Lebanon, and then to the Mediterranean.

Turkey, a NATO country, has defied NATO and reached an agreement with Russia to purchase the latter's most sophisticated missile-defense system, the S-400. Under the $2.5 billion agreement, Ankara would receive two batteries of the antiaircraft missile from Moscow in 2017, and then produce two more batteries in Turkey."

*With the world's attention focused on the question of Russian influence in the United States elections, Russia is making inroads in another region vital to both the United States and Europe, the five North African states on the southern Mediterranean.

Russian and Algerian officials, at a St. Petersburg shipyard in 2017, christened the first of two so-called Black Hole submarines built for the Algerian navy. The same day, news broke that Russia had deployed Special Forces and drones to a base in western Egypt, to bolster a militia leader in neighboring Libya. Late in 2016, the secretary of Moscow's national security council traveled to Morocco. The King invited Russian President Vladimir Putin to repay the visit he had made to Moscow earlier in the year. Also, in Tunisia, Russian tourism increased by 1,000% in 2016, and Russia had signed a deal in the fall of 2016 to build a nuclear power plant.

*Russia's Charm Offensive in North Africa: Its Growing Economic and Military Influence in the Region

By Oren Kessler and Boris Zilberman, Foreign Affairs, April 3, 2017

ArmchairTechInvestor Opinion

Russia and the U.S. are on collision courses in Europe, especially with regard to the small countries that surround Russia and are vulnerable to Russian attack. Russian sanctions are now in place over their meddling in the U.S. presidential elections. Sanctions are also in place because of Russia's annexation of Crimea, and inciting violence in Eastern Ukraine. Russia is also aggressively expanding its influence in the Middle East and Africa.

While the U.S. is embroiled in political chaos in the House and Senate, thanks to Democratic obstinance, and fractures in the Republican Party, Russia is quietly expanding its influence in Africa, the Middle East, and even South America.

Russia Is Being Sanctioned For Interfering in the 2016 Presidential Election: Russia Has Responded Negatively

The U.S. intelligence community has concluded that Russia sought to interfere in the 2016 presidential election. A Russian sanction bill also included sanctions on Iran and North Korea. The bill passed the House by a lopsided vote of 419-3.

A January, 2017 report from the U.S. Intelligence agencies said the Russian interference was directed from the highest level of government. The actions it took included hacking state election systems, and infiltrating and leaking information from party committees and strategists. It disseminated through social media and other entities negative stories on Democratic Nominee Hillary Clinton and positive and negative ones about Donald Trump. The House bill, through negotiations, included a May, 2017 House bill that punished North Korea, and a June bill that punished Iran.

The U.S. Senate approved the sanctions by a vote of 98-2. One part of the bill was contentious in that it may infringe on presidential authority. President Trump will be required to consult with the Congress before he relaxes any of the sanctions on Moscow, or restores Russia's control over the compounds that Obama sanctioned by requiring Russia to send back the diplomats in those facilities for interference in the presidential election. Mr. Trump expressed skepticism about the findings of the intelligence report that preceded the bill. However, he signed the bill for national security reasons, despite believing the bill was seriously flawed.

The sanctions against Russia:

- Included restrictions on the extension of credit to Russian entities;
- Mandated sanctions on those deemed to be undermining cybersecurity;
  - o   As well as those engaging in significant transactions involving the Russian defense and intelligence sectors.

Russia's response was to reduce the U.S. diplomatic presence in Moscow to 455 from slightly over 1000 people, the same number of Russian diplomats operating in the U.S. Many of the people working in the U.S. Embassy and three consulates are local Russia hires, so it is unclear how many U.S. personnel were involved when the changes took effect on September 1, 2017.

ArmchairTechInvestor Opinion

There can be no doubt that Russia interfered in the U.S. presidential elections. Some of the more damaging leaks to Hillary Clinton came from WikiLeaks. What connection the January report found between WikiLeaks and Russia is unclear. It is also clear that the Russians tried to interfere in local balloting at many states, so their denial of innocence rings hollow. There was obviously interference, and within Russia, that could only have happened with the knowledge and presumed approval of Putin.

Russia Is Promoting Terrorism To Enhance Russia's Territorial Ambitions: What Should The U.S. And The EU Do?

Russia In the Eastern Ukraine

Image: Russia in Eastern Ukraine
Image Source: Ukraine Ministry of Defense

Two main areas where Russia has territorial ambitions are Ukraine and the Balkans. The Russian territorial ambitions became apparent when it acquired Crimea, and supported terrorists in the Eastern Ukraine trying to break off from Ukraine. The European Union and the United States fully back Kiev's claim that Russia started and supported the war in order to meddle and disrupt its Western neighbor's affairs, after its February 2014 ouster of a Kremlin-backed Ukrainian regime.

Ukraine's subsequent embrace of the West was followed by Russia's annexation of Crimea, in March 2014, and the takeover of government buildings in the east in April by groups of armed men who swore allegiance to Moscow.

Kiev responded by launching a military offensive to win back the separatist region. But, Russia denies any involvement in the war, despite its soldiers being repeatedly captured or killed in the war zone and tanks and other heavy weapons being spotted crossing the border into Ukraine.

The U.S. has imposed sanctions on Russia, as has the European Union, and other countries. Russia responded by putting in place a total ban on food imports from the U.S., Norway, Canada and Australia. The sanctions contributed to the substantial decline of the Russian Ruble, and a continuing financial crisis in Russia. They also caused economic damage to a number of EU countries, with the total losses estimated at €100 billion. According to Ukrainian officials, the sanctions forced Russia to change its approach toward Ukraine, and undermined military advances in the region. The sanctions will not be removed until Moscow fulfills the Minsk II agreements.

Russia controls two areas of Ukraine, the so-called Donetsk (Donbas) and Luhansk "people's republics", which go by the acronyms DNR and LNR. These areas have a population of 3.5 million. Russia is accelerating the integration of Donbas into Russia. The DNR and LNR have been converting their economies to the Russian Ruble. Russia's objective might not be to totally integrate these regions into Russia, but rather that Russia have control of these regions, not Ukraine. They are doing this in a variety of ways, including taking over companies, issuing Russian passports, and managing the economies or the DNR and the LNR.

ArmchairTechInvestor Opinion

The Ukraine is applying for NATO membership, and attempting to align itself with the west. Relations between NATO and Ukraine date back to the early 1990s, and have since developed into one of the most substantial of NATO's partnerships. Since 2014, in the wake of the Russia-Ukraine conflict, cooperation has been intensified in critical areas. The U.S. needs to continue to support Ukraine, and oppose this and other efforts of Russia to expand its geographical influence, including in the Balkans. In December, 2017, Trump approved sending weapons to the Ukraine.

Foreign Policy-Ukraine

The Ukraine is under pressure from Russia. Russia has annexed Crimea and has supported with weapons a breakaway from the Ukraine by a dissident group in Eastern Ukraine. The U.S. has just begun supporting the Ukraine with weapons, and has been threatened by Russia, for such support being provided.

Russia Annexing Crimea Was The First Step. Step Two Is Russia Interfering In Eastern Ukraine. Where Will It Stop?

Ukrainian Leader Petro Peroshenko met with President Trump in June, 2017 to gain U.S. support in confronting Russian aggression in Eastern Ukraine. Trump, not mentioning the reform agenda, and anti-corruption efforts of Ukraine, called the countries "strategic partners". Following the forcible annexation of Crimea by Russia, in 2014 the Minsk Agreement was adopted by the U.N. The Minsk Agreement was designed to deliver a ceasefire in the eastern Donbas region of Ukraine and alleviate the war in that region. Russia continues to be actively involved in Donbas, despite U.S. sanctions that the U.S. has declared that will not be eliminated until Russia complies with the Minsk Agreement.

According to a Wall Street Journal article by James Marson, Vladislav Surkov, a powerful Russian advisor, was the Moscow point person "in encouraging, organizing, and managing the pro-Russian separatists fighting Ukraine's central government." In the 2000's he served as Putin's chief of staff and helped design the Russian leader's tightly controlled political system. He molded the leadership and structure of the separatists in the Donbas region to bring it under Moscow's control.

* **Kremlin Envoy Playing A Central Role in Eastern Ukraine,** Wall Street Journal, by James Marson, August 20, 2017

The history of Ukraine with Russia is of interest. Soon after the Bolsheviks seized control in immense, troubled Russia in November 1917. One of pre-war Russia's most prosperous areas, the vast, flat Ukraine (the name can be translated as at the border or borderland) was one of the major wheat-producing regions of Europe as well as rich with mineral resources, including vast deposits of iron and coal. Ukraine proclaimed itself a republic within the structure of a federated Russia, then declaring its complete independence in January 1918. In 1922, Ukraine became one of the original constituent republics of the Union of Soviet Socialist Republics (U.S.S.R.). It would not regain its independence until the U.S.S.R.'s collapse in 1991.

ArmchairTechInvestor Opinion

Ukraine is seeking backing in Europe, and would undoubtedly like to become a member of NATO. It was a flashpoint for Russia when a Ukrainian leader who supported Russia was defeated.

The U.S. can show more support for Ukraine by increasing sanctions on Russia and supplying defensive weapons to Ukraine so they can engage with the Russian supplied, and organized separatists in Eastern Ukraine. In early 2018, the arms may already be flowing from the U.S.

The Balkans

Turkey and Russia are threatening to foment the land acquisition ambitions of Balkan countries. The U.N. has traditionally played a role in stabilizing the region, but the countries are now turning to the U.S., if the EU will not extend a helping hand to them. Another alternative is for them to rely on Russia and Turkey.

There are issues between the EU and Russia over attempts by Turkey and Russia to exert influence, and possibly even try to acquire, countries in the Balkans, Serbia and Albania through their proxies in those countries. Russia is supporting the Serbian government to acquire large portions of Bosnia populated by Serbs. Turkey's support could aid Albania in acquiring heavily Albanian Kosovo and Macedonia, where an Albanian minority would like to reunite with Albania. EU membership is being sought by Serbia, Macedonia, Montenegro, Kosovo and Bosnia to thwart the aggressive regional ambitions of Russia and Turkey. With the UK withdrawing from the EU, the EU seems reluctant to add new members with their own territorial issues. For the EU to be a solution, the U.S. will need to step up to help save the Balkans.

The Balkans

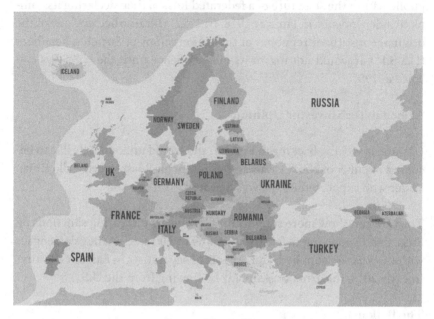

Image: The Balkans
Image Source: Getty Images

NATO

President Trump had characterized NATO as being obsolete, but he has changed his tone to encourage the NATO countries to step up to their defense responsibilities. They have committed to spend 2% of their GDPs on defense, and countries such as Germany and France have not met those responsibilities. It appears that Trump may have goaded some NATO members into moving toward meeting their defense spending obligations to NATO.

Trump's Partial About Face On NATO: It's No Longer Obsolete

NATO is a vital element in providing for the security of Europe, and confronting Russia's territorial ambitions. President Trump has dropped his assessment that NATO is obsolete, but in early 2018, he was still insisting that each of the NATO countries pay 2% of their GDP that they have committed to pay for defense. The U.S. paid 3.61% of GDP for defense in 2016.

Of the 27 other members of NATO, only 4 are spending 2% or more of GDP on defense, including the UK, which spent 2.17% in 2016. Germany has been criticized because it spends only about 1.2% of GDP on defense. NATO Secretary General Jens Stoltenberg met with President Trump in 2017, and made a very good case that NATO members are making an effort to increase defense spending. This meeting appears to have convinced President Trump that the NATO members are trying to move toward meeting their 2% commitments. NATO had a NATO leaders' meeting on May 25, 2017, which President Trump attended. A U.S. initiative was introduced that would have countries committing to specific defense spending goals by 2024, with yearly targets.

Russia annexed Crimea in 2014, in a bloodless coup. It continues to support rebels in the Ukraine that are trying to destabilize the country. This is done in the name of supporting ethnic Russians in meeting their political objectives. This same rationale can be used to support ethnic Russians in other countries to destabilize those countries. The Ukraine has applied for NATO membership, which would require the NATO members to support them in fighting off an aggressive Russia.

There is the belief that Russia's goal is to restore their boundaries to include countries that they view as having been taken from them. Political destabilization of these countries by Russia should be expected. NATO needs to counter this threat by providing physical security, as well standing up to the political subversion of Moscow. In the face of these risks, NATO also wants work with Russia to fight terrorism, and address Europe's immigration crisis.

ArmchairTechInvestor Opinion

NATO is clearly not obsolete. It is the primary obstacle facing Russia in blocking its expansion ambitions. Most of its members appear to be receptive to rebuilding their defense capabilities, and in standing up to Russian efforts to undermine some of its members. This renewed effort should manifest itself over the next 8 years. The NATO Secretary General attributed some of the NATO member commitment to the criticism of President Trump. NATO's renewal appears to be a success story of the Trump Administration.

United Nations

The U.S. has proposed that the U.N. reorganize itself to become more efficient, a proposal that has been accepted without rancor. The U.N. may be able to operate more effectively, but it is the only organization that has been willing to go into places such as Africa to promote peace, fight terrorism, and eliminate human suffering in disadvantaged countries.

The United Nations Is Controversial: However, They Can Be Crucial To Fighting Terrorism in Africa.

The United Nations (U.N.) is a controversial body. It is accused of being blatantly biased against Israel, one the U.S.'s strongest allies. It is also accused of being ineffectual in dealing with Iran, North Korea, and Syria. The U.S. has asked the U.N. to cut costs, and is planning on providing reduced funding to the U.N.

The United States is the biggest U.N. contributor, paying 22% of the $5.4 billion core budget and 28.5% of the $7.9 billion peacekeeping budget. The Trump Budget proposal in 2017 cut about a third from U.S. diplomacy and aid budgets, or nearly $19 billion. This includes cutting some $1 billion from U.N. peacekeeping funding. Trump wants to cap the U.S. peacekeeping contribution at 25%.

The United States is reviewing each of the 16 U.N. peacekeeping missions as the annual mandates come up for renewal by the Security Council in a bid to cut costs. There are 95,301 uniformed personnel in the U.N. Civilian personnel total 15,319. There are 112,207 total personnel. This a substantial local military contribution, compared to the U.S. military presence in terrorist regions such as the Middle East. The U.S. might be a very effective contributor, if it was more involved in training U.N. forces.

In testimony before the Senate Foreign Relations Committee, U.N. Ambassador Nikki Haley sidestepped questions about the size of the proposed cuts, focusing instead on her goal of finding "real value" in the large number of U.N. agencies providing humanitarian aid, demanding clear guideposts for peacekeeping efforts, and working to end attacks on Israel. She said the president's budget "was helpful at putting countries on notice that we are not being taken for granted anymore."

The U.S. is targeting savings of $150 million alone on efforts to scale back the UN peacekeeping mission in Haiti, Haley said. Larger savings will come from reducing the U.S. contribution to the peacekeeping budget to 25% of total costs, from 28.5% in 2017, she said.

Below are the most important U.N. missions:

Central African Republic (CAR)

In the Central African Republic since April 2014. Strength: 13,389. Approved budget (07/2016– 06/2017): $920,727,900.

The CAR conflict is an ongoing civil war in the Central African Republic involving the government, rebels from the Séléka coalition and the Anti-balaka militias.

Democratic Republic of the Congo

In the Democratic Republic of the Congo since July 2010, Strength: 22,199. Approved budget (07/2016 – 06/2017): $1,235,723,100.

Subject to foreign interference since the colonial era, the eastern Congo poses difficult questions about the role of international intervention. The U.N. mission, the largest peacekeeping deployment in the world, has provided crucial support for the DRC's peace process, but many observers argue that it lacks a clear strategy for sustaining the peace and eradicating the plethora of armed groups that remain. Presidential elections originally scheduled for 2016, were delayed to 2018. The Congolese government, Western policymakers, and regional leaders all face pivotal decisions that will determine whether the country can consolidate its democratic progress.

Darfur

In Darfur since July 2007, Strength: 19,797.

Approved budget (07/2016 – 06/2017): $1,039,573,200.

For the past four years, the remote Sudanese region of Darfur has been the scene of a bloody conflict that has led to the death of thousands of people and the displacement of more than two million. The United Nations has described it as "the world's worst humanitarian crisis" and the United States government called it "genocide." The violence and destruction is often compared to the 1994 genocide in Rwanda.

Haiti

In Haiti since June 2004, Strength: 5,063.

Approved budget (07/2016 – 06/2017): $345,926,700.

The U.S. has called for the elimination of funding for the U.N. intervention in Haiti.

Lebanon

In Lebanon since March 1978, Strength: 11,390.

Approved budget (07/2016 – 06/2017): $488,691,600.

The 2006 Lebanon War, also called the 2006 Israel–Hezbollah War and known in Lebanon as the July War, was a 34-day military conflict in Lebanon, Northern Israel and the Golan Heights. The principal parties were Hezbollah paramilitary forces and the Israel Defense Forces (IDF). The conflict started on July 12, 2006, and continued until a United Nations-brokered ceasefire went into effect in the morning on August 14, 2006, though it formally ended on September 8, 2006, when Israel lifted its naval blockade of Lebanon. Due to unprecedented Iranian military support to Hezbollah before and during the war, some consider it the first round of the Iran–Israel proxy conflict, rather than a continuation of the Arab–Israeli conflict.

Mali

In Mali since April 2013, Strength: 14,043.

Approved budget: (07/2016– 06/2017): $933,411,000.

Mali is in the grip of an unprecedented political crisis, one of the most serious since the landlocked West African country gained independence from France in 1960. It was hit by a coup in March 2012, and a rebellion in the north that has caused alarm around the world. The former colonial power has now deployed troops after an appeal from Mali's interim president.

The five main Islamists groups in Mali are Ansar Dine, Movement for Unity and Jihad in West Africa (Mujao), al-Qaeda in the Islamic Maghreb (AQIM), the Signed-in-Blood Battalion and the Islamic Movement for Azawad (IMA).

Abyei, Sudan

In Abyei, Sudan since June 2011, Strength: 4,770.

Approved budget (07/2016 – 06/2017): $268,624,600.

Abyei is a tormented piece of land, locked on the border between Sudan and South Sudan. It has been violently contested since South Sudan split from the north in 2011. There is oil, which the governments of Sudan and South Sudan desire to possess. There is no government in Abyei, no legal justice system and no police force. When South Sudan gained independence, the governments of Khartoum and Juba failed to agree on the border division, leaving Abyei's status unresolved. A United Nations peacekeeping mission, the U.N. Interim Security Force for Abyei (UNISFA), has monitored the situation since 2011. When South Sudan seceded, most of greater Sudan's oil fields went with it. One of these, known as Difra oil field, remains disputed inside the Abyei region.

South Sudan

In South Sudan since July 2011, Strength: 15,873.

Approved budget (07/2016 – 06/2017): $1,081,788,400.

The South Sudanese Civil War is a conflict in South Sudan between forces of the government and opposition forces. In December 2013, President Kiir accused his former deputy Riek Machar, and ten others, of attempting a coup d'état. Up to 300,000 people are estimated to have been killed in the war, including notable atrocities such as the 2014 Bentiu massacre. Although both men have supporters from across South Sudan's ethnic divides, subsequent fighting has had ethnic undertones. Kiir's Dinka ethnic group has been accused of attacking other ethnic groups and Machar's Nuer ethnic group has been accused of attacking the Dinka. More than 3.5 million people have been displaced in a country of about 12 million, with more than 2.1 million internally displaced, and more than 1.5 million having fled to neighboring countries, especially Kenya, Sudan, and Uganda. Fighting in the agricultural heart in the south of the country has catapulted the number of people facing starvation to 6 million, with famine breaking out in some areas.

ArmchairTechInvestor Opinion

The U.N. has a number of important functions, although some, like their climate change and population control efforts, will not be supported by the Trump administration. The U.N. will be driven to be more efficient, and their 16 peacekeeping operations will be reexamined. Much of the peacekeeping efforts are directed at Africa, where governments are weak and tribal rivalries strong. ISIS and al Qaeda find this type of situation inviting. The U.N. could be an even a more important vehicle for fighting terrorism in Africa, if the U.S. gets more involved in their efforts.

Foreign Policy-Africa

African Continental Free Trade Area (ACFTA)

In April 2018, discussions continued that could lead very soon to the formation of ACFTA. Trade among the African countries is very low. Although there are some differences among the African neighbors, the formation of ACFTA could aid the African countries in increasing trade among themselves. The amount of trade between the African countries is a very low 16% of total trade. By comparison, 70% of the trade in Europe is among the European countries. In Asia, the percentage is 51%.

CHAPTER 8

Chinese and U.S. Foreign Policy-Asia, the Arctic and Africa

MAP 1

Russia Fortifying Bases in Arctic Region

● Key regional headquarters ● Confirmed bases Russia is building/upgrading ● Bases Russia may upgrade

1 Bodø, Norway's National Joint Headquarters	**7** Rogachevo	**14** Temp-Kotelny Island
2 Sputnik Base, Pechenga	**8** Vorkuta Air Base	**15** New Siberian Islands
3 Gadzhiyevo Naval Base	**9** Alykel	**16** Wrangel Island
4 Severomorsk, home of Russia's Northern Fleet	**10** Nagurskoye	**17** Mys Shmidta
5 Alakurtti	**11** Graham Bell Island	**18** Anadyr-Ugolny
6 Naryan-Mar	**12** Sredny Ostrov	**19** Vladivostok, home of Russia's Pacific Fleet
	13 Tiksi	

SOURCE: Heritage Foundation research.

IB 4578 ☎ heritage.org

Image: Russian Arctic Facilities
Image Source: Heritage Foundation

The Arctic Is Being Coveted By Russia And China As Well As Others. Will The U.S. Arctic Policy Be Effective?

Foreign Policy-Russia and China-The Arctic

The Arctic is starting to become an important political battlefield of the future. The warming of the polar ice cap will likely reveal large untapped natural resources. Due to sequestration, the U.S. military has struggled in the Arctic. However, with the approval by the Congress of a two-year military and other budget deal in early 2018, that may now change. Although Trump's 2018 Budget will allow substantially increased military expenditures, the Trump policy in early 2018 consists of allowing increased offshore drilling in Alaska. An overall plan for the Arctic has been absent and military funding increases have not yet happened. The lack of a strong Trump policy may be due to his disbelief in climate change. The lack of such a belief could leave the U.S. behind if increasingly warmer temperatures make the Arctic more attractive, particularly for Russia and China, even though China has no direct Arctic presence.

*The Arctic is becoming increasingly important, as warming worldwide temperatures enable shipping to increase through the winter months, and resource exploration becomes more feasible.

In January, 2018, China issued its first strategy paper describing its long-term ambitions for the Arctic, even though it does not have any territory in the Arctic Circle. However, in an effort to bring legitimacy to its future claims, it declared itself a "Near Arctic State". Its expressed interests include shipping, natural resource development, and scientific research. The resources mentioned included oil, gas, minerals, and fisheries. This effort will be an element of China's strategy to become a world power, and surpass the U.S. and other world powers.

***Beijing Stakes An Arctic Claim**, Wall Street Journal, By Eva Dou, January 27, 2018

**Russia is also developing a substantially increased Arctic presence, to restore its previous might in the area. In December, 2015, Russia's news agency Tass declared that Russia had finished equipping six new military bases throughout the Arctic in a move to recreate the country's military presence to levels it had during the Cold War. In total, Moscow's plans involve the opening of ten Arctic search-and-rescue stations, 16 deep-water ports, 13 airfields, and 10 air-defense radar stations across its Arctic periphery.

Once completed, this construction will "permit the use of larger and more modern bombers" in the region, Mark Galeotti, a Russia expert at New York University, wrote for The Moscow Times. "By 2025, the Arctic waters are to be patrolled by a squadron of next-generation stealthy PAK DA bombers."

Russia Just Put The Finishing Touches On 6 Arctic Military Bases, Business Insider, By Jeremy Bender, Dec. 7, 2015

***A new U.S. strategy for the Arctic was outlined by the Obama administration in 2013. The Pentagon said it would seek to expand both its understanding of the Arctic environment and its presence in the region, while also promoting collaboration on a range of issues. In 2013, the United States had stationed about 27,000 military personnel in Alaska.

Despite this number, in some ways Washington is starting from a relatively weak position. Other Arctic countries, particularly Russia and China, have already moved far more aggressively in staking out a presence in the region.

***U.S. Unveils Military Strategy for Arctic**, Inter Press Service, By Carey L. Biron, November 26, 2013

ArmchairTechInvestor Opinion

The Arctic is starting to become an important political battlefield of the future. The warming of the polar ice cap will likely reveal large untapped natural resources. The U.S. estimates that about 15% of the world's remaining oil, up to 30% of its natural gas deposits, and about 20% of its liquefied natural gas are stored in the Arctic seabed.

Due to sequestration, the U.S. military has struggled in the Arctic. Although Trump's 2018 Budget is likely to allow substantially increased military expenditures, the Trump policy in early 2018 consists of allowing increased offshore drilling in Alaska. An overall plan for the Arctic has been absent and military funding increases have not yet happened. The lack of a strong Trump policy may be due to his disbelief in climate change. The lack of such a belief could leave the U.S. behind if increasingly warmer temperatures make the Arctic more attractive, particularly for Russia and China.

Russia-Northern China

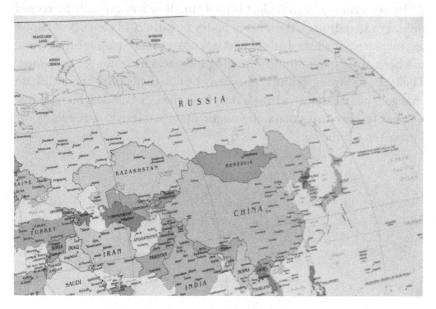

Image: Russia and Northern China
Image Source: Getty Images

Foreign Policy-China

Asia has over half of the world population, and its dominant countries are India, China and Japan. India, China, North Korea, Russia and Pakistan all have nuclear weapons, with nuclear weapons having been essentially supplied by China to North Korea and Pakistan. Iran is likely developing nuclear weapons and ICBMs by collaborating with North Korea. China is aggressively pursuing geographic expansion into the South China Sea, and is developing One Belt, One Road trade routes into Europe and Asia along traditional trade routes to tie those countries economically, politically and militarily to China.

China Has Finally Stepped Up To Enforce Sanctions On North Korea; Will This Lead To Denuclearization Of The Korean Peninsula?

It appears that China is enforcing the most recent U.N. sanctions. A telling consequence may be that border traffic and business activity along the

China-North Korea border has changed dramatically. The lines of people going into North Korea have dropped significantly.

According to businessmen crossing the border:

- New U.N. sanctions on garments caused a dozen or more garment factories to close in North Korea;
- Battery prices have increased by at least 50% from a year earlier;
- Seafood for export from North Korea, has fallen by more than 50%, and is a glut on the market.

Somewhat offsetting these developments are smuggling cross-border and ship-to-ship cargo transfers.

Although the numbers may be somewhat unreliable, it is believed that 90% of North Korean trade is with China. Oil exports by China appear to have dropped to zero, although there may still be crude exports. One international initiative is to get foreign countries to stop using North Korean workers, who are virtual slaves, and provide currency. Many of them appear to be heading back to North Korea, although this probably does not include Russia, which uses many such workers.

In March, 2018, a North Korean cybertheft may have occurred in Turkey, such activities undoubtedly continue. There are also arms sale revenues that continue to be received through sales to the Middle East and Africa.

According to the Chinese government, exports to North Korea were down by one-third in 2017, and down by 82% in December, 2017.

The U.S. continues to put pressure on North Korea, with substantial new sanctions on shipping and trading companies. It has also been reported that the U.S. is interdicting vessels at sea that are involved in trade with North Korea.

ArmchairTechInvesor Opinion

It is estimated that North Korea went through about half of its foreign currency reserves of $3 billion in 2017. The noose is tightening on North

Korea. A breakthrough may have come when President Trump agreed to meet with Kim Joug Un in May, 2018. A precondition by Trump has always been that North Korea be willing to denuclearize the Korean Peninsula. There have been many times when North Korea violated agreements they had made, leading to skepticism about their current Intentions. The U.S. needs to hold these talks, keep increasing sanctions, and propose an agreement that will have a verifiable way of guaranteeing that North Korea abandons its nuclear and missile development activities. Also, one must remember the ruthless power Kim Jong Un has used to consolidate power, including the killing of relatives such as his half-brother and uncle.

China's Tight Grip On Its Domestic Internet Is Another Example Of Its Closed Society And Unfair Trade Practices

*The Chinese Internet, which is very large, is being pursued by U.S. titans that include Apple, Inc., Alphabet (Google), Facebook, and Cisco. Competing with these U.S. companies in China are giant Chinese companies that include Alibaba Group and Tencent. China has organized an annual conference, the Wuzhen World Internet Conference, that is organized by the Cyberspace Administration of China. At a conference held in mid-2017, China mouthed its theme as "Developing digital economy for openness and shared benefits". Apple and Cisco echoed this statement as corporate policy, which sounds good. However, how China operates in their home market is quite different. Despite the theme of the conference by China, and the blind acceptance of the theme by U.S. companies, China has used its conference to promote a "policed Internet" that uses unfair trade practices, such as exist in China.

China's Internet market is walled off from the rest of the world, with Facebook's social network and Google's search results blocked from being used in China. A cyberspace law has been enacted that required Apple to remove some Apps that enabled users to evade China's Internet firewall. Cisco is one of many U.S. companies that have taken the risk of their intellectual property being stolen by forming a joint venture with a Chinese company. This requirement by China is an unfair trade practice.

U.S. Firms Tout China Despite Web Curbs, Wall Street Journal, by Liza Lin, December 4, 2017

Google pulled out of China in 2010, after a cyberattack occurred that was traced to China, and complaints occurred the claimed that Google's content was censored. Since that time Google has had limited operations in China.

Another initiative underway by China is to develop trade relations that extend from Europe to Asia. Added to the transportation infrastructure campaign has been an initiative in 15 areas to expand ties to countries such as the United Arab Emirates (UAE), Thailand and Turkey, that include e-commerce, international standard setting and regulation, presumably such as exists in China.

**China, aided by companies such as Alibaba, Baidu and Tencent, has built one of the most sophisticated citizen surveillance systems, that can include video surveillance, and facial recognition systems, and includes cyberspace. The result is the creation of cities wired for surveillance. The Chinese companies work openly and supportively with the Chinese government to monitor and control their citizens. The companies can push back against any request for information by the Chinese government, but in the end, the government can demand the information.

China's Tech Giants Have a Side Job: Helping Beijing Spy, Wall Street Journal, by Liza Lin and Josh Chin, November 30, 2017

ArmchairTechInvestor Opinion

China has a police state that requires the largest Chinese companies to cooperate in monitoring its citizens both in terms of their everyday actions, but also in enforcing a cyberspace wall that isolates the Chinese population from much of the rest of the world.

Also familiar are the obstacles China places on companies such as

Facebook and Google that have eliminated them from the Chinese market, and allowed Chinese companies such as Alibaba and Tencent to dominate the Chinese internet market.

Tesla Will Be Competing In The Electric Car Industry In China Despite China's Unfair Trade Policies. This Will Benefit China's Worldwide Trade

China has unfair trade practices, such as requiring foreign manufacturers to have a Chinese partner, or pay a 25% import duty, if the car is manufactured outside of China. Tesla seems to be unwilling to give away its technology to a Chinese company partner, and perhaps give away 50% of the local Chinese market to them. Tesla has substantial electric car intellectual property, including wireless car batteries, that it will protect by building an electric car manufacturing plant in Shanghai, thereby avoiding Chinese companies stealing their technology.

Batteries, which are a significant portion of the cost of an electric car, will undoubtedly be able to be imported to the Shanghai plant. This will protect Tesla's electric car battery technology. Tesla will also be able to benefit from the low cost of Chinese manufacturing, by being in Shanghai. This plant will be able to ship to Asian and European markets from this plant, and enjoy the low cost of Chinese manufacturing plants. It will also benefit from the low cost of automobile parts manufactured in China for its export markets outside of China.

China does not allow foreign companies in China to set up manufacturing plants anywhere except in "free trade zones". One of those free trade zones is Shanghai, where Tesla will locate its plant. There are also ten more such free trade zones throughout China.

*Tesla Plugs In Own China Plant,** Wall Street Journal, Tim Higgins, Trefor Moss and Eva Dou, October 23, 2017

China is planning on eventually banning the purchase in China of any car that is not electric. It is requiring any car manufacturer in China to have an electric car model in the next few years. All Chinese car manufacturers will need to have electric car sales in 2019, and have electric cars be 12% or more of their sales in 2020.

China has underway an extensive One Belt, One Road Trade Network that will be open to Tesla and others to export their cars to Europe, Asia and other countries, including Russia. Missing from this list of countries served by the network is India, which also has plans to have all electric cars by 2040.

Tesla will likely have large foreign profits overseas and President Trump has implemented corporate tax reduction policies that make it attractive for U.S. companies to bring back their foreign profits to the U.S. Hopefully he hopes these funds will be invested in the U.S. to create jobs. This could run up against Chinese currency controls that restrict the movement of money out of China.

ArmchairTechInvestor Opinion

China, and their One Belt, One Road Network, is taking advantage of Chinese unfair trade practices. These practices cause foreign companies to set up companies in China to access the Chinese market, and transfer their technology to these local companies. This requiring joint Chinese company ventures, allows China to benefit from the expertise of foreign companies and develop a widespread trade network. U.S. companies such as Tesla, Apple and IBM will, through their foreign subsidiaries in China, meaningfully assist China in their global trade ambitions. It is a brilliant scheme to use unfair trade practices to promote Chinese trade, economic and political influence in the region from Europe to Asia and Africa, and use U.S. companies such as Tesla to do it.

China has stated to the U.S. that it plans to deemphasize trade in the future. The reality is their trade network is also about political influence, military capabilities development, and economic ties with over 60 countries. Important new endeavors will expand China's influence in the Indian Ocean and Africa.

China's Policies, That Require Foreign Companies To Have Chinese Partners, May Be Addressed By U.S. Legislation.

*In early November, 2017, a bill was introduced in the U.S. Congress that will toughen foreign investment rules. The problems that could be addressed include a recent Chinese company's attempt to acquire a U.S. company with a significant amount of semiconductor technology.

This could help China develop its semiconductor industry to compete in the commercial Internet business, and develop sophisticated military systems. The real risk is the transferring of military capabilities to a country that has professed its intention to become the dominant country worldwide in trade and military capabilities. They are very purposeful and diligent in their pursuit of those ambitions.

Identical bills concerning the foreign investment issues were introduced in both the Senate and the House. The bills give additional guidance and requirements to CFIUS, an interagency panel led by the Treasury Department that reviews proposed transactions that raise national security concerns.

Rep. Denny Heck, a Democrat from Washington, was concerned about China, at least partly because of how China's trade policies result in stolen U.S. intellectual property. One of his statements was "China's actions are clear, they are cheating the system. They are evading the rules meant to prevent them from accessing technology critical to our national security and we need to do something to stop them sooner rather than later," he said. "With these changes, we hope to modernize and update the law in order to meet today's threats from around the globe."

CFIUS has become more conservative since President Donald Trump was inaugurated. Since then, they have been more diligent in rejecting a broader range of deals from China.

The bills would also expand CFIUS' power to look at smaller investments and joint ventures, according to sources who have read drafts of the bills.

*Bipartisan Bills Expected to Toughen U.S. Foreign Investment rules, Reuters, Diane Bartz, November 3, 2017

ArmchairTechInvestor Opinion

China has policies that require joint ventures with Chinese companies to do business in China. This results in Chinese joint venture companies, many of which may be owned at lease partly by the Chinese government, being in a position to steal the technology of their joint venture foreign partners.

China's expressed ambitions are to be a world power, and use trade, and military predominance to achieve their goals.

China is not a monolithic country. It has a great diversity of interests, from the rural population to the urban dwellers, to the local governments that have their own significant power. China has used its dominance politically to make China a worldwide threat to the U.S. The U.S. Congress acts slowly, but they will likely adopt the pending legislation that could address at least a part of the threat, the transfer of U.S. technology to China.

Asia Is Of Substantial Interest To The U.S.: What Should Be The Response To China's Aggression?

Asia has over half of the world population, and its dominant countries are India, China and Japan. India, China, North Korea, Russia and Pakistan all have nuclear weapons, with nuclear weapons having been essentially supplied by China to North Korea and Pakistan.

China has been aggressively expanding its influence and geography. There are vast natural resources in the rural parts of China. The natives of China's frontier, the Mongols, Tibetans, and Muslim Uighurs, see their land and ways of life being swept away by a flood of Han Chinese immigrants. When their anger boils over into violence, as it did in 2016 in Lhasa, and in 2017 in Urumqi, the response is usually swift and brutal.

China is involved in a border dispute with India in the Kashmir region. The area is important to India as a contributor to its security.

China has built seven artificial islands in disputed waters of the South China Sea. Satellite images appear to show that China has installed antiaircraft and other weapons on all seven islands. China's President Xi Jinping made a pledge in 2015 not to militarize the islands. The U.S. has aggressively been protecting U.S. and other countries' navigation rights in the South China Sea. The U.S. has sent warships close to the atolls to assert freedom-of-navigation rights. This has raised tensions with China, an indication of their aggressive intentions with regard to those seas.

There are also tensions between China and Japan in the East China Sea. In 2017, those tensions between China and Japan over the contested Senkaku/Diaoyu islands rose as incursions into the disputed waters by Chinese vessels increased. Both countries have increased their military capabilities in the region. China's aggression in the area includes building large naval warships that are used as coast guard ships. Chinas aggression also includes aircraft that have invaded Japanese airspace hundreds of times in 2015 and 2016. Japan has scrambled its Air Self-Defense Force fighters hundreds of times to meet these threats.

Japan, India and the U.S. are confronting China's ambitions in the Indian Ocean by increasing their naval presence. The fear is that China's aggressive expansion in the South and East China Seas will spill over to the Indian Ocean. In recent years, China has been developing ports and other facilities in countries around the Indian Ocean.

In May, 2017, Chinese President Xi Jinping hosted 28 heads of state at a summit about China's One Belt, One Road initiative. China has underway a massive project to build a land and sea network connecting Europe, Asia, the Middle East and Africa. China is planning to spend as much as $3 billion on a trade route infrastructure in over 60 countries. This will include spending on ports, roads, railways, airports, power plants, telecommunications, and other infrastructure, including gas and oil pipelines. Obviously one objective, besides increasing trade, is to get countries to invest in the projects, and thus become beholden to China financially and politically.

ArmchairTechInvestor Opinion

In 2017, President Trump had a meeting with Indian Prime Minister Narendra Modi. The meeting appeared to go well. The U.S. and India have both committed to strengthen the relationship between the two countries. Having India and the U.S. as partners is attractive to both countries for many reasons, including confronting the ambitions of China.

The ten ASEAN countries have a dispute with China in the South China Seas. After over ten years, China has finally agreed to negotiate a maritime code of conduct in the South China Seas. A series of security-oriented meetings have been concluded. However, in view of China's massive size and military build-up, it remains to be seen if the ASEAN countries can get any satisfaction from what is currently the early stages of a vague agreement with China.

The U.S. has in the past been a guarantor of security for the ten ASEAN countries in the South China Seas and elsewhere. At a meeting in 2017, the U.S. reassured the ASEAN countries of its security commitment to the countries in the region, including in the South China Seas.

U.S. North Korea And China Options Were Discussed Lou Dobbs Fox Broadcast: Both Are A Threat, And What Should The U.S. Do?

Lou Dobbs Tonight-Gordon Chang-Some of "The Coming Collapse of China" author's opinions are included below.

China and the U.S. are on a collision course. China is essential to North Korea's ability to develop a nuclear weapons program, and an ICBM missile program.

China provides 90% of North Korea's external trade plus most of their food and oil. China has also provided most of the technology for their missiles. Three launches in 2017 appear to be from China's technology for JL-submarine launched missiles. Also, parts recovered after the launches were provided by Chinese companies. Additionally, in the North Korea nuclear weapons program, some of the semi-processed materials came from China.

To recap North Korea's missile tests, there were 8 in 2015, 16 in 2016, and 23 in 2017, including ICBMs capable of reaching the U.S. The missile test launch program was obviously accelerated in 2017. The missiles are now being carried on mobile launchers, which makes them more difficult to detect. Those mobile launchers are Chinese. The canister in a recent North Korea military parade also looks like it is Chinese.

The U.S. responded by sending a third carrier strike force moving into the Sea of Japan. It might be there partially because of China, to counter possible provocative measures elsewhere.

North Korea has increased its provocations by exhibiting its missile launch capabilities. This is despite China's President's understanding with President Trumps' apparently successful meeting in Mir-A-Lago, Florida. The U.S. issues with China appear to go well beyond North Korea, and could affect our desires that they restrain North Korea, which they have not done in the past. However, it appears this changed in the second half of 2017.

In mid-2017, China launched its third missile in three weeks vowing to send a gift package to the U.S. Coincidentally, a few days later, the U.S. successfully launched a missile from Vandenberg AFB in California to intercept a missile launched from the Ronald Reagan Ballistic Missile Defense Test Site on Kwajalein Atoll in the Marshall Islands 4,200 miles away. This is part of a protective measure shield that can protect the U.S. against missile attacks on the U.S. by North Korea, connected to their nuclear weapons development programs and their missile launch tests or others.

ArmchairTechInvestor Opinion

Developing a responsible response to North Korean weapons development programs, while confronting Chinese worldwide expansion ambitions, is a daunting challenge.

The U.S. sanctioned Chinese and other persons that have been, and are, involved in assisting North Korea in evading sanctions, and assisting the development of North Korea missile, and nuclear activities. The Trump administration's overall response to the joint threats from China and North Korea remains to be seen. A recent agreement in early 2018 for Trump to meet with Kim Jong Un, that appears to have as a precondition the denuclearization of the Korean Peninsula, is a possible positive sign. However, if North Korea is not sincere, it could be one of the steps the U.S. must explore, before moving forward on more aggressive action. China may view North Korea as a subservient country over whom they have total control, which control expands their territorial ambitions, protects their Korean Peninsula border, and extends their political influence.

China Is Enabling The North Korean ICBM And Nuclear Programs, But This Changed

President Trump recently met with the Chinese president, Xi Jinping. The official China Daily newspaper said it was encouraging to see the two-day summit "going as well as it could". There seems to be some movement by China in addressing the nuclear program, and missile development program being developed by North Korea.

In mid-2017 North Korea launched a medium range missile toward Russia. Russia's response was that it did not represent a threat, since they have a missile defense system.

China Enablement of North Korea

Until mid-2017, China has been ignoring sanctions:

- In 2016, China imported $1.2 billion of North Korean coal.
  - o   The U.N. imposed sanctions that limited such shipments to 1 million tons or $53.5 million in the year beginning in December, 2016;
  - o   China Shipped $160 million, or 2 million tons at the beginning of 2017.
  - o   China approved the U.N. restrictions and it agreed not to make any more shipments in 2017.
  - o   This appeared to be a reversal of China policy, and in early 2018, that still appears to be the case.
- Chinese companies were aiding North Korea in importing goods by setting up front companies; and
- Chinese banks are facilitating North Korea in evading financial sanctions.

So far, there is no visible movement in China addressing other issues. North Korean weapons programs are expanding, with exports going to Africa, the Middle East and Southeast Asia. The U.N. issued a report where two particularly egregious incidents documented were the North Korean Embassy in China facilitating the shipment of lithium, a material used to reduce the size of nuclear warheads, and the facilitating a Chinese company is shipping weapons materials from Europe to North Korea.

North Korean Nuclear And Missile Capabilities

North Korea has a uranium enrichment plant that allows it to produce up to 8 nuclear bombs per year. These could be sold to Iran or other terrorists. North Korea completed its sixth nuclear test in 2017. It is also launching medium range missiles, one of which had a range of 500 miles, and followed three failures. It has announced an objective of developing an intercontinental ballistic missile (ICBM) that can carry a nuclear warhead to the U.S. The pending talks between Trump and Kim Jung Un are to be accompanied by missile and nuclear weapons test freezes. North Korea has yet to demonstrate a nuclear missile launch that shows their ability to conquer the task of successful reentry of the warhead from space into the atmosphere.

U.N. Involvement

- The U.N. Security Council has passed a number of resolutions since North Korea's first nuclear test in 2006;
- In 2006, the U.N. demanded that North Korea cease nuclear testing and prohibited the export to North Korea of some military supplies and luxury goods;
- After the second nuclear test in 2009, the U.N. broadened the arms embargo. Member states were encouraged to inspect ships and destroy any cargo suspected being related to the nuclear weapons program;
- In January, 2013 after a satellite launch, the U.N. strengthened previous sanctions by clarifying a state's right to seize and destroy cargo suspected of heading to or from North Korea for purposes of military research and development;
- In March 2013, after the third nuclear test. It imposed sanctions on money transfers and aimed to shut North Korea out of the international financial system;

- In March 2016, after the fourth nuclear test, it further strengthened sanctions. It banned the export of gold, vanadium, titanium, and rare earth metals. The export of coal and iron were also banned, with an exemption for transactions that were purely for "livelihood purposes";
- In November 2016, it capped North Korea's coal exports and banned exports of copper, nickel, zinc, and silver;
- In February 2017, a U.N. panel said that 116 of 193 member states had yet not submitted a report on their implementation of these sanctions, though China had, and;
- In February 2017, China announced it would ban all imports of coal for the rest of the year.

Failed U.S. Policies

The North Korean nuclear program is the reason it receives bribes, and its being ended could be impeded for that reason. These bribes have included:

- The U.S. unilaterally removed nuclear weapons from South Korea in 1991. Yearly shipments of heavy fuels occurred for most of the 1990s;
- South Korea built the Kaesong Industrial Complex inside North Korea in 2003; and
- North Korea was removed from the list of state sponsors of terrorism in 2008.

U.S. Sanctions

President Obama pursued a policy of strategic patience, waiting for the regime to collapse, or change course. This policy was a failure. The United States imposed sanctions in 2016, when President Obama enacted the North Korea Sanctions and Policy Enhancement Act of 2016, which passed the House of Representatives and the Senate with nearly unanimous support. This law:

- Requires the President to sanction entities found to have contributed to North Korea's weapons of mass destruction program, arms trade, human rights abuses or other illegal activities;
- Imposes mandatory sanctions for entities involved in North Korea's mineral or metal trades, which comprise a large part of North Korea's foreign exports; and,
- Requires the U.S. Treasury Department to determine whether North Korea should be listed as a "primary money laundering concern," which would trigger tough new financial restrictions.

South Korea Sanctions

South Korea imposed sanctions against North Korea following the 2010 sinking of the South Korean naval ship, the Cheonan. In 2016 President Park Geun-hye ordered the Kaesong complex shut in retaliation for the nuclear test in January of that year and the rocket launch in February.

U.S. Objectives

Possible objectives can be:

- Regime change; or
- enuclearization of the Korean peninsula;
- The imposition of secondary financial sanctions that will bar Chinese banks that aid North Korea in evading sanctions:
  o Secondary sanctions are both simple and powerful. A foreign bank can process transactions for a bank already facing sanctions (for example, one of the many North Korean banks that have been listed by the United States) or it can maintain its access to the U.S. financial system, but it cannot do both. This is powerful because access to the U.S. financial system also means access to the U.S. dollar, and is necessary for almost any bank anywhere.
- A $1.2 billion penalty was imposed by the U.S. on the Chinese computer company ZTE. They admitted their guilt:
  o Similar penalties can be imposed on Chinese companies that violate sanctions, particularly those that are involved in the weapons industry.

Foreign Policy-China-North Korea

North Korea and the U.S. were on a nuclear collision course. North Korea had stated that it is developing a missile program that will deliver a nuclear weapon to the U.S. Guam, and its U.S. presence there has been threatened also. China had said it will not intervene if the U.S. is attacked, but will side with North Korea, if they are attacked. In early 2018, it began to appear that China was starting to enforce U.N. and U.S. sanctions against North Korea. It appears likely that North Korea will be under severe pressure from the sanctions by 2019, possibly resulting in unrest in the country, unless Russia or Iran help bail them out, particularly through weapons systems purchases. Direct talks occured between Trump and North Korea in June, 2018. Given the history of such talks, the prospects of North Korea agreeing to denuclearize the Korean Peninsula appear to suspect, given the history of North Korean violations of prior agreements.

Foreign Policy-North Korea

The U.N. Adopts Sanctions To Reduce North Korea's Exports By $1 Billion: Will This Deter Nuke and ICBM Development?

After North Korea's first ICBM test, Russia vetoed a U.N. condemnation of the launch. In 2017, the U.N. Security Council, by a vote of 15-0, including yes votes by Russia and China, voted to impose additional sanctions on North Korea, following their second ICBM launch capable of hitting the U.S. The sanctions were designed to reduce North Korea's exports by one-third, or $1 billion. This should deny them some hard currency to finance their nuclear and missile launch programs, should the negotiations started in June 2018 fail.

If these sanctions are effective, they could help in slowing North Korea's programs, but are not likely to eliminate them. Also, clandestine revenue sources include the sale of weapons technology, including what might be shorter-range updated Scud technology, that is capable of launching short-range nuclear weapons. If these weapons get in the hands of terrorists, including Iran, the results could be devastating. The revenues from such sales could offset the impact of the U.N. sanctions. Weapons shipments are only likely to be reduced or eliminated by putting a blockage on

North Korean shipping, North Korea accepting a denuclearized Korean Peninsula, or by regime change.

China seems to finally be having an impact in slowing down the North Korean missile and nuclear programs. China says that it wants a de-nuclearize the Korean Peninsula. It may have stopped North Korean coal imports, at least for 2017, but that, or the U.N. sanctions, are not likely to result in North Korea's nuclear program being dismantled.

Following the Chinese President's visit to the U.S., President Trump believed that China might be helpful in dealing with North Korea. Why is China slow to act? China policy may include the belief that the North Korean threat will drive the U.S. out of Northeast Asia. Secondly, the collapse of North Korea could drive millions of refugees into China. Finally, if South Korea should become the focus of a unified South and North Korea, including regime change in North Korea, that could put nuclear weapons on China's border. In 2017, the U.S. began the process of invoking sanctions against Chinese banks and companies that are working with North Korea to evade financial sanctions, and to help them get parts and technology to develop their weapons programs.

The philosophy of North Korea could include their belief that nuclear weapons assure the survival of their regime. The U.N. and U.S. sanctions have not been effective because, in the past, North Korea has been successful in evading sanctions. Even though North Korea has become increasingly dependent on China, they have economic and diplomatic ties with many countries. Many of these countries are possible buyers of North Korean weapons, despite the U.N. sanctions. Unless the U.N. sanctions can be shown to get North Korea to freeze and then eliminate their nuclear weapons, North Korea will continue to be a nuclear threat to the U.S. and its allies, including South Korea and Japan. But, also Saudi Arabia and Israel are in danger, because of the threat of short range Scud nuclear weapons.

ArmchairTechInvestor Opinion

The U.N. sanctions adopted should be helpful in slowing North Korea's nuclear weapons and ICBM programs, but they are not likely to be successful in stopping those programs before North Korea will be able to launch an ICBM at the U.S., Japan and South Korea. The issue is how to get North Korea to dismantle their nuclear weapons program without the U.S. having to take military action, or achieve regime change. China taking action against North Korea is probably the only other option.

Should South Korea And Japan Be Given Nuclear Weapons? Will That Cause China To Contain North Korea?

When North Korea launched its first intercontinental ballistic missile (ICBM) in 2017, this was viewed as a serious escalation of the threat that North Korea poses to the U.S. and the international community. The Hwasong-14 ICBM that was launched appears to have a range that will put South Korea, Japan, Guam and Alaska in range. More technical feats that need to be accomplished for North Korea to deliver a nuclear weapon to the U.S. West Coast are:

- To increase the range of the missile;
- Miniaturize the warhead; and
- Hardening of the warhead so that it can survive a reentry from space into the atmosphere.

It seems that these technical hurdles are likely to be surmounted in 2018 or 2019 by North Korea, if it resumes its tests. Based upon their threats and actions, if the U.S. does not neutralize the threat, the U.S. will soon be vulnerable to nuclear attack by North Korea.

Since North Korea could continue to threaten the U.S. with a nuclear weapon, relevant is the magnitude of the threat, if the Korean Peninsula denuclearization talks fail. South Korea's population is about 50 million people. Pyongyang, the capital of North Korea has a population of about 2.4 million people. Seoul, South Korea, which is close to North Korea, has a population of 10 million people, and is an immediate threat from North Korea because of the thousands of missiles pointed at it. Japan has a population of 127 million people and the U.S. has a population of 321 million people. North Korea, with a population of 25 million people is a direct nuclear threat to three countries with a population of about 500 million people. Something must be done to neutralize the nuclear threat of North Korea.

North Korea appears to have diplomatic ties with 164 countries, and embassies in 47 countries. Most of the North Korean foreign diplomats are believed to be responsible for developing business and providing funds for their country. Under the Trump administration, more countries are starting to clamp down on North Korea. The U.S. Senate is drafting legislation that would create a "global embargo" on North Korea, according to Senator Cory Gardner (R, CO), who is on the chairman of the Senate Committee on Foreign Relations sub-panel on East Asia.

India and Russia have been trading partners with North Korea, with India being the second largest after China. According to a U.N. report, in 2016, North Korea attempted to export communications equipment to Eritrea through front companies in Malaysia. Also, there were about 50,000 Korean workers in foreign countries. Their wages go to the government, and provide hundreds of millions of dollars in financing for North Korea. By early 2018, many of these workers could be seen returning to North Korea.

The U.S. announced it is leading with diplomatic efforts, but the military remains ready based on its treaties with South Korea and Japan. The U.S. is trying to involve the U.N., but so far has been stymied by Russia. The U.N. had imposed 6 rounds of increasingly severe sanctions on North Korea, which it appears that both Russia and China and their companies have violated. The U.S. plans to introduce a resolution to the U.N. Security Council "that raises the international response in a way that is proportionate to North Korea's escalation". Nikki Haley, the U.N. Ambassador, has told China that their trade with the U.S. is at risk if they violate U.N. resolutions in dealing with North Korea. Future actions, if necessary, could be designed to:

- Cut off major sources of currency to North Korea;
- Restrict the flow of oil to their military and weapons programs;
- Increase maritime and air restrictions; and
- Hold senior officials accountable.

She also said that "We will also look at any country that does business with this outlaw regime". These countries could also be candidates to have their trade with the U.S. impacted.

What Are The Risks That North Korea Will Launch A Nuclear EMP Attack?

North Korea is testing only low-yield nuclear weapons, and has yet to attach them to ballistic missiles. North Korea had expressed a desire to provoke a nuclear conflict with the U.S. The U.S. should take them at their word. In 2017, It was estimated that the North Koreans had about 20 nuclear weapons, and are capable of producing about 5 per year.

An electromagnetic pulse can be produced by a nuclear weapon detonated at a height of 40 miles. It will provide widespread damage to electrical grids and electrical devices. A component of an EMP is a very brief but powerful electromagnetic field that can induce very high voltages in electrical conductors. Damage occurs by causing voltage limits in equipment to be exceeded and happens so fast that ordinary surge protectors cannot effectively protect computers and communications equipment. However, special transient protectors fast enough to suppress this part of an EMP exist and there has been significant progress in hardening critical U.S. systems against EMP.

If the denuclearization talks fail, South Korea could be in immediate danger. Should North Korea detonate a nuclear weapon forty-miles in the air above South Korea, it might knock out all of the electrical power in South Korea. Of course, the U.S. would also be capable of knocking out North Korea's entire power grid. The U.S. has 28,500 troops in South Korea, and more at sea in the area.

Some Russian generals have said that EMP technology was transferred to North Korea in 2004. One of North Korea's missile launches exploded in flight. It is possible that this was a test to see if a missile could be exploded at about 40 miles high. The nuclear weapons North Korea possesses are estimated to be in the 10-20 kiloton range, and are capable of producing EMP effects, with little damage on the ground. EMP technology is far simpler to use than developing an intercontinental ballistic missile (ICBM) that would need to be able to reenter the atmosphere.

A possible EMP attack on the U.S. needs to be taken seriously. A short-range missile launched from a submarine or freighter that reached a height of 40 miles could take out the power grid in the Eastern U.S., and disable the power grid for 75% of the U.S. Also, North Korea has two satellites that orbit over the U.S., and they could serve as a platform for launching an EMP attack on the U.S.

ArmchairTechInvestor Opinion

The nuclear threat from North Korea is real, and like Iran, it needs to be stopped. An EMP attack on the U.S. mainland by North Korea currently is the most likely scenario that needs to be addressed. The power grid in the U.S. needs to be upgraded to survive an EMP attack in the next few years, or in the longer-term future.

Will The U.N. Adopt More Sanctions, and Will China Enforce The Existing And New Sanctions On North Korea?

UNITED NATIONS: The U.N. Security Council met behind closed doors on May 16, 2017 to discuss tightening sanctions on North Korea. U.S. Ambassador Nikki Haley said the United States was working with China on a new sanctions resolution. This could be in addition to the six previous U.N. sanctions imposed, which had so far not worked. Countries that fail to enforce sanctions will expose themselves to possible punitive measures, she warned. New sanctions might include blocking Chinese oil exports to North Korea.

After a President Trump meeting with Xi Jinping, the President of China, suddenly there is an opportunity to confront the cozy relationships of China's companies and banks that have been supporting North Korea in its development of nuclear weapons and intercontinental ballistic missiles.

There are suggestions from some in the U.S. Congress that the U.S. should confront Chinese companies that help North Korea access international markets. Those could include manufacturing companies, wholesalers, and Chinese banks. A possible bank move would be applying secondary sanctions that could be devastating to the Chinese banks by denying them access to the U.S. dollar worldwide.

Russia and China are being pressured to assist with the North Korean problems. This U.N. move could have resulted in the Chinese beginning to enforce U.N. sanctions, and through early 2018 has resulted in the border trade between North Korea and China being significantly disrupted, although it may have declined in the first half of 2018.

Additional information surfaced on an ICBM launch in mid-2017. The missile was characterized as probably a mobile, two-stage, liquid-fueled rocket with a range of 2,800 miles and being capable of reaching the U.S. base in Guam. Over time, this rocket might be adapted to deliver a nuclear missile to the U.S.

Chinese-North Korea-U.S. Objectives

The U.S. might pursue regime change, if the denuclearization talks fail. It might involve China or the U.S. might undertake it with backing from countries such as South Korea and Japan, who are very much at risk to North Korea's nuclear ambitions.

North Korea purged Chinese sympathizers several years ago, and there is probably no love lost by China. If regime change involved China, this could involve the removal of Kim Jong Un, assistance to the impoverished North Korean population, and North Korea remaining an independent country.

Should China not wish to assist the U.S. in removing Kim Jon Un, the U.S. and its allies might pursue a policy to unify North and South Korea. China would like North Korea to be a stable country, but would not like to have a democratic South Korea on its border.

Japan and the European Union have also imposed sanctions on North Korea.

ArmchairTechInvestor Opinion

China has so far shown very little improvement in limiting the weapons activities of North Korea. They have begun to limit coal imports to China from North Korea, which will significantly impact North Korean import revenues. So far, there is no visible attempt by China to address the issue of Chinese companies and banks assisting North Korea in avoiding sanctions, and assisting them in developing and selling weapons.

Russia And China Are Working Together Despite Their Different Ambitions: What Should Be The U.S. Response?

China and Russia are each a threat to the U.S. in many different ways. One might presume that each is pursuing their own global goals, but there is evidence that in certain ways they are acting in concert with each other. One example is the U.N. Security Council. Each country has a veto over any actions by the body. North Korea is an example of China and Russia colluding. North Korea is under sanction by both the U.S. and the U.N. Following the 2017 North Korean threats, including a hydrogen bomb nuclear threat, and intercontinental ballistic missile (ICBM) threats to Japan, Guam and the U.S., the U.N. passed a resolution to impose sanctions on North Korea that was severely watered down by Russia. The U.S. wished to restrict oil shipments to North Korea and totally banned North Korean workers being used in other companies, and these sections were watered down by Russia before the sanctions were passed. The U.S. has suffered threats from North Korea that would involve ICBMs with nuclear warheads being delivered to South Korea, Japan, Guam and the U.S. All of these possible targets, should they be attacked, would likely involve a U.S. nuclear response to destroy the missile and nuclear facilities of North Korea.

There are other reasons to believe there will be Russian-Chinese co-operation in the future. The most obvious reason is that democracy is the biggest threat to both of these totalitarian countries, and the U.S. presents the major threat. Russia has been supplying advanced fighter aircraft and surface-to-air missiles that are being deployed by China in the contested South China Sea, where China is building military armed manufactured islands. China threatens international trade in that area and threatens American trade protections for countries such as South Korea, the Philippines, and Japan. China has become a big lender to and investor in Russia in recent years.

Both China and Russia are engaged in cyber warfare. Russia obviously made an effort to influence the U.S. presidential elections. They have made similar efforts in Europe.

*China and Russia's Dangerous Entente, Wall Street Journal, By Alexander Gabuev, October 4, 2017

**North Koreans In Russia Work 'Basically In The Situation Of Slaves' New York Times, by Andrew Higgins, July 11, 2017

ArmchairTechInvestor Opinion

Both China and Russia pursue their own territorial ambitions. China's strongest focus is on the South China Sea and Taiwan, as well as regions on their One Belt, One Road Network. Russia is focused on countries surrounding it that have in the past been under its control. Russia has no particular interest in North Korea, other as a customer for its petroleum products. However, the relationship between Russia and China provides a good reason for Russia to support China as it deals with North Korean issues created by increasing U.S. and U.N. sanctions on North Korea. The U.S. could aggressively move to block oil shipments to North Korea, which would be a big blow to its military buildup.

The U.S. needs to continue to treat Russia and China both as adversaries, and yet work with each them on some issues where there are mutual interests.

Both Russia and China hire North Korean workers who are basically slaves. Their wages are remitted to North Korea, and are a source of support for the North Korean military program. U.S. Customs and Border Protection says it is ready to block U.S. imports of seafood, as well as any other goods, produced by North Korean laborers who work in China. This is just one example of goods that are produced by North Korean laborers that might be exported to the U.S.

ISIS Attack On Hamas Makes Clear Hamas' Shift In Funding And Policies: Will Palestine Be Unified?

An ISIS bomber killed a Palestinian guard in 2017, making it clear that Hamas is on the side of the U.S. in fighting ISIS. The military wing of Hamas, the Izz ad-Din al-Qassam Brigades, is listed as a terrorist organization by the U.S. The Israeli Ministry of Foreign Affairs states, "Hamas maintains a terrorist infrastructure in Gaza and the West Bank, and acts to carry out terrorist attacks in these territories and Israel." In 2017, Israel announced an $800 project to block tunnels Hamas had used to launch attacks in Israel.

Trump has underway an initiative to promote a Palestine that includes Hamas and the Palestinian Authority as a unified Palestinian government. Hamas has dropped its objective of the destruction of Israel. The Palestinian Authority governs the West Bank and Hamas runs Gaza. A unified Palestine could then negotiate a peace with Israel. One issue has been how to unify Palestine. Recent changes seem to make that more likely. They primarily involve the financing of Hamas. Also, Hamas rejects the ISIS goals of Sharia law and a Caliphate, and is seeking an independent Palestine.

Hamas has strained ties with Iran and Syria over its backing of Syrian rebels. Gulf states have not followed through on their pledge in 2014 to help rebuild Gaza after Hamas' war with Israel. However Qatar did provide about $400 million per year of infrastructure funding. But, this was cut off in 2017 by the economic blockade of Qatar by the gulf states that include the UAE, Saudi Arabia, and Egypt.

The Palestinian Authority has reduced its funding for Palestinian Authority employees in Gaza and cut off funding for Gaza's main power plant, and for electricity provided by Israel. This caused power blackouts. Hamas has run Gaza with an iron fist for ten years. However, in 2017 there has been public discontent due to these public service outages, and other public services issues. The financial pressure and public unrest has caused Hamas to form a link with and get funding from Egypt. ISIS fighters have been using Gaza as sanctuary to attack Egypt. In return for

Hamas' help in keeping ISIS out of Gaza, Egypt is providing funding for Hamas.

ArmchairTechInvestor Opinion

Negotiating a peace agreement between Israel and Palestine requires a unified Palestine. It is not certain that Hamas and the Palestinian Authority can be unified. However the loss of funding for Hamas, and it being funded by Egypt, could bring Hamas closer to the reality that their survival may depend on uniting with the Palestinian Authority, and honoring their statement that they no longer are seeking the destruction of Israel. Their continuing attacks on Israel will be an indicator whether Hamas is willing to recognize Israel and develop an agreement that recognizes Palestine and Israel as independent countries. To make this happen, an agreement on how to jointly enjoy Jerusalem will need to be negotiated. With the U.S. now recognizing West Jerusalem as Israel's capital, a peace agreement will need to recognize East Jerusalem as being under the jurisdiction of Palestine.

Foreign Policy-India

India has a population greater than China. China and India are unfriendly toward each other. India and Pakistan are also territorial rivals, with Pakistan being backed by China, and conducting terrorist raids on India. The U.S. is confronting Pakistan because of the fact that Pakistan is financing terrorism in Afghanistan, and harboring terrorists. India can provide a partnership with the U.S. that will confront both Pakistan and China, and provide a joint relationship as a foil to China's territorial ambitions, particularly in the Indian Ocean.

*India has become the large country with the highest growth rate, replacing China. Both countries have about the same size populations, but India has lagged China in developing its economy. India's economic growth problems have improved. In the last quarter of 2017, India's economy grew by 7.2%. In the first half of 2017, Mr. Modi voided most of the currency in circulation and put in a nationwide goods and services tax, causing uncertainty and consternation that took the economy below a 6% growth rate. The reforms implemented by Mr. Modi were aimed at stemming

corruption and aiding cashless transactions. The banks in India are struggling and a $32 billion capital infusion was implemented in October 2017.
Areas of the economy are growing but exporters are struggling

***India's Growth Zooms to Global Lead, Wall Street Journal, by Anant
Vliay Kala, March 1, 2018**

**The U.S. Is Developing Ties To India Knowing They Have Strong Ties
To Iran And Russia**

*On a visit to India in 2017, by the U.S. Secretary of State, Rex Tillerson,
India and the U.S. agreed to increase regional security and prevent
other countries from providing a safe haven for terrorists. The U.S. and
India plan to have talks with Afghanistan to increase regional stability.
Unlike talks that Russia had with Afghanistan to seek peace, that included Pakistan, and did not condemn them for financing and providing
a safe haven for terrorists, these talks will confront the Pakistani issues.
Pakistan's terrorist issues, should they grow, could undermine the stability of Pakistan. This could engender having their nuclear weapons fall
into the hands of terrorists. However, China's support for Pakistan could
reduce the risk of Pakistan's nuclear weapons falling into terrorist hands.

The U.S. has offered advanced military weapons to India, and hopes to facilitate a relationship between India and Japan. These weapons are being
offered despite the fact that Russia is supplying weapons to India, and in
October, 2017 India held joint military exercises with them.

With regard to the Iran relationship, India has renewed its financial relationship with Iran following the signing of the Iran Nuclear Agreement.
It has a port project called Chabahar. India sees the project as a possible
deterrence to the development of Pakistan's port of Gwadar, which is
now fully run by China. India, Afghanistan and Iran signed a trilateral
trade treaty for developing the Chabahar port project and beyond. Also,
Iran has invited China and Pakistan to participate in the Chabahar Port
project. India's objectives in developing the port project appear to be
severely compromised. Pakistan and China seem likely to be involved in
the project.

As of 2017, India owes Iran $6 billion for oil, which is being paid gradually. Tehran agreed in 2016 to keep the giant Farzad B gas field exclusively for Indian investment.

India has a strong relationship with Russia. In October, 2017, they held a joint military exercise with Russia that included India's army, navy and air force. This was the first such military drill with Russia.

Russia has managed to maintain security partnerships with both India and Pakistan. At about the same time India and Russia held their military drills, Russia announced that Pakistan held negotiations with Russia on the purchase of S-35 warplanes. This is part of a broader Russian strategy in South Asia that showcases Russia's increasing power in the international community. It also highlights Russia's interest in directly competing with the United States and China for influence in the Asia-Pacific region.

The relationships of Russia and Pakistan are based upon joint efforts to combat international terrorism in Asia. To convince the Indian government of Moscow's commitment to cracking down on facilitators of terrorism, Russian President Vladimir Putin supported India's counter-terrorism raid in Kashmir after the 2016 Uri attacks, and openly praised India's counter-terrorism policies during his meeting with President Modi in June, 2017.

An additional Russian objective is to serve as a mediator to both India and Pakistan to address their issues in Kashmir. This seems to be of more interest to Pakistan than to India. However, from Russia's standpoint, they have stayed unbiased in dealing with differences between India and Pakistan.

Russia has even sponsored peace talks in Afghanistan to solve their terrorist problems. Moscow has given Pakistan a prominent diplomatic profile in the peace talks it has hosted on the Afghanistan crisis. This has served to convince Pakistan that it is impartial in its relationships with both India and Pakistan. This contrasts with the U.S. approach of supporting Afghanistan, and criticizing Pakistan for supporting terrorists, and allowing them to have a safe haven in Pakistan.

*U.S. India Agree to Bolster Security, Wall Street Journal, by Niharika Mandhana, October 25, 2017

ArmchairTechInvestor Opinion

The relationship the U.S. has with India is a complex one. India has declined to enter into a formal alliance with the U.S., probably because of their strong ties to both Iran and Russia. Such an alliance would undoubtedly undermine those relationships. However, India is a developing country and has a population almost the same size as the 1.4 billion people in China.

The U.S. relationship with China is a complex one. The U.S. needs them to attempt to de-nuclearize the Korean peninsula by shutting down the North Korean nuclear weapons and ICBM development programs. China has mixed feelings about this because of the possibility of the North Korean government failing, the possibility of having a democratic South Korea on their border, and millions of refugees streaming into their country from North Korea. As of June 2018, China is attempting to insert itself in the Korean Peninsula denuclearization discussions between the U.S. and North Korea.

To strengthen the Asia region, the U.S. is trying to develop a relationship between India and Japan to fight China's aggressive actions in the South China Seas. The U.S. is also trying to involve India in Afghanistan as a participant in bringing stability to Afghanistan, and fighting Pakistan's terrorist support.

Also, the U.S. is working to develop a military relationship, including supplying weapons, with India.

India Has A Larger Population Than China: It Could Be The Ideal Partner In Confronting China

*India has some of the same problems that the U.S. has with China. There has been a confrontation on the Indian border with China. China began to build a road on disputed territory that India believes threatened its security. This confrontation created a rift such that Indian consumers were avoiding Chinese companies, and the public was calling for retaliation. China has much to lose by alienating the Indian consumers. China has a huge trade surplus with India, and as with the U.S., India claims that China is violating World Trade Organization rules, and is dumping product in its country. This claim is prevalent in other countries besides the U.S.

China-Indian Trade Hits Geopolitical Snag, Wall Street Journal, Eva Dou, September 1, 2017

**There is definitely a rivalry going on between China and India, which goes beyond the border dispute. Financially, China had been growing faster than India, but in early 2018, that has changed. The Indian rupee has been growing faster than the Chinese yuan currency. The Indian economic growth rate is expected to be 7.2% in 2018. The growth rate in China has been slowing, and is projected to be 6.5% in 2018. Much of the future success of India is predicated on the continued political success of Prime Minister Narendra Modi, who in 2017 met with Trump in Washington.

India Separates Itself From The Pack, Wall Street Journal, Corinne Abrahms & Desipesadad Nayak, September 8, 2017

ArmchairTechInvestor Opinion

India has a larger population than China, and perhaps the political situation is stable enough in India to allow it to reach its GDP potential. In any case, India's objectives are for the most part aligned with those of the U.S., and it could be a strong partner for the U.S. in confronting the expansionist objectives of China.

India And The U.S. Have Substantial Common Interests: The Differences Should Be Solvable

President Trump and Indian Prime Minister Narendra Modi met at the White House in a very hospitable environment. India is the world's largest democracy, with 1.3 billion people. They appear to be very suspicious of and competitive with China, and therefore a natural democratic ally of the U.S. Areas in which the U.S. has common interests include:

- Combating terrorism;
- Stabilizing Afghanistan; and,
- Improving trade relationships.

With regard to terrorism, the U.S. has sanctioned Mohammad Yusuf Shah, the head of Hizb-ul-Mujahideen, a terrorist group that India is fighting in the Kashmir, where India is also facing Pakistan. In early 2018, the U.S. is downgrading its relationship with Pakistan and increasing its support for Afghanistan. Mr. Modi highlighted that India has played an important role in rebuilding Afghanistan.

U.S. exports to India are about one-half of U.S. imports. The U.S. trade deficit with India was $24.4 billion in fiscal 2016. U.S. officials want trade barriers on agriculture and intellectual property reduced. Natural gas imports by India could grow substantially, as energy imports are of significant interest to India. India expects U.S. energy exports to total about $40 billion in the coming years. The U.S. and India share very strong computer, software and Internet development capabilities and technologies. India is a large user of H1B visas. It has companies that have invested $15 billion in 35 states in the U.S. U.S. companies have invested $20 billion in India. There are 3 million Indians living in the U.S. Manufacturing operations for the F-16 U.S. fighter jets could be moved to India in the near future. India plans to buy 200 U.S. aircraft. India has substantial satellite manufacturing operations and deployments planned, and could provide surveillance of the South China Sea. India is also considering buying the MQ-9 maritime surveillance drone.

At home, India is working with U.S. companies on 100 smart cities, the massive modernization of ports, airports, roads and rail networks. This should result in billions of dollars in revenues for U.S. companies. This is equivalent to what China is doing with its OBOR Initiative whereby Chinese companies are brought into countries to help them develop their infrastructure.

ArmchairTechInvestor Opinion

The meeting of Prime Minister Modi and President Trump was an opportunity for the two leaders to get to know each other. The joint Indian-U.S. interests are significant, including large investments by U.S. and Indian companies in each other's countries. Fighting terrorism, and confronting China together are likely to be significant joint efforts. Those are just a few of the significant joint interests and activities that Modi's visit to the U.S. enhanced.

Foreign Policy-Japan

Japan finds itself in the middle of a showdown between the U.S. and North Korea over nuclear weapons and intercontinental ballistic missiles that North Korea is developing, apparently with the expressed intention of attacking the U.S. China is the wildcard in this confrontation, and if the U.S. should equip or encourage Japan to have nuclear weapons, China could be additionally encouraged to restrain North Korea, assuming a failure of the U.S.-North Korean denuclearization negotiations.

Should Japan Go Nuclear In Response To North Korea's Aggression?

*North Korea launching an ICBM over Japan has brought to the forefront the issue of whether Japan should go nuclear, or rely on the U.S. to protect them, as they have done since World War II. However, the issue is much broader. Kim Jung Un, the President of North Korea, has as an objective to drive the U.S. out of East Asia, and drive a wedge between the U.S. and its partners, including Japan and South Korea. Japan has nuclear power plants, and it is believed that they could very quickly produce their own nuclear weapons, perhaps in months. North Korea's nuclear and ICBM actions could push Japan in that direction.

Should Japan go nuclear, it is possible that Taiwan would follow suit and work with Japan to develop its own nuclear weapons. The Japanese public is divided, but some within Japan are pushing for Japan to nuclearize and thereby join the great nuclear powers. Also, the U.S. has had volatile foreign policies, and Japan could be freed to a certain extent from those political uncertainties.

Russia could benefit from a nuclear Japan, if it reduced the U.S. influence in the region, and advanced their interests at the expense of China, particularly if both China and Japan were competing for influence with Russia.

The U.S. interests in East Asia could be furthered by a nuclear Japan, and even South Korea, if they served as a check on Chinese ambitions in the region.

Alternatively, the U.S. will need to continue paying most of the costs to contain China. This seems like the most likely route, even if Japan and South Korea were to go nuclear. North Korea will still continue to be a threat, and the shipping lanes in the South China Sea will still be under threat from China's expansionist policies. The U.S. will still need to protect the region from China, even if the Korean Peninsula is denuclearized.

Does Trump Want a Nuclear Japan? Wall Street Journal, By Walter Russell Mead, September 4, 2017

ArmchairTechInvestor Opinion

There is no other country in the world with the defense might of the U.S. that might be capable of standing up to China, particularly in the South China Sea. So, the U.S. presence there is likely to continue in any case. The U.S. is likely to be a bystander with respect to Japan choosing to go nuclear. If Japan should go nuclear, and Taiwan chose to do so also, the U.S. would be better off, as it would not have to confront Chinese antagonism and violation of the One China Policy if it aided Taiwan in going nuclear. Taiwan going nuclear might put it in a better position to forestall China taking over Taiwan as they did in Hong Kong, where they have subverted Hong Kong freedom and democracy.

Foreign Policy-Philippines

The Philippines has taken on crucial importance in the U.S. battle against ISIS. With ISIS on the verge of defeat in Syria and Iraq, their fighters are looking for other Muslim countries where they might reestablish a Muslim caliphate beachhead. Trump has recently strengthened the relationship with a controversial head of government, Rodrigo Duterte, and is supporting the Philippines in defeating ISIS in their country. Duterte is making overatures toward China.

The Philippines Have Taken On Crucial Importance: This Could Be A Big Win For Trump

The Philippines have gotten notoriety in the U.S. for several reasons. A frosty relationship with the Philippines developed under Obama. President Rodrigo Duterte had a bloody first year in office, killing over 8,000 people in an anti-drug campaign beginning in June, 2016. President Trump visited with president Duterte at the White House. The visit was supposedly soliciting support to oppose North Korean aggression. However, there are other reasons for the U.S to have a relationship.

China is claiming the South China Sea as their territorial domain, and building islands, on which they are locating military facilities. In mid-2017, China sent three naval ships to visit President Duterte, and they were well received at the President's hometown. President Duterte has reversed Philippine policy, and instead of using the U.S. as a partner to oppose China, is seeking Chinese investment.

The Association of Southeast Asian Nations (ASEAN) had a meeting in 2017 at which the China South China Sea situation was not mentioned, despite the Philippines having some claims in the South China Sea. The U.S. has pulled out of the TransPacific Partnership (TPP), weakening the U.S. in opposing China's global trade ambitions, although the Philippines is not a member.

The Philippines has ISIS terrorist problems on the Muslim island of Mindanao, where a 60-day period of martial law was declared in mid-May, 2017. This area has entrenched poverty and poor education that has alienated the residents from the Philippines' Roman Catholic majority, making them susceptible to radicalization. Ipsnlon Hapilon, with Abu Sayyaf, is the ISIS leader in the Philippine area.

The island of Mindanao has a population of about 22 million people, and has a number of terrorist organizations. As ISIS has lost territory in Syria and Iraq, fighters have gone to Mindanao, aided by porous borders and lax immigration policies. The Philippine army launched a raid on the terrorist group Abu Sayyaf's hideout in the city of Marawi, a city of over 200,000. It was an attempt to capture the terrorist leader Ipsnilon Hapilon. Hapilon is on the U.S. most wanted list, and has a price tag of $5 million on his head. The group is known for kidnapping and beheading foreign tourists. They live off of ransoms and other illegal activities. The leader was not caught and the Maute group, another ISIS terrorist group was called in to join attacks in the city. About 500 terrorists attacked the city. They cut power and captured several facilities, including city hall, and a Catholic church. A priest and others were captured.

At the time of the attack, Duterte was in Moscow, where agreements were to be signed. He met with Vladimir Putin, and asked the Russians to supply guns to fight the terrorists. He immediately came home, and declared martial law.

Over two hundred had been killed, and a surprisingly well-armed terrorist organization was hunted house-to-house. The deaths included 58 security forces, about 200 terrorists, and a small number of civilians. The terrorists came from Saudi Arabia, Yemen, Indonesia, and Malaysia. Tens of thousands of residents were fleeing, and kidnappings happened.

The Mautes are reputed to be the force behind the attack. Omar and Abdullah Maute are part of an aristocratic land owing clan. They could have been planning to take control of Marawi, and were prematurely interrupted when the initial attack by the Philippine army occurred.

ArmchairTechInvestor Opinion

The Philippines have become very important in many respects. They are developing investments from China, and seeking arms to fight ISIS from Russia. They are also the nexus of a thrust by ISIS to infiltrate the Philippines, Indonesia, and Malaysia. Those three countries have banded together to form a naval force to fight the terrorists, and their supply, ransom and hijacking activities. The U.S. Special Forces has been aiding The Philippines in Marawai. The Philippines contact, which President Trump has opened up, could be a major achievement in the South China Sea area.

Foreign Policy-South Korea

Korea's new President has succeeded in arranging talks between the U.S. and North Korea. In addition to being instrumental in the Korean Peninsula denuclearization negotiations, It appears that South Korea is also on a path to defend itself against North Korea, including perhaps completing the full deployment of the U.S. THAAD missile defense system, depending on how the denuclearization negotiations proceed with North Korea.

South Korea In The Middle Between The U.S. and China And North Korea and THAAD Are The Biggest Issues

President Trump met with South Korean President Moon Jae-in. Issues that were discussed included North Korea and bilateral trade issues.

In 2016, the U.S. imported $69.9 billion of South Korean goods and exported $42.3 billion, for a $27.6 billion trade deficit with South Korea. In the scheme of things, this is a relatively small trade deficit. However there are specific issues, such as South Korea dumping steel, and automobile trade barriers, which will be discussed in future bilateral trade negotiations.

The U.S. Terminal High Altitude Area Defense (THAAD) missile system, which is designed to shoot down short, medium, and long-range missiles, is being deployed in South Korea. Two of six missile launch platforms have been installed in South Korea, and the final four have been delayed, supposedly for an environmental study. However, Chinese dissent could be the reason.

China opposes THAAD. It fears it can reduce China's military leverage. The U.S. will be working with South Korea and Japan to build out what might become a broader and more comprehensive missile defense system. China is also worried that the radar system employed by THAAD could be used to track Chinese missile launches. The U.S. contends that the system is not capable of serving that purpose. President Moon told the U.S. Congress that he would not seek to reverse or cancel the THAAD missile defense system.

China is a much larger trading issue for South Korea than it is for the U.S. The value of its exports to China is more than double the exports to the U.S. For South Korea, exports are a very large 46% of GDP. China has threatened more economic repercussions if THAAD installations continue, but those negotiations are likely to take a back seat to denuclearization negotiations.

U.N., U.S. and other sanctions are in place to stop North Korea from developing nuclear weapons. The U.S. had asked the President of China to deter North Korea's weapons programs. The U.S. has pressed for additional sanctions on North Korea, and has imposed sanctions on a Chinese bank, and three other Chinese companies that have been fronts for North Korea in China, or enabling North Korea in the development of their nuclear and ballistic missile programs. President Moon had suggested meetings with North Korea, a highly popular position in South Korea. However, this approach has not been successful for the last 50 years, as North Korea has continued to develop its weapons programs. However, President Trump scheduled such a meeting for June, 2018, and denuclearization discussions are in the early stages of being able to complete an agreement.

In confronting North Korea, the preferred solution would have been to overthrow the current North Korean regime, and consolidate North Korea and South Korea. In a 2013 paper, RAND estimated that reunification between north and south could cost about $2 trillion, $500 billion for military operations, another $500 billion for damages, and $1 trillion for building the North's economy.

ArmchairTechInvestor Opinion

North Korea is the most important issue for South Korea, and North Korea's nuclear weapons and missile launch programs need to be decisively confronted. North Korea has sophisticated weapons systems manufacturing operations. The U.S. needs to impede the improvement of their nuclear program and disable the development of their ICBM development program designed to deliver a nuclear weapon to the U.S. It is the hope of the U.S. that this threat can be eliminated by the current discussions and a subsequent verifiable denuclearization agreement and program.

South Korea Faces Difficulties In Dealing With China: Will The THAAD Missile Defense System Remain Deployed?

South Korea's newly elected leader, Moon Jae-in, has promised to engage with North Korea, which he has so far done successfully, despite his overtures being met by an accelerated missile launch program by North Korea. Mr. Moon, a moderate, replaced Park Geun-hye, a South Korean conservative, who is in jail facing corruption charges.

The U.S. has been deploying the THAAD missile defense system in South Korea, which has met with resistance from China. China's military and intelligence hackers, plus so-called patriotic hackers, have been targeting South Korea's government, military and defense companies. China has denied the hacking, which originated in Chinese cities, one of which is a home to North Korean hackers also.

Other moves taken by China, in retaliation for Lotte Group leasing land where the THAAD missile system is located, include what South Korea has characterized as unlawful economic pressure. In addition, tour packages have been cancelled, and regulatory measures taken against South Korean companies.

Following Mr. Moon's election, China expressed a willingness to normalize relations with South Korea. China expressed its commitment to stopping North Korea's nuclear program, and maintaining stability on the Korean Peninsula. However, the THAAD is still an issue.

With regard to the THAAD, President Trump wanted South Korea to pay for the $923 million THAAD system, but apparently backed off of that position, after getting resistance from South Korea. Mr. Moon is still in favor of the system, but apparently wants to get formal government approval. Two THAAD systems have been deployed, and Mr. Moon has complained that four additional systems were being deployed, without him being told about them by the military.

ArmchairTechInvestor Opinion

The THAAD missile defense system is a major irritant to China. We expect South Korea to keep the system, and it remains to be seen what will be China's attitude toward South Korea, if that is the case. Not addressed by China is whether they will attempt to help curtail the North Korea's missile test program, which is a major issue for South Korea, Japan and the U.S. Since China was doing little to stop this program, the U.S. decided, in concert with South Korea, to confront North Korea directly. It appears that the talks between the U.S. and North Korea in June 2018, have left China out of the negotiation process. China's weakness in dealing with North Korea could be the reason for this occurrence.

Foreign Policy-Africa

African Continental Free Trade Area (ACFTA)

In April 2018, discussions continued that could lead very soon to the formation of ACFTA. Trade among the African countries is very low. Although there are some differences among the African neighbors, the formation of ACFTA could aid the African countries in increasing trade among themselves. The amount of trade between the African countries is a very low 16% of total trade. By comparison, 70% of the trade in Europe is among the European countries. In Asia, the percentage is 51%.

CHAPTER 9

Chinese and U.S. Foreign Policy-Middle East

North Africa and Middle East

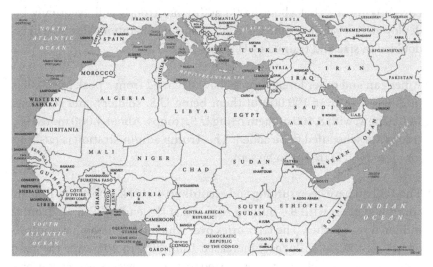

Image: North Africa and Middle East Map
Image Source: Getty Images

Foreign Policy-Middle East

Foreign Policy-Afghanistan

Afghanistan has Taliban supporters among its politicians and is under serious threat from a resurgent Taliban. The Taliban is financed by Pakistan, and has a safe harbor there. The U.S. has a resurgent relationship with Afghanistan that is necessary to stop the Taliban and al-Qaeda. A complicating factor in Afghanistan is that about 10% of the people are addicted to opium, which drives the drug trade and can finance terrorism. The U.S. policy in Afghanistan is under review, including the size of U.S. forces there, which in mid-2018, had been increased by about 4,000 troops. The U.S. has threatened Pakistan with the elimination of about $2 billion of U.S. military aid.

Taliban Talks May Be Undertaken In Afghanistan: Are They Likely, And Could They Be Successful?

President Trump's recently announced strategy for Afghanistan is under review. He is believed to endorse an open-ended commitment, but that currently means that about 4,000 additional troops will eventually be deployed. At the same time the Afghan special operations forces, will be doubled in size and trained by U.S. and NATO advisers.

American and other foreign forces have declined from a peak of 150,000 in 2009, with over 100,000 of them being U.S. soldiers, and to about 14,000 now, with 8,400 of them being U.S. troops. About 4,000 more U.S. troops are scheduled to be added. The Trump administration is pushing for more NATO troops to be sent.

The Taliban have been surging and according to a U.N. report, the Taliban controlled areas with 8.4 million Afghans at the end of 2016, up from 5 million a year earlier. The territories over which the Taliban has control, or has significant influence, increased from 30% to 40% over the year 2016. Any sustainable solution will need to involve successful negotiations with the Taliban. The Haqqani group and the Taliban are both financed by Pakistan, and have safe havens in Pakistan. For this reason, the U.S. is reducing its support for Pakistan, and the relationship is deteriorating.

Middle East Map

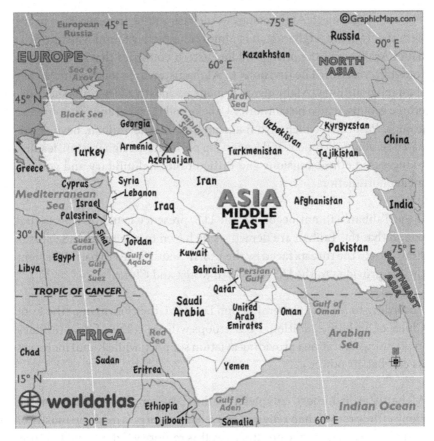

Image: Middle East Map
Image Source: Worldatlas

Also being questioned is Trump's declaration that the U.S. government would no longer pursue "nation-building" in Afghanistan and elsewhere. The United States has invested billions of dollars in aid, advisers and projects to help build Afghanistan's democracy and economy since the fall of the Taliban regime in 2001. As of early 2018, U.S. support for Afghanistan is increasing.

ArmchairTechInvestor Opinion

The easy solution in Afghanistan would seem to be to negotiate a peace with the Taliban. Afghanistan is almost completely Sunni Muslim, as is Saudi Arabia, and the other Middle Eastern countries that have aligned to fight terrorism. The divisions in Afghanistan are along ethnic rather than religious lines. Afghanistan is made up mostly of Pashtun and Tajik ethnic groups. It also has minority Uzbeks and Hazaras and other smaller groups. Pashtuns, which also make up most of the Taliban, have dominated senior government and leadership positions in Afghanistan, leading to increased ethnic tensions and difficult internal military and government coordination.

If the Taliban will not negotiate, the U.S. presence could be a perpetual one so that the Taliban are denied a safe haven to attack the U.S. This is similar to to the threats faced by the U.S. in South Korea to battle the joint threats provided to the U.S. by North Korea and China.

According to Marine General Joseph Dunford, the chairman of the Joint Chiefs of Staff, the additional U.S. troops will assist the Afghan military in planning operations providing aviation support, while Kabul increases its combat air power.

Afghanistan is almost completely Sunni Muslim, but its divisions lie along ethnic rather than religious lines. The country is made up mostly of Pashtun and Tajik ethnic groups, as well as minority Uzbeks and Hazaras and various other smaller groups. Pashtuns, which also make up most of the Taliban, have dominated senior government and leadership positions, leading to increased ethnic tensions and difficult internal military and government coordination.

According to a Fox News article by Hollie McKay, the Taliban is attempting to take Kunduz, which is situated at a key logistical juncture with highways linking Kabul to the south, Sher Khan Bandar to the north and Mazar-e Sharif to the west. The Taliban has gradually infiltrated the city, and the government has not provided the resources to fight them.

Several officials cautioned Fox News that Kunduz, even if Afghan forces soon retake Taliban areas, would inevitably fall to the Taliban again unless local support for terrorists is rooted out and ethnic rivalries are addressed. Furthermore, the government forces themselves are not as strong as they should be, with leaders said to be put in place, not based on performance or experience, but on tribal and family connections.

An Afghan local noted that Afghans themselves need to be the foot soldiers. They are the ones who are familiar with the area itself. More U.S.-led air support would be of helpful, However, ensuring fair representation among ethnic groups and stamping out corruption in military leadership, putting the most capable in the top jobs rather than those with the right connections, are fundamental. The Afghans themselves need to be the soldiers, and are the ones who are familiar with the areas themselves. While more U.S.-led air support would be of benefit, ensuring fair representation among ethnic groups and stamping out corruption in military leadership, putting the most capable in the top jobs rather than those with the right connections, are crucial. This should be a viable objective for the U.S. and allied troops in Afghanistan.

ArmchairTechInvestor Opinion

Afghanistan is a difficult battlefield because of government corruption, and the need to vet the people to identify Taliban supporters. The locals can be organized to fight the Taliban or ISIS, and the best locals should be put into positions of authority. It is also difficult because of many Pashtun Taliban in powerful positions in the government in Kabul.

Foreign Policy-Egypt

Egypt receives substantial foreign aid from the U.S. despite its human rights abuses. The major positive in supporting Egypt is the aid it provides to the U.S. in fighting terrorism, including terrorists that bombed Coptic Christian churches in Egypt. Egypt is funding Hamas, which is designated by the U.S. as a terrorist organization, to help it fight ISIS in the Sinai Peninsula. Egypt is also a supporter of Israel. To achieve a Palestinian peace with Israel, Hamas will likely need to eliminate its military presence in the Sinai and Gaza.

Despite Egypt's Alleged Human-Rights Abuses, The U.S. Is Likely To Continue Providing Foreign Aid.

Egypt has a history of human rights abuses. According to Amnesty International, "The old patterns of human rights abuses under Hosni Mubarak remain in place." Egypt has suffered a number of human rights setbacks since the removal of Mohamed Morsi from the presidency in July 2013. Security forces killed about 1,000 people on August 14, 2013, during the sit-ins by Morsi's supporters. In early 2018, the ability of activists to express their views has declined, particularly in the media outlets.

Egypt is number two to Israel in receiving foreign aid from the U.S. At a Senate Appropriations committee meeting in 2017, a bipartisan panel of experts on Egypt-U.S. relations urged Congress to rethink its annual $1.5 billion aid package to Cairo, as the country fails to improve its human rights record. Egypt is criticized for not using the money to fight terrorism. It is claimed that the fighter jets the U.S. is supplying to Egypt are not effective in fighting terrorism. However, the success of Russia, working with Assad in Syria, might argue to the contrary.

In 2017, President Abdel Fattah el-Sisi declared a state of emergency after two suicide bombings on Coptic churches killed at least 45 people. The attacks, for which Islamic State claimed responsibility, struck worshippers in the town of Tanta and the Egyptian port city of Alexandria, as they celebrated Palm Sunday. Egyptian fighter jets carried out 6 strikes against camps near Derna in Libya, where the militants responsible for attack are believed to have been trained.

al-Sisi was criticized for "selling" Egyptian territory, after deciding in April 2016, to hand over two Red Sea islands to Saudi Arabia.

Why the Red Sea islands are important:

- Sanafir and Tiran are islands that lie about 4km (2 nautical miles) apart in the Red Sea;
- Tiran sits at the mouth of the Gulf of Aqaba, on a strategically important stretch of water called the Strait of Tiran, used by Israel to access the Red Sea;

- The islands are uninhabited, apart from Egyptian military personnel and multinational peacekeepers;
- Egyptian troops have been stationed on the islands since 1950 at the request of Saudi Arabia; and
- Israel captured the islands in 1956 and 1967, subsequently returning them to Egypt both times

ArmchairTechInvestor Opinion

Egypt is an important element in fighting terrorism, as a member of Gulf Countries fighting terrorism. This group numbers almost fifty countries. Three Gulf countries and Egypt accused Qatar of supporting terrorism and destabilizing the region. Qatar, which shares its only land border with Saudi Arabia, has rejected the accusations, calling them "unjustified" and "baseless." Yemen and the Maldives also cut ties with Qatar.

In addition to the anti-terrorism gulf country group, Egypt also has a relationship with and has recognized Israel. This could be very helpful in attempting to get Israel and Palestine to arrange a peace agreement that recognizes both Israel and Palestine as independent countries. Egypt is supporting Hamas financially to protect Egypt from ISIS. This financing is sorely needed by Hamas, and Egypt. Since Egypt is providing needed financing for Hamas, they could be crucial in negotiating a peace agreement.

It seems likely that Trump will continue foreign aid for Egypt.

Foreign Policy-Hamas

The U.S views Hamas as a terrorist organization. However, Hamas will be vital if a Palestine-Israel Peace Agreement is to be reached. Hamas has limited financial resources, and is using a pact with Egypt to provide financing. The agreement has Hamas working to defend Egypt from ISIS. For there to be a Peace Agreement, the Palestinian Authority will need to govern a unified Palestine that includes Hamas. The major obstacle is how to disarm Hamas so that a situation like that in Lebanon, where Hezbollah has its own military, does not occur in Palestine.

ISIS Is Driving Hamas Into The Arms Of Egypt And Israel. Will A Palestinian Peace Be The Result?

* In August 2017, an ISIS militant killed a Palestinian security guard near a crossing between the Gaza Strip and Egypt. This was the first ISIS attack on Hamas. After this, Egypt began funding Hamas, as a deterrent to attacks against Egypt by ISIS. An offshoot of ISIS, Sinai Province in the Sinai Peninsula, attacked Egypt twice in two weeks in 2017. These attacks were aimed at robbing a bank. ISIS no longer has its financial resources in Iraq and Syria, and appears to be using terrorism to secure local financing.

*Terror Group Strikes Egypt, Wall Street Journal, By Rory Jones and Dalia Kholaif, October 20-21, 2017

** Iran Extends Its Reach in Syria, Wall Street Journal, By <u>Dexter Filkins</u>, June 9, 2017

Those attacks occurred after Egypt helped negotiate reconciliation between Hamas, which rules the Gaza Strip, and the Palestinian Authority (PA), which rules the Sinai Peninsula. They have agreed to form one government, which the Palestinian Authority will run, and the PA will presumably support a financially stressed Hamas, in addition to the financial support being provided by Egypt.

During mid-2017, rockets were fired at Israel from the PA controlled Sinai. These might be militants independent of the PA, or they might have had the approval of the PA. There have been negotiations between the PA and Israel to develop a peace agreement that would recognize Israel, and form a country, Palestine.

ArmchairTechInvestor Opinion

ISIS is unwittingly driving Hamas into the arms of Egypt, and into accepting the right for Israel to exist, at least in words. With Egypt having a good relationship with Israel, Egypt promoted the unification of the Palestinian Authority and Hamas. President Trump has espoused getting a peace agreement between a united Palestine and Israel. The U.S.

is providing foreign aid to Egypt. Egypt could be helpful in getting Israel and Palestine to negotiate a peace agreement, particularly with Hamas being supported financially by Egypt.

If the PA is sincere in seeking peace, the rocket attacks on Israel do not bode well for an agreement. Another deal breaker for Israel, regarding the unification of the PA and Hamas, is that Hamas will keep its military arm in the unification with the PA, at least for now. If Israel is likely to recognize Palestine as a country, Hamas will undoubtedly need to be disarmed and the PA will need to stop the launching rockets at Israel.

One never knows about peace between Israel and Palestine, but the pieces are increasingly being put in place to make that happen. This could be a big achievement for President Trump, one that many of his predecessor presidents have not been able to accomplish.

Foreign Policy-Hezbollah

Hezbollah has a substantial political presence in Lebanon, and is vehemently anti-Israel. It is also a proxy militant fighter for Iran, and has an important role with Russia and Iran in Syria, including helping run the communities where it is a fighter. Hezbollah is also active in Latin America. U.S. operatives have been apprehended that appeared to be developing plans to attack the Panama Canal, and execute terrorist activities in the U.S.

Iran Is Financing Terrorism In The U.S. Through Hezbollah: Iran and Hezbollah Are Enemies Of The U.S. Will the U.S. Recognize This Reality?

A Wall Street Journal editorial in late 2017 provided details that indicate that Iran is, through a surrogate, Hezbollah, recruiting U.S. citizens to terrorize the U.S. and also Panama. Iran appears to provide about $200 million per year of financing to Hezbollah. The U.S. is at war with Iran and Hezbollah. An Iran sponsored Hezbollah, is fighting on behalf of Assad in Syria, and with Iran supplied missiles. Hezbollah is threatening Israel with a war in Israel, from its base in Lebanon. Israel faces the threat of being attacked from Lebanon and an Iran sponsored contingent on its other border with possible Syria and Iran sponsored hostile forces.

*Hezbollah has been recruiting supporters in the U.S., including two identified in late 2017. They had been planning terrorist activities in the U.S. and Panama, where Hezbollah has perpetrated terrorist activities going back to the early 2000's.

In October 2017, a joint FBI-NYPD investigation led to the arrest of two individuals who were allegedly acting on behalf of Hezbollah's terrorist wing, the Islamic Jihad Organization (IJO). At the direction of their Hezbollah handlers, one person allegedly "conducted missions in Panama to locate the U.S. and Israeli Embassies and to assess the vulnerabilities of the Panama Canal and ships in the Canal," according to a Justice Department press release. The other allegedly "conducted surveillance of potential targets in America, including military and law enforcement facilities in New York City." In the wake of these arrests, the director of the National Counterterrorism Center warned: "It's our assessment that Hezbollah is determined to give itself a potential homeland option as a critical component of its terrorism playbook, and that is something that those of us in the counterterrorism community take very, very seriously." These cases, one official added, are "likely the tip of the iceberg."

* **How Trump Is Going After Hezbollah in America's Backyard**, Politico, By Matthew Levitt, November 30, 2017

The Trump administration runs a counter-Hezbollah campaign that is an interagency effort. It includes leveraging diplomatic, intelligence, financial and law enforcement tools to expose and disrupt the logistics, fundraising and operational activities of Iran, the Qods Force and the long list of Iranian proxies. These include Hezbollah snf other Shia militias in Iraq and elsewhere. But in the words of Ambassador Nathan Sale, the State Department coordinator for counterterrorism, "Countering Hezbollah is a top priority for the Trump administration."

Hezbollah, the Party of God, is a Shia Islamist political, military and social organization that wields considerable power in Lebanon. It began as a movement in the 1980's, with the support of Iran, during the

Israeli occupation of Lebanon. Israel withdrew from Lebanon in 2000. Hezbollah took this opportunity to strengthen its military capabilities, and used those resources against Israel in the 2006 war. Its military capabilities rival those of the Lebanese army. It has also expanded its political activities, and effectively has veto power in the Lebanon cabinet. It adds political instability in Lebanon, but is popular in the Shia community.

Hezbollah has been fighting in Syria on behalf of the Assad regime. As the war in Syria escalated, thousands of Hezbollah militants went to fight for Syrian President Bashar al-Assad, proving decisive in helping pro-government forces recover ground lost to rebels, particularly along the Lebanese border. They appear to be honing their village running skills, with the objective of expanding beyond their base in Lebanon.

Hezbollah's involvement in Syria, however, has sharpened sectarian tensions in Lebanon, where Sunni militants have targeted the group in a series of bombings.

Hezbollah is designated as a terrorist organization by the U.S. and other western powers, Israel, the Gulf Arab countries and the Arab League.

ArmchairTechInvestor

Iran is using its proxy, Hezbollah, to find sympathizers in the U.S. that can undertake acts of terror. This is no different than what ISIS is doing, and makes it clear that beside ISIS, Iran and Hezbollah are also trying to attack the U.S. at home. Another Iranian proxy is the Houthis in Yemen, making it clear that the U.S. needs to support Saudi Arabia and the UAE in Yemen. With the increasingly global reach of many terrorist organizations, the U.S. needs to recognize that it is at war with the terrorists.

Potential Iranian Routes to the Mediterranean

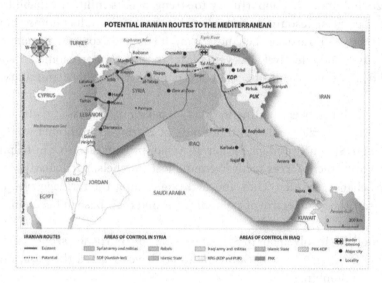

Image: Potential Iranian Routes to the Mediterranean Map
Image Source: Map Reprinted With Permission of the
Washington Institute for Near East Policy

Iran has stepped into the void created by the Obama administration withdrawal from Afghanistan, Syria and Iraq. Iran is involved in the fighting, along with Russia, in Syria. Its hope is to develop a supply route from Iran through Syria and Iraq to Lebanon and the Mediterranean.

Iran Is Executing On Its Plan To Extend Its Shiite Influence And Gain A Supply Route To The Mediterranean.

Iran has a two-pronged attack to extend its influence in Iraq. It has militias that are integrated with the Iraqi government forces to fight ISIS. It also has political influence in Iraq.

It was thought that the Iraq election in 2018 would pit pro-Iran Nouri al-Maliki, the former prime minister, against Haider al-Abadi, the current prime minister. Mr. Abadi has developed strong ties with the U.S. The election was expected to be close, and a continued allegiance of Iraq to the U.S. was not assured. Abadi is working to reduce the influence of the

Iran- backed militias in the military, even though they have been very helpful in the fight against ISIS. In the election, a totally unexpected result appeared to occur. The winner of the election was the Sadrists, followers of the religious leader Muqtada al-Sadr, and the Iraqi Communist Party. The coalition has pushed an anti-corruption and anti-sectarian campaign. There is a complicated process that will determine who becomes the prime minister. There are five Shiite political groups who are likely to determine the nature of the government, and it will take alliances among these groups to determine a winner.

Iraq is a majority Shiite country, and the legislature in Iraq has some strong supporters of Iran, also a Shiite country.

Iran, and its proxy, Hezbollah, have been working with Assad and Russia to recapture land lost to ISIS and other militants in Syria.

In Raqqa, Iraq, U.S. forces backed a coalition of Kurds and Arabs known as the Syrian Democratic Forces (SDF). They control land in Northern Syria, and could control Raqqa after a peace is reached. Following the war, the control of Raqqa by the SDF could be an important impediment to Iran's ability to ship weapons through Raqqa to Mosel, the route that was previously the core supply route for ISIS. The Iran weapons route now appears it could go through the northern part of Iraq and Syria, where it could face U.S. resistance. Alternatively, it could go south through Baghdad, and then west through Southern Iraq and on to Damascus in Syria. From there it go could North through Homs to Tartus, on the Mediterranean, or through Lebanon to the Mediterranean. It appears probable the Iran will be able to secure a route to the Mediterranean, unless they are blocked from going through both Northern and Southern Syria. A link to the Mediterranean going through Lebanon to Iran would allow weapons to be supplied by ship to Iran's wholly controlled weapons supply line.

ArmchairTechInvestor Opinion

The U.S. presence in Iraq and both Northern and Southern Syria could provide a roadblock to Iran developing a supply line to the Mediterranean. It will be very important for the U.S. to continue to work with the Kurds and Iraq, and hope that the new government will be neutral to both Iran and the U.S., which may happen.

Iran Leader Reelected

Hassan Rouhani was elected president of Iran in 2017, having garnered a substantial 67% of the vote. The turnout was strong, with the poles being open for an extra 5 hours.

Prior to the voting, the U.S. signed a sanctions waiver at the very last minute. However, the U.S. is now going beyond the content of the Iran Nuclear Agreement, and has implemented sanctions that initially addressed Iran's missile development program. They cover 7 individuals and entities, including a Chinese-based network.

The Iran Election Is Unlikely To Change Iranian Policy: Their Terrorist And Missile Development Activities Need To Be Addressed

On May 19, 2017 Iran elected its next president. The two major issues were probably the Iran Nuclear Deal, which allowed Iran to resume oil exports to Europe, the conclusion of passenger plane deals, and the economy.

The reelected incumbent president, Hassan Rouhani, negotiated the nuclear deal, and is considered to be a moderate. Trump's opposition to the nuclear deal could have aided Rouhani, because of fear that the election of Ebrahim Raisi, the hard-liner, could again isolate Iran. Raisi was allegedly involved in the 1988 mass execution of thousands of prisoners. He is also the favorite of Ayatollah Ali Khamenei, Supreme Leader of Iran.

Raisi also had the support of two major clerical bodies that declined to endorse anyone in the last presidential election. He had pledged to support the poor with a monthly cash payment equivalent to $65, which is about a sixth of what a menial laborer makes in a month.

According to a report in Al Jazeera, since taking office, Rouhani has brought inflation down to 6.5% from 40% in 2013. In addition, Iran had a 12.5% increase in growth during his initial presidential term.

However, unemployment rates for men and women were at 21.8% and 10.4%. at the time of the election, Youth unemployment was at 30%. This surely weighed heavily on the minds of the voters. During the televised presidential debates, Raisi lashed out at Rouhani for Iran's slow economic growth.

Trumps' opposition to the Iran Nuclear Deal has raised serious questions about the deal itself, and whether Iran will be able to build a nuclear weapon at the end of the ten year deal. Also at issue is Iran's aggression in Yemen, Syria, and Iraq, and its support of proxy militias that include Hezbollah in Syria, Panama and the U.S., and the Houthis in Yemen. Additionally, Iran has economic problems at home and in early 2018, may be stretched thin in its support of terrorist activities.

The U.S. Congress requires the President to report on whether Iran is meeting its nuclear obligations. Not included in the Iran Agreement are any limits to Iran's development of ballistic missiles, and they continue to do tests. Technically these tests may not violate U.N. resolutions, and were not covered by the Iran Nuclear Deal. In 2017, Trump certified that Iran had not been meeting its Nuclear Deal obligations.

ArmchairTechInvestor Opinion

President Trump has questioned the Iran Nuclear Agreement. Language was included in the Agreement that prohibits Iran from ever developing nuclear weapons, even after the ten-year period ends. However, the question of how to enforce that on a long-term basis needs to be addressed by the U.S. Also, Iran's missile development activities and support of terrorism in the Middle East need to be controlled. As of early 2018, the U.S. is essentially at war with Iran, even though war has not been declared. The question of regime change in Iran is always a possibility, because of Iran's theocracy and autocratic domination of its people.

The U.S. Has Taken Some Steps to Confront Iran, Including Initiating Sanctions on Chinese and Russian Entities.

The U.S. is fighting in court for a temporary travel ban to 6 countries. It bars travel to the U.S. for 90 days from six predominantly Muslim countries., Sudan, Syria, Iran, Libya, Somalia and Yemen. This initiative includes

Iran, and is part of a renewed effort to confront Iran's moves to expand its presence in the Middle East. This travel ban has essentially been approved by the Supreme Court, but applies only to those that do not have a U.S. familial relation. As of early 2018, additional determinations are pending.

The State Department has evidence that Iran is providing missile support to the Houthi rebels in Yemen. Saudi Arabia and the United Arab Emirates (UAE) are targeting the Iranian backed Houthi rebels, including Al Qaeda. The U.S. reversed an Obama policy, and is again providing military support, including precision-guided weapons, to Saudi Arabia and the UAE.

The Houthis have targeted U.S. ships in the region and are a threat to commercial vessels in the Persian Gulf. The Houthis appear to be a Hezbollah-like Iranian proxy in Yemen.

In another U.S. initiative, the U.S. has put sanctions on individuals and entities that have provided support for Iran's ballistic missile program. The sanctions applied target 30 individuals & entities from 10 countries sanctioned for transferring missile technology or flouting export controls on Iran, North Korea and Syria. Twelve are Chinese and eight are Russian. Of these, 11 are companies and individuals that have provided materials to Iran's ballistic missile program.

In mid-2017, 14 Senators introduced a bipartisan bill to increase sanctions on Iran for support of terrorism, weapons transfers, and human rights violations.

ArmchairTechInvestor Opinion

The Trump Administration is substantially increasing the pressure on Iran, including questioning the Iran Nuclear deal. We believe the Trump initiatives above are the beginning of a substantially increased U.S. initiative that includes confronting Iran's nuclear weapons initiatives.

Foreign Policy-Iraq

Iraq has been taken off of the list of countries on the Trump travel ban. The U.S. has been instrumental in helping drive ISIS out of Mosul, and substantially weakening them in Iraq. The U.S. has been supplying weapons to the Kurds, to the dismay of Turkey. A Kurdistan state might have been set up in Iraq, but a Kurdish vote to become a separate country appears to have scuttled that effort. The Kurds are fractured now, and appear to have been a small factor in the recent election. Supporters of Iran are in the government of Iraq, and the leader of Iraq has yet to be decided as of June, 2018.

Iraq Appears To Have A Moderate Government. Can The U.S. Trust Iraq As a Future Partner?

The Kurds are in control of Iraqi territory in the north. Iraq has not agreed to allow the Kurds have their own country, Kurdistan, in Iraq. Two things are complicating the situation. Iraq had an election in 2018 that could bring into power radical Shiites that oppose the Kurds. The Kurds also have a presence in Syria, Iran and Turkey and all of these countries oppose the Kurds getting their own country, fearing that the Kurds in their countries will be encouraged to try to produce similar results in those countries.

According to an article by ex-ambassador John Bolton, who is now Trump's National Security Advisor, the Kurds are not monolithic. The Kurds in Syria, whom, the U.S. is backing, are apparently linked to the Marxist PKK in Turkey. The U.S. has branded the PKK a terrorist organization, and is working with Turkey to fight terrorism, including the PKK. However, the U,S, was selling weapons to the Kurds in Syria, and fought beside them to defeat ISIS in Mosul and in Northern Syria. The U.S. provides the Kurds, known as the YPG, in Syria with air power and special forces assistance. Facing resistance from Turkey, a weak NATO ally, the U.S. parceled out weapons as they were required in Raqqa, and took steps to prevent those weapons being used by the PKK in Turkey. Besides small arms, the YPG was given anti-tank weapons. The U.S. views the Kurds as a separate fighting force, not a terrorist group. Since Raqqa is primarily Sunni, their Muslim partners in the Syrian Democratic Forces (SDF), of which the YPG is a partner with the Arab groups, are likely to play the role of integrating with the local Sunni population. The Kurds made up the largest part of this 50,000-fighter group. The battle for Raqqa started in June, 2017, and defeated was a determined ISIS force. Another nearby area that still had an ISIS force was Deir ez-Zour province, which is oil-rich. Assad, allied with Russia and Iran, took that region back from ISIS. Raqqa was to be the SDF's last major battle, and the SDF might remain in control of Raqqa, during the post-ISIS period in Syria.

The situation in Iraq is quite different. The Iraqi Prime Minister is Haider al-Abadi. Over a 3-year period, Abadi has managed to narrow the gaps between the warring Shiites and Sunnis. He managed to balance the competing interests of Iran and the U.S., while rebuilding the Iraqi security forces. President Trump removed Iraq from the immigration ban, strengthened the U.S.-Irag ties. Iraq's security forces are in the final stages of defeating ISIS in Mosul, with the final battle being waged in the Old City. This completed the recovery from ISIS after them taking much of Iraq in 2014, and declaring the Caliphate defeated in Mosul.

Iran has a major influence in Iraq. Iran is the largest Middle Eastern Shiite country, and was determined not to lose Iraq to the Sunnis. Through Grand Ayatollah Ali al-Sistani, the preeminent Shiite cleric in Iraq, Shiite militias were formed and trained by Iran's Revolutionary Guard. The forces were supposed to be under the control of Iraq. The bond with Iraq could give Iran a supply route from Iran through Syria and Iraq to Hezbollah in Lebanon. Complicating this goal could be the presence of the Kurds in Northern Iraq and Syria.

The U.S. has also been very active militarily in Iraq. The U.S. has spent more than $1 billion to train and equip the Iraqis and fund U.S. troops in Iraq. The support includes advanced arms and air support. The Iraqi military personnel have pledged to be non-sectarian, which facilitated the U.S. assistance.

ArmchairTechInvestor Opinion

The U.S. faces challenges to the continuing loyalty of Iraq, because of the strong military reliance of Iraq on Iran. Also, the elections in 2018 could increase the power of radical Shiites. The U.S. needs to continue to work with the Iraqi government, with the hope that radical Shiites will not gain control. It may also want to continue to support the Kurds.

Iran And The U.S. Are Working Together in Iraq. Will That Continue Once ISIS Is Defeated?

President Trump removed Iraq from the temporary travel ban in recognition that the U.S. and Iraq are working together to defeat ISIS. That Iraqi, Kurdish and Iranian campaign had significant success in driving ISIS from Iraqi cities. The last remaining stronghold for ISIS in Syria was Mosul.

In Eastern Mosul, which was liberated from ISIS in 2017, life is coming back to normal. Trees are being planted, and downed wires repaired. Retail establishments are reopening. Products banned by ISIS, such as cell phones, and women's lingerie, are reappearing.

Western Mosul has historically been a less prosperous area. Five bridges around the area were knocked out to eliminate ISIS supply lines. The fight had came down to door-to-door fighting in the Old Town area, which is less than 10% of Western Mosul. The recaptured areas of Western Mosul are in need of rebuilding, as is underway in Eastern Mosul.

When Obama abandoned Iraq in 2011, it left the door open for Iran to increase its presence, and ISIS, formed by the remnants of Saddam Hussein's Sunni regime, captured large parts of the country in 2014. Iran has its supporters in the government, but it appears that Haidi al-Abadi, the Prime Minister, is interested in maintaining relationships with both the U.S. and Iran, with military help from the U.S. being very important. However, Iran has Shiite proxy militias fighting in Iraq, that give it a strong influence. Further complication the situation is the uncertainty caused the 2018 election.

The Kurds have their own separate region, Kurdistan, in Northern Iraq. Iran has a strong presence in this region. The U.S. support of the Kurds in Syria could be an important element in helping the U.S. stay involved in Iraq.

ArmchairTechInvestor Opinion

What will happen now that ISIS is defeated, and a peace accepted by Assad in Syria, is not clear. President Trump's aggressive moves to confront Iran's regional ambitions could work against the U.S. in Iraq, because of the foothold the U.S. allowed Iran to establish. Since ISIS is still likely to be a terrorist threat in the country, the U.S. could be important militarily on a long-term basis. Trump's move to reestablish relations with Iraq was a prudent one. Also, his move to arm the Kurds in Syria appears to have been a successful one, despite the anger from Turkey in response to this move.

Foreign Policy-ISIS

The U.S. has been instrumental in defeating ISIS in Iraq and Syria. ISIS has also been largely defeated in Libya. However, despite the defeats, ISIS is attempting to wage a terrorist war from ungoverned parts of Syria, and by expanding elsewhere, including to the Philippines and Africa.

The Trump Administration Was Instrumental In The Defeat Of ISIS In Iraq And Syria

Since the Trump administration took office, an objective in the Middle East has been to defeat ISIS in Iraq, Syria and elsewhere. In Iraq, the government has a strong Iranian element. Despite that factor, the U.S. had successfully revived a relationship with Iraqi Prime Minister Haider al-Abadi.

*The Iraq stronghold and capital for ISIS had been Mosul. Iraq's security forces suffered huge casualties in the nine-month-long battle to take back the city of Mosul. In August 2017, they completed taking back the ISIS stronghold of Tal Afar, one of the last urban areas held in Iraq by the militant extremist Sunni group, American defense officials said. According to the New York Times, an estimated 1,000 Islamic State fighters were believed to have been in Tal Afar. This could have been a brutal and bloody last stand, the officials said, because Tal Afar had been encircled by Iraqi and Kurdish forces, making it difficult for the fighters to flee in large numbers. The battle in Iraq to defeat ISIS in the populated areas has been won.

* Revived After Mosul, Iraqi Forces Prepare to Battle ISIS in Tal Afar, New York Times, By Helene Cooper, AUG. 18, 2017

With regard to Syria, the story is quite different because of the presence of Iran, Hezbollah, and Russia supporting the Assad regime. After the ISIS defeat in Raqqa, their headquarters in Syria, ISIS was essentially defeated in Syria. The U.S. had supported the Kurdish led Syrian Democratic Forces that led the fight against ISIS in Raqqa. They have been successful in controlling a large portion of Northern Syria. The U.S. has also supported some militias in Southern Syria on the Jordan border. It appears that those two areas might be able to remain independent of Syria, should there be a peace agreement.

ArmchairTechInvestor Opinion

The U.S. appears to have largely achieved its goal of defeating ISIS in Syria and Iraq. It will be important for the U.S. not to abandon their partners, the Kurds in Northern Syria, and the militant groups in Southern Syria, once a peace agreement has be reached with Assad. This will give the U.S. a presence that could serve to thwart Iran's ambitions of creating a supply line from Iran through Syria and Iraq to Hezbollah in Lebanon, and connecting this supply line with the Mediterranean.

In Iraq, there were elections in 2018. It will be important for the U.S. to support the winner in that election, and work to develop a continuing relationship that supports Iraq in what will be a continuing fight against ISIS, that will still be present in remote areas.

Also, the fight against ISIS is spreading to places such as Libya and the Philippines, as the losing fighters in Syria and Iraq seek to develop other strongholds where they can launch attacks against the U.S. and Europe.

ISIS Is Morphing Into A More Global Terrorist Threat: Does This Increase U.S. Vulnerability

ISIS has lost the basis of its self-described caliphate, in what were losing battles in its two largest cities, Mosul in Iraq, and Raqqa in Syria.

The losses in Iraq and Syria have caused ISIS to encourage their militants to go to other areas. Those include the Philippines, and Indonesia, where ISIS is launching renewed attacks. An important threat to the UK and Europe is the citizens in those countries that have gone to fight for ISIS, and are returning to their own countries. This is likely to escalate the frequency of ISIS sponsored attacks, such as has occurred in the France and Belgium.

In 2017, ISIS attacked the Iran parliament building and the tomb of Ayatollah Khomeini, killing at least 12 people. ISIS sympathizers have been recruited in Iran, expanding their influence. Iran has been fighting ISIS in the Middle East.

ArmchairTechInvestor Opinion

ISIS lost badly in Iraq and Syria, negatively impacting their ability to attract recruits. They need successes to be able to remain attractive to Muslim recruits. The U.S. has done a good job in fighting Shiria believing terrorists, President Trump's extreme-vetting process for immigrants from countries that have large Muslim populations should assist in attracting Muslims, particularly those that do not believe in Shiria law.

Foreign Policy-Israel

President Trump has renewed the U.S. relationship with Israel, which deteriorated when Obama developed the Nuclear Agreement with Iran. Nuclear weapons and ballistic missiles in the hands of Iran are a threat to Israel. Israel is also threatened by Iran arming Hezbollah in Syria and Lebanon. Israel is worried about having enemies on the borders of both Syria and Lebanon. Israel is working with the U.S. to develop a successful peace process with Palestine. However, the U.S. is moving its Israeli embassy to West Jerusalem, might seem like a setback to a Palestinian peace. However, this position by the U.S. could shape a Palestinian entity in East Jerusalem, and take this element off of the table in Palestinian peace negotiations that would end up with Palestine having parts of Gaza and the Sinai.

Israel-Under Pressure From Iran And Hezbollah In Syria: Will It Lead To War?

*In 2017, Israel launched strikes in Syria that were apparently aimed at weapons storage facilities, a military training facility, and facilities that were used to store chemical weapons. This was part of an overall picture that has Iran using the war in Syria to establish a permanent presence in that country, once ISIS is defeated and the war winds down. Iran's Revolutionary Guard apparently has the backing of Russia in Syria. Iran has helped Hezbollah stockpile thousands of missiles to be used the next time there is a war between Hezbollah and Israel.

The fear is that the U.S. will be dragged into such a war. However, the U.S. has indicated it is only in Syria to kill ISIS. Also, the U.S. is supporting the Kurds in Syria, and will probably be asked to provide long-term support. It is likely that ISIS, despite a defeat in Syria, will continue to have a rural presence, and the ability to launch random strikes in Syria. Iran will continue to have a presence in Syria, and the U.S. will need to articulate its long-term strategy there.

*The Next Middle East War, Wall Street Journal Editorial, September 8, 2017

**In another development in Syria, the Syrian government broke a 3-year siege by ISIS by surrounding oil-rich Deir ez-Zour province, where ISIS apparently congregated following its defeats in the north in Raqqa, where the U.S. is supporting the Kurdish led coalition that has defeated ISIS. The U.S. and Russia have an agreement to avoid clashes in Syria. Much of ISIS's leadership and assets were believed to have been located in Mayadeen, about 30 miles south of the city of Deir ez-Zour, which has been recaptured by President Bashar al-Assad's Syrian forces. ISIS no longer controls the oil assets in the area, which it used to finance its operations.

**Syrian Military Advances, Ramping Up Pressure On ISIS, Wall Street Journal, by Maria Abi-Habib & Nour Alakraa, September 6, 2017

***The Kurdish lead Syrian Democratic Forces (SDF) control land areas outside the control of Assad, and there is an issue of how these areas will be segregated, and ruled, once ISIS is defeated. American's military had planned to push south along the Euphrates River, and seize the cities of Mayadeen and al-Bukamal on the Iraqi border. That is the region that has most of the oil and gas reserves in Syria. The rapid defeat of ISIS in Deir ez-Zour blocked the route the SDF was going to take to get to Mayadeen and al-Bukamai. The U.S. wants a soft partition of Syria along the Euphrates River, but that plan may now be in jeopardy. Syria and Iran have no interest in such a soft partition. It is possible that Assad will eventually attack the SDF, and that could bring the U.S. into the conflict, or require the U.S. to eliminate their support for the Kurds. Also, important to Iran is whether they can control a land link between Tehran, Syria and Hezbollah in Lebanon.

***In Syria, A New Conflict Looms As ISIS Loses Ground,** Wall Street Journal, by Yaroslav Trofimov, September 8, 2017

ArmchairTechInvestor Opinion

The U.S. backed the Kurds in Syria, and has withdrawn support for them in Iraq because of the vote to make Kurdistan a separate country there. The issue of Iran and Russia having a continuing presence in Syria post-ISIS is an important one for Israel, and if war breaks out between Hezbollah/Iran and Israel, the U.S. could become a participant also. The U.S. seems to have a working relationship with Russia in Syria. There have been some close brushes with conflict, particularly with Assad, and the U.S. will have to decide at some point on its long-term policy in Syria.

Foreign Policy-Jordan

The U.S. has a strong relationship with Jordan, which also has a good relationship with Israel. Jordan could be a factor in protecting U.S. Muslim partners in Southern Syria on the Jordanian border, should a Syria peace agreement be negotiated with Syria, Russia and Iran.

A More Aggressive U.S. Policy In Syria: The U.S. Is Protecting Its Muslim Partners On The Jordan Border

In looking at Syria and what may be the final political settlement, Jordan is on the southern border of Syria, and rebels supported by the U.S. had control of territory in that Syrian region. Maghaweer al-Tharwa is described as an elite rebel group that, along with the U.S. and other rebel groups, occupies Tanf, which is close to a base where the U.S. has been training rebel troops.

The U.S. launched an airstrike against a Syrian tank group that is part of the Assad government's army. They had been advancing on Tanf for a week, and were a threat. President Trump gave the authority to local U.S. officers to pursue the war as they see fit. This was the first such strike in Syria to defend a U.S. supported position.

The U.S. alerted the Russians that they would undertake the strike if Assad's troops advanced on Tanf. The Russians warned Assad not to undertake that action, but he ignored the warning. The result appears to be that a tank, and 4 vehicles were destroyed, in addition to 8 Assad regime fighters being killed, and others wounded.

ArmchairTechInvestor Opinion

The first U.S. attack in Syria was launching 59 tomahawk missiles in response to a Syrian regime poison gas attack, in violation of U.N. restrictions on Syria. This was an alert to the Syrian regime that the U.S. will not ignore their poison gas atrocities. The attack by the U.S. in the Tanf area was a further message that the U.S. will defend U.S. supported rebel fighters in Syria. This could also be a message to Turkey not to attack U.S. supported Kurdish fighters in Northeastern Syria.

Foreign Policy-Kurds

The Kurds have territorial ambitions in both Iraq and Syria. In Northern Syria, they tried to set up a separate country, and the Iraq government rebuffed that initiative. Although the U.S. supports the Kurds in both Iraq and Syria, the U.S. did not support the Kurds in trying to set up a separate country in Iraq. In Syria, it remains to be seen if the Kurds will eventually control a region of the country. That seems unlikely in view of the effectiveness of the Russians and Assad in recapturing a substantial portion of Syria that had been lost to what Assad calls terrorists.

The Kurds' Ambitions To Have Their Own Country Took A Giant Setback With Iraq Taking Control Of Kirkuk, And The Oil Fields.

*The Kurds in Iraq took a giant gamble in holding a referendum to approve establishing their own country in Kurdistan, which is part of Syria. The referendum won vast approval, but received no support from surrounding countries, and their U.S. partner in defeating ISIS in Iraq. The Kurds had control of substantial oil assets in Kirkuk and surrounding areas.

*__Iraq Clash Raises Fear of Wider Conflict__, Wall Street Journal, by Ali A. Nabban, and Isabel Coles, October 16, 2017

**The Kurds have their own area, Kurdistan, in Northern Iraq, which has been operated autonomously. The Kurds' referendum caused the Iraqi government to draw a line in the sand, and begin reasserting their control over the areas controlled by the Kurds that are not a part of Kurdistan, and therefore disputed. The Kurds had expanded the territory they controlled in the North by about 40% while they were working with the U.S. to defeat ISIS. Iraq began by attacking Kirkuk unexpectedly. They took the municipal facilities, and surrounding oilfield areas. This shut down operators such as Chevron, many of whose workers sought safety in surrounding areas. Iraq also shut down the exits to Kurdistan, creating additional problems for the oil field workers.

**__Kurd Clashes Delay Chevron__, Wall Street Journal, by Benoit Faucon, October 19, 2017

Iranian Shiite militias that are working with the Iraqi government and are backed by Iran drove the reassertion of Iraqi control over Kirkuk and the oil areas. Once ISIS is fully defeated and the disputes between Iraq and the Kurds resolved, Iran will undoubtedly try to continue to operate in Iraq, perhaps independently of the Iraqi government. In any case, Iran could continue to have substantial military influence in Iraq, despite the possible efforts of the Prime Minister Haider al-Abadi to reduce the military influence of Iran.

ArmchairTechInvestor Opinion

Iraq is a country where the U.S. will continue to be challenged by Iran. If the U.S., under the Trump administration, tries to abandon the Kurds, it is likely to face the same fate as Obama did when he withdrew from the Middle East. The U.S., under Trump, could lose influence and be forced back into the country by Iran and other militants, including ISIS.

The Kurds Had An Opportunity To Create Their Own Country in Iraq: It Didn't Happen

The Kurds voted overwhelmingly in favor of Kurdistan becoming independent of Iraq. The turnout was 72% and 93% voted in favor of establishing their own country, Kurdistan. Iraq had allowed the Kurds to operate as an independent region in the Northern part of Syria. The U.S. along, with other Western countries, opposed the Kurds holding the election. The objective of the Kurds was to use the vote to negotiate with Syria to establish their own separate country. Those possible negotiations did not happen and the election backfired.

Kurdistan is landlocked, and therefore subject to a possible economic blockade. It had control of Kirkuk, which has substantial oil fields. Iraqi Prime Minister Haider al-Abadi had said that Iraq does not recognize the vote and there were no plans for talks with the Kurdish leaders. The Afghanistan parliament authorized Abadi to deploy troops to disputed areas and to regain control of the oil wells, which he did.

*Iraqi Kurds Back Independence in Referendum, Wall Street Journal, by Israel Coles and Ali A Nabhan, September 28, 2017

The Kurds are also working with other militants in Syria in the Kurd led Syrian Democratic Forces (SDF). They have been successful in driving ISIS out of Raqqa in Northeast Syria, and attempted to move to the Southeast. They had captured a huge Conoco gas plant from ISIS, substantially denting their revenue sources. The revenues of ISIS have declined 80% in the last two years according to IHS Conflict Monitor. The objective of the SDF is to prevent Assad from taking back control of Syria and he needs to control the oil and gas resources to do that.

U.S.-Backed Forces Seize Gas Plant From Militants, Wall Street Journal, by Raja Abdulrahim, September 25, 2017

ArmchairTechInvestor Opinion

The Kurds essentially control an area in Northern Iraq called Kurdistan. They would like to split off from Iraq, and establish a new country called Kurdistan. Control of this area has been ceded to the Kurds by Iraq. The Kurds are tenacious fighters. It seems highly unlikely that Kurdistan will become an independent country. There were many issues would have needed to be resolved, such as the borders, and developing amicable relationships with their neighbors, Iran, Turkey, and Iraq, that would allow Kurdistan to have trade relations with other countries. The issues for the Kurds to overcome to have their own country, are substantial, particularly because of the animosity they have in relations with Turkey and Iran. Controlling oil resources was an important element of their possible success, and they lost that when they lost Kirkuk to a surprise attack by Iraq.

Foreign Policy-Kurds

The Kurds have territorial ambitions in both Iraq and Syria. In Northern Syria, the tried to set up a separate country, and that initiative was rebuffed by the Iraq government. Although the U.S. supports the Kurds in both Iraq and Syria, the U.S. did not support the Kurds in trying to set up a separate country in Iraq. In Syria, it remains to be seen if the Kurds will eventually control a region of the country. That seems unlikely in view of the effectiveness of the Russians and Assad in recapturing a substantial portion of Syria that had been lost to what Assad calls terrorists.

The Kurds' Ambitions To Have Their Own Country Took A Giant Setback With Iraq Taking Control Of Kirkuk, And The Oil Fields.

*The Kurds in Iraq took a giant gamble in holding a referendum to approve establishing their own country in Kurdistan, which is part of Iraq. The referendum won vast approval, but received no support from surrounding countries, and their U.S. partner in defeating ISIS in Iraq. The Kurds had control of substantial oil assets in Kirkuk and surrounding areas, which were recaptured by the Iraqi government.

*Iraq Clash Raises Fear of Wider Conflict, Wall Street Journal, by Ali A. Nabban, and Isabel Coles, October 16, 2017

**The Kurds have their own area, Kurdistan, in Northern Iraq, which has been operated autonomously. It appears that the Kurds referendum caused the Iraqi government to draw a line in the sand, and begin reasserting their control over the areas controlled by the Kurds that are not a part of Kurdistan, and therefore disputed. The Kurds had expanded the territory they controlled in the North by about 40% while they were working with the U.S. to defeat ISIS. Iraq began by attacking Kirkuk unexpectedly. They took the municipal facilities, and surrounding oilfield areas. This shut down operators such as Chevron, many of whose workers sought safety in surrounding areas. Iraq also shut down the exits to Kurdistan, creating additional problems for the oil field workers.

ArmchairTechInvestor Opinion

Iraq is a country where the U.S. will continue to be challenged by Iran. If the U.S., under the Trump administration, tries to abandon the Kurds, it is likely to face the same fate as Obama did when he withdrew from the Middle East. The U.S., under Trump, could lose influence and be forced back into the country by Iran and other militants, including ISIS.

Foreign Policy-Palestine/Israel

President Trump has pledged to do whatever it takes to get a Palestine-Israel peace agreement. A precondition to such an agreement is likely to be for Hamas and Gaza to form a single government with the Palestinian Authority, which runs, the West Bank. Recently, such an alliance was proposed and accepted by Hamas. The other main issues are:

- The recognition of Israel;
- How to demilitarize Hamas; and
- How to share Jerusalem.

President Trump Has Predicated A Successful Palestinian Peace Agreement With Israel On The Unification of Palestine. Will It Happen?

The Palestine Authority, which controls the West Bank and is led by Mahmoud Abbas, and Hamas, has a recent leader, Yahya Sinwar, and controls the Gaza Strip. Sinwar was jailed by Israel in 1988 and spent the next 23 years in prison, where he was a key leader of Hamas members in the Israeli prison system. Hamas has two wings, the political arm, and Izzedine al-Qassam, an armed wing.

Talks have been underway between the Palestinian Authority and Hamas to bridge a gap that has existed for ten years, unify the Palestinians under one organization, and negotiate a peace agreement with Israel. The Palestine Authority has said that any agreement for unification of the West Bank and the Gaza Strip under the Palestine Authority must include the disarming of the armed wing of Hamas. This would avoid a situation like that in Lebanon where Hezbollah has its armed group that operates in parallel with the Lebanese army. This disarming has been resisted by Hamas for obvious reasons. The members of the armed wing would suddenly be disbanded and disarmed. It seems unlikely that Sinwar will be able find a solution to this dilemma and this seems to be the biggest hurdle to a unified Palestine emerging. However, Hamas' financing sources are seriously depleted, and they may feel they need to have access to the financial resources of the Palestinian Authority. Also, their financing is heavily dependent on Egypt.

*Palestinian Talks Hit an Impasse, Wall Street Journal, by Rory Jones, October 4, 2017

ArmchairTechInvestor Opinion

The Trump administration has set a goal that has not been achieved by many past administrations. It seemed like a Herculean task to unite Palestine into one organization that could negotiate a peace agreement with Israel. Finally, the financial weakness of Hamas has a chance of making peace possible. The military wing of Hamas will probably need to be disarmed to achieve peace, and Hamas will have to recognize Israel. The obstacles are still large but there is a glimmer of hope that Palestine can be unified and peace can be negotiated with Israel.

Israel-Palestine Peace Deal: Will Trump Get It Done?

President Trump has pledged to "do whatever is necessary" to bring about an Israeli-Palestinian peace deal where both sides can live together in peace and harmony. The peace talks stalled in 2014.

Mahmoud Abbas is the President of the Palestinian Authority, which rules the West Bank. Rival Hamas is listed by the U.S. as a terrorist organization, and occupies the Gaza Strip. Both Palestinian entities are very different and efforts to get a peace accord between Israel and both entities will likely continue to be difficult. However, Trump is the master of the deal, and who knows. In the U.S. budget, funds to the West Bank and the Gaza Strip are expected to see an increase of 4.6 percent for the 2018 fiscal year, from $205 million in 2017 to $215 million.

Mr. Abbas, who in 2017 visited President Trump in the White House, has been trying to unify Palestinian territories, which has been difficult since Hamas took control of the Gaza Strip 10 years ago.

In a secret vote, Hamas has selected a very hawkish Yahya Sinyar as its political leader in the Gaza Strip, a replacement for the current political leader, Ismail Haniyeh. The U.S. has Yahya Sinyar on its list of terrorists. The current overall leader of Hamas, Khaled Meshaal, resides in Qatar, and Ismail Haniyeh is expected to challenge him for the overall leadership. The four chapters overseen by the overall leadership are:

- Gaza;
- The West Bank;
- Israeli prisons; and,
- Areas outside Palestinian territories.

Hamas has expressed the desire for a fully sovereign state with Jerusalem as its capital. And, its Charter no longer refers to the Muslim Brotherhood, from which it evolved, and which was shut down by Egypt, after it abused its power following its successful election.

Although Hamas dropped its call for the destruction of Israel, activities and teachings, and a new Charter that make a peace deal difficult include:

- Israel is not recognized;
- A Palestinian state is envisioned in the territories captured by Israel in the 1967 war; and
- An ambition expressed is the long run desire to take all Israeli territories.

An Israeli spokesman for Benjamin Netanyahu said there are continuing Hamas calls for the genocide of all Jews and the destruction of Israel. And, there is continuing bombardment of Israel from Gaza. Neither the U.S. nor Israel believes there has been a fundamental shift in Hamas' actions despite the rhetoric of Hamas. The activities of Hamas going forward will determine their current intent.

Hamas appears to be under pressure on many fronts. They include:

- Ties with Syria and Iran are strained over Hamas support for Syrian rebels;
- Gulf states that have deepened their ties to Israel have not delivered the funds promised for the rebuilding of the Gaza Strip after Hamas' 2014 war with Israel;
- Egypt, and other Gulf States, such as Saudi Arabia, the United Arab Emirates have designated Hamas as a terrorist organization; and,
- Turkey restored its diplomatic relationship with Israel in 2016.

Israeli activities that make peace talks difficult include:

- For security reasons, Israel says it will not return to pre-1967 borders;
- Israel has put tight restrictions on goods flowing in and out of Gaza, resulting in dire economic conditions; and,
- Israeli settlements total around 400,000 and Israelis live in about 130 separate settlements;
  - o This doesn't include East Jerusalem;
  - o Settlements have been established in every corner of the West Bank, giving the Israeli military a reason to be present

throughout the territory and making it difficult to create a viable Palestinian state. The settlement locations and the roads that connect them make Palestinian movement difficult;

o   There are many Palestinian refugees that would like to return to Israel;

o   Jerusalem is an issue and Israel has the support of the U.S. to establish their capital there; and

o   Terrorism is a huge issue.

ArmchairTechInvestor Opinion

A starting point in negotiating a peace agreement will be for Hamas and the Palestinian Authority to reach an agreement that will make the Gaza Strip and the West Bank into a unified Palestinian state. This is only likely if the two territories can be unified under Abbas, or Hamas changes its territorialism ambitions, and terrorist activities, which is probably unlikely. How the Israeli settlement issue will be resolved, is uncertain, but there are many Palestinians in Israel, so perhaps the Israeli police presence could be reduced over time. If there was a true peace, the terrorist issue will have to be addressed by the Palestinians and the Israelis. Immigration of Palestinians into Israel is an issue, but perhaps the numbers can be scaled back to provide comfort to Israel that Israelis will still be in a substantial majority. A sharing of Jerusalem would need to be negotiated. The issues are daunting, but any movement that Trump can initiate could reduce the tensions, even if a peace agreement is not reached immediately.

Foreign Policy-Qatar

Qatar is a U.S. ally and the U.S. has its largest Middle East military base there. Qatar has a relationship, based upon a joint gas field, with Iran. It is likely providing financial support to the Muslim Brotherhood and other terrorist organizations. For this reason, the UAE, Saudi Arabia and Bahrain have blockaded Qatar, pushing Qatar toward Iran, which is supplying food and other goods to them.

Qatar Is A U.S. Ally, But It Has Serious Differences With Saudi Arabia And Its Allies. What Will Happen?

The U.S. has its largest military base in the Middle East in Qatar. It directs the U.S. military operations in the Middle East.

Saudi Arabia, the United Arabs Emirates (UAE), Egypt and Bahrain cut off diplomatic relations with Qatar, and implemented policies such as closing ground routes to Qatar, and blocked Qatari vessels and aircraft from their waters and airspace. This essentially isolated Qatar. Qatar's only land border is with Saudi Arabia.

Iran is attempting to take advantage of this rift by sending food to Qatar. Iran has also allowed Qatar to use its air and sea lanes after the Saudi-led Arab group suspended all flights to and from Doha, and severed diplomatic ties. Some Saudi Arabia companies also are supplying food to Qatar, in violation of the blockade.

Qatar is accused of hosting and supporting terrorism, and providing financing to terrorist organizations that include Hamas and The Muslim Brotherhood, but previously they have said that these organizations are not terrorist groups.

The measures are more severe than during a previous eight-month rift in 2014, when Saudi Arabia, Bahrain and the UAE withdrew their ambassadors from Qatar, alleging Qatari support for militant groups.

Rex Tillerson, the former Secretary of State, signed a memorandum of understanding (MOU) with Qatar to jointly fight terrorism. On the eve of Tillerson's arrival in the region in 2017, documents were leaked purporting to show secret agreements that Qatar had signed several years ago, probably in 2014, agreeing not to support the Muslim Brotherhood or other groups opposed to its Persian Gulf neighbors. In a joint statement carried by the Saudi press agency, the Arab states said that the agreements confirm beyond any doubt Qatar's failure to meet its commitments. During the current crisis, the Arab states have linked Qatar to a host of opposition and militant groups in the region.

Iran has a relationship with Qatar through gas interests that are in a contiguous gas field. Iran is apparently inserting itself into a breach between Qatar and other Middle East countries and is supplying food and other goods. The U.S. is afraid that the rift with the Saudi-led Arab countries could push Qatar further into the arms of Iran. The U.S. relationship with Qatar could reduce the threat posed by Iran.

ArmchairTechInvestor Opinion

The MOU with Qatar is not an agreement until it is finalized. The documents leaked showing Qatar has apparently violated past agreements not to fund terrorist groups, like the Muslim Brotherhood, make the MOU's impact very uncertain. However, it will give the U.S. a chance to see if Qatar is now sincere, particularly because the Saudi led group that the U.S. is supporting can supply facts about Qatar's ongoing activities on a realtime basis.

Saudi Arabia Hosted Trump: And, The Saudi Power Structure was In Flux

President Trump visited Saudi Arabia at the time they had organized a 2-day event that included 50 Arab heads of state that back a unified Arab response to ISIS in Yemen, Syria and Iraq. Times have changed in that Trump was standing up to Iran, whereas Obama had a frosty relationship with Saudi Arabia and others because he favored Iran sharing the Middle East with the Sunni countries, including Saudi Arabia. That policy resulted in Iran flexing its muscles in Syria, Iraq and Yemen, where they have supported proxy militias that include Hezbollah in Syria and the Houthis in Yemen. The Houthi forces launched a major operation in southwestern Yemen, in mid-2017, striking the United Arab Emirates (UAE)-backed Southern Resistance units inside the Ta'iz Governorate. Backed by the Yemeni Republican Guard, the Houthi Forces inflicted heavy damage on the defenses of the Southern Resistance near the coastal city of Mocha, while also killing at least ten fighters in the process. According to Hezbollah's official media wing, the Houthi forces destroyed a large number of UAE-supplied military vehicles in the Ta'iz Governorate. The UAE and Saudi Arabia are fighting together in Yemen.

King Salman is 81, was hosting Trump, and had not yet named his successor. A rising star, Deputy Crown Prince Mohammad bin-Salman (MBS), who is considered an outsider, was leading a modernization of Saudi Arabia, when he was only 31. He was subsequently named as the Saudi successor. Women will apparently have a much larger role, and are being allowed to drive cars. Entertainment, which used to be banned, is now allowed. The conservatives opposed these changes, but were not been able to block them.

Saudi Arabia has had zero growth in its economy. It needs to transition to a broader economy. It also needs to instill a work ethic in its population that has traditionally relied on oil revenues for its income.

ArmchairTechInvestor Opinion

Trump's visit to Saudi Arabia in 2017 was important in many respects. The Saudis, the UAE, and other middle eastern countries, are the most important allies in fighting terrorism. The Saudis have recognized Israel and are working with them to confront ISIS. Also, there were 50 countries that attended the meetings in Saudi Arabia, that can all be supporters of an anti-ISIS coalition.

Important will be whether the Sunni countries can organize into an effective unit to fight ISIS and Iran. Also, Saudi Arabia is groping for a way to develop non-oil businesses. Helping Saudi Arabia modernize their economy could go a long way in the U.S. rebuilding rapport with them and their allies.

Foreign Policy-Saudi Arabia

President Trump has renewed ties to Saudi Arabia. They have become a focal point to unite Sunni Muslim countries to fight ISIS. Saudi Arabia is restructuring its economy, has plans to take its oil company, Aramco, public, and is undertaking action to silence the radical clerics in its country. It is also leading a blockade of Qatar. Complicating the U.S. relationship is a Saudi relationship with Pakistan.

Saudi Arabia Unveils Up To $370 Billion Of U.S. Investments And A Global Islamist Terrorist Center As Well As The Saudi Drive To Diversify Its Economy

Saudi Arabia has talked for some time about its need to diversify away from oil. Some initial steps have been taken in that direction. The first step was to make Aramco, their state-owned oil company, a public company. This will result in hundreds of billions of dollars that can be used to fund economic diversification. Aramco said it signed 16 accords with 11 companies valued at about $50 billion. One initial deal, worth $15 billion, was signed with General Electric Co. The Aramco public offering could face severe problems, particularly because of the relationship of the Saudi government to Aramco.

The U.S. and the Saudi Defense Ministry also negotiated a package of about $110 billion, according to a White House transcript.

Deputy Crown Prince Mohammad bin-Salman (MBS), who is 32, and a strong advocate of economic and social modernization, will drive the economic diversification. Important to those efforts will be the development of knowledge-based businesses, and presumably building those businesses in Saudi Arabia.

The Saudi's and SoftBank of Japan have invested in a $93 billion high-tech fund, of which the Saudis indicated they would invest up to $45 billion, and which is targeted at $100 billion. This is the SoftBank Vision Fund. The head of the SoftBank, Masayoshi Son, had previously told Donald Trump that the fund would invest $50 billion in U.S. tech companies, and create 50,000 U.S. jobs. Examples of the kinds of investments already made include:

- $1.4 billion in an early stage Indian mobile payments company, Paytm;
- $1.2 billion in a U.S. internet-satellite startup, OneWeb. SoftBank led a $502 million round for a U.K. virtual world startup, Improbable; and
- Led a $130 million fundraising for Bay-Area microbe designing robot company, Zymergen.

They have a large pipeline that includes genome sequencing, virtual-reality simulations, games, autonomous driving, and biotechnology. The fund took longer than expected to get launched because of Saudi desires on how the fund would be managed. Mohammad bin-Salman led the negotiations, with a vision that the fund would provide Saudi Arabia knowledge that would help them develop their country, and also the wider Gulf Region.

The Saudi's have committed $20 billion to a Blackstone U.S. Infrastructure fund in the U.S. The fund is expected to total about $40 billion, and with another $60 billion of debt it could invest a total of $100 billion. The total Saudi investment in this fund could be about $50 billion. The largest previous fund was a $15.8 billion fund of Global Infrastructure Partners, which is located in New York. Infrastructure funds are growing rapidly. In 2016, $56 billion was invested in infrastructure funds, with an additional $29 billion invested in Q1 2017. Many of the investments are targeting airports, pipelines, roads, utilities and other U.S. public projects. Also, non-traditional investments, such as hospitals, are being considered. Such funds typically have a lifetime of ten years, but the Blackstone fund has no termination date.

Honeywell International Inc., Nabors Industries Ltd., Exxon Mobil Corp. and Lockheed Martin Corp. were among other U.S. companies to sign accords, after American corporate leaders met local business heads in Riyadh.

Raytheon Co. will work with Saudi Arabia Military Industries on defense-related projects and technology development. It will establish Raytheon Arabia in Riyadh, the company said in a statement. Saudi Arabia Military Industries was set up to help reduce reliance on foreign purchases and to diversify the economy away from oil.

ArmchairTechInvestor Opinion

President Trump was impressive in opening up relations with Saudi Arabia that had stalled under President Obama. The trip to Saudi Arabia by Trump was an ideal time to announce Saudi-U.S. deals that included:

- $110 billion of investment by Aramco in U.S. companies;
- $50 billion of U.S. investment by SoftBank Vision Fund; and
- What could be $100 billion of U.S. infrastructure investment by Blackstone.

The U.S. and Saudi Defense Ministry also negotiated a package of about $110 billion that included tanks, fighter jets, combat ships and the THAAD missile defense system, according to the White House.

Also impressive was the Saudi commitment to establish a center to combat global Islamist terrorists in conjunction with the representatives from 54 Arab and Muslim countries that attended the two-day event in mid-2017.

Saudi Arabia Is A Key Link In Fighting ISIS

Saudi Arabia's Ambassador to the U.S. outlined their policies and the strong ties they share with the U.S. The U.S. strike in Syria, resulting from a sarin chemical weapons attack by the Assad regime, struck a resonant cord with the U.S. Middle Eastern allies, including Saudi Arabia. Iran and Hezbollah, along with Russia, are supporting the Assad government. Together they are responsible for over 400,000 deaths, and half of Syria's population of 22 million is displaced.

Saudi Arabia did not believe that Assad could be a part of a peaceful solution in Syria. Saudi Arabia's air force used a base in Turkey to attack ISIS in Syria, so they are involved beyond Yemen. The peace in Syria could be in conjunction with the 2012 Geneva I declaration. Such a solution might result in three regions being formed. Turkey and the Kurds are in different areas of the north. Baghdad is in the middle on the west coast, and Jordan is on the border in the South. However, with the successes that Russia and Iran have had on behalf of Assad, the outcome of peace negotiations has shifted toward an Assad driven solution.

Saudi Arabia is sandwiched between Yemen and Iraq. In Yemen, Saudi Arabia, with U.S. backing, is fighting the Houthis. Like Hezbollah, the Houthis are an Iranian surrogate. It is clear that Iran, the Houthis, and

Hezbollah are U.S. enemies in the Middle East. Iran provides a sanctuary for the leaders of al Qaeda.

ISIS and al Qaeda are also U.S. enemies, not only in the Middle East, but also in Africa. ISIS has lost control of the cities it has dominated in Iraq and Syria, and lost its caliphate potential. This could result in al Qaeda and ISIS working together, despite their differences.

Saudi Arabia is the leader of a 41 Sunni-majority Middle Eastern country group that some have called the "Muslim NATO". A mission of it is to fight ISIS, as well as to meet threats to member countries, including confronting militia groups in Libya and Boko Haram in West Africa. Their first meeting was scheduled in Saudi Arabia, and they expected to be militarily operational by the end of 2017.

Pakistan is a partner of Saudi Arabia, and has sent 5,000 troops to guard their southern border with Yemen.

ArmchairTechInvestor Opinion

The U.S. is in an undeclared war with Iran, Hezbollah, and the Houthis in the Middle East and Africa. Saudi Arabia is perhaps the U.S.' most important partner, but Afghanistan, Iraq, Jordan and Egypt are also important partners in that war. The U.S. tried to get Russia to abandon its support for Assad in Syria, which was an unsuccessful undertaking.

Foreign Policy-Syria

Iran, Hezbollah and Russia are supporting Syria in their fight to regain control of their country from militants that include the Kurds in the North. As a result of Russian intervention, Syria has signed with Russia a 49-year lease for an air base in Syria. It seems possible that Syria might be partitioned. Whether Assad will sign a peace agreement to that effect is questionable because of his military gains with Russia's help.

The U.S. Withdraws Support For Syrian Rebels: The U.S. Is Losing And Russia/Iran Are Winning.

A covert program to provide military support for moderate Sunni-Arab rebels in Northern Syria was ended before President Trump's recent meeting with Russia's Vladimir Putin. Support had been supplied by the U.S. to those rebels since 2013. This withdrawal of support was a surprise, and makes Bashar al-Assad stronger in his quest, with the support of Iran and Russia, to regain control of a fractured Syria. The withdrawing of support for the moderate Syrian rebels by the U.S. could be recognition that Russian backing for Assad had turned the tide against the rebels, and perhaps President Trump hoped he could reach some accords with Russia, such as cease-fire regions, in Syria.

Russia has signed a 49-year lease for Hmeymim air base. Russia has used the base to assist Assad since 2015. The base is well equipped, having an advanced S-300 air defense system, Russian troops, and offensive capabilities that include Sukhoi SU-35 fighters and attack helicopters. Further consolidating its long-term presence, Russia has signed a military agreement with Syria that provides for an expansion of Russia's Tartus naval base on the Syrian coast. The agreement is a 49-year lease that could automatically renew for a further 25 years, according to Tass, the Russian news agency. Tass said the expansion would provide simultaneous berthing for up to 11 warships, including nuclear-powered vessels, more than doubling its present known capacity there. Russia has largely won the war in Syria for Assad, Iran, and Iran backed proxy rebel group Hezbollah.

Following a Trump meeting with Putin in Germany, a limited cease-fire was agreed to for Southeastern Syria, where the U.S. has military bases, supports rebels fighting the Assad regime, and Jordan is the neighboring country. This is an area of Syria where the U.S. may have a continuing presence, after a peace agreement is agreed to in Syria.

*In 2017, Turkey was fighting ISIS on the northwestern Syrian border with Turkey. Turkey had endorsed the Assad regime, so is not likely to attempt to claim the territory it controls in Syria, once a peace agreement is reached.

The U.S. fought alongside the Kurdish YPG forces on the northeastern Syrian border with Turkey. The Kurds were a very effective ally of the U.S. in fighting ISIS in Syria. The Kurds control about 20,000 square miles or Syrian territory. In late April, 2017, Turkey launched dozens of airstrikes against the Syrian Democratic Forces (SDF), including the Kurdish YPG, which is backed by the U.S. Over 30 Kurds were killed. The Kurds were reported to have had about 25,000 fighters in Syria. The U.S. has announced that it supplied small arms, machine guns, and possibly vehicles to the Kurds.

ArmchairTechInvestor Opinion

Russia has solidified a long-term relationship with Syria that includes a major military air base and naval facilities in Syria, including nuclear-armed ships. Iran and Hezbollah have made major advances in Syria by aligning themselves with Russia and Assad. The best the U.S. can hope for is that Hezbollah and Iran do not maintain military presences in Syria. It does not seem probable that the U.S. will prevail on this issue. However, a war with Israel could begin over this issue.

U.S. backed militias in the Northeast, including the Kurds, and in Southeastern Syria on the Jordanian border could provide the U.S. with an opportunity to maintain a presence in Syria that could be an offset to Russia, Iran and Hezbollah. However, for this to occur, the U.S. will need to continue to arm and train the militias in those regions, with the support of Jordan in the Southeastern part of Syria.

With All of the Different Combatants in Syria, What Should the US Do?

This book looks at the participants in six different Syrian regions in the Syrian civil war, and how eliminating ISIS was the number one objective, defeating al Qaeda was a secondary objective, while looking for a long-term solution for Syria.

If Russia, Iran and Syria believe that they cannot recapture all of Syria, peace negotiations may be possible. Russia is likely to be the key to a peace settlement, and the US will need to be resolute in confronting Russia.

Russia will need to constrain Assad to stop the conflict, and accept a decentralized political solution.

Two of the regions are in the North, with Turkey being the dominant foreign influence in one of them on the west, and in the northeast the Kurds have expanded their influence. U.S. forces are backed a coalition of Kurds and Arabs known as the Syrian Democratic Forces (SDF). Turkey is at war with the Kurds in Turkey. The U.S. had discussed setting up safe zones in Syria, and one likely location could be along the Turkish border, and another being in Kurd controlled territory.

Jordan has millions of Syrian refugees, and its border with Syria could become a safe zone in the South. Moderate Muslim groups are in the Syrian areas bordering Jordan.

Saudi Arabia is not participating in the Syrian war by supplying troops, but it is supporting Islamist groups. It is on the eastern border, and has about 2 million Syrian refugees.

ArmchairTechInvestor Opinion

The war in Syria is a very complex one. The Regions in the Northwest involving Turkey, the Northeast involving the Kurds, and in the south on the Jordanian border could be regions that might be involved in peace negotiations.

The U.S. Issues With Turkey Are Significant: Can Our Relations Improve?

The U.S., and Turkey are both NATO members and the U.S. has Incirlik Air Base in Turkey. Also, both countries are against ISIS. Will those common interests be enough to facilitate improved relations?

Foreign Policy-Turkey

A tenuous situation exists between the U.S. and Turkey, which is a NATO member. The U.S. has agreed to help Turkey fight terrorists in their country. The Kurds are considered by Turkey to be terrorists, but the U.S. has helped the Kurds in Syria and Iraq, but has not endorsed the Kurds in their referendum on establishing a new country, Kurdistan, in Iraq.

The U.N. Human Rights Office released a report criticizing Turkey for its actions against the Kurdish People's Democratic Party. Turkey stripped many of their representatives of their votes. They are accused by the U.N. of violence against people living in 30 towns and neighborhoods, where curfews were imposed following the failed 2016 coup. The report said that a half million people were displaced, and human-rights violations occurred, including the large-scale destruction of homes. Also, Turkey has asked for the extradition of Fethullah Gulen, whom Turkey says masterminded a failed coup in July 2016. The U.S. has not acceded to this Turkish request.

Turkey had a referendum, in April, 2017, to subvert democracy by allowing President Erdogan to remain in power for 10 years, following his second term reelection.

Turkey has expanded its military presence in Syria to create a buffer zone against the Kurds. This appears to have been more important than its opposition to ISIS.

Turkey has criticized the Trump labeling Islamic terrorism as an issue. It has also criticized the U.S. 6-country temporary travel ban.

The Erdogan move to consolidate his power, and possibly try to impose an Islamic state, is anathema to U.S. values of the separation of church and state.

Turkey and U.S. Are At Odds Over U.S. Support For The Kurds In Syria: There Are Many Issues

Turkey was fighting ISIS on the northwestern Syrian border with Turkey. The U.S. was fighting alongside the Kurdish YPG forces on the northeastern Syrian border with Turkey. The Kurds have been a very effective ally of the U.S. in fighting ISIS in Syria. The Kurds control about 20,000 square miles or Syrian territory.

Both the U.S. and Turkey have designated the Kurdistan Workers Party in Turkey, the PKK, as a terrorist organization. The PKK has had an ongoing battle with Turkey over Kurdish territory in Turkey. Turkey considers both the YPG and the PKK to be enemies, and related organizations.

In late April 2017, Turkey launched dozens of airstrikes against the YPG and Syrian Democratic Forces, which is backed by the U.S., and Northern Syria, after giving the U.S. only one-hour notice of the impending strikes. Over 30 Kurds were killed, and the U.S. did not report any casualties. The Kurds called the attack by Turkey an act of war.

The Kurds announced that they had captured the largest dam in Syria, the Tabqa Dam. There were no other major urban regions on the road to Raqqa, which is 25 miles away. Presuming that ISIS would be defeated in Raqqa, Turkey is afraid that the Kurds will retain the property that they have captured.

Despite Turkey being a NATO member, and the U.S. having Incirlik Air Base in Turkey, Turkey had indicated it would continue attacking the Kurds and the U.S. in Syria.

The U.S.-Turkish relationship was poor at the end of the Obama administration, and now has a new issue in Syria, the U.S. backing of the Kurds. President Recap Tayyip Erdogan met with President Trump in mid-2017. The relationship appears to remain strained. A sore point for the U.S. was ruthless behavior by Erdogan's bodyguards while they were in the U.S.

CHAPTER 10

Chinese and U.S. Climate Change, Energy, and Renewables Development

Climate Change

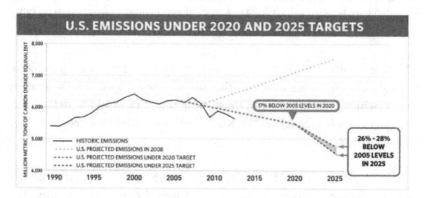

Image: U.S. Carbon Emissions Targets
Image Source: U.S. Environmental Protection Agency (EPA)

Climate Change

President Trump has withdrawn from the Paris Climate Accord on the basis that he does not believe the science of climate change is proven. His assumption is that the restrictions under the Accord unfairly punish American businesses, particularly in competing with China. China does not plan to stop increasing its carbon emissions until after 2030, and there is no guarantee it will do that, even then.

The Trump Team Debates Climate Change: What Are The Evidence And The Issues?

NASA has published very good outlines of the causes of climate change, and the present and possible future consequences. President Trump apparently does not believe climate change is real. The U.S. is reexamining whether it should be a participant in the Paris climate agreement. This is made difficult by its agenda to revive the coal industry, and develop additional oil and gas supplies, including expanding offshore drilling.

There is a real split on Trump's team. Steve Bannon, at the time Trump's top strategist, favored withdrawal from the Paris agreement, as did Scott Pruitt, the EPA administrator. Rick Perry, the Secretary of Energy, seems to believe the Paris Agreement should be renegotiated. Rex Tillerson, then the Secretary of State, and Trump's family members and advisers Ivanka Trump and Jared Kushner, appear to favor being in the Agreement.

China vs. U.S. Carbon Reduction Issue

China's contribution to carbon emission reductions appears to be a major Trump administration issue, since China's emissions are not forecasted to peak until at least 2030.

On June 30, 2015, China formally submitted its intended nationally determined contribution (INDC) to the new global climate agreement concluded in Paris. China committed to the following actions by 2030:

- Peaking of carbon dioxide emissions around 2030 and making best efforts to peak early; and
- Lowering carbon dioxide intensity (carbon dioxide emissions per unit of GDP) by 60% to 65% from the 2005 level.

By contrast, the United States had committed to reduce its greenhouse gas emissions by 26-28% below the 2005 level in 2025, and to make "best efforts" to reduce emissions by 28 percent. Carbon emissions from the United States have been dropping since the year 2000.

Climate Change Causes

A layer of greenhouse gases, primarily water, but including carbon dioxide, methane, and nitrous oxide ("greenhouse gases"), blankets the earth, and holds the average temperature to about 59 degrees Fahrenheit. The main cause of the current global warming trend is human caused expansion of the greenhouse effect, higher temperatures that result from the atmosphere trapping heat, instead of letting it radiate into space. Greenhouse gases, such as those generated by the use of fossil fuels to generate energy, block heat from escaping and can increase global temperatures.

Human Contributions

In the United Nations' Fifth Assessment Report, the Intergovernmental Panel on Climate Change, a group of 1,300 independent scientific experts from countries all over the world concluded there's a more than 95% probability that human activities over the past 50 years have warmed our planet.

Industrial activities have raised atmospheric carbon dioxide levels from 280 parts per million to 400 parts per million in the last 150 years, and the increases are continuing.

Scientific and Visual Evidence

There is a vast amount of scientific evidence that confirms the buildup of carbon dioxide in the atmosphere, and its effect in raising global temperatures. And, the buildup of greenhouse gases is accelerating.

The evidence for rapid climate change is compelling:

- Sea level rise:
    o   The global sea level rose 8 inches in the last century, and the rate of increase in the last 20 years is about double that rate.
- Global temperature rise:
    o   The earth's average temperature has risen by 2.0 degrees Fahrenheit since the late 19th century, driven by human-made emissions, with the U.S. being a very large contributor:
        ♣   Most of the warming occurred in the last 35 years, with 16 of the 17 warmest years on record occurring since 2001.
            •   Not only was 2016 the warmest year on record, but eight of the 12 months that make up the year, from January through September, with the exception of

June, were the warmest on record for those respective months.

o   The number of record high temperature events in the United States has been increasing, while the number of record low temperature events has been decreasing, since 1950. The U.S. has also witnessed an increasing numbers of intense rainfall events.

- Warming oceans:
  o   The oceans have absorbed much of the increased heat:
    ♣ The top 2,300 feet of the ocean has increased in temperature by 0.3 degrees Fahrenheit since 1969.
- Shrinking ice sheets:
  o   The Greenland and Antarctic ice sheets have decreased in mass:
    ♣ Data from NASA shows Greenland lost150 to 250 cubic kilometers (36 to 60 cubic miles) of ice per year between 2002 and 2006; and
    ♣ While, Antarctica lost about152 cubic kilometers (36 cubic miles) of ice between 2002 and 2005.
- Declining Arctic sea ice:
  o   Both the extent and thickness of Arctic sea ice has declined rapidly over the last several decades.
- Extreme events:
  o   Glaciers are retreating worldwide, including in the Alps, Himalayas, Andes, Rockies, Alaska and Africa.
- Ocean acidification:
  o   Since the beginning of the Industrial Revolution, the acidity of surface ocean waters has increased by about 30%. This increase is the result of humans emitting more carbon dioxide into the atmosphere and hence more being absorbed into the oceans. The amount of carbon dioxide absorbed by the upper layer of the oceans is increasing by about 2 billion tons per year.
- Decreased snow cover:
  o   Satellite observations reveal that the amount of spring snow cover in the Northern Hemisphere has decreased over the past five decades and that the snow is melting earlier.

ArmchairTechInvestor Opinion

There is almost universal agreement that climate change is real. The Intergovernmental Panel on Climate Change (IPCC), which includes more than 1,300 scientists from the United States and other countries, forecasts a temperature rise of 2.5 to 10 degrees Fahrenheit over the next century.

*Temperatures in the U.S. in 2017 were slightly below those in 2016, but 2017 was ranked as the third hottest year since records began being kept in 1880. Most of the warming occurred in the last 35 years, with 17 of the 18 warmest years on record occurring since 2001. NASA calculates that temperatures in 2017 were 1.62 degrees Fahrenheit hotter than the 30-year period from 1951 to 1980.

*2017 Among Warmest Years on Record, Wall Street Journal, by Robert Lee Hotz, January 19, 2018

The global sea level has risen by about 8 inches since reliable record keeping began in 1880. It is projected to rise another 1 to 4 feet by 2100. This is the result of added water from melting land ice and the expansion of seawater as it warms. Recent results indicate that the high end of current estimates may be too low.

The U.S. may have a moral obligation to be a part of the Paris Accords. The U.S. has been a major contributor to past carbon emissions retained in the atmosphere. The major contributor to climate change in the future will be China, because of the size of their population, and their rapid economic growth. A goal of the U.S. might be to renegotiate the terms of its and China's participation. However, this does not seem to be in prospect for the Trump administration or a reorganized Chinese government.

Climate Change Is Real And 2017 Was Among The Three Warmest Years Ever Recorded.

*The five warmest years since records began being kept in 1880 all occurred since 2010, according to NASA. Also, according to NASA, global average temperatures were 1.62 degrees warmer than the mean temperature from 1951 to 1980. There are fluctuations that occur, including variations in the sun, ocean changes such as El Nino and volcanic events, but the trends are unmistakable.

*2017 Among Warmest Years on Record, Wall Street Journal, by Robert Lee Hotz, January 19, 2018

ArmchairTechInvestor Opinion

There is some question about whether President Trump believes climate change is real. He did pull out of the Paris Climate Accords. However, one can argue that he did so in the belief that the Chinese, because their carbon emissions are not scheduled to peak until 2030, were burdening U.S. businesses with unnecessary costs that reduce their competitiveness.

President Trump Has Decided To Exit The Paris Climate Accord, But May Renegotiate The Terms. What Are The Consequences?

Twenty states and Washington, DC have adopted their own greenhouse emissions targets. The Paris Accord sought U.S. reductions of 26-28% below 2005 levels. Twenty-nine U.S. states require utilities to sell a prescribed amount of renewable energy in their states. Some states, such as Texas, are ramping up renewable energy, such as wind power, because prices are competitive. This will aid the U.S. clean tech industry. The states will largely assure that the Paris targets are pursued. Some states approved the withdrawal. West Virginia's Senator Capito said it would aid their coal industry, which has been devastated by Obama's anti-coal policies.

China, which is the largest emitter of greenhouse gases, and whose emissions are committed by China to peak in 2030, said it would continue to meet its obligation. There are transparency issues with respect to China actually meeting its commitment. However, one of President Trumps' objections to the Agreement was that the U.S. would reduce its fossil fuel emissions significantly, while China would continue to build new coal plants until 2025. China is also investing heavily in clean technologies, such as solar, and will be a difficult competitor in those areas.

An additional stumbling block for President Trump was a provision that developed countries would financially support underdeveloped countries, including India, by financing their renewable fuels efforts to the tune of $100 billion per year in 2020. Trump objected to foreign countries forcing the U.S. to make what he considered to be foreign aid. This would have added tens of billions of dollars per year to the U.S. deficit. Additionally, Obama signed the Accord, but the Congress did not ratify it.

Trump supports fossil fuel development in the U.S., including natural gas and the large fracking industry. Fracking is controversial because of the possibility that underground water supplies may become polluted. The state and local governments can address these issues. They will also be addressed by the EPA, which despite being weakened by Trump, cannot unilaterally disregard environmental impacts from fossil fuels, including carbon and fracking.

ArmchairTechInvestor Opinion

It will take until 2020 for the U.S. to officially withdraw from the Paris Accords. It does not seem likely that U.S. involvement will be renegotiated. Because of state renewable fuel activities, and market realities, coal will not likely make much of a rebound, except for exports to China and other countries still building coal power plants. Other than the elimination of U.S. financing for underdeveloped countries, the effect of Trump's Paris Accord withdrawal does not appear to be a negative for the U.S. And, it will not have much of an effect on rising ocean levels and global temperature increases.

Energy-Coal & Nuclear Power

The Market For Energy Is Widening. Coal And Nuclear Are Becoming Less Competitive And Solar And Wind Are Becoming More Competitive With Natural Gas

President Trump is trying to save coal and nuclear power, presumably because he believes they are safer at times of national catastrophe. He is proposing subsidies to reward their presumed reliability. Solar and wind can be unreliable because of the variability of their sources, wind and the sun. The Trump policies are facing the challenges of an energy generation industry that is about flat in terms of demand.

The recovery of inexpensive natural gas from shale deposits has been a driver in the electrical energy distribution market. However, this is being matched by the declines in the cost of the renewables solar and wind.

Power Shift Drives a Slide in Prices, Wall Street Journal, by Erin Ailworth and Russell Gold, November 30, 2017

The main drivers of the energy industry are the fact that energy usage is not growing because of such things as more energy efficient devices, including home appliances. Also, businesses and homeowners are doing things such as using solar power on their facilities and homes to reduce their energy demands from energy providers.

Older energy facilities, particularly coal and nuclear plants, are being retired because they are not cost competitive. According to Lazard, an investment banker, electrical energy costs $60 per megawatt of power, on average. This compares with $102 for a coal burning plant, and about $150 per megawatt hour for a nuclear-powered plant. However, there are still two nuclear plants in Georgia that are struggling to be completed.

Wind and solar power costs are competitive with natural gas in many regions of the U.S. According to Lazard, utility grade crystalline solar sells for $49.50 per megawatt-hour (MWH) and wind is about $45 per MWH. Natural gas, in the recent past, was used as a base power source that could handle peak loads. Natural gas can still be used to fill in at the times when solar and wind are not generating power. The three provide a very cost effective and reliable long-term source of power when the power generating facilities are planned in a way to mitigate the variability of solar and wind.

ArmchairTechInvestor Opinion

The energy market directions for coal and nuclear power are not likely to be changed by the Trump administration. The costs of solar and wind are competitive with natural gas. Coal is the big environmental polluter.

The nuclear waste disposal issue is unresolved, and it needs to be stored safely for 10,000 years. China continues to build coal power plants, and exports of coal to China may help the U.S. coal industry through 1930, but after that coal will likely resume its death spiral. The only hope for nuclear power seems to be the smaller plants that are being developed by early stage companies that might sell such plants internationally.

Trump Ordered Energy Study, But Not Much Help Provided For Coal And Nuclear Power

In April 2017, Energy Secretary, Rick Parry, authorized a study of the electric grid. Coal and nuclear energy have been declining in use, and the study, which was released in August 2017, provides little help in reviving the fortunes of these two fuel sources that President Trump has been advocating.

The report says that cheap natural gas, driven by fracking, is the primary cause behind recent coal and nuclear plant closings. Mr. Perry said, "It is apparent that in today's competitive markets, certain regulations and subsidies are having a large impact on the functioning of markets and thereby challenging our power generation mix." Renewable sources, such as wind energy and solar, and expanding regulations and subsidies, have been secondary causes.

The Energy Department report recommendations included:

- Recommending changes in how electricity is priced to recognize the benefit of steady power;
- Faster permitting of fossil fuel plants; and
- More research and development is needed to better integrate solar and wind power into the electric grid in the U.S. In the past nuclear power and coal-fired power plants have provided baseline power to the U.S. power grid. As they have declined, natural gas power plants have continued to increase their usage from about 35% in the past to about 50% in 2017.

The report also argues that it is important to have power plants with a reliable source of fuel. Natural gas can be in short supply in the winter months, when its use surges, and delivering fuel through pipelines can be impacted. For coal and nuclear plants, fuel can be available at the site year-round. These plants might be compensated for that security. However, this is really subsidizing coal and nuclear power.

ArmchairTechInvestor Opinion

The Report provides little benefit to the coal and nuclear power industries. They are likely to continue to decline because of the lower cost of natural gas, with clean energy being only a secondary factor in their declines. Nuclear power is considered to be a clean source of energy, despite the dangers and costs of nuclear power waste disposal. Some states, such as California, will continue to support clean energy use for power generation, assuring the continued success of clean fuels.

Energy-Coal

The real opportunity for coal is to export it to countries such as China. China has been criticized for a 40% increase in coal imports from North Korea in the first quarter of 2017. However, in April 2017, Reuters reported that China began rejecting North Korean coal shipments, and there were 600,000 tons of coal sitting at various ports, and another 2 million tons that had been rejected by the Chinese and were stranded in Chinese ports. China said in February 2017 that it was suspending North Korean imports for the rest of 2017. In a change in policy, no coal was exported from the U.S. to China from late 2014 to 2016, but by February of 2017, U.S. coal shipments to China totaled over 400,000 tons.

Coal Industry Revival? Trump Ignores Climate Change Scientific Conclusions: Exports May Help

President Trump signed an executive order early in 2017 that eliminated some restrictions on fossil fuel production, and boosted the use of fuels such as oil, natural gas and coal. This fulfills a campaign promise to bring back coal mining jobs.

The executive order ran counter to many environmental and energy industry trends. There is a worldwide effort underway to enact a climate change initiative, the Paris Accords. Trump has withdrawn the U.S. from that Accord. U.S. utilities are converting coal power plants to less expensive and cleaner burning natural gas plants. The order also ignores scientific evidence the fossil fuels are building up in the atmosphere, and are the cause of global warming. The United Nations has developed forecasts of the impact of global warming, and groups like the American Association for the Advancement of Science have validated the science that underlies global warming trends.

The development of solar power and wind turbines has produced clean energy that can compete with the cost of coal. Coal mining jobs have been declining for decades, and now number only about 75,000. Renewable fuels, including solar, biofuels and wind, now account for about 650,000 jobs.

ArmchairTechInvestor Opinion

Coal's days in the U.S are numbered as a fuel source, unless inexpensive ways can be found to stop the coal from going into the atmosphere. That means carbon dioxide must be collected and buried at the power plant site to eliminate these emissions. The cost of recapturing and burying the carbon dioxide is very high, and numerous projects to do this cost effectively have failed. Meanwhile, cleaner energy sources such as natural gas, wind and solar have come down significantly in cost, and in the case of natural gas, increased substantially in capacity. China and other countries continue to rely on coal, and its best hope is to become an export to those countries.

Energy-Coal-China

Coal is unlikely to be revived in the U.S. because of the high emissions of carbons. The cost of carbon removal from coal is proving to be prohibitive, and many states, such as California, ban the use of coal as a fuel source in power plants. However, China is still building new coal power plants and China should be a good buyer of coal exports, as may smaller countries.

Energy-Natural Gas

Natural gas prices from the fracking of shale are so low that they are driving nuclear power and coal power out of business. Natural gas is also a relatively clean fuel. Because of the quantity of natural gas, and the low prices, the export market for natural gas in the form of liquid natural gas (LNG) is very large. Russia has been interfering in the U.S. energy industry, to promote its oil and gas interests.

There is a growing worldwide market for LNG. The fracking of shale deposits in the U.S. has created a large supply of gas that can be converted to LNG and then shipped internationally. President Trump is a strong proponent of the U.S. developing its world export markets, including LNG.

Trump Promotes Coal And Nuclear Energy-Clean Energy Will Continue Grow, But Coal and LNG Exports Should Increase

Overall gas, wind and solar make up 40% of U.S. energy needs, up from 22% ten years ago, according to the U.S. Energy Information Administration. Over the last 5 years, 30% of the coal plants have closed. Nuclear power plants are also closing. Between 2013 and 2023, 11 of 65 nuclear power plants are expected to close.

Natural gas has been the main engine of change. Prices are so low that U.S. coal usage is likely to continue to lose market share. Natural gas is the cleanest fossil fuel, and increasingly plentiful and inexpensive. Overall, natural gas has increase from 52 billion cubic feet (bcf) in 2006 to 79 bcf in 2015. Fracking was only 29% of natural gas production in 2006. Fracking made up 67% of the production of natural gas in the U.S. in 2015. The U.S. liquid natural gas (LNG) market offers an export opportunity for natural gas. Natural gas U.S. energy delivery is expected to grow from 72.2 bcf in 2016 to 76.2 bcf in 2018, a 5.5% increase.

Eastern European countries like Poland and the Baltic states have already suffered past episodes of Russian energy bullying. Now, they are increasingly unnerved by Russia's tense showdown with NATO over Ukraine, Syria, and other possible political issues. But they also remain heavily reliant on Russian energy. The U.S. would like to reduce Europe's reliance on Russian energy, and has just announced that Poland, where Trump had a meeting, will for the first time import U.S. produced LNG. This could be the start of a broader strategy to reduce European Russian energy dependence, and increase U.S. energy jobs.

Energy-Renewables

Wind power and solar power make up about 10% of energy generation in the U.S. Wind power is expected to grow by 26% through 2019. Although solar is a much smaller percentage of power generation than wind, it is expected to grow by about 52% by 2019.

Wind electricity generating capacity was 81 gigawatts at the end of 2016. The U.S. Energy Information Administration (EIA) estimates that wind electricity will grow by 26% to 102 gigawatts at the end of 2018. Wind is an important clean energy source that is taking market share from oil, nuclear and coal.

Total utility scale solar generating capacity was 21 gigawatts at the end of 2016. Solar is forecast to increase to 32 gigawatts at the end of 2018. Although the growth is expected to be 52% over that two-year period, solar will add a little over 50% of the additional capacity wind is expected to provide. Not included in these forecasts are the substantial investments being made by businesses and residences in solar replacement of traditional energy provided by local electric utilities.

ArmchairTechInvestor Opinion

Despite President Trump pulling out of the Paris Accords, clean energy will continue to grow in the U.S., partially driven by states such as California that has restricted the use of coal and other carbon polluting energy sources in the state. Wind and solar will be the largest sources of clean electrical energy production.

Exports of coal and LNG are likely sources of increased U.S. trade and job creation.

Energy-Natural Gas

**Liquid Natural Gas (LNG) From The U.S. Should Be Able To Capitalize
On The Growing Worldwide Market For LNG.**

*Liquid Natural Gas (LNG), which is turned into a liquid so that it can be
transported, is turning into a global market, particularly because of the
historically low price of natural gas. Asia, including China, is becoming a
growing market for LNG. According to the International Energy Agency
(IEA), 90% of the global growth in LNG will come from emerging and
frontier countries by 2022, with most of the growth coming from China.

Countries that are isolated, such as Japan and South Korea, do not have
supplies that are affordable using pipelines, and are therefore natural
markets for LNG. LNG supplies are running low in countries such as
Pakistan, Bangladesh and the Philippines. As demand growth slows at
traditional markets, such as Japan and South Korea, smaller markets
will become 20% of the LNG market by 2022, according to IEA. What is
driving the market is a shortage of electricity.

In 2015, 40% of natural gas moved by sea, and the total is expected to
surpass that of pipelines by 2040 according to the International Energy
Agency. Thirty-nine countries import LNG, up from 17 ten years ago.

The costs of LNG import facilities are expensive, and prohibitively so for
some smaller countries, with a typical import facility costing $4 billion.
However, floating offshore LNG import facilities are significantly less
expensive. Pakistan is building one such LNG import terminal to import
LNG from Oatar. Bangladesh is seeking financing to complete such a
terminal in their country.

Natural gas demand from traditional markets, such as Australia, Japan,
South Korea and New Zealand, is forecasted to decline to 206 billion
cubic meters in 2022, from 218 billion cubic meters in 2016, according
to IEA.

The U.S. is developing markets in China, with facilities located in
Shanghai and Guangdong receiving gas from Texas and Pennsylvania.
China should be a growing U.S. customer.

The price of LNG is an issue. Spot prices in 2017 were $5.74 per million BTUs. This is about $1 higher than prices in Europe. If the price of LNG declines, Europe could be an attractive market as an alternative to Russian gas.

As LNG terminals are opened in more countries, the market for LNG will become more competitive. At any given time in 2017 there were about 170 LNG tankers on the oceans, up from 150 a year earlier, according to a tracker firm, ClipperData. LNG shipments are growing about 7% a year. New sources of LNG are being developed in the U.S. and elsewhere, and the price of LNG is expected to decline.

*Emerging Markets Pick Up Slack In LNG, Wall Street Journal, Demi Guo, August 30, 2017

ArmchairTechInvestor Opinion

President Trump has been saying that exports of coal and natural gas will be good for the U.S. balance of trade. It appears that the U.S., with new supplies of gas coming from shale fracking, will be able to capitalize on the growing global demand for LNG.

Oil & Gas From Shale, And Renewable Energy Are Making The U.S. Energy Independent

President Trump has declared that the U.S. will seek "Energy Dominance" as a break with the Obama era. This will be pursued through natural gas (LNG), coal and petroleum exports. What does this objective mean, and how realistic is this objective?

*In 2016, energy production in the U.S. was equal to 86% of consumption, with the difference being net imports of petroleum.

President Trump has emphasized renewing U.S. production of coal, which has been declining and was down to 17% of energy production in 2016, and nuclear power, which was 10% of energy production in 2016. Renewable energy was 12% of U.S. energy production.

Coal production could increase in the U.S., primarily through shipments to China, which has promised that its carbon emissions will peak in 2030. Natural gas and petroleum production in the U.S. will increase, if there continue to be substantial increases in oil and natural gas from shale fracking.

Several recent changes in U.S. energy production have occurred that will contribute to President Trump's objective of reaching Energy Dominance.

- Coal production peaked in 2008 and trended down through 2016. The primary reason for the general decline in coal production in recent years is the decrease in coal consumption for electricity generation. It appears unlikely that the production of coal for U.S. consumption will increase;
- Natural gas production in 2016 was the second largest amount after the record high production in 2015. More efficient and cost-effective drilling and production techniques have resulted in increased production of natural gas from shale formations. Gas production from shale fracking could increasing be used for U.S. power production and for LNG exports;
- Crude oil production generally decreased each year between 1970 and 2008. In 2009, the trend reversed and production began to rise. More cost-effective drilling and production technologies helped to boost production, especially in Texas and North Dakota, including oil from shale fracking;
- Natural gas plant liquids (NGPL) are hydrocarbon gas liquids that are extracted from natural gas before the natural gas is put into pipelines for transmission to consumers. NGPL production has increased alongside increases in natural gas production. In 2016, NGPL production reached a record high; and
- Total renewable energy production and consumption both reached record highs 2016. Increases in energy production from wind and solar helped to increase the overall energy production from renewable sources. Energy production from wind and solar were at record highs in 2016.

*U.S. Energy Information Administration, September 5, 2017, U.S. Energy Facts Explained

ArmchairTechInvestor Opinion

The U.S. has been making progress in energy independence, primarily through oil and natural gas production from fracking, but also from the development of wind and solar energy. Exports of natural gas (LNG) and coal are starting to increase. Coal shipments to China will aid the U.S. coal industry, but will not make the U.S. more energy independent. A similar statement can be made with regard to LNG shipments, such as to Europe. This will aid the U.S. shale fracking industry, but will not reduce U.S. dependence on foreign oil.

Trump has not been promoting renewable energy, but has been promoting the U.S. use of coal and nuclear power. This appears to be a losing strategy. Renewable energy, and improvements in automobile mileage efficiency, are likely to continue to reduce U.S., foreign oil dependence, despite Trump's rejection of climate change, and the withdrawal from the Paris Accords. It appears to be likely that coal or nuclear energy will continue to decline in the U.S., and will therefore not contribute to U.S. energy independence.

China and Russia are dominating the exporting of nuclear reactors, and several U.S. power companies have visions of exporting nuclear reactors, despite the fact that their reactors are made by Toshiba, a Japanese company that bought Westinghouse out of bankruptcy.

Environmental Protection Agency

An area that is of vital importance is the regulation that surrounds the EPA. Nuclear power and coal are two areas that the Trump administration is focusing on with regard to reducing energy regulation. Trump's disbelief in climate change is also driving EPA environmental regulation reduction.

President Trump has proposed that regulations issued by the Environmental Protection Agency (EPA), which are imposing what he calls unreasonable environmental costs, be revisited. New regulations can be frozen, but it is likely that regulations that are in effect will have to be studied to determine if the regulations are unreasonable.

The Media Has Characterized the Trump Environmental Protection Agency (EPA) Changes as Massive. What is the Reality?

The most immediate change was the freezing of new regulation adoption, and the requirement that 2 regulations be eliminated for each new one. An example of such a regulatory impact is the freezing of a new regulation that would require dentists to eliminate mercury from their waste emissions. Other U.S. policy issues are on the table.

Another change could be EPA budget changes. The EPA budget is forecasted to be $8.3 billion in fiscal 2017. As much as a 25% reduction has been discussed in the media. This would save about $2.1 billion. With respect to the budget, this is a very small amount compared to a $54 billion increase in defense spending. It has also been suggested that EPA employment would decline by about 3.000 employees, or about 20%. Such changes have been delayed until at least 2019, due to a 2-year budget approved by the Congress.

The Army Corps of Engineers (ACE) has been directed to review and reconsider the controversial Waters of the U.S. rule. This rule change is expected to be lengthy, since it will be handled on a case-by-case basis, as permits are required.

The Supreme Court has issued a decision on which wetlands are protected under the Clean Water Act. It set a new test for when a water body should be covered. Anthony Scalia issued a much narrower opinion on navigable waters, and the ACA has been directed to consider this opinion. Any changes would have to go through a lengthy rulemaking process.

Nuclear Power-U.S.

The status of the U.S. nuclear power industry is precarious. There are only two nuclear power plants under construction. They are Georgia Power's two Vogtle plants that use the Westinghouse AP1000 reactors. Westinghouse declared bankruptcy and is now owned by Toshiba. Several companies are developing smaller, more scalable, nuclear power plants, presumably for the export market.

Is Nuclear Power Vital To The U.S. Energy Industry?

*Nuclear power has many attractive features, despite the nuclear waste disposal issues. It is a clean energy source. It is a reliable energy source in that it will generally continue operating at the time of a natural disaster. The Trump administration hopes to give credit to both coal and nuclear power because of their self-contained nature and the resilience this gives them. There appears to be increasing political support for reforming the nuclear licensing process, and improving the incentives for nuclear power. For nuclear power to be cost effective, particularly with regard to natural gas, there will likely be a need for financial incentives. However, there are nuclear startups that are building smaller plants that may be cost competitive.

There are two new nuclear power plants being built, both of them in Georgia. The plants are only partially complete, and financial support from the Trump administration will likely be required to complete them.

*Does Nuclear Power Have a Robust Future in the U.S.?, Wall Street Journal, by Rich Powell and Jason Bordoff, November 13, 2017

ArmchairTechInvestor Opinion

Nuclear waste disposal is the Achilles heel of the nuclear power industry. It will be very expensive to store the waste underground for 10,000 years, and a location and the storage technology has not been fully developed. Arguments for nuclear power include the fact that they are viewed as a clean energy source, and provide a vital military technology.

A negative for power plants generally in the U.S. is that there is little or no growth in the industry. Thus, new power plants are generally replacements of older power plants, and with the low cost of natural gas plants, it is difficult to make a case for nuclear power based upon past plant designs and sizes. There are startups designing smaller nuclear plants that may even be competitive with gas. There is an international market for nuclear power that could be served if a U.S. companies that have designed smaller nuclear plants could penetrate that market. That market has been characterized as being a $10 trillion market over the coming decades. Having

U.S. companies provide those plants provides some protection against nuclear proliferation. However, Russia and China are in the worldwide nuclear market, and they have been responsible for nuclear proliferation to countries that include Pakistan, Iran and North Korea.

Trump Wants To Revive U.S. Nuclear Plants: There Are Substantial Roadblocks

The status of the U.S. nuclear industry is precarious. There are only two nuclear power plants under construction. They are Georgia Power's two Vogtle plants that use the Westinghouse AP1000 reactors. Westinghouse declared bankruptcy and is now owned by Toshiba. The two reactors are forecasted to cost about $19 billion. The project needs to be approved by the Georgia Public Utilities Commission. It is also contingent on getting U.S. tax credits and receiving a bankruptcy settlement of $3.7 billion from Toshiba.

The company, which has partnered with three other utilities on the project, said it expected the new reactors would cost roughly $19 billion and come online in 2021 and 2022. The project is also backed by $8.3 billion in Federal loan guarantees awarded by the Obama administration. The project is 44% complete, and the total cost is expected to be about $25 billion.

In July 2017, South Carolina Scana Corp. abandoned efforts to build two similar reactors at V.C. Summer, because of delays and cost overruns. That decision left Georgia as the American nuclear industry's sole hope for a near term project.

Utilities in other states have found the cost of large new reactors prohibitive. Duke Energy Florida announced it would spend $6 billion expanding solar power while abandoning plans for a nuclear plant in Levy County estimated to cost about $22 billion.

*Nuclear power still provides 20 percent of the United States' electricity, the largest source of carbon-free power. Over a dozen older nuclear plants around the United States are retiring early because of low natural gas prices. Maria G. Korsnick, head of the Nuclear Energy Institute, an industry group, said that share could fall below 10 percent by midcentury, if retirements continue and few new units are built.

A revival of nuclear power would depend on several factors, Ms. Korsnick said, none of them assured. States would need to act to support their existing fleets of financially troubled reactors, as New York and Illinois have done. Georgia Power would need to finish its AP1000s, allowing the United States to export the technology to the rest of the world.

Other companies would also have to develop smaller, more advanced reactors, meant to be easier to build than the hulking light-water reactors of old. In January 2017, Oregon-based NuScale Power submitted the first application for a small modular reactor to Federal regulators, but the technology remains unproven, and the company does not expect to build its first working reactor until the 2020s.

China is building 20 nuclear reactors, including four AP1000s.

*The U.S. Backs Off Nuclear Power. Georgia Wants to Keep Building Reactors, New York Times, By Brad Plumer, Aug. 31, 2017

ArmchairTechInvestor Opinion

Since Toshiba owns the technology used to develop the AP1000 reactors that are used in Georgia, and are the only new nuclear plants being built in the U.S., it seems unlikely that U.S. suppliers will be able to successfully compete for foreign nuclear reactor sales. Toshiba is attempting to raise financing to eliminate financing issues surrounding its recovery out of bankruptcy.

Small modular reactors are being developed that could provide NuScale with a foreign market opportunity.

With regard to U.S. nuclear power use, it is likely to decline, despite the interest the Trump administration has in promoting nuclear power.

Trump Is Trying To Revive Nuclear Power: What Are The Issues?

Nuclear power faces competition from natural gas, solar and wind power. President Trump has initiated a study to develop a plan for nuclear power plants. It is likely to include what to do with regard to the aging power plants, and examine the costs and other issues of a new generation of power plants. Subsidizing at-risk nuclear reactors to keep them online through 2020 would require an estimated $2.9 billion annually according to Bloomberg New Energy Finance. There is also the issue of whether to compensate the operators of nuclear power plants for their ability to provide zero carbon energy.

Another issue is an array of regulatory challenges, and how to fix them, including a costly government licensing process for new nuclear plant designs.

A major issue that is not often discussed is how to provide long-term storage of nuclear waste, and the cost and safety of the storage facilities. A House committee in 2017 approved legislation that would revive research on permanently storing spent radioactive material at Yucca Mountain in Nevada. The nuclear waste storage issue is controversial.

Energy Secretary Rick Parry is a supporter of nuclear power, and has vowed to make the U.S. the leader in its development. There is an international market for nuclear reactors that will be filled by other countries such as China or Russia, if the U.S. is not a leader.

ArmchairTechInvestor Opinion

Nuclear power will continue to be a large international industry. An example of the negative effects is the nuclear power capabilities transferred by Russia to Iran that formed the core of their nuclear weapons ambitions. The U.S. needs to continue developing the industry, if only for international nuclear reactor sales.

The proposed budget of the Trump administration would reduce Energy Department funding by 28 percent, including the support for small modular reactors, and advanced large light-water reactors. The nuclear power industry developments proposed by Trump could help it regain is place as a future source of clean energy, assuming sufficient government financial support is provided. These funding changes are on hold.

* **Trump's Plans for a Nuclear Revival Will Begin With a Study,** Bloomberg, by Jennifer A Dlouhy, June 29, 2017

Nuclear Waste

The biggest issue for nuclear power may not be its cost; it could be how to safely dispose of the nuclear waste. The U.S. government has taken responsibility for this problem, and as is not atypical of government, it still has not solved the problem. Yucca Mountain was selected as the site for nuclear waste disposal 30 years ago, and the U.S. has not yet even begun to build the facility.

Storing Nuclear Waste For 10,000 Years Needs To Be Done: It Is Still An Issue

The biggest issue for nuclear power may not be its cost; it could be how to safely dispose of the nuclear waste. The U.S. government has taken responsibility for this problem, and as is not atypical of government, it still has not solved the problem after 30 years. Yucca Mountain was selected as the site for nuclear waste disposal 30 years ago, and the U.S. has not yet even begun to build the facility.

The issue of nuclear waste disposal is not a trivial one. Radioactive (or nuclear) waste is a byproduct from nuclear reactors, fuel processing plants, hospitals and research facilities. Radioactive waste is also generated while decommissioning and dismantling nuclear reactors and other nuclear facilities. High-level radioactive waste is primarily uranium fuel that has been used in a nuclear power reactor and is "spent," or no longer efficient in producing electricity. Spent fuel is thermally hot, as well as highly radioactive, and requires remote handling and shielding. Nuclear reactor fuel contains ceramic pellets of uranium 235 inside of metal rods. Before these fuel rods are used, they are only slightly radioactive and may be handled without special shielding.

*There are 121 locations in the U.S. that currently store spent fuel. The objective is to eventually ship fuel that requires long-term storage to Yucca Mountain. Yucca Mountain was designated as the permanent underground storage site for nuclear waste in 1987. The objective is to store high-level nuclear waste safely for at least 10,000 years. It was supposed to open in 1998, but was put on permanent hold by Obama.

President Trump has included $120 million in the budget to restart the licensing process for Yucca Mountain.

*Trump Administration Revives Nevada Plan as Nuclear Waste Piles Up, Wall Street Journal, by Kris Maher, May 9, 2017

ArmchairTechInvestor Opinion

Nuclear waste disposal is still an issue that has not been resolved. Nevada politicians are against locating the disposal facility in Nevada because of possible risks to the water supply, and because of the long-term nature of the storage required. President Trump is aware of the issue, and has proposed funding to solve the problem. Whether the funding will be sufficient is questionable.

The cost of nuclear waste disposal is not reflected in the current cost of nuclear power, and therefore the current use of nuclear power is creating a liability for future generations.

CHAPTER 11

Chinese and U.S. Education and Technology: Artificial Intelligence, Bitcoins and Blockchain Technology, CyberSecurity and Quantum Computing

Chinese Education

Chinese education is directed particularly at the 89 million Communist Party members. They are the core of a new thrust under President Xi to integrate the Communist Party with all of the operations of government, including promoting blind obedience to the edicts of the Xi presidency. These efforts are also being accompanied by extremely strict surveillance of the Chinese population, a virulent anti-corruption campaign, and a long-term vision for China to become the dominant country in the world. Consistent long-term commitments, and technology development and acquisition, will be the keys to that Chinese vision. The U.S. will face a significant challenge globally from China over the next 20 years. The important issue will be whether the world's leading democracy, the U.S., can continually focus, because of the continuity issues of a democracy, enough to remain competitive.

U.S. Education

The objectives of the Department of Education:

- Children and parents should have school options where the children can learn, grow and be safe;
- There should be no one delivery mechanism of education choice; and
- Open enrollment, tax credits, home schools, magnets, charters, virtual schools, education savings accounts and choices not yet developed all have their place.

There are no virtually no content political agendas to U.S. education, with the exception that science, technology and math (STEM) policies that rely on U.S. companies for tech development, are often emphasized.

Technology

There are numerous new technologies being developed that will have important governmental importance. We will outline those technologies in this China vs. U.S. 2018 book, and outline the governmental issues.

Artificial Intelligence

The U.S. Is Leading The Charge Toward Artificial Intelligence, But The Rest Of The World Is Close Behind

Artificial intelligence (AI) is in its infancy, and robotics is an early application of the technology, but the scope of AI's influence will be much broader. It involves harnessing the power of computers to replace human tasks. There are those that believe that the U.S., China and India are the leaders in the development of AI technology. The technology itself is partly software, and partly semiconductor technology that enables devices to make decisions at very rapid speeds.

In the semiconductor arena, NVIDIA has been the leader in developing graphics displays. Qualcomm and Broadband Technologies have each developed smartphone and network capabilities that enable many of today's smartphones, including those of Apple. Broadcom made an unsolicited $110 billon dollar bid to acquire Qualcomm. Qualcomm rejected the bid. The U.S. stopped the acquisition on national security grounds.

Intel competes directly with NVIDIA in providing AI calculations for large corporations.

China-Artificial Intelligence

AI is going to be an international horse race, and China has indicated that it wants to dominate the area. The Chinese government has laid out an ambitious plan for a $150 billion AI industry, saying in July 2017 that it wants China to become the world's "innovation center for AI" by 2030.

ArmchairTechInvestor Opinion

Artificial intelligence has improved enormously since the 1950's. Brad Peery, the author, had an artificial intelligence focus in his undergraduate electrical engineering program at Stanford. In those days you could beat the weatherman's forecast for the Bay Area for the next day by forecasting that the next day was going to be just like the current day.

Silicon Valley giants, such as Facebook, Amazon, Google and Tesla, are investing billions in using computers to replace human tasks. In China, however, the biggest push towards AI is coming from the government. In India, the main shift towards AI is coming from companies that make up its $150 billion tech outsourcing industry. The U.S. and India do not rely on the government for their AI, as do dictatorships such as China, North Korea and Iran.

With the power of today's computers, AI, and its potential to understand today, and forecast tomorrow, has become an international technology imperative for governments that want to remain secure and safe.

Bitcoins and Blockchain Technology

The bitcoin blockchain network was the first application of what is likely to be a blockchain technology revolution. Bitcoins are very volatile, and the bitcoin blockchain network has limited capacity. It would be overwhelmed by just one credit card application such as Visa. The banks are likely to drive the development of additional blockchain networks. The features that are the most attractive are smart contracts and distributed ledgers. Other coin applications, such as Ethereum and colored coins, will be developed.

The SEC Has Launched An Investigation Into Possible Digital Currency Offering Violations Of The U.S. Securities Laws: This Is the Beginning of SEC Regulation

*The SEC has initiated a sweeping probe into possible securities violations by digital coin offering companies and advisors. Subpoenas and information requests have been issued to numerous companies involved in the raising of capital for digital coin or token companies (ICOs). The standards required of such companies may be substantially less than for initial public offerings (IPOs). The money can be raised for even small niche products. According to SEC Chairman Jay Clayton: "Many promoters of ICOs and cryptocurrencies are not complying with our laws".

As of February, 2018, coin offerings have raised $1.66 billion, and could be on the way to surpassing the $6.5 billion raised in a hot 2017 market, according to Token Report, a research and data company. Many of the projects for which money has been raised, originate outside of the U.S.

A blockchain technology risks study is underway at MIT. The statement has been made that $270 million to $317 million of the money raised for coins has likely gone to fraud or scams, according to Christian Catalini, an MIT professor.

In one of the first SEC initiated actions, Dallas-based AriseBank, is apparently under investigation for claiming to it plans to buy a U.S. bank with the $600 million it claims it has raised. The SEC halted the offering in January 2018. Many other offerings have apparently been delayed by increased SEC scrutiny.

An element of the increased scrutiny by the SEC relates to simple agreements for future tokens (SAFTs), which allow existing investors to buy coins or tokens prior to their being offered to the general public. The profits can typically be flipped or sold before the offerings.

*SEC Launches Crypto-Probe, Wall Street Journal, by Jean Eaglesham and Paul Vigna, March 1, 2018

ArmchairTechInvestor Opinion

Digital coin and token offerings in the U.S. are in the initial stages of being investigated and regulated by the SEC. This area is likely to be extensively regulated, but not as closely regulated as traditional IPOs.

In China, the government is controlling capital outflows from China. One issue is the anonymity of blockchain technology asset transfers.

Bitcoins and Blockchain Technology Are Revolutionizing The Transfer Of Asset Ownership

*Bitcoins were invented in 2008 by an unknown inventor. They are a unique creation that allows assets to be transferred securely, and anonymously, bypassing the need for the buyer and seller to verify the validity of the other party. Initially bitcoins were used to buy and sell commercial items. A seller of an item would set a price for the item he wished to sell. The buyer would purchase bitcoins. They can be purchased in a variety of ways. One of the most convenient could be to set up an account with a bitcoin vendor. Those bitcoins could be transferred to a vendor that accepts bitcoins as a payment source. The vendor doesn't need to know the buyer. Bitcoins are bought anonymously, and the purchase transaction is completed seamlessly over the bitcoin network. An entity, called a miner, is used to complete the transaction, and miners are paid in bitcoins when they are successful in completing a transaction. The miners compete with each other to complete the transaction, and the miner that successfully completes the transaction is paid for its services.

* **Distributed Ledgers, Smart Contracts, Business Standards and ISO 20022,** Swift, Information Paper

**Another way to use bitcoins might be to set up what amounts to a bitcoin account with a bank. An example of such a situation is a company, ChromaWay, working with LHV Bank in Estonia. LHV Bank, which is the largest Estonian financial group, wanted a secure technology for implementing a euro-based payment solution. In 2016, their Cuber project was launched. This ChromaWay app basically provides an alternative to cash. Instead of being dependent on bitcoin price fluctuations, users hold reclaimable tokens representing Euros. Cuber becomes a new kind of open platform that takes advantage of blockchain innovation and bitcoin security, but eliminates bitcoin price fluctuations.

**Brad Peery, the author of this book, is an Advisor to ChromaWay. ChromaWay was the original developer of colored coins that allow asset transfers over the bitcoin blockchain network. ChromaWay is in the process of moving its headquarters from Sweden to the U.S.

Blockchain technology is much broader than just bitcoins. It provides robust security for any kind of cryptocurrency. It is a very powerful technology that can provide efficiencies and technological benefits that make it capable of performing complex operations. This is where the idea of smart contracts comes in. Smart contracts allow complex transactions to occur without intermediary intervention. Smart contracts can create accounting transactions that result in distributed ledgers that reside on a blockchain network. They can reduce or eliminate the need for individual participants in a transaction to keep their own accounting ledgers.

Colored coins, which was developed by ChromaWay, can be use as a way to transfer assets over a blockchain network, including the bitcoin blockchain network. Any kind of asset can be transferred. Examples are real estate properties, and stocks and bonds. Any type of asset that has commercial value can be transferred over a blockchain network.

There are other kinds of blockchain networks besides the bitcoin blockchain network. A company called Ethereum has its own blockchain network, and has a currency similar to bitcoins, called ethers, which are similar to bitcoins, and have their own value. Blockchain technology will become pervasive when the banks adopt it.

Kodak is developing an application. They are developing their own blockchain network. Following its filing for bankruptcy in 2012, Kodak has been regenerated as a digital photography company. It is launching new blockchain platforms KODAKOne and KODAKCoin, in partnership with Wenn Digital.

KODAKOne will be an "image rights management platform". It will help photographers register new work and warehouse their existing work. These works can then licensed within Kodak's new platform.

KODAKCoin will be an "a photo-centric cryptocurrency" which allows photographers and agencies to "take greater control in image rights management". Photographers can receive payment for licensing their work immediately upon sale. It will also allow them to sell their work on a secure blockchain platform.

https://kodakcoin.com

Bitcoin futures contracts are being offered. Bitcoin ETFs are being developed. And, the Fed is looking at ways to incorporate bitcoins into their operations. This is a way of using a new currency that is not backed by an asset such as gold, or by a governmental body or bodies.

An issue for bitcoins is their volatility. They have gone from about $100 per bitcoin in 2016 to $16,000 per bitcoin in late 2017. The biggest issue with bitcoin fundamentally is that the transaction rate using miners occurs at about seven transactions per second and is not fast enough to serve such applications as bank credit card applications. In contrast, Visa's peak is 47,000 transactions per second, and that is just one company.

ArmchairTechInvestor Opinion

Many of the largest banks are working to standardize blockchain networks. The elements of blockchain networks that make them useful include smart contracts that make complex transactions possible, and distributed ledgers. If these elements can be standardized, then a bank might have its own blockchain network that might interconnect seamlessly with another banks separate blockchain network, but each of these networks might be private to each of the banks. This can greatly simplify the user authentication process, as each bank can have its own process.

CyberSecurity

Cybersecurity is a much broader topic than is generally believed. It can go all of the way from attacking on a widespread basis the Internet connections that are vital to conducting daily life and commerce, to ElectroMagnetic Pulse (EMP) atomic bombs that can be dropped at high altitude to disable a countries electrical grid and communications, as North Korea has threatened to do to the U.S.

CyberSecurity Is The War Of The Future: What Can Be Done To Guard Against It?

In terms of U.S. national cybersecurity, the most aggressive threats to the U.S. are Russia, China, North Korea, ISIS, and Iran. China is expanding in the South China Sea, and Russia has accessed Crimea, and is threatening the Ukraine by trying to acquire Eastern Ukraine. Those are just examples of the geographic intentions of China and Russia. Both are focused on territorial expansion either geographically or in terms of economic or structural influence. ISIS, Iran and North Korea are direct threats to the U.S. if they get nuclear weapons, and ISIS is engaged in inciting terrorist attacks in the U.S., either through direct planning of an attack, or inciting others, particularly those who have the luxury of citizenship, or unfettered travel opportunities, to launch such attacks.

State sponsors of terrorism have made recent attacks on the U.S., and attacks have been made elsewhere. China has stolen intellectual property in the U.S. North Korea made an attack on Sony. Russia has made attacks on elections in France and the U.S. Some of the state sponsored attacks are criminal activities.

*Who Is Hacking the U.S.?, Wall Street Journal, Gregory Touhill and James Woolsey, March 7, 2017

Underway in the U.S. is information sharing on cyber attacks between the Federal government and business. Left out of the information loop are medium size and small businesses.

**Another security risk is created by cloud computing. Cloud computing purchased from Amazon and Microsoft allows corporate individuals to bypass their corporate IT departments to get an immediate solution to a data problem. Many of the data security problems occur when the service is configured to allow outside vendors or others access to their data. This can expose the whole corporate database to outside attack.

**An Unexpected Security Problem in the Cloud, Wall Street Journal, by Robert McMillan, September 17, 2017

***A recent phenomenon is ransomware, where a virus infects a computer and a payment must be made to regain access to ones data. Even worse is NotPetya, which can lock a user out of his data, but the data is not able to be unlocked, and is thereby lost forever to the data owner. Data shows that criminals launch hundreds of millions of attacks daily, and 60% of them are ransomware attacks.

***The Disturbing Inevitability of Cyberattacks, Wall Street Journal, by Brian E. Finch, August 21, 2017

ArmchairTechInvestor Opinion

Attacks on business and individual databases are inevitable. From personal experience, the two easiest ways to get infected are by opening email attachments from sources unknown to the recipient, and accessing data sources on the Internet that are unknown to the user. However, there are obviously security threats that can be avoided by frequent updates to the software being used on the Internet, which are often done automatically by the vendor.

The problems of cybersecurity for the U.S. government are monumental, because of the size of the government workforce, and that careless users can do damage to the databases.

The U.S. Has Raised The Importance Of Meeting CyberSecurity Threats. Will Those Initiatives Make The U.S. Safer?

President Trump, responding to the cybersecurity threats coming from countries such as Russia, China and North Korea, stated that the U.S. Cyber Command will be elevated to a "Unified Combatant Command," putting it on an equal footing with existing organizations that oversee military operations in the Middle East, Europe and the Pacific. This unit was a part of the Pentagon, and has now taken on its own importance. Before his inauguration, Trump vowed to make Cyber Command more important. Its new role might include the development of additional cyber weapons meant to deter attacks on the United States.

The unit reached "initial operating capacity", meaning all 133 teams consisting of roughly 5,000 staffers, could execute missions on a basic level. By the end of the 2018 fiscal year, those 133 Cyber Command teams will swell to 6,200 personnel as the organization hits "full operating capacity."

An important continuing threat to the U.S. is ISIS. Cyber Command is attempting to block the digital payments systems of ISIS and infiltrate their communications channels that give directions and recruit new fighters. These efforts have had only limited success. ISIS has been a difficult foe. It establishes new accounts, platforms and devices when stymied by America's digital weapons.

ArmchairTechInvestor Opinion

There is a potential cyber threat that might involve putting weapons in space meant to disable vital functions such as communications systems or vital infrastructure such as electrical grids or water systems.

A very important potential new threat is quantum computing, which will become so powerful that it may be able to very quickly crack existing computer passwords and codes. The threshold is about 100 qubits of capacity. Intel announced at CES the development of a 49-qubit quantum computer. It is not viable as a defense for local computers because it must be operated at very low temperatures.

Quantum Computing-CyberSecurity-U.S. and China

Countries such as China, Russia, the U.K., the European Union, and Australia are in a race to develop quantum computers, as are companies such as IBM, Intel, Microsoft and Alphabet (Google). The winners of the race will be able to quickly obsolete existing cybersecurity technologies and systems. They will instantaneously be able to break their security codes.

Quantum Computing Will Dominate CyberSecurity: The Stakes Are High And The U.S. Must Win The Race

Quantum computers use quantum mechanics to provide extremely fast computers. How do these computers work? In quantum mechanics, photons and electrons can exist in two states at the same time. Instead of using ones and zeros like existing computers do, a quantum bit, a qubit can be both a one and a zero at the same time and do two computations at once. As qubits are added, the computer power grows exponentially, instead of linearly like today's computers. This is like a gigantic cloud computing world within one computer. This will allow quantum computers of the future to perform calculations thousands of times faster than supercomputers do today. Large quantum computers of the future will almost instantaneously be able to break encryption systems that use ones and zeros today.

Blockchain technology and the bitcoin network are supposedly secure, but that will not be the case in the future unless quantum computers protect them.

The development of quantum computers is necessary for the protection of U.S. computer networks, particularly when they are linked together. The U.S.'s large companies such as IBM, Google, Microsoft, Apple, AT&T and others will be the larger companies developing quantum computing capabilities to protect their computer networks, and defeat the protections of other networks.

Computers with 10 qubits of capacity already exist. China is apparently the leader in quantum computer research. In mid-2017, it launched the first satellite capable of transmitting quantum data. It is building the world's largest quantum computing facility. Its focus is on code-breaking, and supporting its military with quantum navigation systems for stealth submarines. It appears to be getting close to getting a 40-qubit quantum computer prototype. Staying up with China in quantum computing will likely be the next military frontier for the U.S.

The U.S. Congress has held hearings to understand quantum computing, and hopefully to undertake something at least equivalent to the $10 billion China has pledged to become the worldwide leader developing this worldwide weapon that could make all current cybersecurity efforts obsolete. The U.S. has a National Quantum Initiative that will need to be undertaken and given substantial funding. The U.S. is behind, but U.S. companies recognize what needs to be done, and are committing corporate research and development money to accomplish the task. About 100 qubits of quantum computing capacity is apparently needed to instantaneously obsolete existing data security systems.

*The Computer That Could Rule the World, Wall Street Journal, by Arthur Herman, October 27, 2017

ArmchairTechInvestor Opinion

There appears to be little doubt that the development of quantum computers will be equivalent militarily to the development of the atomic bomb in World War II. The U.S. is getting a late start, but luckily the U.S. has companies that will likely be able to keep up with the quantum computing developments in China. However the U.S. still needs to make this a major defense spending focus. The Congress does not seem to be far enough along to make this the priority that it should be. Hopefully the U.S. politicians will see the threat that quantum computing presents to the U.S. computer network, and its defense network and computing facilities.

CHAPTER 12

U.S. Infrastructure, Air Traffic Control and Inland Waterway Systems

Infrastructure-U.S.

As a starting point in looking at infrastructure spending planned by Trump in the U.S., the U.S. is projected spend about 20% of the total, with state and local governments being about 40%, and private entities spending about 40%. President Trump has targeted $1.5 trillion of infrastructure spending. This will be funded partly by the Federal government, along with non-Federal funding of prioritized and expedited projects.

AP and The New York Times Mischaracterize Trumps Infrastructure & Other Plans. What Will They Really Be Like?

The Trump administration has promised a $1 billion increase in infrastructure spending. They have not said that U.S. infrastructure spending would not increase. A New York Time article on June 3, 2017 said that Trump plans to shift infrastructure spending to cities, states and business. This statement is clearly inaccurate. Since the Trump program is new spending, it is not a shift in spending. An important objective will be to attract private capital through public-private partnerships.

The Times also said that Trump plans to sharply curtail Federal government infrastructure funding. Again, this is not true, since Federal infrastructure funding will increase. One example is the possibility of about $200 million of Federal tax reductions for private companies. This is a form of Federal funding, even though it is encouraging private infrastructure project spending.

The Associate Press (AP) also had a tainted overview of a week of Trump meetings to discuss their infrastructure plans. It said that an infrastructure plan has been "stymied in Congress and overshadowed by White House controversies". This is not accurate. The Congress has not undertaken infrastructure spending consideration, and although the liberal media and the Democrats have raised so far baseless claims of Russian collusion with the Trump campaign in the election in 2016, the infrastructure plans are on an undeterred separate track, and could be identified in more detail. If Trump can develop a plan that increases significant private investment, this will be a major accomplishment.

Additional Associate Press bias included: "Job growth has slowed in recent months instead of accelerating as the president predicted." This is not true. April 2017 was a slower month, but jobs have increased by over 1 million in 2017, and at 4.3% in April 2018, the unemployment rate is at the lowest level it has been in the last two decades.

AP claimed, "Trump has said he has tax legislation moving through Congress but his effort has been stalled and no bill has been written." This is again misleading. Tax reform is a very complex issue. With the Democrats largely obstructing Trump efforts, crafting a tax bill, which can be passed by the Republican majority in the House and Senate, may be difficult. The tax reform bill was in the early stages of being developed, although passing one in 2017 was the objective. It was passed in 2017.

AP again stated: "His budget plan released during his foreign trip included math errors that enabled the White House to falsely claim that its tax plan would deliver both faster growth and a balanced budget." There may be some truth in this assertion, although there was no defense of a math error being present in the budget. The truth is that the budget is an early stage document that needs to show a balanced budget to get through the legislative process, again because of Democratic obstruction, and a possible Senate filibuster. The budget did have economic assumptions that appear to be unreasonable, particularly the starting growth rate after fiscal 2017, and it appeared to not include the revenue impacts of corporate and personal tax reductions, and infrastructure spending. However, these issues will need to be addressed in an updated budget, once the tax reduction details have emerged. This may occur by the end of 2018.

ArmchairTechInvestor Opinion

The Trump $1 trillion infrastructure plan is on track, and more details will become available, probably in 2018. Particularly important will be the efforts to develop public-private partnerships. The projects are expected to include roads, bridges, waterways, electrical power distribution, and airway systems.

Trump Has Outlined His Infrastructure Plans: The Budget Shows The First Year Of This Plan

Spending on inland waterways, and updating the air traffic control system are two examples of important possible private projects. The 2018 Budget includes $200 billion of spending to pursue these initiatives. The U.S. government will be designing a suite of programs and identifying partners that can include states, localities, and private infrastructure stakeholders;

The U.S. plans to reevaluate its role in overall infrastructure spending. Some key principals include:

- When Federal funds are provided, they should be awarded to projects that address problems that are a high priority from the perspective of a region or the country, or projects that lead to long- term changes in how infrastructure is designed, built, and maintained;
- The Federal Government should support more communities moving toward a model of independence;
- The Federal Government provides services that non-Federal entities, including the private sector, could deliver more efficiently. The administration will look for opportunities to appropriately divest from certain functions, which will provide better services for citizens, and potentially generate budgetary savings; and
- The private sector can provide valuable benefits for the delivery of infrastructure, through better procurement methods, market discipline, and a long-term focus on maintaining assets. While public-private partnerships will not be the solution to all

infrastructure needs, they can help advance the countries most important regionally significant projects.

In addition to the $200 billion, these proposals are also in the 2018 Budget:

- The Budget proposes that a non-governmental entity be created to manage the air traffic control system. This entity could be used to work with a private investor that would finance and operate a modern air traffic control system;
- The Veterans Administration (VA) has old facilities that are often located in places that are different from where they should be located, where veterans most need care. The Budget proposes to allow the VA to lease out facilities, and increase the speed of pursuing facility renovations. Future reforms will encourage public-private partnerships and reduce barriers to acquisition, contracting, and disposals;
- The Power Marketing Administration (PMA) has transmission infrastructure assets (lines, towers, substations, and rights of way) that could be leased out so the private sector could fulfill transmission functions; and
- Separately, the Budget proposes to reform the laws governing the Inland Waterways Trust Fund, including establishing a fee to increase the amount paid by commercial navigation users of inland waterways. These revenues could fund future capital investments.

ArmchairTechInvestor Opinion

President Trump has proposed a $1 trillion infrastructure program. The 2018 Budget includes $200 billion for this program. We expect that money to be used over perhaps five years, and if public or private investors can provide $800 billion, or 80% of the capital, a $1 trillion increase in infrastructure spending program is possible. Two programs sorely in need of being upgraded are the U.S. air traffic control system, and the U.S. inland waterways, and their lock systems that allow commerce to flow cost effectively.

Trump's infrastructure program is underway. It is unclear if it will be successful. Projects have not yet been proposed for transportation systems, and highways, just to mention two additional project opportunities. The U.S. is not organized the way China is and allows them to fund a $4-8 trillion One Belt, One Road Initiative that could make investments in about 70 countries. Attached to those investments will be financial, political and even military obligations required of the countries in which China invests. Most of the countries need additional infrastructure spending financial help.

Air Traffic Control

The 2017 U.S. Budget proposed that a non-governmental entity be created to manage the air traffic control system. This entity could be used to work with a private investor that would finance and operate a modern air traffic control system.

A New Air Traffic Control System Is Possible: Will The Congress Step Up And Make It Happen?

The Trump infrastructure plan began to unfold with a proposal to overhaul our nation's air traffic control system. The system includes 300 air traffic control systems and about 30,000 employees. The air traffic control system is seriously antiquated, and many attempts have been unsuccessful in trying to upgrade it.

The good part of the system is that it has been very effective from a safety standpoint. There are about 50,000 flights per day. There hasn't been a fatal crash by a U.S. airline in eight years. However there have been many near misses. Canada has successfully deployed a modern air traffic control system that can become a model or template for an upgraded U.S. system. The Federal Aviation Administration (FAA) would continue to provide safety oversight

The Trump plan for an upgraded U.S. system is very interesting. The existing system would be transferred from the FAA to a non-profit company. User fees would fund the system. A concern in Congress is that the airlines will dominate the operation of the system. This concern has been met by setting up a 13-member board of directors that only includes two seats for the airlines. Another concern is that such a system would not be usable by smaller airports. It would seem that any airport that today has an FAA system should be capable of being upgraded. There are many smaller airports that do not have an FAA system, and perhaps some of them could be added to a much more efficient system using modern technology.

President Trump said that a new air traffic control system would increase safety and reduce wait times. A new system would likely be based upon a modern GPS system instead of the existing 1945 vintage radar system. Besides the improved accuracy of such a GPS-based system, other modern benefits include many ways of actually tracking the planes, directing them on their routes, and particularly planning and directing their landings.

ArmchairTechInvestor Opinion

The challenge in upgrading the existing antiquated air traffic control has two components. The first is the design of the system, which should advance more quickly because of a successful Canadian system. The second challenge is to transition from the existing system to a new system. This will probably require running dual systems, with airports being transferred to the new system one at a time. The existing air traffic control system is seriously outdated, and hopefully a government, that is seriously inadequate at running businesses, will begin to develop some new effective models for developing public operations.

Inland Waterway Systems

The 2017 Budget proposed to reform the laws governing the Inland Waterways Trust Fund, including establishing a fee to increase the amount paid by commercial navigation users of inland waterways. These revenues could fund future capital investments for aging inland waterways infrastructure.

Trump Shortens Infrastructure Planning Cycle: However Climate Change Modifications Are Controversial

President Trump signed an executive order eliminating environmental orders implemented by the Obama administration, and shortening the time for getting approval of Federal highway projects to two years. The objective is to eliminate and update permitting regulations for roads, pipelines, bridges and other transportation projects. A key element of the new executive order rolls back standards set by former President Barack Obama that required the Federal government to account for climate change and sea-level rise when building infrastructure.

President Trump has proposed a $1 trillion plan to update the nation's infrastructure. Few details have been given on the plan, but we expect it to evolve project by project. An outline of the plan is that the U.S. will provide $200 billion, and private industry and local governments will provide the remainder. The one plan that has been offered is the replacement of the nation's antiquated air traffic control system. The new system that is being proposed would replace World War II radar systems with current GPS technology. This seems like a needed improvement. To meet the Trump plan's financial objectives, this would need to involve a private or non-profit non-Federal organization operating the system.

Trump is belligerently opposed by the Democrats on issues such as the approval of Trump nominees for government positions, and opposition to healthcare reform. However, there could be bi-partisan support for infrastructure rebuilding.

The plan to reduce the time for obtaining Federal approval for a project begins by having one lead agency work with other review parties to complete environmental reviews and other permits for a project. All permit decisions are required to be made within 90 days. Agencies will have a goal of two years to process environmental reviews of major projects.

A major change in permit requirements is eliminating climate change requirements for project designs. The Federal Flood Risk Management Standard, established by Obama as an executive order in 2015, is eliminated. Reinstated is the previous standard adopted under Jimmy Carter in 1977. However, state and local agencies may adopt more rigorous standards. For example, if California, which has endorsed climate change as being real, wants to adopt the Federal Flood Risk Management Standard, they may.

The Obama rule gave Federal agencies three options to flood-proof new infrastructure projects. They could:

- Use the best available climate change science;
- Require that standard projects like roads and railways be built two feet above the national 100-year flood elevation standard; and
- Require that critical buildings like hospitals be built three feet higher; Or they could require infrastructure to be built to at least the 500-year flood plain. The order only applied to government development.

ArmchairTechInvestor Opinion

President Trump promised to simplify the process of getting infrastructure projects, such as roads, approved more quickly by simplifying the process. Not only has the process been simplified, but also, time limits have been set on getting agencies to approve or reject projects.

Some progress has been made in identifying infrastructure projects that might be built. A project that has been proposed is the need to renew our river lock systems, which are very old, and assure users of river goods transportation that this mode of product delivery, such as agriculture, will have long-term viability.

Climate change science adopted by the United Nations (U.N.) states that the median estimate is that global temperatures will rise by 3 degrees Fahrenheit, and the oceans will rise by 3 feet over the next 100 years. Trump does not believe in climate change, and has thus eliminated costly measures to build structures that will survive if the oceans do rise at the rate predicted by the U.N.

We believe climate change is real. The last three ten-year periods have each been the warmest in modern history. The build-up of carbon in the atmosphere is undeniable. The effects of carbon in the atmosphere are also undeniable in reflecting back sunlight from the atmosphere, and causing higher ocean temperatures. Projects built near the coasts should recognize that climate change is probably real, either in determining where the project is located, or by taking measures to guard against that possibility.

CHAPTER 13

U.S. Legal and Law Enforcement-Housing, Inner Cities, Supreme Court and Other Court Appointments

Housing and Urban Development (HUD)

HUD Is Being Reorganized In A Way That Should Make Home Ownership Available To Millennials.

The Department of Housing and Urban Development (HUD) provides rental assistance to low-income and vulnerable households and helps work-eligible families achieve self-sufficiency. The President's 2018 Budget requested $40.7 billion in gross discretionary funding for HUD, a $6.2 billion or 13.2 percent decrease from the 2017 annualized level. However, such cuts have been postponed until at least 2019 due to the two-year U.S. budget that has been approved.

Fannie Mae and Freddie Mac are the core loan programs of HUD. They both went bankrupt during the 2008-09 housing meltdown, and were essentially acquired by the U.S. government. The Obama administration was prepared to close them. President Trump appointed Ben Carson to lead HUD. HUD has decided not to close Fannie Mae and Freddie Mac. The Congress has not yet addressed the future of those two loan programs, but it seems probable that both will be merged into one program. Both programs package loans originated by lenders such that they can be resold, allowing lenders the flexibility of not having to provide long-term financial support for the loans they originate.

One of HUD's goals is to allow college graduates to manage student debt and still be able to afford housing. Graduates that take on student loans to pay for college often end up with very large debt to income levels. A proposal has been made to include college loans with financing undertaken to buy a home, so that both can be paid off together as a home is being purchased. To give opportunities of affordable homeownership, Carson said they are creating a circumstance to buy a condominium with "FHA banking."

Vision Centers are being established in low-income areas, providing mentorship programs, childcare, and basic instruction, Carson said. The centers provide advantages that stable families provide, and on which children from disadvantaged homes miss out.

ArmchairTechInvestor Opinion

HUD, along with Fannie Mae and Freddie Mac, provide invaluable services to the housing market. If both of them charge a fee for the services they provide in reducing the risk of making home mortgages, those fees can be used to offset the costs of the mortgages that fail. Theoretically, this can reduce the risk to the U.S. government in supporting the home mortgage market.

The goal of including college loans along with a mortgage in the financing of a home purchase will make it much easier for students with college loans to be able to purchase a home, and benefit financially from owning a home that they might otherwise not be able to purchase.

Also, setting up Vision Centers in disadvantaged communities should provide additional benefits not otherwise available to minorities and other disadvantaged citizens.

Inner Cities

Trump's Inner Cities Plans Have Yet To Materialize: What Are The Prospects For Improvement?

In August 2016, on the campaign trail, Donald Trump declared to urban black voters in Michigan. "You're living in poverty, your schools are no good, you have no jobs, and 58% of your youth are unemployed." He has also said: "And I'll tell you, we're spending a lot of money on the inner cities, We're going to fix — we're fixing the inner cities. We're doing far more than anybody's done with respect to the inner cities. It's a priority for me. And it's very important." He has pledged to spend a lot of money on the inner cities. He has said he will reduce crime, increase jobs, and improve education. What are the facts so far? The unemployment of black and Hispanic minorities has dropped to record lows as of mid-2018.

Trump's proposed 2018 budget cut Housing and Urban Development by 13% and eliminated the Community Development Block Grant (CDBG) Program, potentially saving $3 billion. According to the budget blueprint released in March 2017, CDBG, which provides grants to cities and states for a variety of community development programs, "has not demonstrated results." That assessment is not shared by the U.S. Conference of Mayors, which sent Congress a letter in July 2017, urging its members to support the CDBG program at a level of $3.3 billion in 2018. "CDBG is one of the most effective Federal programs for growing local economies and for providing a lifeline to families and communities with proven results," the mayors' letter states. "It has provided funds in every state, including housing investments, public infrastructure improvements, and economic development, while also providing public services, including services for seniors, youth, the disabled, and employment training. This program helps more than 1,200 cities, counties, states, and rural areas that meet the needs of low- and moderate-income people and communities." The mayors of more than 350 U.S. cities signed the letter.

In the area of education, Trump has proposed increases in school choice programs for low-income families. The biggest increase would be in Title 1 funding, which is awarded to schools with high numbers of children from low-income families. The department's budget proposed an additional $1 billion for Title 1, up to $15.9 billion, to provide funding for a new school-choice program called Furthering Options for Children to Unlock Success, or FOCUS. The grant money would be awarded to school districts "with open enrollment systems that allow Federal, State, and local funds to follow students to the public school of their choice," the department budget says.

Inner Cities Crime

On the crime front, Trump has shifted some existing resources in an effort to reduce violent crime in the cities. In June 2017, Attorney General Jeff Sessions announced the Justice Department would partner with 12 cities to combat violent crime as part of a program called the National Public Safety Partnership. In Chicago, the U.S. Bureau of Alcohol, Tobacco, Firearms and Explosives (ATF) in June 2017 sent 20 ATF agents in an attempt to reduce gun violence in that city.

Michael F. Crowley, a senior fellow at the Brennan Center for Justice at the New York University School of Law, has done a review of nine Federal grant programs that could potentially reduce violent crime in the coming fiscal year. Crowley's analysis found a slight decrease in violence-related grants.

Crowley, who worked as a budget analyst in the White House Office of Management and Budget under both Republican and Democratic presidents, said there are two major Federal grant programs for combating crime: the Edward Byrne Memorial Justice Assistance Grant Programs, known as Byrne JAG, which provide general operating funds based on a formula, and the Community Oriented Policing Services, or COPS, grant for hiring police officers. According to Crowley, Trump's proposed budget would have increased funding for COPS, but decrease it for Byrne, resulting in a net reduction of $55.1 million, or nearly 12 percent, in the two major programs. These possible changes have been delayed by the 2-year budget approval negotiated with the Democrats.

Overall, there would be a net reduction of about $7.1 million, or 1 percent, across nine grant programs that could potentially address violent crime, according to Crowley's analysis.

With regard to jobs in the inner cities, not much has been said about that element of the overall inner cities plan. To the extent that crime can be reduced and education improved, the jobs outlook in the inner cities can also improve. Record lows of minority unemployment were achieved by Trump as of mid-2018. Trump gets virtually no recognition for this achievement by the liberal media.

ArmchairTechInvestor Opinion

There is no one key to inner cities improvements. Budget cuts of 13% were planned for the Housing and Urban Development Department. It is claimed by the Trump administration that there is significant waste. Ben Carson has taken the helm of HUD, and it will be up to him and his staff to make HUD more efficient. The jury is still out as to whether the Trump administration can improve the inner cities, where drugs are rampant, and education is poor. Any improvements will take a generation or more, but Trump professes to have the interest in fighting crime, improving the job outlook, and improving education through school choice. Fighting drugs and gangs will likely be an important element of producing positive change.

Law Enforcement & Department of Justice

The Department of Justice is the driving force behind improving the immigration system, in conjunction with the border wall. The objective is to reduce the number of drug dealers and other criminals that are illegally in the United States. The sanctuary cities are a major impediment to enforcing the immigration laws.

Supreme Court

The Supreme Court Is Helping Trump In His War On The 9th Circuit Court's Intransigence

Neil Gorsuch, at the relatively young age of 49, faced a grueling approval process in the U.S. Senate, despite his obvious qualifications as a Supreme Court Justice. This included a filibuster by the Democrats that was defeated by a Republican rule change. The final vote was 54-45, with only two Democratic Senators voting yes. His approval provided a 5-4 Republican majority in the Supreme Court.

There will be many important issues that will face the Court. The most high-profile case that was facing the Supreme Court was Trump's executive order providing a temporary travel ban on people coming from six Muslim countries. Judges in Hawaii and Maryland suspended this travel ban on the basis that the order was based upon religious grounds. The Trump administration had argued that the temporary ban was needed to prevent terrorists from coming to the U.S., and to allow the U.S. time to develop more-stringent vetting procedures.

A Trump appeal to the Supreme Court was successful in allowing the travel ban to proceed, but with immediate family members and those with legitimate U.S. interests, such as being in school in the U.S., being allowed to enter the U.S. The presumption of the Court was that Trump would prevail when the full case was heard, which did happen.

The Ninth Circuit Court of Appeals, a liberal court in San Francisco, defied the Supreme Court's order by extending the order to include grandparents, aunts, uncles, nieces, brothers-in-laws as well as refugees with no claim on the U.S. The Supreme Court stayed this ruling. As of March 2018, the Supreme Court had not issued a final ruling.

ArmchairTechInvestor Opinion

The Constitution appears to allow the President to restrict travel, if it is in the national interest. Many of the circuit courts of appeal do not appear to be strict constitutionalists, particularly the 9th Circuit Court of Appeals. Justice Gorsuch now gives the Supreme Court 9 Justices, allowing it to avoid 4-4 split decisions on controversial issues.

One of Trumps biggest victories so far is getting Senate approval of Justice Gorsuch. He is likely to support strict interpretations of the Constitution, as envisioned by its drafters, as opposed to those who wish to change the meaning of the Constitution on the basis that times have changed.

Other Judicial Appointments

In 2017, President Trump appointed twelve Federal appellate judges, a record for a president in his first year in office.

CHAPTER 14

Regulation-Banks, Communications and the Environment

Chinese Regulation

China is going through a thorough reorganization of its Communist Party and the functioning of its state activities, such as governing the direction of the economy. This functioning is done by edict. There are essentially no contracts and no judicial system to solve disputes. Failure to follow the edicts can lead to severe retribution, including arrest for actions such as corruption.

U.S. Regulation

President Trump has been reducing regulations. He has promised that there will be two existing regulations eliminated for every new regulation. Bank regulation under the Obama administration is typified by Dodd-Frank. There is no substantial issue that the large banks are able to comply with the legislation, but that it is a significant burden for smaller banks, severely restricting their operations and growth.

Environment And Energy

The Trump administration is promoting nuclear energy, and the fossil fuel industry, including coal. Coal is inherently an environmentally un-friendly fuel source because of the pollution it causes, and its contribution to global warming. Nuclear is considered to be a clean fuel source except that its waste disposal, which needs to be stored underground for about 10,000 years, has not been solved.

Fossil Fuels

Trump is attempting to promote fossil fuels, is opening up new areas where oil and gas exploration can occur, such as in Alaska, and attempting to reduce regulatory restrictions on fossil fuel exploration and delivery.

Dodd-Frank-Banks

In 2017, the House has passed a Dodd-Frank reform bill. That was the first of three pillars for bank reform completion. The second event was the Treasury Department issuing its prescription for banking sector regulatory reform. It may be some time before the third pillar is done, the Senate addressing the Dodd-Frank issue. Dodd-Frank is very technical and complex.

House Passed Dodd-Frank Rewrite: Will The Senate Follow Suit?

Dodd-Frank was passed in 2010 as a financial reform prescription to avoid another economic collapse, such as occurred in the housing crash in 2008-2009. The regulations were targeted at the large banks, but have had a profound negative impact on the medium size banks. President Trump says that regulations such as Dodd-Frank are negatively impacting the U.S. Economy.

A threshold of $50 billion in size was the cutoff established to separate the banks that would come under the act from those that would not. The largest bank, J.P. Morgan Chase has $2.5 trillion in assets, and the tenth, Capital One, has $300 billion in assets. Banks with $50 billion in assets certainly do not pose a risk to the U.S. economy. There are 37 banks above this threshold. In revising the bill, the threshold might be set between $250 billion and $500 billion or it might depend on the riskiness of the bank. The larger banks use depositor assets as capital to reach a 5% threshold of capital required for making a loan. Changes might be to make loans dependent on actual capital in the bank, instead of deposits by customers

Although the Senate will certainly change the House Financial CHOICE Act, the changes in the House bill are numerous:

- There is a Consumer Protection Bureau that will be restructured;
- Stress tests on the banks are designed to make sure they don't undertake actions that are too risky. The Fed-administered tests may have improved banks' risk management and transparency. However, the testing procedures have created uncertainty. These will be revised, and might be applied at as long as two-year intervals;

- An Orderly Liquidation Authority, designed to wind-down a failing bank, has been eliminated;
- Banks with assets above $50 billion, and below as much as a 10 times higher threshold, will no longer need to comply with the Act.

Mortgage lending by small banks is an issue. Increased lending will be promoted by minimizing a rule about qualified mortgages. The rule increases the costs of lending to higher risk borrowers and often precludes banks from holding mortgages on their books. Modifying the rules may allow local banks to increase mortgage lending.

The Volcker Rule limits proprietary trading by banks, and attempts to reduce speculation. Defining the differences between speculation and market making has been difficult. The Volcker Rule has been eliminated.

A very controversial element has been the fiduciary rule, which mandates that financial advice must be in the client's best interest. It's set to be implemented, and the Department of Labor has said it wouldn't enforce the rule until January 1, 2018.

The Financial CHOICE Act could face difficulties in the Senate, and because of Democratic intransigence, might be broken into smaller bills to allow the Republicans to use the reconciliation process to avoid a Senate filibuster.

Armchair Politician Opinion

Dodd-Frank's objective of reducing the risks being undertaken by large banks is a good objective that has forced large banks to reexamine the risks they undertake. However, it has been heavy-handed, increasing substantially the costs of complying with the Act, particularly for small banks. Its revision is sorely needed.

The Financial CHOICE Act's outcome is uncertain, because of the question of when and if the Senate might act. It is being hailed as a Trump victory because of it passing the House. Whether it becomes a true victory remains to be seen.

The Treasury Released a Bank Regulation Proposal: It Supplements Dodd-Frank Reform Efforts

The House has passed a Dodd-Frank reform bill in 2017. That was the first of three pillars for bank reform completion. The second event was the Treasury Department issuing its prescription for banking sector regulatory reform. It may be some time before the Senate addresses the Dodd-Frank issue. Dodd-Frank is very technical and complex.

The Treasury Report, can be summarized as:

- Improving regulatory efficiency and effectiveness by critically evaluating mandates and regulatory fragmentation, overlap, and duplication across regulatory agencies;
- Aligning the financial system to help support the U.S. economy;
- Reducing the regulatory burden by decreasing unnecessary complexity;
- Tailoring the regulatory approach based on the size and complexity of regulated firms and requiring greater regulatory cooperation and coordination among financial regulators; and
- Aligning regulations to support market liquidity, investment, and lending in the U.S. economy.

The Treasury recommendations are outlined below.

Addressing the U.S. Regulatory Structure

Both Congress and the financial regulatory agencies have roles to play in reducing overlap and increasing coordination within the U.S. financial regulatory framework. Treasury recommends that Congress take action to reduce fragmentation, overlap, and duplication in the U.S. regulatory structure. This could include consolidating regulators with similar missions and more clearly defining regulatory mandates.

Refining Capital, Liquidity, and Leverage Standards

Treasury offers a number of recommendations aimed at both decreasing the burden of statutory stress testing and improving its effectiveness by tailoring the stress-testing requirements based on the size and complexity of banks. For the statutory, company-led annual Dodd-Frank Act stress test (DFAST), Treasury recommends raising the dollar threshold of participation to $50 billion from the current threshold of $10 billion in total assets.

Providing Credit to Fund Consumers and Businesses to Drive Economic Growth

Treasury has identified numerous regulatory factors that are unnecessarily limiting the flow of credit to consumers and businesses and thereby constraining economic growth and vitality. Some of these regulatory factors also unnecessarily restrict the range of choices and options for borrowers, particularly consumers, through undue restrictions on a bank's ability to design and deliver responsible lending products.

Improving Market Liquidity

The cumulative effect of a number of bank regulations implementing Dodd-Frank may be limiting market liquidity. Maintaining strong, vibrant markets at all times, particularly during periods of market stress, is necessary to support economic growth, avoid systemic risk, and therefore minimize the risk of a taxpayer-funded bailout.

Allowing Community Banks and Credit Unions to Thrive

In order to promote the orderly operation and expansion of the community banking and credit union sector, Treasury recommends that the overall regulatory burden be significantly adjusted. This is appropriate in light of the complexity and lack of systemic risk of such financial institutions. The capital regime for community banks having total assets less than $10 billion should be simplified, which can be achieved by providing for an exemption from the U.S. Basel III risk-based capital regime and, if required, an exemption from Dodd-Frank's Collins Amendment.

Advancing American Interests and Global Competitiveness

Treasury recommends increased transparency and accountability in international financial regulatory standard-setting bodies. Improved inter-agency coordination should be adopted to ensure the best harmonization of U.S. participation in applicable international forums. International regulatory standards should only be implemented through consideration of their alignment with domestic objectives and should be carefully and appropriately tailored to meet the needs of the U.S. financial services industry and the American people.

Improving the Regulatory Engagement Model

In conducting its review of the depository sector and the regulatory engagement model, Treasury has identified areas for review and further evaluation to improve the effectiveness of regulation. The role of the boards of directors (Boards) of banking organizations can be improved to enhance accountability by appropriately defining the Board's role and responsibilities for regulatory oversight and governance. A greater degree of inter-agency cooperation and coordination pertaining to regulatory actions and consent orders should be encouraged, in order to improve the transparency and timely resolution of such actions.

Enhancing Use of Regulatory Cost-Benefit Analysis

While Congress has imposed discrete cost-benefit analysis requirements on independent financial regulatory agencies, including the CFTC, SEC, FDIC, Federal Reserve, OCC, and CFPB, these agencies have long been exempt from Executive Order 12866. As a result, the financial regulators have not adopted uniform and consistent methods to analyze costs and benefits, and their cost-benefit analyses have sometimes lacked analytical rigor. Federal financial regulatory agencies should follow the principles of transparency and public accountability by conducting rigorous cost-benefit analyses and making greater use of notices of proposed rulemakings to solicit public comment.

Encouraging Foreign Investment in the U.S. Banking System

Treasury considers foreign investment in the U.S. banking system to be an aid to diversifying the risk of the financial system and propelling economic growth. Among other reasons, such investment and related connection back to the home jurisdiction of these banks can frequently enhance a bridge of further foreign corporate investment in the United States. The application of U.S. enhanced prudential standards to foreign banking organizations (FBOs) should be based on their U.S. risk profile, using the same revised threshold as is used for the application of the enhanced prudential standards to U.S. bank holding companies, rather than on global consolidated assets.

ArmchairTechInvestor Opinion

Dodd-Frank's objective, reducing the risks being undertaken by large banks, is a good objective that has forced large banks to reexamine the risks they undertake. However, it has been heavy-handed, increasing substantially the costs of complying with the Act, particularly for small banks. Its revision is sorely needed. The House passed the Financial CHOICE Act in 2017. However, The Financial CHOICE Act's outcome is uncertain, because of the question of when and if the Senate might act. It is being hailed as a Trump victory because of it passing the House. Whether it becomes a true victory remains to be seen. The Treasury Department report supplements this effort and provides non-legislative means of reforming bank regulation.

Federal Communications Commission (FCC)

The FCC regulates the communications industry, including common carriers and Internet service providers. Pending before the commission is a proposed merger between AT&T and Time Warner. The Trump administration has challenged the merger on anti-trust grounds. The outcome was decided by the courts in mid-2018 in favor of letting the merger proceed. The FCC will oversee the development of a 5G network in the U.S. An important application for this, the latest U.S. upgrade, will be artificial intelligence.

The FCC Adopted Revised Rules For Network Neutrality That Will Spur Innovation On The Internet-Many New Products Should Emerge

*The FCC adopted the latest version of "net neutrality" during the Obama administration, in 2015. Internet service providers were classified as common carriers. The concept was that carriers treat all traffic on their network equally. That is, that small users should be charged the same rates as large users, despite the amount of their traffic. The unfounded assumption was that carriers' costs are equal for small and large customers. This ignores the fact that Internet customer handling costs are larger for small customers, and assumes that there are no economies of scale in network traffic costs for small and large customers.

**The Federal Communications Commission (FCC) repealed the net neutrality rules. The new rules require broadband communications carriers to disclose when they limit or control speeds, such as speeding up live sports programming. This will allow the carriers' customers to choose packages and pricing that meets their needs. It is also claimed that the changed rules will increase the carriers' investment in broadband wireless and fiber infrastructure, and support the growth of content. Apple plans to spend $1 billion on content to compete with Amazon, Netflix and YouTube. Streaming services will be customized to compete with the cable companies by providing smaller customized bundles that will be less expensive than bundled cable services. Disney is buying 21st Century Fox to compete with Netflix.

FCC Vote Promises to Reprice The Net, Wall Street Journal, by John D. McKinnon and Ruan Knutson, December 12, 1017

****FCC Reverses Rules on Net Access,** Wall Street Journal, by John D. McKinnon, December 14, 2017

ArmchairTechInvestor Opinion

In delivering content for customers, it is important that the carriers not favor their own content, or block their competitors' content. With those caveats, it is better to have less regulation than more. On that principal, eliminating the net neutrality rules will allow more innovative services to be operated. The typical cable systems bundle programming packages in a way that includes many programs not wanted by a typical consumer. The net neutrality rule elimination will allow streaming services to be customized in ways that will promote choice. We also believe it will promote network innovations in fiber and broadband wireless that will benefit more rural areas.

The requirement that the carriers provide the details of their services and alliances should make the activities of the carriers transparent, and subject to anti-trust or anti-competitive scrutiny.

CHAPTER 15

China vs. U.S. 2018 Conclusions

China-XI Reorganization-Territorial Ambitions, Political Influence, Trade

While the U.S. is emphasizing its policy of negotiating bilateral trade agreements, China is doing just the opposite. It has developed a trade agreement, called the Regional Comprehensive Economic Partnership with 16 countries making up 39% of global GDP. China is the main trade competitor of the U.S. on the global stage. It has an ambitious project called the One Belt, One Road Network that will connect about 70 countries to China economically, and as joint investors. These types of activities can result in relationships that go far beyond trade and can involve joint investment, political and military relationships.

China's One Belt, One Road Network

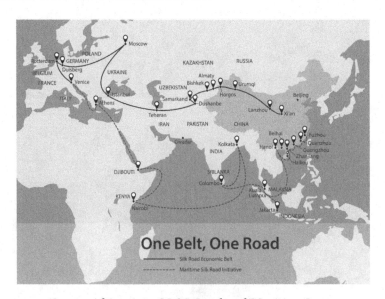

Image: Africa-Asia OBOR Road and Maritime Loops
Image Source: Getty Images

Political and State Organizations-Xi Reorganization and Economy-China

Xi Jinping has become China's President for life. This occurred in early 2018. This will bring profound changes to the way China is operated. The management of the Chinese economy is one case in point. Liu He, who is a Harvard graduate, has assumed leadership of the economy, including the financial system and the industrial sector, over which Xi Jinping previously presided. In October, 2017, Mr. Liu produced an economic blueprint for running China's economy, "Xi Thought". Regulation, particularly of the central bank, will be a very important responsibility.

A reorganization of the whole Chinese country has begun. The Communist Party is being integrated with all of the state operations to provide a unified plan for eventually replacing the U.S. as the dominant world power. Central to that plan is the One Belt, One Road Initiative that is aimed at expanding Chinese control beyond a China that already includes regions such as Tibet to the North, and the South China Seas. Taiwan will be rigorously pursued to incorporate it into the China Empire. Also included in the plan and vision is to extend Chinese influence through their trade plan to about 70 countries in the Indian Ocean, Europe, Asia and Africa.

Conclusions Issues

The main issues that we will cover in this conclusions chapter are:

- China has underway continuing efforts to acquire the intellectual property of U.S. companies in China and in the U.S.;
- U.S. companies are subject to discrimination by the Chinese government in seeking to invest in China;
- China has a One Belt, One Road (OBOR) Initiative to form political, economic, and military relationships in about 70 countries in Asia, Africa, the Middle East, and Europe;
- China is improving its military capabilities by making substantial investments and through its OBOR Initiative;
- The U.S. deficit with China could provide most of the financing for China's OBOR Initiative; and

• China's objectives are long-term threats to the U.S. and its democracy. The status of U.S. defense and political initiatives is outlined.

China Trade-World Trade Organization (WTO)

China has used the national security threat issue as a way to protect Chinese companies. China was admitted to the WTO in 2002 and is still considered to be an emerging country under the World Trade Organization rules, showing how antiquated is the WTO.

Chinese And U.S. Companies: Examples Of The Different Treatment They Receive In The Mainland China Market

The technological war with China has begun. It remains to be seen whether U.S. companies can do business in China without giving away their technology. The U.S. is pushing back on the Chinese theft of the intellectual property of U.S. companies.

Companies such as ZTE and Huawei are finally being restricted because of the business they do in the U.S. that could provide a threat to U.S. security.

U.S. and other foreign tech companies are severely restricted in accessing the China market. The restrictions vary by sector, but the most onerous restrictions are on providing Internet access to their databases and search services to their customers.

Only three Chinese companies, Alibaba Group Holding, Baidu and Tencent Holdings, are allowed to directly access the Internet in mainland China. All foreign companies must use these companies to access the Internet, providing Chinese companies with an Internet monopoly.

Alibaba

*Alibaba Group Holding is one of three companies, including Tencent Holdings, and Baidu that dominate e-commerce, social media, and mobile payments. With China moving toward what could be mostly an all-electric automobile market by 2030, providing a variety of subscription services to vehicles is viewed as an extremely large market opportunity in China, but also perhaps elsewhere. For example, Renault is forecasting that it could achieve a fivefold increase in revenues by 2023 as a result of its ability to sell automobiles on Alibaba's platform.

Baidu

***Baidu is one of the three companies that dominate e-commerce, social media, and mobile payments in China. In particular it provides search and mapping services. With China moving toward what could be mostly an all-electric automobile market by 2030, providing a variety of subscription services to vehicles is viewed as an extremely large market opportunity in China, but also perhaps elsewhere.

Broadcom

Broadcom is a very large semiconductor company based in Shanghai. It attempted a hostile takeover of Qualcomm, which has an impressive portfolio of intellectual property patents. The U.S. rejected the attempted acquisition on the grounds that such an acquisition could jeopardize national security and the development of 5G Internet technology in the U.S. 5G will become crucial for developing advanced services such as artificial intelligence.

Following its failure to acquire Qualcomm, Broadcom is attempting to acquire U.S. software company, CA. The U.S. may also block this acquisition on the basis that Broadcom is furthering China's goal of being a leader in semiconductors and software

Huawei

Huawei is a Chinese telecommunications equipment manufacturer. It is the world's largest wireless equipment manufacturer and the third largest smartphone maker. The company is making an investment in the United Kingdom. The UK has set up a facility, run by Huawei, to examine the intricacies of their own equipment. U.S. politicians have expressed concern that the company's equipment can be used to gather intelligence for

China or even disable U.S. equipment. Even equipment in other countries
might also be used for spying on the U.S. or network control purposes.
The House and Senate have each introduced bills to address the Huawei
risk. Huawei counters that it is an employee-owned company and is respected in 170 countries around the world.

South Korea's largest carrier's CEO called Huawei a "concern". Australia
ruled out Huawei for its Solomon Island undersea cable deployment despite the fact that Huawei is an advisor to it on its development of a 5G
wireless network.

Tencent Holdings

Tencent Holdings is a Chinese Internet company. Because the Chinese
Internet is very tightly controlled by the Chinese government, Tencent
Holdings is in a very enviable position. One important capability is their
ability to provide GPS mapping services. Driverless vehicles could be an
extremely important application. Vehicle manufactures will need to use
an Internet company to provide driverless vehicle services. China could
eliminate the sale of internal combustion engine cars in China beginning
in about 2030.

Xiaomi

Xiaomi, is one of the largest cellphone makers in the China, and has
a $46 billion market capitalization. It has high quality cellphones that
rival Apple in looks, but are inexpensive. It has completed an Initial
Public Offering (IPO) that could have a valuation of $100 billion or more.
Xiaomi is essentially an Internet company. Its China market share was
12% in 2017 and its shipments grew 50% to 96 million units. However,
the company is risky and subject to the vagaries of hardware development
companies with low margins. On revenues of $15.2 billion, it had profits
of about $1 billion. By contrast Apple had a market capitalization of about
$900 billion in early 2018. In China, non-Internet companies are generally
banned from using GPS for self-driving vehicles and existing providers
such as Xiaomi are very much in demand to provide future services for
self-driving electric vehicles.

Zejiang Geely-Daimler-Volvo

Geely has become the premier Chinese vehicle manufacturer by connecting with Western automaker technology. Geely went to Ford to buy Volvo for $1.8 billion. Relying on the manufacturing expertise of Volvo in Sweden, the design vision of a seasoned Western car designer, it has had increasing success both worldwide and in China. China is going toward all-electric vehicles, and Volvo plans to have 90% of its vehicles electric or hybrid by 2020. It has manufacturing plants in China and Europe and has a U.S. plant that will open in the U.S. in 2018.

Daimler

Daimler has said it plans to begin assembling Mercedes-Benz vehicles in 2018 from a $1 billion facility shared with Renault-Nissan in Aguascalientes in Mexico. In February 2018, Li Shufu, the chairman of Chinese automaker Geely, bought Daimler stock, worth $9 billion. Geely will not own the stake. It will be held by an investment vehicle known as Tenaclou3 Prospect Investment Ltd., according to a filing. The purpose of the Geely investment in Daimler is not clear, but because Geely is working to improve the quality of its vehicles, particularly in the luxury vehicle area, that is very likely a reason.

ZTE

ZTE and Huawei are two Chinese companies that could pose a threat to the U.S. broadband communications networks. ZTE has become the fourth largest cellphone supplier in the U.S. The UK banned the use of ZTE equipment because of concerns that China could force the company to infiltrate the UK's broadband communications infrastructure. China essentially requires Chinese companies that wish to do business in China to pledge allegiance to China. This can result in those companies being used to spy on countries where they do business. This is the equivalent of the U.S. requiring Apple to spy on behalf of the U.S. government, which they would not do.

China-Semiconductor Investments

China announced plans to significantly improve the competitiveness of its state and Chinese semiconductor companies when it launched a $21.8 billion semiconductor development fund in 2014. A U.S. Trade Representative's report on March 22, 2018 declared the 2014 fund as an effort by government agencies and state-owned companies to meet Chinese national strategic objectives.

China has also announced a new fund that could total about $47.4 billion. Important semiconductor industry sectors it will support are likely to include microprocessors and graphic processors. The objective is to reduce China's dependence on foreign semiconductor products from companies such as Qualcomm, IBM and Nvidia.

China-Quantum Computers

China is apparently the leader in quantum computer research. In mid-2017, it launched the first satellite capable of transmitting quantum data. It is building the world's largest quantum computing facility. Its focus is on code breaking, and supporting its military with quantum navigation systems for stealth submarines. It appears to be getting close to getting a 40-qubit quantum computer prototype.

The U.S. Congress has held hearings to understand quantum computing. China has pledged $10 billion to become the worldwide leader developing this weapon that could make all current cybersecurity efforts obsolete.

Alphabet (Google)

Google is blocked in China, and unlike Apple, it has not been able to limit the download of apps sufficiently to be able to enter the Chinese Internet search market.

Amazon

Online Internet retailers in China are not allowed to sell directly. This requires Amazon to go through a complicated process that severely limits

its capabilities in China, compared with the big three allowed Chinese company Internet providers. In China, the Amazon website is operated by local companies owned by Chinese nationals in order to meet ownership and licensing requirements.

Apple

Apple did well in the December quarter of 2017, increasing revenues by 11% in the Asia-Pacific region, but is losing market share in the huge smartphone markets in China, India and other Asian countries. Taking significant market share is Xiaomi. Which has inexpensive smartphones, and feature rich smartphones that compete with Apple's X. The X sells for about $1,000.

China is issuing demanding cybersecurity requirements. It is requiring that all cloud data be located on servers in China, including encryption keys. Apple has said that the keys will be stored in a secure location, it will retain control of them, and hasn't put in any backdoors. However, Chinese seizure is always a possibility, or it could require that Apple give them specific keys. The U.S. Congress is very concerned about these keys being stored in China

This could make the data vulnerable to Chinese surveillance. Apple also removed 700 apps that allow users to bypass Internet restrictions. Other restrictions include censoring content, and having to set up joint ventures with Chinese companies. Chinese companies assemble most smartphones.

IBM

U.S. companies such as Tesla, Apple and IBM will, through their foreign subsidiaries in China, meaningfully assist China in their global trade ambitions. It is a brilliant scheme to use unfair trade practices to promote Chinese trade, economic and political influence in the region from Europe to Asia and Africa, and use U.S. companies such as IBM does it.

Staying up with China in quantum computing, and trying to get to a 100-qubit quantum computer will likely be the next military frontier for the U.S. Countries such as China, Russia, the U.K., the European Union, and Australia are in a race to develop quantum computers, as are companies such as Intel, IBM, Microsoft and Alphabet (Google). The winners of the race will be able to obsolete existing cybersecurity technologies and systems.

Qualcomm

In 2013, Chinese government officials invaded the Beijing and Shanghai offices of Qualcomm. After a 15-month investigation, regulators saddled the company with a $975 million fine. In addition to the fine, Qualcomm:

- Was branded a monopoly;
- Was forced to reduce prices;
- Had to move more of its technical manufacturing to China;
- And, help boost the technological abilities of Chinese companies.

By 2018, a growing number of American companies "have complained that China has pressured them into sharing their technology in similar ways".

Qualcomm, which is a worldwide leader in semiconductors used in cellphones, wireless communications networks and semiconductor technology, was threatened by an unfriendly takeover by Broadcom, a Singapore-based company. The U.S. blocked the acquisition on national security grounds. There were several concerns. The acquisition of Qualcomm could have reduced U.S. superiority in semiconductors. It could also have reduced the U.S. lead in next generation 5G broadband networks. Qualcomm has a large business in China, and China has threatened to block Qualcomm has made an offer to acquire NXP Semiconductors, an important part of its growth strategy.

Qualcomm has developed 5G wireless networks that are used throughout the world. It was in a hostile takeover situation that could have resulted in a Singapore company, Broadcom, taking over the 5G networks being developed in the U.S. These networks will significantly improve the performance of artificial intelligence networks. The two risks were that:

- China could have been in control of the networks that are used to deliver artificial intelligence in the U.S., and are very important to military systems; and,
- China might have used Chinese companies, including Huawei, the second largest supplier of 5G networks worldwide, to infiltrate the U.S. broadband communications networks;
  - o Chinese companies have sworn allegiances to China, or they wouldn't be allowed to operate in China. This presumable applies to Broadcom.

The Treasury department blocked the Broadcom acquisition of Qualcomm.

Tesla

Tesla has substantial electric car intellectual property, including wireless car batteries, which it will protect by building an electric car manufacturing plant in Shanghai, thereby avoiding Chinese companies stealing their technology. It will pay a 20% import tax on vehicles sent to mainland China.

China does not allow foreign companies in China to set up manufacturing plants anywhere except in "free trade zones". One of those free trade zones is Shanghai, where Tesla will locate its plant. There are also ten more such free trade zones throughout China.

China uses unfair trade practices, such as requiring foreign manufacturers to have a Chinese partner, or pay a 25% import duty, if the car is manufactured outside of China. Tesla seems to be unwilling to give away its technology to a Chinese company partner, and perhaps give away 50% of the local Chinese market to them.

Batteries, which are a significant portion of the cost of an electric car, will undoubtedly be able to be imported to the Shanghai plant. This will protect Tesla's electric car battery technology. Tesla will also be able to benefit from the low cost of Chinese manufacturing, by being in Shanghai. This plant will be able to ship to Asian and European markets from this plant, and enjoy the low cost of Chinese manufacturing plants.

It will also benefit from the low cost of automobile parts manufactured in China for its export markets outside of China.

China-Intellectual Property Theft Issues

There are substantial intellectual property theft issues that the U.S. has leveled against China both in the U.S. and regarding U.S. companies operating in the Chinese market. The Committee on Foreign Investment in the U.S. (CFIUS) screens foreign investments in the U.S. to determine whether they are a threat to U.S. national security. The U.S. has passed legislation in the House and Senate that would revise the Committee on Foreign Investment in the U.S. (CFIUS) legislation. A compromise bill had not yet been agreed upon by the two chambers as of June 2018. President Trump had proposed broadening the legislation to go beyond national security interests to include such issues as China making small venture capital investments in the U.S. However he may have relented on tightening the scrutiny.

The focus of additional restrictions on China could involve scrutiny of more transactions, including possible limitations on state-owned companies. An export-import section could examine the treatment of U.S. companies doing business in the China market.

The issues of intellectual property theft from U.S. companies also extends to China. It has a plan, "Made in China 2025" that details 10 areas of technology that Chinese companies will try to dominate by 2025. From a military standpoint, the most important areas are information technology, aerospace, maritime, robots, and advanced materials. China has been downplaying its Made in China 2025 policies, but it is probable that these policies will continue to be pursued aggressively.

Two factors of importance in the China market are that there are only three Chinese companies that are allowed to directly access the web and foreign companies must go through them to use the Internet. The second important factor is that foreign companies must have Chinese partners with whom they must share their technologies to do business in China.

International trade with China has two aspects that are crucial to understand the situation. On one hand, China imposes tariffs on foreign companies that want to export into the China mainland market. The size of these tariffs is substantial, including 25% on vehicles exported from the U.S. There are also Chinese industries that are protected under an outdated WTO that still treats China as an emerging country and allows them protections for sectors that are vital to their national defense. The U.S. has imposed tariffs on steel and aluminum that are based upon these industries being vital to the U.S. national defense, and domestic manufacturing needs to be revitalized. This is in line with what China is still allowed to do under the antiquated WTO structure.

Made in China 2025

1. Information Technology:
   a. Semiconductor chips;
   b. Computers;
   c. Cloud computing systems;
   d. Industrial censors;
   e. Artificial intelligence; and
   f. Quantum computers.
2. Robots
3. Aerospace:
   a. Airplanes;
   b. Jet engines; and
   c. Civilian space industry.
4. Maritime:
   a. Ships; and
   b. Out-at-sea engineering equipment and systems.
5. Railways
6. Smart Vehicles:
   a. Electric; and
   b. Hybrids.
7. Renewables:
   a. Geothermal
   b. Hydro;
   c. Solar; and
   d. Wind.

8. Farming:
   a. Equipment
   b. Genetically modified organisms; and
   c. Tractors.
9. Materials:
   a. Advanced basic materials; and
   b. Strategic materials
      i. Rare earths
      ii. Alloys.
10. Drugs and Devices:
   a. Biotechnology;
   b. Drug development; and
   c. Hospital equipment.

China Has Underway A One Belt, One Road (OBOR) Initiative To Invest In 70 Countries To Improve Its Financial, Trade And Military Relationships: This Is A Major Challenge For The U.S.

China Trade-One Belt, One Road Initiative

This paragraph is a final portion of the Conclusions Chapter of the China vs. U.S. A Police State vs. a democracy book. China has underway a massive project, One Belt, One Road, to build a land and sea network connecting Europe, Asia, the Middle East and Africa. China is planning to spend as much as $4-$8 trillion on a trade route infrastructure project in about 70 countries in Africa, Asia, the Middle East and Europe. This will include spending on ports, roads, railways, airports, power plants, telecommunications, and other infrastructure, including gas and oil pipelines. The network has been designed by and implemented by China. The countries on the network will individually be nodes on the network. There six economic corridors on the network. China says that the infrastructure is for the purpose of enabling economic growth in some of China's surrounding countries.

The trade deficit with China appears likely to remain above $360 billion per year, despite President Trump's efforts to reduce it. Over 10 years such a trade deficit could be viewed as providing financing for 90% of a $4 billion OBOR intitiative by China.

The corridors are the:

- China-Indochina Peninsula Economic Corridor (CICPEC);
- China-Mongolia-Russia Economic Corridor (CMREC);
- China Pakistan-Economic Corridor (CPEC);
- Bangladesh-China-India-Myanmar Economic Corridor (BCIMEC)
- China-Central and West Asia Economic Corridor (CCWAEC); and
- New Eurasian Land Bridge (NELB).

China-Indochina Peninsula Economic Corridor (CICPEC)

The Indochina Peninsula Economic Corridor starts in Kunming, China and has two corridors that run south from China through Vietnam, Laos, Thailand and Cambodia. There is also a western corridor that runs west in China from Kunming, to Myanmar and then south to link up with an East-West Corridor that goes through Thailand and Laos. In the south, there is also a second east-west corridor that links up with the north-south corridors.

The coastal states in Southeast Asia such as Vietnam, Cambodia, the Philippines, Thailand, Malaysia, Myanmar, Brunei, Singapore and Indonesia and the only landlocked country Laos would take part in the OBOR to build highways, railways and sea ports to realize the China-Indochina Peninsula Economic Corridor and the 21st Century Maritime Silk Road. However, Myanmar, Thailand, Cambodia, Malaysia and Vietnam would provide nodes connecting the Belt and Road. The Belt stands for the continental sections of the Silk Road while the Road is the maritime domain of the Silk Road.

China-Mongolia-Russia Economic Corridor (CMREC)

The Russia-Mongolia-China Road Corridor runs from Tianjin in China north through Mongolia to Ulan Ude in Russia. The corridor is supposed to open in 2018. This is the development of a central railway corridor, organizing transit trucking activities on the Tianjin-Ulaan Baatar-Ulan-Ude route and paving a road along this route. "Chinese Foreign Minister Wang Yi, said construction of a transport corridor linking the three countries

helps support economic development, and encourages Mongolia's participation in international affairs."

China Pakistan-Economic Corridor (CPEC)

The China-Pakistan economic corridor is being established to develop
modern infrastructure projects that include roads, railroads and power
plants. A 250-mile Multan-Sukkur section of the Peshawar-Karachi
Motorway began construction in 2016 for completion in August 2019.

Gwadar Port in Pakistan is financed and operated by China Overseas
Port Holding Co., It started operations in November 2016. Located at
the mouth of the Persian Gulf, it is close to the Straits of Hormuz, and
the Gwadar Port provides China with an important shipping route to
the Middle East. In April 2017, China provided a loan of $1.2 billion to
Pakistan to help it with a currency crisis. The Port city population is
mostly Chinese and represents an example of how China can expand its
operations beyond China using the OBOR initiative. This is particularly
important in port cities that expand China's maritime military footprint.

Bangladesh-China-India-Myanmar Economic Corridor (BCIMEC)

China is setting up economic corridors in alliance with other countries, with one covering Bangladesh, India and Myanmar (i.e. the BCIM
Economic Corridor). The Corridor will link India's Kolkata with China's
Kunming, with Myanmar's Mandalay and Bangladesh's Dhaka among
the key points." The Port of Dhaka is a major river port on the Buriganga
River. The Chinese government has pledged to finance multi-billion infrastructure projects in Bangladesh.

China-Central and West Asia Economic Corridor (CCWAEC)

This is one of the main axes of the new Silk Road; it connects the Chinese
province of Xinjiang to the Mediterranean Sea, through Kazakhstan,
Kyrgyzstan, Tajikistan, Uzbekistan, Turkmenistan, Iran and Turkey. It
follows the ancient Silk Route. This initiative will be completed by bilateral cooperation agreements between China and Central Asia states.
This corridor aims to better connect all the regional economies to China

but also to Europe and thus offers a new intercontinental communication network that will open up Central Asian states. This corridor requires the construction of numerous transportation and energy infrastructures from the Middle East to China. It is supplemented by various measures aiming at increasing trade among all states involved in the OBOR.

New Eurasian Land Bridge (NELB)

The New Eurasian Land Bridge runs from northern China through Russia to Europe.

To stimulate investment with an aim to diversify its economy, the Russian government is providing a wide array of incentives for investors developing new product, technology in the energy efficiency, nuclear engineering, space technology, medicine and IT industries. Other key sectors for development include pharmaceutical and medical, real estate, innovations and technology, infrastructure, aluminum, iron and steel, lead, platinum-group metals, precious metals, nickel, copper, zinc, coal, telecommunications, transportation, agriculture and food and gas."

The Ukraine crisis made Russia embrace the OBOR Initiative by:

• Beginning confrontation with the West and Russia's deteriorating economy due to U.S.-led sanctions and falling oil prices left Moscow little choice;
• Without Ukraine, the second-largest post-Soviet economy and a market of about 44 million people, Moscow's hopes to create an integrated bloc that would be on par with the European Union and other centers of global economic power were essentially dashed;
• Lacking a market of sufficient size to create its own viable geo-economic area, Russia was left with the only option of moving into another nation's economic orbit;
• Russia joined the China-controlled Asian Infrastructure Investment Bank in March 2015; but
• The most decisive step came a few months later in May 2015, when Xi and Russian President Vladimir Putin met in Moscow

and pledged to work toward a "link-up" between Russia's Eurasian Economic Union (EEU) and China's OBOR Initiative.

China's OBOR Involvement

China is providing financing in the form of high interest loans. China is being accused by many of using the loans to put many small countries in default, and to thereby take over the projects that they have financed.

With many of the projects being port development, these joint ventures with the countries could allow China to expand their naval presence throughout Asia, Africa and the Middle East.

The U.S. Is Ahead Of China In Developing Space Technology, But Is Being Challenged In Other Defense Areas

Worldwide threats to the U.S. are increasing from China, Russia, ISIS, Iran and North Korea. President Trump has achieved defense spending increases for fiscal 2018 that will only begin to restore the U.S. defenses to the level they were at in 2009. It will take a decade or more of defense spending increases to restore U.S. military capabilities.

China's Defense Budget

*China's defense budget is expected to reach $173 billion in 2018, compared to $716 billion expected for the U.S. in 2019. 2018's defense budget comes to about 1.3% of China's 2017 GDP of $12.4 trillion. Analysts don't consider China's publicly announced defense spending to be entirely accurate, since defense equipment projects account for a significant amount of "off book" expenditures.

China is nearing completion of a reduction of its military forces by 300,000, taking the total to 2 million and still has the largest military in the world.

Shanghai military expert Ni Lexiong said China was seeking to avoid a full-on arms race based on quantity of weapons, choosing instead to invest in high-tech systems and training. China's range of weapons is impressive. They include:

- A second aircraft carrier they are about to launch;
- Stealth fighters they are integrating into their air force;
- An array of advanced missiles that are long-range and able to attack sea and air targets;
- In April 2017, it launched a 50,000-ton carrier built entirely on its own.
- A nuclear-powered attack submarine equipped is considered only slightly inferior to the U.S. Navy's mainstay Los Angeles class boats;
- Their guided-missile destroyers are at the forefront of China's naval technology;
    o Such vessels stand to alter the balance of power in the Indo-Pacific, where the U.S. Navy has long been dominant, and regional rivals such as Japan and India are stepping up their presence.
    o Most navy ships already have anti-ship cruise missiles, with longer ranges than those of their U.S. counterparts.
- China has begun equipping combat units with a stealth fighter jet that is competitive with fifth-generation jets such as the U.S. F-22 and F-35; and
- China's missile technology is also impressive.

All three of China's sea forces, the navy, coast guard and maritime militia, are the largest of their types by number of ships, allowing them to "maintain presence and influence in vital seas," according to Andrew S. Erickson of the U.S. Naval War College's China Maritime Studies Institute.

China has a wide range of both defensive and offensive weapons systems. Their navy is predicated on having a large number of smaller ships. The U.S. is moving its navy in that direction. The U.S. has a huge superiority in aircraft carriers, which serves the U.S. well in operating in Asia, and somewhat offsets China's land-based aircraft presence.

The U.S. is also far superior in its space-based weapons systems being developed by NASA, and a range of commercial competitors, such as Space-X. U.S. space technology allows the Space Station to be accessed, and Space-X has plans for a Mars mission that it hopes will be developed by 2024.

Space-based weapons systems will become an important element of future U.S. defense capabilities.

The 2018 U.S. Defense Budget

The U.S. faces a range of defense challenges, including China, ISIS, Iran, Russia, and North Korea. President Trump has indicated that defense spending will increase, with nuclear weapons, fighter aircraft, and the U.S. Navy having been mentioned.

A good way to look at defense spending is as a percentage of Gross Domestic Product (GDP). was forecasted to be 4.4% of GDP in fiscal 2017.

U.S. Defense-Nuclear Weapons-China, Russia and the U.S.

Two initiatives being pursued by the Trump administration are:

- To upgrade U.S. missile systems, including the Minuteman system, and nuclear systems such as our nuclear submarines;
- And, upgrade U.S. missile defense systems. In early March 2018, Russia announced a new missile capability that they claim makes their nuclear missiles undetectable by U.S. missile defense systems.

This appears to have been posturing by Russia prior to the reelection of Putin.

Two Nuclear Issues Are Upgrading U.S Current Nuclear Missile And Missile Defense Systems

Two initiatives being pursued by the Trump administration are:

- To upgrade our missile systems, including the Minuteman system, and nuclear systems such as our nuclear submarines; and,

- Upgrade U.S. missile defense systems;
  - o   In early 2018, President Putin of Russia made the statement that Russia has nuclear missiles that can evade U.S. missile defense systems;

Systems such as the Aegis Missile Defense at sea, and the Terminal High Altitude Area Defense (THAAD) on land, are the two systems the may be able to destroy missiles that don't go into space.

North Korea's testing of intercontinental ballistic missiles comes as the U.S. still has reliability issues with its homeland missile defense system. There is no guarantee it will destroy any incoming nuclear warhead from North Korea. The ground-based interceptors in Alaska and California, have been tested, but, U.S. government agencies have critiqued the test as not being realistic, said John Park, director of the Korea Working Group at the Harvard Kennedy School.

At the same time, Russia and China are upgrading their nuclear capabilities. Pakistan, India and Israel continue to build new nuclear weapons and delivery systems. Air Force officials worry increasingly about the Minuteman's ability to penetrate adversaries' future missile defense systems.

The Pentagon has begun work to replace the Minuteman fleet with a new generation of missiles and launch control centers, with a test flight program scheduled for launch in the mid-2020s.

The ICBM missile defense system of the U.S. appears to be unreliable, despite a successful missile intercept in 2017. The Minuteman missile system needs to be upgraded to allow it to be successful in evading missile defense systems of others. Similar upgrades are needed for ship missile launch systems. The threat from North Korea is real, and the U.S. needs substantial improvements in its offensive and defensive missile systems.

Improvements to the U.S. missile programs, including submarine, aircraft, and the ground-based Minuteman 3 missile system are long overdue, particularly in view of the increasing threat from Russia and North Korea. The first phase, the initial design, is underway and Boeing and Northrop have been selected to compete for this phase.

The first phase of a U.S. land-based missile program replacement for the Minuteman 3, deployed in silos in the Great Plains, is underway. The first phase is a $700 million design phase, and Boeing and Northrop have been selected to compete for this business.

The replacement comes at a time when China and Russia are modernizing their nuclear forces, and there is growing risk from North Korea, which has demonstrated an ICBM that might be able to reach the U.S., and in 2017 detonated successfully a hydrogen bomb that they will attempt to put on the ICBM missile tip. As of July 2018, there is no guarantee that U.S. talks with North Korea on the denuclearization of the Korean Peninsula will be successful.

After languishing for years due to budget cuts under the Obama administration, the GBSD program has finally been instituted as one leg of the triad of nuclear missiles, which include submarine launched missiles, and aircraft launched nuclear missiles.

This program will compete for defense dollars with contracts for new naval vessels, such as aircraft carriers, and jet fighters.

U.S. Defense-Air Force

Trump Is Trying To Restore Air Force Readiness: Will He Be Successful?

The Air Force is at its smallest level ever, and less than half of its planes are combat ready. While Trump is attempting to restore our military capabilities, it will take some time to restore the Air Force's readiness.

According to Maj. Gen. Jim Martin, the Air Force budget director, the budget addresses critical shortfalls while building a larger, more capable and more lethal Air Force.

Addressing readiness deficiencies, the budget funds, among other elements:

- Flying hours to executable levels and weapons system sustainment to near capacity;

- Two additional F-16 training squadrons and ensures advance weapons schools and combat exercises are fully funded to restore full-spectrum readiness long-term;
- The Intercontinental Ballistic Missile Program;
- The space procurement strategy;
- The nuclear enterprise;
- Munitions to support ongoing operations; and
- Replenishing current inventories.

Delaying modernization has become a trend in recent years, allowing potential adversaries to narrow the capability gap. This budget addresses modernization by:

- Advancing recapitalization of the current fighter and tanker fleets by procuring 46 F-35A Lightning and 15 KC-46 Pegasus aircraft;
- Continuing modernization efforts for the 4th and 5th generation aircraft;
- Continuing efforts from fiscal 2017 to maximize munitions production capacity to sustain global precision attack capabilities.

The research, development, test and evaluation investments saw notable growth in 2017, and are designed to pay significant future dividends through game-changing technologies that, when fielded, will increase lethality and provide the joint force a technological advantage.

The F-35 is the core next generation aircraft program, and will replace several existing Air Force planes. The Air Force is putting much of its aircraft eggs in this basket.

U.S. Defense-Navy

It is planned to increase the Naval fleet from 275 to 350 ships, but this will take additional resources. The 2018 budget adds 8 additional ships. The Navy would like to add one additional carrier to the current eleven. It is likely that the Navy will become more mobile in response to the current threats, particularly from Russia and China, which are also increasing their Navies.

In 2017, President Trump promised to expand the current Naval fleet from 275 to 350, which is near the 355 that the Navy Department was recommending. The U.S. is on the way to 308 ships, but building up to 350, or more, will likely require significant additional shipbuilding resources. However, the numbers can be reached in different ways. The current U.S. program is built around carriers. Another possibility is to add ships that create a more mobile Navy, which may be better suited to the current threats we face, particularly from Russia and China.

Trump's 2018 budget includes 8 additional ships, which are likely to be small surface ships. The U.S. has 11 aircraft carriers, and, although it will take at least a decade, the Navy would like to add one more to the fleet. To reach a 350 ship level will take decades, which will be complicated by ship retirements. The U.S. has a substantial competitive advantage, particularly when confronting China, in submarines.

Senator John McCain said the Navy should focus investment on undersea warfare, where the U.S. has an advantage, and should procure two to three manned submarines per year in 2020, and four per year starting in 2021, to give industry time to ramp up to meet the government's need.

The Navy is likely to be rebuilt in ways that will allow the U.S. to effectively confront Iran in the Persian Gulf, China in the South China Seas and the Indian Ocean, and Russia worldwide, while substantially expanding the U.S. submarine fleet.

U.S. Defense-Space

SpaceX and other space companies are competing against NASA. These satellite launch systems are smaller than some being developed by NASA. Lockheed Martin and Boeing are the primary contractors on NASA's SLS/Orion satellites. They include a very powerful Space Launch System rocket, which is being developed by Boeing for NASA.

SpaceX is successfully competing against NASA using reusable rockets. It has launched a spacecraft to the Space Station. SpaceX has executed successful launches of its reusable Falcon 9 space launch system. Falcon 9 engines are reused by landing them on an ocean platform. Its spacecraft are also recovered after reentry. SpaceX has announced a new launch system, BFM that is planned to send a payload to Mars by 2024. This is a much larger launch system than the Falcon 9.

SpaceX is projecting that by successfully recovering launch engines and space capsules, it will significantly reduce the costs of its space launches. Their plan is for as many as 52 launches in 2019, following the 18 launches in 2017. It is unclear whether launch costs are coming down as much as expected.

India and China Space Programs

India and China are also planning their own space launches for others. They are both expected to be competitors of SpaceX. China has strenuously objected to India's space activities.

China Space Program

China offered to build telecommunications satellites for Afghanistan, Sri Lanka and Nepal, where India is offering free use of their satellites. China is developing a trading network called One Belt, One Road. It is an ambitious project that includes a traditional land-base trading route from China to Europe. It also includes satellite expenditures that are expected to be about four times those of India.

U.S. Space Program

The U.S. space program is about $40 billion per year, and appears to be about six times that of China. In addition to SpaceX, other competitors in this arena are Richard Branson's One-Web Ltd., China-based startups One-Space and ExPace. Astrome Technologies, an Indian start-up company plans to launch 150 satellites to provide wireless communications to difficult-to-reach locations. In 2017, Team Indus, a Bangalore-based Indian company, planned to launch a moon-lander in a Google Lunar XPrize competition.

SpaceX, and NASA budget cuts, appear to be putting pressure on NASA to reduce the costs of the SLS/Orion. Lockheed and Boeing are already talking about 50% cost cuts in the future.

Renewed space competition is underway, and Elon Musk's SpaceX appears to be a leader in the race. However, some large competitors could emerge, many of them driven by Indian space launch capabilities. Space is an important frontier that is drawing many participants. It is also important to the U.S. from a defense standpoint, particularly with North Korea developing nuclear weapons, and ICBMs capable of delivering them to the U.S., or putting them into orbit.

SpaceX-Mars Flight By 2024

SpaceX has continued its success with its Falcon 9 space launch system, launched 18 launch vehicles in 2017. It has a strong customer base, including one with NASA to deliver supplies to the Space Station.

Elon Musk unveiled plans for a giant new Big Fucking Rocket (BFR) that could be used to launch a Mars vehicle by as early as 2022, or 2024. This could be as much as 10 years earlier than planned by any other company or country. It will be the biggest rocket ever built, with a capsule larger than a superjumbo airliner. SpaceX's current customers are commercial customers and the Pentagon.

Hypersonic Missiles

President Trump said he planned to discuss with Russian President Vladimir Putin ways to substantially reduce the number of nuclear weapons the U.S. and Russia have stockpiled. But both nations are racing to develop an entirely new kind of weapon.

When Putin showed off what he said was a hypersonic cruise missile, he gave the world a brief glimpse into a secret arms race. It pits the U.S. against Russia and China in a contest to build weapons that can fly 10,000 miles per hour.

"It's quite an advantage if anybody could ever do that," said John Wilcox, vice president at Northrop Grumman.

The company built the first hypersonic aircraft back in 2004. It only flew for about 10 seconds. But Northrop Grumman is now conducting tests as part of the Pentagon's Top Secret efforts to develop hypersonic weapons that can fly longer and farther.

Wilcox took CBS News into a test chamber on condition we would not reveal its location. It is a giant air gun that fires bursts of gas at incredible speeds and pressure to simulate the conditions of hypersonic flight.

"The gases come down the air gun and hit right back here at the plate," Wilcox explained.

The gases burst through the steel plate. That, plus temperatures of 2,000 degrees are what a hypersonic aircraft would have to survive.

"If we have a test article that we're trying to emulate in the conditions of the hypersonic flight, it'll be in here," Wilcox said.

Wilcox estimates a working hypersonic weapon is still five to 10 years away.

The Pentagon has declared hypersonics its number one technical priority, but the official in charge of the program recently acknowledged that the U.S. is playing catch up to Russia and China.

BIBLIOGRAPHY

Prologue

House memo states disputed dossier was key to FBI's FISA warrant to surveil members of Team Trump
Fox News, By Alex Pappas, Catherine Herridge, and Brooke Singman, February 2, 2018

Fusion co-founder: Dossier author feared Trump was being blackmailed, CNN Politics, By Jeremy Herb, Manu Raju and Marshall Cohen, CNN, Updated January 10, 2018

Embattled FBI admits it can't verify dossier claims of Russia, Trump campaign collusion, The Washington Times, By Rowan Scarborough, December 25, 2017

Bill Clinton, AG Loretta Lynch meet on tarmac in Phoenix, CBS News, By Emily Schultheis, June 29, 2016

FBI investigating Clinton Foundation for pay-to-play: reports, New York Daily News, By Christopher Brennan and Denis Slattery, Updated, January 5, 2018

FBI On Hot Seat Over 'Insurance Policy' Against Trump Election
Senator: 'Some officials took actions beyond expressing their political opinions'
WND, By Chelsea Schilling, 12/14/2017

Introduction-Obama Legacy Issues, Recent U.S. International Issues, Trump State of the Union Address-2018-Achievements-2017, Plans-2018, ABC Response to State of the Union Address, Trump Has Addressed Significant U.S. Weaknesses, Worldwide Threats, China vs. U.S.-2018 Book Overview

Worldwide Threats Hearing, Senate Intelligence Committee, Dan Coates-Director of National Intelligence, February 14, 2018

Chapter 1-China vs. U.S-Economy, Regulation, Territorial Ambitions-Trade, Xi Reorganization, One Belt, Growth, Jobs, U.S. Immigration, Chinese International, China vs. U.S.-Trade, Trans Pacific Partnership, Nafta, Visas, WTO, U.S. Investment, Currency, U.S. Trade Deficit and Jobs

Beijing Sees Growth of 6.5% This Year, Wall Street Journal, by Lingling Wei and Chun Hong Wong, March 5, 2018

China Moves to Forestall Growth Slowdown, Wall Street Journal, by Lingling Wei, April 18, 2018

Trusted Xi Ally Set to Guide China Economy, Wall Street Journal, by Lingling Wei, February 27, 2018

Yuan Weakness Revives Manipulation Debate, Wall Street Journal, by Saumya Vaishhampayan, May 5, 2018

China Speeds Push for Electric Vehicles, Wall Street Journal, by Yoko Kubota and Trefor Moss, Sept. 28, 2017

China's Taxes on Imported Cars Feed Trade Tensions With U.S., New York Times, By Keith Bradsher, March 20, 2017

Trump's Pacific Trade Tear, Wall Street Journal Editorial, November 11, 2017

Re-Entry to Trade Deal Won't Be Cheap, Wall Street Journal, by Bob Davis, April 16, 2018

Tackling China's Protectionism, Wall Street Journal Editorial, March 20, 2018

Yuan Weakness Revives Manipulation Debate, Wall Street Journal, by Saumya Vaishhampayan, May 5, 2018

China Draws Gas Out of Global Market, Wall Street Journal, By Sarah McFarlane and Nathaniel Taplin, January 24, 2018

https://www.ceicdata.com/en/indicator/china/labour-productivity-growth

Chapter 2-China's One Belt, One Road Trade Initiative

China's Connectivity Strategy in Southeast Asia, Science, Technology and Security Forum, Dr. Puyam Rakesh Singh, August 18, 2017

One Belt, One Road, Wikipedia, May 18, 2018

Why Greece is banking on China's modern-day Silk Road to help its economic recovery, South China Morning Post, By Catherine Wong, December 26, 2017

Three Examples of China Using Its One Belt, One Road Network Initiative To Project An Increase In Military Power Are In Sri Lanka, Pakistan And Djibouti

China's Belt and Road Initiative is Being Blamed for Sri Lanka's Hambantota Port Problems. But the Real Story is Rather Different, Silk Road Briefing, April 23, 2018

China's vast foreign investment program comes at a sharp cost to human rights and good governance, Foreign Policy, By Richard Fontaine and Daniel Kliman, May 16, 2018

Beijing is using commercial bridgeheads to give its warships staying power in the Indian Ocean, Foreign Affairs, By Keith Johnson and Dan De Luce, April 17, 2018

The Belt and Road Initiative: Country Profiles, Hong Kong Trade Development Council, May 17, 2018

Beijing is using commercial bridgeheads to give its warships staying power in the Indian Ocean. Foreign Affairs, By Keith Johnson and Dan De Luce, April 17, 2018

Belt and Road has promise for Ethiopia, Africa: envoy
By Hong Xiao and Wang Linyan, China Daily USA, May 11, 2017

China welcomes Madagascar to join Belt and Road construction
Source: Xinhua March 27, 2017-03-27, Editor: huaxia

China, Morocco sign MOU on Belt and Road
Source: Xinhua|, November 17, 2017, Editor: Mengjie

South Africa's dilemma in the Belt and Road Initiative: Losing Africa for China?, Friedrich-Ebert-Stiftung, by Tamara Naidoo, February 26, 2018

Tunisia hopes boost in Chinese investment can ease economic woes, Al-Monitor, Sarah Souli, March 19, 2018

The Belt and Road Initiative: Country Profiles, Hong Kong Trade Development Council, May 17, 2018

China's Connectivity Strategy in Southeast Asia, Science, Technology and Security Forum, Dr. Puyam Rakesh Singh, August 18, 2017

The Belt and Road Initiative: Country Profiles, Hong Kong Trade Development Council, May 17, 2018

China's One Belt One Road Initiative, WHAT IS BELT AND ROAD INITIATIVE?, Medium, By Markus Patrick Chan, September 9, 2017

Thailand To Integrate The EEC With China's One Belt One Road Initiative, Thailand Business News, By Olivier Languepin, March 2, 2018

China's Connectivity Strategy in Southeast Asia, Science, Technology and Security Forum, Dr. Puyam Rakesh Singh, August 18, 2017

Money talks: China's belt and road initiative in Cambodia, Global Risk Insights, by Qi Lin, January 7, 2018

Russia-Mongolia-China Road Corridor to be Ready in 2018 Silk Road Briefing, September 8, 2017

Mongolia, a new link in the Belt and Road initiative, OBOReurope, April 10, 2017

Russia-Mongolia-China Road Corridor to be Ready in 2018 Silk Road Briefing, September 8, 2017

Pakistan learns the downside of taking infrastructure money from China, China giveth, and China taketh away. CNBC Asia-Pacific, Nyshka Chandran, December 12, 2017

The BCIM economic corridor: Prospects and challenges, Observer Research Foundation, K. YHOME, February 10, 2017

Xi Jinping's infrastructure initiative will help power-starved South Asian nation fire up more manufacturing capacity, South China Morning Post, April 10, 2017, Sidney Leng

One Belt-One Road Initiative and MYANMAR" Connectivity: Synergy Issue and Potentialities, Global New Light of Myanmar, Than Zaw, March 11, 2018

The Belt and Road Initiative: Country Profiles, Hong Kong Trade Development Council, May 17, 2018

China's Belt and Road Initiative Is Stoking Tensions with India, The National Interest, Mitchell J. Hays, November 16, 2017

The Belt and Road Initiative: Country Profiles, Hong Kong Trade Development Council, May 17, 2018

Relations between China and Azerbaijan are growing fast and Azerbaijan has great potential to become a valuable partner in the

Silk Road project, Malik Ayub Sumbal is the Editor in Chief of Eurasia Media Network and The Caspian Times., China Daily European Weekly, January 20, 2017

As Western banks leave, China adds Brunei to new silk road, Reuters, By Praveen Menon, March 4, 2018

Practitioners' perspectives, Kazakhstan and the Belt and Road, GRATA Law Firm, Shaimerden Chikanayev, April 27, 2017

Majlis Podcast: What Does China's One Belt, One Road Project Mean For Central Asia?, OBORwatch, December 6, 2016

What's Next for the Belt and Road in Central Asia?, Three regional presidents attended the Belt and Road Forum in Beijing last weekend. By Catherine Putz, May 17, 2017

Tajikistan – transport leader reveals how TIR in China will open up vast opportunities" for the region, IRU, September 5, 2017

Belt and Road a 'great opportunity': Uzbek official
China Daily, By Ren Qi, December 12, 2017

Turkmenistan dreaming: Gurbanguly Berdimuhamedow's big bet on Belt and Road, Financial Review, by Andrew Clark, April 27, 2018

China stands to gain in Iran after US quits nuclear deal, AFP, Julien Girault, May 17, 2018

Why is Turkey so eager to be led down the Belt and Road?, East Asia Forum, Nicol Brodie, October 28, 2017

China wants closer ties with Indonesia, says Premier Li Keqiang, The Straits Times, Feb 9, 2018. Goh Sui Noi

China's Belt and Road: What's in it for Malaysia? The Borneo Post, September 3, 2017, Sunday Rachel Lau

Nepal joins China's 'One Belt, One Road' initiative, possibly alarming India, South China Morning Post, October 10, 2017

What does China's Belt and Road mean for NZ?, Newsroom, Sam Sachdeva, July 21, 2017

Nomura: Philippines a winner, but also most at risk, under China's 'Belt and Road' By Ian Nicolas Cigaral (philstar.com) - April 17, 2018

Belt and Road Initiative a focal point for Singapore's ties with China, The Straits Times, By Danson Cheong, April 8, 2018

One Belt, One Road, One Korea?,The Diplomat, By Maximilian Römer, February 10, 2018

One Belt One Road – A Unique Opportunity For Sri Lanka, by Dr Palitha Kohona, February 10, 2018

The Belt and Road Initiative: Country Profiles, Hong Kong Trade Development Council, May 17, 2018

China, Albania agree to expand cooperation under Belt and Road, 16+1 framework, Xinhua|, Yameni, April 18, 2017

Chinese defense minister meets with Bosnia and Herzegovina counterpart, China Military, EditorYao Jianing, May 17, 2017

Bulgaria can Open the "New Silk Road" to Central and Western Europe, Novinite.com, April 29, 2018

China, Croatia could enhance ties under Belt and Road Initiative: ambassador, Xinhua|, Yang Yi, September 15, 2017

Why Greece is banking on China's modern-day Silk Road to help its economic recovery, South China Morning Post, By Catherine Wong, December 26, 2017

One Belt, One Road" initiative brings more than infrastructure to Central and Eastern Europe, Xinhua|, Editor, Mu Xuequan, October 8, 2017

Beijing's Balkan backdoor, Politico, By Matthew Karnitschnig, July 13, 2017

The Impact of China's One Belt, One Road on Romania, Geopolitical Monitor, By Marcela Ganea, December 19, 2016

As China Moves In, Serbia Reaps Benefits, With Strings Attached, New York Times, By Barbara Surk, Sept. 9, 2017

PM at summit of Central and Eastern European countries and China, Government of the Republic of Slovenia, November 29, 2017

The Belt and Road Initiative: Country Profiles, Hong Kong Trade Development Council, May 17, 2018

Belt and Road Initiative spells opportunities for Austria-China cooperation, Xinhua, April 7, 2018

Belarus and One Belt, One Road, alternative oil, SCTO, Belarus state press digest, May 20, 2017

China's gift to Europe is a new version of crony capitalism, The Guardian, Martin Hala, April 20, 2018

China Eyes Estonia as Smartest and Nearest Port for EU Access, Silk Road Briefing, July 20, 2017

China's Relationship With Hungary Is Being Tested As The EU And Russia Apply Pressure, David Hutt, September 5, 2017

Riga Port has the potential to become a significant transit hub for the New Silk Road, Embassy of the Republic of Latvia, June 4, 2018

Lithuania's investments within the framework of 'One Belt One Route' projects, Coordinating Secretariat for Maritime Issues, "16 + 1", October 26, 2017

Maldives Crisis Could Stir Trouble Between China and India, New York Times, By Mujib Mashal, February. 14, 2018

Can a China-Moldova free-trade deal give Beijing a foothold in Eastern Europe?, South China Morning Post, Liu Zhen, December 29, 2017

China, Poland, and the Belt and Road Initiative - the Future of Chinese Engagement in Central and Eastern Europe, Geopolitica, Alicja Bachulska, December 12, 2017

Putin's Silk Road gamble, The Washington Post, By Artyom Lukin. February 8, 2018

Do the Central European media show caution towards China?, Matej Šimalčík, East Asia Forum, Institute of Asian Studies, February 14, 2018

As Trump Is Distracted, The Chinese Are Moving In On Ukraine. Newsweek, By Nolan Peterson, December 12, 2017

China's Belt and Road Meets Trump's Afghanistan Plan

Could China play the good cop while the U.S. plays the bad cop? The Diplomat, By Yu Fu, December 21, 2017

Making sense of Belt and Road – The Belt and Road country: Armenia EUROMONEY, By: Chris Wright, September 26, 2017

China's 'One Belt, One Road' is a 'win-win' for GCC – Bahrain Minister, GulfInsider, May 13, 2018

Greening the belt and road: opportunities for Egypt, Middle East Institute, By Deborah Lehr and Yasser Elnaggar January 23, 2018

With Port Project, Georgia Seeks Place on China's Belt and Road. Georgian infrastructure remains underdeveloped, which could leave Anaklia disconnected, Eurasianet, Bradley Jardine, February 21, 2018

China and Israel to enhance trade cooperation through the "One Belt, One Road" Initiative, ChinaGoAbroad, May 25, 2018

China's One Belt, One Road initiative to benefit Jordan — ambassador, The Jordan Times, By Mohammad Ghazal, November13, 2017

Kuwait's Silk City project expected to top $100B, Daily Sabah, March 8, 2017

Kuwait's Silk City is key project in China's One Belt One Road initiative, AME info, March 22, 2018

Lebanon's Tripoli keen for active role in Belt and Road initiative, Xinhua, November 11, 2017

The Belt and Road Initiative: Country Profiles, Hong Kong Trade Development Council, May 17, 2018

Oman To Become A Key Part Of China's Silk Road, Oilprice.com, By Zainab Calcuttawala, September 7, 2017

China Has a New Middle East Peace Plan, What's new in Beijing's latest proposal and what does it tell us about China's views and intentions concerning the region?, The Diplomat, By Yoram Evron, August 14, 2017

How Qatar Row Could Impact China's One Belt, One Road Project Sputnik International, Aleksey Nikolskyi, August 6, 2017

Belt, Road initiative will help Saudi Arabia realize 2030 vision, ambassador says, ChinaGoAbroad, Xinhua, May 25, 2018

China and UAE move a step closer to opening a 'Belt and Road Exchange', CNBC, Sam Meredith, April 24, 2018

China and Yemen's Forgotten War, US Institute of Peace, By I-wei Jennifer Chang, January 16, 2018

Chapter 3-Trump Budget, Economic Assumptions, Budget Strategy, Tax Reductions, Immigration, Entitlement Programs, Household Debt, Debt: U.S. National Debt And Fed Portfolio Balances, Deficit, and Government Funding and the Debt Ceiling

Economy, Markets Rev Up, Wall Street Journal, by Josh Mitchell and Nick Timiraos, November 30, 2017

New Record for Household Incomes, Wall Street Journal, By Ben Leubsdorf, September 12, 2017

Weakened Nafta, WTO Pave Way for Conflict, Wall Street Journal, by Greg Ip, October 18, 2017

A Nafta Collapse Would Carry Risks, Wall Street Journal, By Jacob M. Schlesinger, October 15, 2017

Trump's Pacific Trade Tear, Wall Street Journal Editorial, November 11, 2017

China Speeds Push for Electric Vehicles, Wall Street Journal, by Yoko Kubota and Trefor Moss, Sept. 28, 2017

China's Taxes on Imported Cars Feed Trade Tensions With U.S., New York Times, By Keith Bradsher, March 20, 2017

New Record for Household Incomes, Wall Street Journal, By Ben Leubsdorf, September 12, 2017

Understanding U.S. Productivity Trends From the Bottom-up, Wall Street Journal, by Joseph Parilla and Mark Muro, Wednesday, March 15, 2017

5 Facts About The National Debt, Pew Research Center, By Drew Desilver, August 17, 2017

Trump, Schumer agree to pursue plan to repeal the debt ceiling. Washington Post, By Damian Paletta and Ashley Parker September 7, 2017

Alibaba Looks to go Home, Wall Street Journal, by Julie Steinberg and Liza Lin, March 17, 2018

Beijing Could Recruit Help to Clean Up Anbag's Mess, Wall Street Journal, by Jacky Wong, February 21, 2018

China's Tech Giants Take to the Road, Wall Street Journal, by Trefor Moss and Liza Lin, March 19, 2018

Huawei's Breadth Raises Concern, Wall Street Journal, by David George-Cosh, February 24, 2018

Caution Over Huawei Grows, Wall Street Journal, By Dan Strumph and Paul Vieira, March 21, 2018

Hot Xiaomi Carries Big Risks, Wall Street Journal, by Li Yuan, March 17, 2018

Beijing Dials Up Pressure on Xiaomi, Wall Street Journal, Stella Yifan Xie, March 2, 2018

Chapter 4- Chinese Local Investment Objectives, Economy, Capital Investment, Consumer Investment, Chinese Companies, Financial Markets

Alibaba Looks to go Home, Wall Street Journal, by Julie Steinberg and Liza Lin, March 17, 2018

Beijing Could Recruit Help to Clean Up Anbag's Mess, Wall Street Journal, by Jacky Wong, February 21, 2018

China's Tech Giants Take to the Road, Wall Street Journal, by Trefor Moss and Liza Lin, March 19, 2018

Huawei's Breadth Raises Concern, Wall Street Journal, by David George-Cosh, February 24, 2018

Caution Over Huawei Grows, Wall Street Journal, By Dan Strumph and Paul Vieira, March 21, 2018

Tencent-Backed Travel Company Is Cruising Toward IPO, Wall Street Journal, By Julie Steinberg and Liza Lin, March 10, 2018

Hot Xiaomi Carries Big Risks, Wall Street Journal, by Li Yuan, March 17, 2018

Beijing Dials Up Pressure on Xiaomi, Wall Street Journal, Stella Yifan Xie, March 2, 2018

Chapter 5-U.S. and Foreign Tech Companies in China-Company and China Market Access Background

Qualcomm May Be Collateral Damage in a U.S.-China Trade War New York Times, By Ana Swanson and Alexandra Stevenson, April 18, 2018

China Plans Fund to Boost Semiconductors, Wall Street Journal, By Yoko Kubota, May 5, 2015

Why Google Quit China—and Why It's Heading Back, The Atlantic, by Kavin Waddell, January 19, 2016

Amazon Warns of Ending India and China Operations Due to Complicated Laws, International Business Times. By Jerin Mathew, November 3, 2014

Asian Rivals Put Apple Under Pressure, Wall Street Journal, by Newley Purnell, March 2, 2018

Apple's Cook Plays Along With China, Wall Street Journal, by Yoko Kubota, February 27, 2018

Apple Puts iCloud Keys in China, Wall Street Journal, by Robert McMillan and Tripp Mickle, February 26, 2018

Nuclear Missile Overhaul Falls to Small Pool of Contractors
Wall Street Journal, By Doug Cameron, August 27, 2017

China Humiliates Another Western Company, Wall Street Journal, by Michael Auslin, February 21, 2018

Tone-Deaf: Facebook's Russia Bungle, Wall Street Journal, By Deepa Seethharaman, Robert McMillian and Georgia Wells, April 3, 2018

Facebook and the Tools of Uprising, Wall Street Journal, by Christopher Mims, February 20, 2018

The Computer That Could Rule the World, Wall Street Journal, by Arthur Herman, October 27, 2017

Lockheed Pursues Longer Jet Pack, Wall Street Journal, March 10, 2018, by Doug Cameron, March 10, 2018

Justices to Hear Microsoft Case on Email Storage, Wall Street Journal, By Brent Kendall and Nicole Hong, February 27, 2018

Justices Grapple With Microsoft Case, Wall Street Journal, by Brent Kendall and Nicole Hong, February 26, 2018

Microsoft's Legal Cloud Cover, Wall Street Journal, Editorial, February 27, 2018

For Qualcomm, Yet More Fights Are on the Card. Wall Street Journal, by Ted Greenwald, March 20, 2018

Treasury's Qualcomm Reversal, Wall Street Journal, Editorial, March 6, 2018

The Qualcomm Question, Wall Street Journal, Editorial, March 5, 2018

China's Tech Giants Have a Side Job: Helping Beijing Spy, Wall Street Journal, by Liza Lin and Josh Chin, November 30, 2017

Tesla Plugs In Own China Plant, Wall Street Journal, Tim Higgins, Trefor Moss and Eva Dou, October 23, 2017

Bipartisan Bills Expected to Toughen U.S. Foreign Investment rules, Reuters, Diane Bartz, November 3, 2017

China and Russia's Dangerous Entente, Wall Street Journal, By Alexander Gabuev, October 4, 2017

North Koreans In Russia Work 'Basically In The Situation Of Slaves' New York Times, by Andrew Higgins, July 11, 2017

U.S. India Agree to Bolster Security, Wall Street Journal, by Niharika Mandhana, October 25, 2017

China-Indian Trade Hits Geopolitical Snag, Wall Street Journal, Eva Dou, September 1, 2017

India Separates Itself From The Pack, Wall Street Journal, Corinne Abrahms & Desipesadad Nayak, September 8, 2017

Does Trump Want a Nuclear Japan? Wall Street Journal, By Walter Russell Mead, September 4, 2017

Chapter 9-Chinese and U.S. Foreign Policy-Middle East

How Trump Is Going After Hezbollah in America's Backyard, Politico, By Matthew Levitt, November 30, 2017

Iraq Clash Raises Fear of Wider Conflict, Wall Street Journal, by Ali A. Nabban, and Isabel Coles, October 16, 2017

Kurd Clashes Delay Chevron, Wall Street Journal, by Benoit Faucon, October 19, 2017

U.S. Refocuses on Pakistan 'Havens', Wall Street Journal, by Saeed Shah, October 20, 2017

Terror Group Strikes Egypt, Wall Street Journal, By Rory Jones and Dalia Kholaif, October 20-21, 2017

Iran Extends Its Reach in Syria, The New Yorker, By Dexter Filkins, June 9, 2017

Revived After Mosul, Iraqi Forces Prepare to Battle ISIS in Tal Afar, New York Times, By Helene Cooper, August 18, 2017

The Next Middle East War, Wall Street Journal Editorial, September 8, 2017

Syrian Military Advances, Ramping Up Pressure On ISIS, Wall Street Journal, by Maria Abi-Habib & Nour Alakraa, September 6, 2017

In Syria, A New Conflict Looms As ISIS Loses Ground, Wall Street Journal, by Yaroslav Trofimov, September 8, 2017

Iraqi Kurds Back Independence in Referendum, Wall Street Journal, by Israel Coles and Ali A Nabhan, September 28, 2017

U.S.-Backed Forces Seize Gas Plant From Militants, Wall Street Journal, by Raja Abdulrahim, September 25, 2017

Palestinian Talks Hit an Impasse, Wall Street Journal, by Rory Jones, October 4, 2017

Chapter 10-Chinese and U.S. Climate Change, Energy, and Renewables Development

2017 Among Warmest Years on Record, Wall Street Journal, by Robert Lee Hotz, January 19, 2018

Power Shift Drives a Slide in Prices, Wall Street Journal, by Erin Ailworth and Russell Gold, November 30, 2017

Does Nuclear Power Have a Robust Future in the U.S.?, Wall Street Journal, by Rich Powell and Jason Bordoff, November 13, 2017

The U.S. Backs Off Nuclear Power. Georgia Wants to Keep Building Reactors, New York Times, By Brad Plumer, Aug. 31, 2017

Trump's Plans for a Nuclear Revival Will Begin With a Study, Bloomberg, by Jennifer A Dlouhy, June 29, 2017

Emerging Markets Pick Up Slack In LNG, Wall Street Journal, Demi Guo, August 30, 2017

U.S. Energy Facts Explained, U.S. Energy Information Administration, September 5, 2017

Trump Administration Revives Nevada Plan as Nuclear Waste Piles Up, Wall Street Journal, by Kris Maher, May 9, 2017

SEC Launches Crypto-Probe, Wall Street Journal, by Jean Eaglesham and Paul Vigna, March 1, 2018

Who Is Hacking the U.S.?, Wall Street Journal, Gregory Touhill and James Woolsey, March 7, 2017

An Unexpected Security Problem in the Cloud, Wall Street Journal, by Robert McMillan, September 17, 2017

The Disturbing Inevitability of Cyberattacks, Wall Street Journal, by Brian E. Finch, August 21, 2017

The Computer That Could Rule the World, Wall Street Journal, by Arthur Herman, October 27, 2017

An Unexpected Security Problem in the Cloud, Wall Street Journal, by Robert McMillan, September 17, 2017

Chapter 11-Chinese and U.S. Education and Technology: Artificial Intelligence, Bitcoins and Blockchain Technology, CyberSecurity and Quantum Computing

SEC Launches Crypto-Probe, Wall Street Journal, by Jean Eaglesham and Paul Vigna, March 1, 2018

Distributed Ledgers, Smart Contracts, Business Standards and ISO 20022, Swift, Information Paper

Who Is Hacking the U.S.?, Wall Street Journal, Gregory Touhill and James Woolsey, March 7, 2017

An Unexpected Security Problem in the Cloud, Wall Street Journal, by Robert McMillan, September 17, 2017

The Disturbing Inevitability of Cyberattacks, Wall Street Journal, by Brian E. Finch, August 21, 2017

The Computer That Could Rule the World, Wall Street Journal, by Arthur Herman, October 27, 2017

Chapter 13-Chinese and U.S. Regulation-Banks and Financial Systems, Communications and the Environment

FCC Vote Promises to Reprice The Net, Wall Street Journal, by John D. McKinnon and Ruan Knutson, December 12, 1017

FCC Reverses Rules on Net Access, Wall Street Journal, by John D. McKinnon, December 14, 2017

Chapter 14-U.S. Legal and Law Enforcement-Housing, Inner Cities, Supreme Court and Other Court Appointment

FCC Vote Promises to Reprice The Net, Wall Street Journal, by John D. McKinnon and Ruan Knutson, December 12, 1017

FCC Reverses Rules on Net Access, Wall Street Journal, by John D. McKinnon, December 14, 2017

Chapter 15-China vs. U.S. 2018 Conclusions

President Eases His Approach On China, Wall Street Journal, by Bob Davis, June 26, 2018

Made in China 2025: Beijing's big ambitions from robots to chips, Reuters, Adam Jourdan, April 20, 2018

Printed in the United States
By Bookmasters